NUMBER FOUR:

Texas A&M University Economics Series

Toward a Theory of the Rent-Seeking Society

Toward a Theory
OF THE
Rent-Seeking Society

Edited by

JAMES M. BUCHANAN, ROBERT D. TOLLISON,

and GORDON TULLOCK

Texas A&M University Press

COLLEGE STATION

Library of Congress Cataloging in Publication Data

Main entry under title:

Toward a theory of the rent-seeking society.

(Texas A & M University economics series; no. 4)
Includes bibliographical references.
1. Rent (Economic theory)—Addresses, essays, lectures.
2. Transfer payments—Addresses, essays, lectures. 3. Industry
and state—Addresses, essays, lectures. I. Buchanan, James M.
II. Tollison, Robert D. III. Tullock, Gordon. IV. Title: Rent-
seeking society. V. Series: Texas A & M University, College Station. Texas A & M University economics series; no. 4.
HB401.T68   333'.012   79-5276
ISBN 0-89096-090-9

Manufactured in the United States of America
FIRST EDITION

Contents

Preface

TITLES are important, all the more so when the object of a book is to introduce a new subject matter to one's fellow economists and other interested social scientists. *Rent seeking* is a term that was introduced to economics by Anne O. Krueger, whose paper on this subject is reprinted in this collection, and it is meant to describe the resource-wasting activities of individuals in seeking transfers of wealth through the aegis of the state. The modern literature on rent seeking, to our knowledge, dates from Gordon Tullock's 1967 paper in the *Western Economic Journal*, which is also reprinted in this volume. Although rent seeking will normally arise in the context of artificial interferences with markets by the state, this is not the only setting in which rent seeking may occur. Indeed, the issue of the boundaries of the domain of rent-seeking behavior, as several of the following essays will argue, is not fully resolved at this point. As we say, this book is "toward" a theory and not a final statement of a theory.

Moreover, as with most economic analysis, the reader will find a blending of positive and normative elements of analysis in the papers presented here. Many of the scholars who contributed to this volume will offer positive-predictive analyses of the course of rent-seeking activities in the economy. What features of legislatures explain, for example, the success of interest groups in obtaining legislation favorable to their cause? Other authors have as their main interest the development of the equilibrium properties of the rent-seeking society and an assessment of the degree to which the rent-seeking society deviates from the economists' "optimal" configuration of the economy.

To repeat, however, we are not offering here a definitive analysis of rent seeking. We are offering something analogous to a travel guide, such as it is, to those scholars who might be attracted to work in this area. Indeed, our guide does not even provide a good road map. We are dealing here with wilderness territory, and though we feel sure that there is plenty of clear water and virgin timber in the wilderness, the best we can do for now is to offer the reader some good stopping places along the way.

We should stress that we canvassed carefully for the papers in this collection, both from previously published and unpublished sources. We should not, however, be surprised if we have missed some relevant and applicable papers. We do not present this book as an exhaustive collection of papers on rent seeking, an attempt that in itself would be wholly inappropriate for an emerging area of study. Our objective is quite different: to generate new interest in rent seeking, interest that will stimulate further work.

We would also like to express our appreciation to those of our colleagues at the Center for Study of Public Choice at Virginia Polytechnic Institute and State University who have helped in the preparation of this book: Donna Trenor, George Uhimchuk, Iris Bowman, and Betty Ross, without whose efforts the project should have surely faltered.

Several of the chapters that follow are reprints of papers already published. These papers appear as they did in their original sources of publication, except for minor stylistic changes. Permission to reprint has been granted by the holders of the copyright in each case. Needless to say, we appreciate the cooperation of the various authors and publishers in allowing us to reprint these papers.

"The Welfare Costs of Tariffs, Monopolies, and Theft," by Gordon Tullock, originally appeared in the *Western Economic Journal* (now *Economic Inquiry*) 5 (June, 1967): 224–232, and is reprinted by permission of the publisher. Anne O. Krueger's paper, "The Political Economy of the Rent-Seeking Society," originally appeared in the *American Economic Review* 64 (June, 1974): 291–303, and is reprinted with the permission of the author and the publisher. The paper by Richard A. Posner, "The Social Costs of Monopoly and Regulation," originally appeared in the *Journal of Political Economy* 83 (August, 1975): 807–827, and is reprinted with the permission of the author and the University of Chicago Press.

The paper by Keith Cowling and Dennis C. Mueller, "The Social Costs of Monopoly Power," originally appeared in the *Economic Jour-*

nal 88 (December, 1978): 727–748, and is reprinted by permission of the authors and Cambridge University Press.

The paper by Harold Demsetz, "Economics as a Guide to Antitrust Regulation," originally appeared in the *Journal of Law and Economics* 19 (August, 1976): 371–384, and is reprinted with the permission of the author and the University of Chicago Law School. "The Transitional Gains Trap," by Gordon Tullock, first appeared in *The Bell Journal of Economics* 6 (Autumn, 1975): 671–678, and is reprinted by permission from the publisher. Tullock's paper, "The Cost of Transfers," originally was published in *Kyklos* 4 (December, 1971): 629–643, and is reprinted with the permission of the publisher. Edgar K. Browning's paper, "On the Welfare Cost of Transfers," appeared in *Kyklos* 2 (April, 1974): 374–377, and is reprinted by permission of author and publisher. Tullock's paper, "More on the Cost of Transfers," also appeared in *Kyklos* 2 (April, 1974): 378–381, and is reprinted by permission of the publisher. Michael L. Goetz's paper, "Tax Avoidance, Horizontal Equity, and Tax Reform: A Proposed Synthesis," originally appeared in the *Southern Economic Journal* 44 (April, 1978): 798–812, and is reprinted by permission of author and publisher.

List of Contributors

Barry Baysinger, Texas A&M University
H. Geoffrey Brennan, Virginia Polytechnic Institute
Edgar K. Browning, University of Virginia
James M. Buchanan, Virginia Polytechnic Institute
Roger Congleton, New York University
Keith Cowling, University of Warwick
Harold Demsetz, University of California, Los Angeles
Robert B. Ekelund, Jr., Auburn University
Roger L. Faith, Virginia Polytechnic Institute
Michael L. Goetz, Temple University
Anne O. Krueger, University of Minnesota
Dwight R. Lee, Virginia Polytechnic Institute
Robert E. McCormick, University of Rochester
Dennis C. Mueller, University of Maryland
Daniel Orr, Virginia Polytechnic Institute
Richard A. Posner, University of Chicago
Robert D. Tollison, Virginia Polytechnic Institute
Gordon Tullock, Virginia Polytechnic Institute

I.
Introduction

1

Rent Seeking and
Profit Seeking

by

JAMES M. BUCHANAN

RENT SEEKING, as a specific term, emerged in applied economic theory only in the 1970's. The behavior that it describes, however, has been with us always, and there is surely no prospect that it will fade away. Behaviorally, rent seeking has become more important because institutional changes have opened up opportunities that did not exist in the nineteenth and early twentieth centuries.

What is *rent seeking*? The words seem clear enough at first reading, but economists will sense the ambiguities. Rent seeking does not refer to the behavior of landlords who collect rents on real property. This everyday usage of the word *rent* had best be put in the closet. We move somewhat closer to understanding when we introduce the definition of *rent* found in standard textbooks of economic theory. Rent is that part of the payment to an owner of resources over and above that which those resources could command in any alternative use. Rent is receipt in excess of opportunity cost. In one sense, it is an allocatively unnecessary payment not required to attract the resources to the particular employment. This textbook definition contains ambiguities, some of which will be discussed briefly in this introductory chapter. Nonetheless, the basic definition offers a starting point for any attempt to clarify the meaning of *rent seeking* as a general concept.

So long as owners of resources prefer more to less, they are likely to be engaged in rent seeking, which is simply another word for profit seeking. Traditional economic models of social interaction are based on the presumption that persons seek to maximize present values of expected income streams, and a central demonstration of economic theory involves the relationships between such individual profit seeking and desired social results. Since Adam Smith, we have known that the profit-seeking activity of the butcher and baker ensures results beneficial to all members of the community. Only through such activity do markets work in getting resources allocated efficiently among competing uses, in getting production and distribution organized, and in establishing prices as standards of comparative value. In an idealized model of market order, profit seeking as an activity produces consequences neither predicted nor understood by any single participant, but "good" when evaluated as a characteristic of the order itself. In such respect, therefore, profit seeking in an ordered market structure generates external economy; in Pigovian terminology, the social marginal product of profit seeking exceeds private marginal product.

In the preceding paragraph, I have deliberately shifted the terms from *rent seeking* to *profit seeking* as the discussion proceeded. My purpose was to call to mind the familiar proposition that the behavior of persons in trying to maximize returns on their own capacities or opportunities can be socially beneficial in an ordered market structure, behavior that we may here describe to be "profit seeking." The selfsame behavior under a different set of institutions, however, may not produce socially beneficial consequences. The unintended results of individual efforts at maximizing returns on opportunities may be "bad" rather than "good." The term *rent seeking* is designed to describe behavior in institutional settings where individual efforts to maximize value generate social waste rather than social surplus. Again I should emphasize that at the level of the individual decision makers, the behavior, as such, is not different from that of profit seeking in market interactions. The unintended consequences of individual value maximization shift from those that may be classified as "good" to those that seem clearly to be "bad," not because individuals become different moral beings and modify their actions accordingly, but because institutional structure changes. The setting within which individual choices are made is transformed. As institutions have moved away from ordered markets toward the near chaos of direct political allocation, rent seeking has emerged as a significant social phenomenon.

Economic Rent

It is useful to return to the definition of *rent* or *economic rent* found in the textbooks. If the owner of a resource unit is paid more than the alternative earning power of that unit, more than opportunity cost, there seems to be no allocative necessity for such excess. The resource unit would have been directed toward the observed employment for any payment above cost, even an infinitesimally small sum. "Economic rent," viewed in this perspective, seems to be a genuine "social surplus" and, indeed, it is this apparent characteristic of rent that has spawned monumental confusion among those who do not fully understand the market process.

In an ordered market structure, the potential attractiveness of economic rents offers the motivation to resource owners and to entrepreneurs who combine resources into production. And it is the action of entrepreneurs that must drive the system. By seeking always to find new opportunities to earn economic rent and to exploit more fully existing opportunities, profit-seeking entrepreneurs generate a dynamic process of continuous resource *re*allocation that ensures economic growth and development, again as an unintended consequence. The role of economic rent in a market structure cannot be properly understood apart from this dynamic.

In the process described, two relevant features of rent require special mention. First, in market systems, all economic rent tends to be eroded or dissipated as adjustments take place through time. Above-cost payments to any entrepreneurs or resource owners must attract other profit-rent seekers to enter identical or closely related employments. As such entry proceeds, rents earned initially are driven down and, in the limit, disappear altogether. In the conceptualized equilibrium of market adjustment, economic rents are eliminated, and all resource owners, including those who have entrepreneurial capacities, earn rates of return established competitively in the whole market system. Second, in the dynamic adjustment process, which, of course, never attains the conceptualized equilibria of the models, economic rents may be negative as well as positive. Resource owners and entrepreneurs who err in their predictions or who over-adjust to apparent opportunities that do not materialize may earn less than opportunity costs. This existence of negative rents or losses adds symmetry to the adjustment process and, of course, accelerates resource reallocation.

For completeness, the time dimension of economic rents should be discussed briefly. Economic rent to the owner of a resource that is explicitly locked in to a single use because of its physical characteristics (a particular machine, building, or human talent) may be positive in some short-run sense, but the resource may have little or no prospect of earning an alternative return comparable to that earned in the particular usage. Hence, the owner will have no incentive to reallocate. At the same time, however, the particular investment may be earning negative economic rent in some long-run or planning sense. The earnings may be less than comparable investments could earn in alternative uses. In such a setting, despite positive "quasi-rents," to use a Marshallian term, the negative economic rent applicable to initial allocation will ensure that no additional resources shift toward the particular usage. Reallocation away from the usage will take place via disinvestment as physical facilities wear out and are depreciated.

The Dissipation of Rents in Markets

We are concerned with the net attractiveness of opportunities for new investment. It will be useful to examine in elementary detail the process through which economic rents arise and are dissipated through time in ordered market structures.

Consider a situation where some person, a potential entrepreneur, discovers a use for a resource or a combination of resources that had not been previously discovered.[1] No one else in the economy is aware of this potential opportunity. The entrepreneur organizes production and commences sale of the new commodity or service. By definition, he is a pure monopolist during the initial period. He may be able to secure a return over and above what he might earn in any alternative employment. He receives "economic rent" on his entrepreneurial capacity. And, indeed, it is the prospect of such rent that motivates the activity in the first place. It is important to emphasize,

[1] See Israel Kirzner, *Competition and Entrepreneurship* (Chicago: University of Chicago Press, 1973), for a thorough discussion of the entrepreneurship role.

however, that the rent reflects the *creation* of added value in the economy rather than the diversion of value that already exists. The entrepreneurial activity of *rent creation* is functionally quite different from that of *rent seeking*. The fact that the innovating entrepreneur is observed to be receiving rent sends out signals to other noninnovating but potentially imitating producers of the new commodity or service. Unless overt barriers to entry exist, other producers will enter the market and sell the new commodity or a close substitute for it. Output on the market will expand; price will fall. The initial monopoly position, and hence the economic rent, of the innovator is eroded to the benefit of consumers generally. In the ultimate equilibrium, the consumers secure the full benefit of the new product. Rents received by producers are dissipated in the dynamics of competitive market adjustment. Resources come to be allocated efficiently between the production of the new commodity and other uses in the economy.

Freedom of entry is critically important in the generation of allocative efficiency in a developing, changing economy. If the entry of those producers who are attracted by the rents of the innovating entrepreneurs is effectively blocked, there will be no dissipation of rents, and, of course, no shift of resources toward the production of the new product. Output will not be forced above monopoly limits, and price will not fall.

Rent Seeking without Social Return

To this point, the analysis has been straightforward elementary economics. Where does "rent seeking" come in? We need only to modify the setting by postulating a particular type of entry restriction. We may do this with a simple, and historically factual, example. Suppose that, instead of discovering a new commodity or service or production process, an innovating entrepreneur discovers a way to convince the government that he "deserves" to be granted a monopoly right, and that government will enforce such a right by keeping out all potential entrants. No value is created in the process; indeed, the monopolization involves a net destruction of value. The rents secured reflect a diversion of value from consumers generally to the favored rent seeker, with a net loss of value in the process.

Suppose that a courtier persuades the queen to grant him a royal monopoly to sell playing cards throughout the kingdom. The courtier so favored will capture sizable monopoly profits or economic rents, and this will be observed by other persons who might like to enter the industry. But their entry is effectively prevented by enforcement of the royal monopoly privilege. What the queen gives, however, the queen may take away, and the potential entrants are not likely to sit quietly by and allow the favored one among their number to enjoy his differentially advantageous position. Instead of passive observation, potential entrants will engage actively in "rent seeking." They will invest effort, time, and other productive resources in varying attempts to shift the queen's favor toward their own cause. Promotion, advertising, flattery, persuasion, cajolery—these and other attributes will characterize rent-seeking behavior.

The contrast between the unintended consequences of this behavior and that which characterizes profit seeking in the competitive market process is striking. Rent seeking on the part of potential entrants in a setting where entry is either blocked or can at best reflect one-for-one substitution must generate social waste. Resources devoted to efforts to curry the queen's favor might be used to produce valued goods and services elsewhere in the economy, whereas nothing of net value is produced by rent seeking. In the competitive market, by comparison, resources of potential entrants are shifted directly into the *production* of the previously monopolized commodity or service, or close substitutes; in this usage, these resources are more productive than they would have been in alternative employments. The unintended results of competitive attempts to capture monopoly rents are "good" because entry is possible; comparable results of attempts to capture artificially contrived advantageous positions under governmentally enforced monopoly are "bad" because entry is not possible.

Rent seeking, when used in this book, refers to the second model in all of its varieties, to activity motivated by rent but leading to socially undesirable consequences.

Rent Seeking and Governmental Action

At the beginning of this chapter I stated that rent seeking continues to gain importance in modern political economy because institutions have changed and are continuing to change. So long as governmental action is restricted largely, if not entirely, to protecting individual rights, personal and property, and enforcing voluntarily negotiated private contracts, the market process dominates economic behavior and ensures that any economic rents that appear will be dissipated by the forces of competitive entry. Furthermore, the prospects for economic rents enhance the dynamic process of development, growth, and orderly change. If, however, governmental action moves significantly beyond the limits defined by the minimal or protective state, if government commences, as it has done on a sweeping scale, to interfere piecemeal in the market adjustment process, the tendency toward the erosion or dissipation of rents is countered and may be wholly blocked. Rents must remain, however, and the signals emitted to potential competitors remain as strong as they are under standard market adjustment. Hence, attempts will be made to capture these rents, and resources used up in such attempts will reflect social waste, even if the investments involved are fully rational for all participants. Rent-seeking activity is directly related to the scope and range of governmental activity in the economy, to the relative size of the public sector.

The more apparent opportunities are those modern examples most closely analogous to the royal grant of monopoly introduced illustratively above. If supply is arbitrarily restricted and price is allowed to rise to market-clearing levels, rents accrue to those who secure the "rights" to engage in the activity. Governmental licenses, quotas, permits, authorizations, approvals, franchise assignments—each of these closely related terms implies arbitrary and/or artificial scarcity created by government. Whether such scarcity is reasonable governmental policy is not my concern here. Regardless of reason, such scarcity implies the potential emergence of rents, which, in turn, implies rent-seeking activity. Persons will invest genuinely scarce resources in attempts to secure either the initial assignments of rights to the artificially scarce opportunities or replacement assignments as other initial holders are ousted from privileged positions. In either case, and despite individually rational investments ex ante, valuable resources will be wasted in the process.

Few questions will be raised concerning the emergence of rent seeking when governmental action creates and supports monopoly positions and effectively prevents entry. Rents emerge because prices are not allowed to be brought down to competitive levels by expanding supply through the entry of new producers. Rent-seeking of a different, but still wasteful, sort emerges, however, when governmental action interferes with markets in order to keep prices below rather than above competitive levels. With simple monopoly, and with the familiar examples noted above, rents emerge because *genuine* supply price falls below the actual price charged, with demand price being allowed to adjust to the latter in order for the market to clear. The surplus, the rent, accrues to the seller, the person who possesses the "rights" to market the commodity or service. Consider, however, the obverse setting, where the *genuine* demand price lies above the actual demand price authorized to be charged, with supply price being allowed to adjust to the latter in order for the market to clear. As in the obverse case, the wedge between the genuine demand price and the genuine supply price, both of which reflect opportunity costs to buyers and sellers respectively, generates rents. In the second case, the rents accrue, not to sellers (who may, here, be competitively organized), but to purchasers or buyers who hold the artificially scarce "rights" to enter the market on the demand side. In the first case, the potential entrants who are thwarted are on the supply side, potential producer-sellers who will, unless constrained, enter and drive price down, hence dissipating rents. In the second case, there are potential entrants on the demand side, potential buyers who will, unless constrained, enter and drive prices up, hence dissipating rents. The analysis, as such, is fully symmetrical. The assignment of a "right to buy" something at, say, $1,000 below what would be a competitively determined price, has the same value as the assignment of a "right to sell" something at $1,000 above a competitively determined price. The signals transmitted are comparable in the two cases, and they will generate comparable if not identical rent-seeking behavior.

If allowed to function within a set of laws and institutions that protect individual property rights and enforce contracts, markets will allocate resources among alternative uses so as to ensure tolerably efficient results. But economists have concentrated far too much attention on efficiency and far too little on the political role of markets. To the extent that markets are allowed to allocate resources among uses, political allocation is not required. Markets minimize resort to politics. Once markets are not allowed to work, however, or once they are interfered with in their allocative functioning, politics must enter. And political allocation, like market allocation, involves profit seeking as a dynamic activating force. It would be absurd to conceive of a market process in which resources are either permanently locked in particular allocations or in which entrepreneurs are not continually searching for more profitable opportunities. Although it is perhaps less apparent, it would, nonetheless, be equally absurd to think that a politically determined allocation of resources could be frozen once and for all and that resource owners and entrepreneurs would not continually seek more profitable opportunities in politics as in markets. The motive force of profit seeking, or rent seeking, does not vary across the two institutional forms. The difference lies in the unintended results. Political reallocation, achieved via rent seeking, does not reduce or eliminate contrived scarcity. In politics, rent seeking, at best, replaces one set of rent seekers with another.

Political Allocation without Rent Seeking?

Earlier I associated the level of rent-seeking activity in a society with the size and scope of government activity in the economy. This proposition can be tested empirically, and the results of such a test would, I think, corroborate the relationship suggested. Such a test would necessarily draw data from the real-world actions of governments rather than from idealized constructions of what governments and politics might be. However, for completeness if for nothing else, I should examine the possibility that direct political allocation might take a form such that rent-seeking activity would not take place.

Rent seeking emerges under normally predicted circumstances because political interference with markets creates differentially advantageous positions for some persons who secure access to the valuable "rights." From this fact, we may derive a "principle." If political allocation is to be undertaken without the emergence of wasteful rent seeking, the differential advantages granted to some persons as a result of the allocation must be eliminated. This principle in turn suggests that all persons in the community must be allowed equal access to the scarcity values created by governmental intervention in the market economy. For example, if government decides to restrict the production or sale of a commodity, thereby creating the opportunity for economic rents, each person in the community must be granted an *equal* share in the prospective rents. If this sharing is announced in advance and becomes generally known, it will not be rational for anyone to invest resources in trying to secure differential advantages. Even this scheme is not certain to eliminate rent seeking, however, since, if it is known that government can assign equal shares, it might also be predicted that unequal shares could be assigned. Only if the equal-sharing rule could somehow be permanently implemented in each-and-all-possible scarcity-value distributions could we predict the total absence of rent seeking, even at the most basic level.

A more plausible means of assigning "rights" to contrived scarcity values would be for government to distribute such "rights" randomly in each situation. In this setting, all persons have equal expected values of rights, and they have little or no incentive to engage in rent seeking. Once again, however, some persons may predict a possible departure from the random distribution process until and unless the process itself becomes widely accepted as an untouchable rule or procedure for all political allocation.

Once we recognize that, under either of the two procedures suggested, much of the political motive for governmental interference with markets would disappear, the presumption of the validity of the empirical proposition relating rent seeking to size of government is strengthened.

Three Levels of Rent Seeking

Rent-seeking activity may occur at several levels, and I shall introduce a single example to indicate this prospect. Suppose that, for whatever reason, a municipal government decides to limit the number of taxicabs. (Whether this decision itself is desirable or undesirable need not concern us here.) If the valued licenses are to be distributed among potential entrants by bureaucratic authority, rent seeking of the most familiar sort previously discussed will, of course, take place. Suppose, however, that, after having settled on the number of taxicab licenses to be issued, the municipal government auctions those valued "rights" among prospective entrants. This procedure will directly and immediately convert the licenses into private property rights, which, we may also assume, are to be fully marketable. No rent seeking of the basic sort previously discussed will take place.

The government will secure the full values of the contrived scarcity, however, and the presence of rents at the level of the municipal budget suggests that rent seeking may shift to a second level. Potential political entrepreneurs may now seek to enter, not the taxicab industry directly, but the set of political-bureaucratic positions or occupations with access to the receipts of the auction. Both politics and the "civil service" will become differentially productive employments if rents are allowed to remain available to those persons fortunate enough to occupy the rent-access positions.

Let us extend our example further, however, to indicate that yet a third level of rent seeking may emerge. Suppose that government officeholders can expect to secure competitively determined salaries and perquisites. Suppose that there are no rent components present in any of the personal rewards to those who hold positions in government. In this setting, the economic rents that arise because of the contrived scarcity, transferred initially to government via the auction procedure, must be returned to all taxpayer-beneficiaries in the community. Unless, however, these rents are returned or passed through the budget in some nondifferential or random manner, rent-seeking activity at a third level will be aimed at securing differential shares in the total values. Suppose that the taxicab licenses are auctioned and that government officeholders are competitively paid, but that funds are returned to citizens in some inverse relationship to income and/or wealth. Even in such a highly restricted model, rent seeking may take a form of attempts on the part of persons to shift into activities that do not generate the type of income or wealth measurable for purposes of qualifying for receipt of rents.

The taxicab example is useful in illustrating at least three levels where rent seeking can occur once a contrived scarcity is created by governmental action. If the "rights to recover" rents are not distributed equally or randomly among all persons and are not auctioned, prospective entrants will engage in rent seeking through efforts to persuade authorities to grant differentially advantageous treatment. The familiar figure of the Washington lobbyist offers the illustration here. Most of the early work on rent seeking involves analysis of this sort of activity. In a broader sense, however, the second level of rent seeking may even be more important. If the salaries and perquisites of government positions contain elements of economic rent, if salaries and perquisites are higher than those for comparable positions in the private sector, prospective politicians and bureaucrats will waste major resources in attempts to secure the favored posts. Excessive education and training (notably, perhaps, among lawyers who are aiming at political office), excessive spending on political campaigns—these offer rent-seeking examples of this second type. Quite apart from the two primary levels at which rent seeking can take place, activity at the third level involves attempts by persons and groups to secure differentially favorable treatment or to avoid differentially unfavorable treatment, defined, not in terms of particular opportunities, but in terms of treatment by the governmental fiscal process. Faced with a prospect of differentially favorable or differentially unfavorable tax treatment by government, a person or group may (1) engage in lobbying effort; (2) engage directly in politics to secure access to decision-making power, and/or (3) make plans to shift into or out of the affected activity. Resources may be wasted at all three levels simultaneously, despite the rational motivation to engage in such activity at each stage.

Conclusions

As the introductory examples have suggested, analysis of rent seeking is little more than applied price theory of the traditional variety. Such analysis does, however, turn much of modern economics inside out. The latter tends to commence with the presumed structure of an ordered market, and its analysis tends to be concentrated on spinning out even more elegant and rigorous "proofs" or "theorems" about the idealized model of the competitive process. But let us be honest. How much more do we know about market process than Adam Smith knew that is of practical relevance?

The analysis of rent seeking, as the contributions in this book indicate, shifts attention to interactions and to institutions outside of and beyond the confined competitive market process, while applying essentially the same tools as those applied to interactions within the process. The analysis of rent seeking is, therefore, properly designated as *institutional economics* in a very real sense. The analysis also falls within *public choice*, especially if the latter is defined methodologically as the extension of the basic tools of economics to nonmarket interaction. Indeed, the previously used rubric, "theory of nonmarket decision making," allows rent seeking to be included directly under its umbrella. As many critics, both friendly and unfriendly, have noted, public choice theory and the economic theory of property rights have several affinities. Rent seeking analysis can readily be incorporated within the property-rights approach, and, as with public choice, the theory of rent seeking can be interpreted as an appropriate extension.

The primary purpose of this book is to collect the most relevant contributions to the analysis of rent seeking and by so doing to call more attention to the opportunities for further inquiry. As the contents of this book suggest, the subject remains new, and opportunities for productive and relevant research seem almost unlimited. The book contains the early bits and pieces of a line of inquiry that can be, should be, and will be extensively expanded. In the process, additional institutional and historical detail will be elaborated; additional empirical tests will be conducted; additional rigor will characterize the formal analysis. We shall come to know much more about rent seeking. As, when, and if we do, we may hope that some contribution may be made in shifting public attitudes toward constitutional reform that will reduce rather than continue to expand rent-seeking opportunities in our society.

2

Rent Seeking as a Negative-Sum Game

by

GORDON TULLOCK

I have just sold one house and bought another. As it happened, the transaction was completed very quickly, taking less than seventy-two hours, and, during that time, the realtor who managed both of these transactions spent something under four hours talking to me, to the person who bought my old house, and showing us around. For this rather short period of time, he collected commissions totaling about $5,000. If we regard this as a return on the time he spent on this specific transaction, it represents $1,250 an hour, which gives him an hourly rate similar to that of the president of a large corporation.

Obviously, this is not the proper way to explain his income. In addition to the actual sales effort, he has many other expenses. He maintains a well-equipped office complete with a radio beeper that makes it possible for him to be reached anywhere within fifteen miles of Blacksburg. He is very well informed about the local real estate market; indeed, it was this very fine information, together with his ability quickly to discern people's needs for housing from rather brief conversations, that led to the extreme speed with which this transaction was completed. There are also advertising costs, time involved in creating the impression on his clients of great efficiency and helpfulness, and simple "waiting" time involved in his business.

If we consider all these factors, it is doubtful that he makes an excessively high return on his investments. Note, however, that the bulk of his costs occurs before, and is not directly related to, any given individual transaction. He invests over a long period of time in acquiring information, specialized abilities to deal with clients, and a good reputation; the payoff comes in the form of relatively rare but lucrative commission payments.

To take one (probably fairly small) example, I have seen him and his partner selling to farmers, a group of hippies, and to university professors. They must maintain a sizable wardrobe right in the office to change clothes between these various activities, because they certainly look like farmers, college professors, or hippies at the appropriate time. All this is perfectly normal, and I presume all of us would agree that the realtor is probably earning only a normal return on these resources, his personal talents counted among them.

There is, however, one more preliminary investment in the sale of real estate I have not mentioned: it is necessary for him to take an examination before he can become a realtor at all. Although the subjects covered in the examination are not totally irrelevant to his business, they are not so closely connected that the resources he invests in studying for the examination can be said to have a direct return at the same rate as those shown above. He earns a return on his complicated wardrobe by continuously using it. He earns a return on the resources he invested in passing the examination because the existence of the examination means that the real estate business is not quite as competitive as it otherwise would be.[1] Hence, his income is slightly higher.

For the purpose of this paper, I am going to call income derived from *this* kind of resource investment a "rent," and "rent seeking" is the effort to obtain such income. Thus, an individual who invests in something that will not actually improve productivity or will actually lower it, but that does raise his income because it gives him some special position or monopoly power, is "rent seeking," and the "rent" is the income derived. Note that his is different from the normal economic meaning of rent seeking, but not so radically different that we must seek out a new word.

Let us now turn to a somewhat similar situation. In imperial China the highest status and wealth positions, other than that of the imperial family itself, were occupied by high officials in the bureaucracy. Entrance into the bureaucracy was by way of a very, very difficult competitive examination. Its difficulty can be seen by the fact that only about a hundred people a year in all of China passed. Further, of

---

[1] The exam is actually fairly easy and hence the effect is small, but it does go in this direction.

those who passed the examination, only a minority—those who finished very near the top—really had much chance for high government office.

The returns to those people who *did* rise to high position by becoming a grand secretary, viceroy, and so forth, were very great indeed. The imperial government did not believe in saving money on the compensation of its high-level executives, although as a matter of fact a good deal of this compensation came in the form of fees for specific services rather than salaries. There was substantially no other occupation in China that could lead to anywhere near the same type of income, power, and prestige possessed by the high official. It is fairly certain that high officials of equivalent talent could have been hired at lower salaries had there been some method of determining their suitability.

As a result of this institution, there were immense investments of resources all over China in preparation for the examinations. The examinations have had a bad press because they contained sections on poetry and good handwriting. Nevertheless, to a considerable extent they were devoted to the kind of problems that might actually affect governmental performance. Hydraulic engineering, a critical view of history, and a good knowledge of the basic philosophy that was supposed to guide the Chinese government were clearly important in passing the examination.

Here again, the return, once one became a high official, was to a large extent a return on talents and work invested long before. Further, there was an immense gamble here. The number of people who spent a great deal of time and energy preparing for the examination was a very high multiple of those who finally reached the top rank. Of those who did invest large amounts of time in an attempt to pass the examinations, the overwhelming majority were eliminated in the first stage, which meant that they actually got no return at all on their educational efforts, except insofar as there may have been a direct consumption return. The remainder would receive a relatively small return, except for those few who became very high-ranking officials.[2]

Presumably, the individuals investing resources in preparation (or, more commonly, in the preparation of their children) for the exam-

---

[2] This is to some extent an oversimplification, but I think it is basically correct. For a more detailed account, see almost any history of China.

ination invested these resources only to the point where the marginal expected return matched that on other possible resource investments. In practice, it was like a lottery in which a large number of people buy tickets and only a few win. Of course, in this case the winners were not selected by luck—or at least not primarily by luck. There is, I take it, little doubt that the people who passed the examination with high scores were in fact geniuses. Still, when the formal education of a child who was preparing for the examination began, no one could tell whether he was going to pass or not; hence, the initial investment was made under conditions of stochastic risk.

The situation, looked at economically, is unusual. Individuals were entering into a high-risk activity and investing resources in a way that discounted both the probability of failure and the extremely high rate of return if success were achieved. Nevertheless, it is hard to avoid the impression that the system was economically wasteful. The education given to the students preparing for the exam was of little or no use in any walk of life other than government. Further, most of the people who passed the examination and received minor government jobs would make only modest use of their highly intensive and expensive educational backgrounds. It was not necessary that a Hsien magistrate at the bottom of the official system be deeply learned in Chinese philosophy and history and be well up into what psychologists would call the "genius" category. In the great days of the British Empire, the district commissioners who held somewhat similar jobs were selected essentially for personality traits rather than for learning and high intelligence. They seem to have done about as good a job as the Chinese Hsien magistrates.

Even at higher levels, it is not obvious that China gained a great deal from the extremely high qualifications of her senior officials. They may have invested the bulk of their superior knowledge and intelligence in maneuvers and intrigue rather than in actual governmental efficiency. Still, most visitors to China before about 1800, when the system was functioning well, admired it.

It will be seen that this system raised the same problems that modern education does with respect to the capital investment–screening problem. It is not clear whether the examination impelled people to acquire valuable capital or simply screened out the inherently brightest people. Probably it did both. In any event, it is clear that the bulk of the people who participated in the process did not gain from it, regardless of its social effect. They entered into a gambling game, in which they lost.

From the standpoint of individual parties, it is not clear whether this game is a positive-sum, zero-sum, or negative-sum game.[3] To anticipate, and put simply what is really a quite complicated line of reasoning, the game can be positive, zero-sum, or negative-sum from the individual's standpoint, depending on certain parameters. Unfortunately, the empirical work necessary to determine the real-world parameters has not been done and will be extremely difficult.

From the social standpoint, however, it is clear that this was a negative-sum game. Assuming, as I think we can assume, that the very large amount of learning undertaken by the candidates for the examination was partially screening and partially capital investment, and that the capital investment failed for those people who did not complete the examination, it is clear that the total social cost must have been much greater than the social benefit, regardless of the rationality or irrationality of the individual resource investments.

The problem is that the individual invests resources in a form in which they are not readily transferable to other uses. If, for example, the imperial Chinese government had sold government positions at auction, it would have obtained a quite different type of candidate, but the funds invested would have been useful for something else. When the individual candidate invested the same amount of resources in learning to write Tang dynasty poetry of a somewhat stuffy nature, it was just as rational from his standpoint, but society has lost these resources, except insofar as having one more producer of rather stuffy Tang dynasty poetry may have a positive value.

If we assume that the type of officials obtained by the examination were a great asset to China, that their value exceeded the cost of generating them, counting the cost of having all those people study Confucian classics all over China, and that there was no other less expensive way of obtaining the result, then the society would have gained from the institution. The situation would be rather similar to what we see in retail trade. People are always opening new restaurants, some of

---

[3] See chapter 6 of this volume for a mildly mathematical preliminary investigation of this type of game.

which go busted. Resources invested in the restaurant are wasted,[4] but we regard that as a necessary cost for maintaining an efficient restaurant industry. The imperial Chinese examination may have been an example of the same kind of thing. I have no doubt that it did produce a superior civil service, but I suspect that the cost was greater than the benefit.

If the benefit was greater than the cost, then this activity would not meet our definition of rent seeking, although it would clearly resemble the rent-seeking situation. Even so, we would prefer to select the same quality of candidate without expenditure of all these resources. This "waste" of resources does not occur if the investment takes the form of paying a fee that may then be used. The same reasoning applies if it is invested in some resource, human or otherwise, that pays a positive and continuing return at the existing marginal rate of interest. The student who had invested a great deal of time and effort in preparing for the imperial examinations and failed had invested a great deal of resources and produced no personal or social gain. Similarly, those very numerous people in India or Kenya, for example, who go to the local equivalent of a university and then remain "unemployed" for many years while they maneuver for government jobs are making a large investment that may have no return at all. The situation resembles the potlatches of the Pacific Northwest, where prestige and power were obtained by physically destroying valuable objects. The one who destroyed the most in the way of valuable products "won" the game and increased his prestige and influence.[5]

The situation may be contrasted with the custom of buying government jobs for cash, until recently quite common on the continent of Europe. The French government is a particularly good example, and most of the jobs held by French civil servants under the *ancien régime* were obtained by purchase. It should be emphasized that not just anyone could purchase a job and that after someone had purchased it he was subject to a good deal of control and supervision (mainly by people who had purchased their supervisory jobs), but the fact remains that one had to put up a large sum of money for the job. This

---

[4] It may have resale value.

[5] I have always been doubtful about the anthropological discussion of these potlatches, and hence I would not like to certify the statement above as true. Nevertheless, this is what the anthropologists say happened.

money was then regarded as ordinary government income and spent. Once again, the person buying the right to collect a particular tax in Orléans was making an investment in much the same way that the restaurant proprietor did. In this case, although he created no capital assets, the money he paid was at least used for government expenditures, such as extending Versailles.

Another outstanding example of a somewhat similar institution was the officer corps of the British Army prior to about 1860. Almost all officers of the rank of colonel or below had purchased their commissions and then purchased their promotions. They were compelled to spend time in each rank (at least one day), but they could buy a lieutenant's commission, spend a day as a lieutenant, sell that commission and buy a captain's commission, and so on. Many wealthy men who wanted to be colonels went through exactly that process. Generals were not appointed by this method.

It is notable that, although this system has been very widely criticized, there seems to be no obvious evidence that it worked badly. The British Army, staffed in this manner, undeniably had the best infantry in Europe. Further, it is notable that their very long record of military success was obtained without anything very outstanding in the way of higher command. Essentially, these "purchasing" officers appear to have been superb trainers and leaders of men. Why this is so, I do not know.

If we turn to the French example, although many people have criticized the *ancien régime*, the fact remains that during the period of two hundred years before the French Revolution (the period in which this system operated), France was usually accepted as the most powerful and progressive state on the continent of Europe. Certainly it would be hard to argue that its government was worse than its contemporaries.

William Niskanen has offered an argument for this type of government, an argument that is not intended to be conclusive but that does have some interest. If one bought an office under these circumstances and were later found guilty of bad performance, he could be removed from the office and the purchase price would *not* be refunded. Thus, in essence, the individual was posting a large bond for good performance. Bad performance would lead to forfeiture of the bond, but good performance would mean that either he could eventually sell the job to someone else—like a British Army officer's commission—or leave it to his heirs. As a third possibility, it would terminate with his death. In the latter case, of course, the price paid for the office was actuarially discounted for the life span of the individual who would hold it. Further, in the latter case, the amount forfeited in case of bad behavior would fall progressively as the incumbent aged.

Thus, we have several different types of "investment" that will produce a rent. In the first, an ordinary capitalist investment is made with the object of obtaining rent in the future. Granted there is a speculative element, it is quite possible the rent will not be obtained; however, real assets are created by the investment, and therefore society is better off, although perhaps not as well off as it would have been had the investment been successful. The second type is the case in which the rent is obtained by actually purchasing the right to collect it, as in the case of the young man who purchased the job of lieutenant in the Light Brigade in 1853. In this case, no social assets are produced, but at least there is no waste, since the payment goes to someone who gains from it. It is a pure transfer operation.

People who object to the second kind of rent seeking characteristically object only if the income source that is purchased is some kind of government employment. If I purchase an income stream by buying government bonds, they do not object. But if I buy the right to be customs inspector, they do. The objection to my purchase of the right to be customs inspector is apparently based on two distinct arguments. The first is that the person who can afford to buy the job may not be the best qualified man for it. In a perfect capital market, of course, this would not be true, but capital markets are certainly not perfect. The second objection is that the individual will use his job to repay himself for his "investment" and obtain further gains if he can. Whether this is an objection or not depends entirely upon the type of supervision the individual faces. If the supervision is of good enough quality that he maximizes his return by efficient service, then the argument would fall to the ground. Presumably, in most cases the performance is not that well supervised, but still it is not obvious that supervision in such cases would be worse than supervision for people who have obtained jobs in other ways. Hence, it is not obvious that this system would lead to poorer performance than other systems. The question of good or bad performance depends on rewards and penalties as they are administered during the course of the job, not on how one got the job.[6] If supervision is known to be very good, one would anticipate that the amount bid for the job, or the rent of the job, would be lower than if the supervision of the job were bad and it was possible to steal.

Our final case, and the one to which this paper is primarily devoted, concerns obtaining a rent by competition in what I suppose we may call a potlatch—in wasting resources. This is a situation in which a job will be given to one of a group of people, all of whom have invested a great many resources in seeking the job, with these resources useless for any other purpose. There is, therefore, a loss to society on those resources invested by the unsuccessful job seekers and a good deal of loss on those resources invested by the successful job seekers as well if the resource investment does not improve their efficiency in the job they seek out.

As we shall see below, the "rent-seeking economy" leads to further waste, but let us temporarily consider only this one particular waste—the waste of resources used in obtaining employment. Anne Krueger has looked into the issue of the returns to those engaged in organizing foreign exchange regulations in India and Turkey. She showed that the gain obtained by these people was about 7 percent of the gross national product in one case and about 15 percent in the other.[7] If we assume that the people who obtained these jobs were not simply selected at random, that they had maneuvered for the job and that the people maneuvering for each customs inspectorship invested resources that totalled about the present value of that inspectorship, this would mean that a capital value, perhaps 70 to 150 percent of the gross national product, was dissipated in obtaining these jobs.

Note that the fact that the individual customs inspector may be compelled to kick back to his superiors does not change this conclusion. His superiors will have had to maneuver for their jobs, and their superiors, and so on. What happens is that a very large quantity of resources is transferred from the productive sector to an activity that pays off for the individual participant but does not increase the

---

[6] This ignores temporarily our previous comment about the quality of the job seeker.

[7] Anne O. Krueger, "The Political Economy of the Rent-Seeking Society," chapter 4 in this volume.

consumer surplus for other citizens. Indeed, from my own experience in Asia, it seems to me that this cost is one of the basic reasons for Asia's backwardness. Asian countries have been doing this for a very long time.

It should be noted in this connection that Krueger's numbers apply to only one aspect of the centralized economic control maintained in both India and Turkey. When we consider that there is very much more in the way of such rent-seeking activity, it is clear that the economic waste must be extremely high.

So far we have been discussing what we might call a mature system of government rent seeking, one that has been in existence a long time and in which resources have adjusted to their long-run best use. In practice, probably most rent-seeking economies in the world today have many large incomes that are windfalls rather than the result of investment.[8]

This situation occurs because many of these governments are newly established, and it seems very doubtful that anyone anticipated that these large gains would be available at the time the individual young intellectual first turned his attention to political matters. For example, presumably many of the district commissioners in Ghana actually made quite modest investments in political maneuvering in the British colonial period, and then, when the Nkrumah dictatorship was established, found themselves in very high-paying jobs. In general, this would be true throughout the former colonial world. The previous colonial governments were not completely free of bribery and corruption, but there was less than there has been since then. Further, the people who collected these payments previously are now gone, and the new holders of these sinecures (in the technical sense of the word) generally got them much more easily than their successors will.

In another context, we may contrast the career of Thomas Corcoran ("Tommy the Cork") with that of a present-day graduate of Harvard Law School who is considering entrance into the Washington legal business. It seems very dubious that Corcoran, at the time he was going through law school, or even when in the early depression years he was recommended for a job in Washington by one of his for-

---

[8] See Donald L. Huddle, "An Estimate of Import Surplus under a Disequilibrium System," *Public Choice* 5 (Fall, 1968): 113–120.

mer professors, thought seriously about a permanent career negotiating with government agencies that at the time did not even exist. He got in early, however, and through great natural talents, application, and good connections became an extremely wealthy man.

In contrast, the present-day lawyer coming out of Harvard has had this idea in mind for a long time. He works on it in order to get into Harvard Law School (which in Corcoran's day was fairly easy), and then he quite deliberately takes a job in Washington at comparatively low pay for the purpose of developing the appropriate capital. Further, since he faces much competition in Washington, it is most unlikely that he will be able to achieve what Corcoran achieved so easily.

This is not an example of rent seeking but of rent avoidance (to be discussed below); however, the time structure is the same as in many existing governments where rent seeking is important. The resource cost of the high income of the present district commissioner in Ghana did not occur at the time he was maneuvering for the position, because in those days it was a relatively low-cost operation. It occurs in the present day when many citizens of Ghana, observing his success and large income, are devoting themselves to the attempt to get such jobs in the future.

Now let us consider a few additional costs of the rent-seeking economy. Note that these costs will depend to a considerable extent on the assumption that the rent is obtained by soliciting bribes for performance or nonperformance of duties. I think that this is normal in most of the countries we think of as rent seeking, although when I turn to American applications, this particular problem will be relatively small.

Suppose that an individual wanting to start a factory in Ghana contemplates the situation. First, he must obtain the necessary customs import license to import his equipment. This may or may not involve foreign exchange controls as well, depending on whether the person is a foreigner who is making a new commitment in Ghana or someone who is using funds that have been derived from Ghana at some time in the past. Once the equipment is in the country, he must move it to the potential investment site and begin construction. This will normally involve him with a totally different set of officials than those involved in passing the entrance of the equipment. Further, the district commissioner in the area where he is establishing his plant must be pacified. There are also other officials. There may be lawsuits, in which case judges will be involved. The use of public utilities may require special side payments, and so on.

The problem with these very large sets of payments is that they are not coordinated. The fee to the government that would maximize government revenue would be a single fee on the whole transaction. The fee to the customs inspector that will maximize his revenue, plus the fee to whoever arranges transportation, plus the fee to the district commissioner, and so forth, is likely to total much more than the revenue-maximizing fee for the government as a whole. The reason for this is the usual rule that when there are a number of stages in production and a monopoly on each one, the output (unless all monopolies can reach an agreement) is apt to be low and monopoly payments per unit high.

We usually face such a monopoly situation in this kind of government activity. The result is that the total fees are markedly larger than those which would optimize the revenue of the government, even if we assume the government had no other objective. In consequence, the investments that are made pay very high fees, but a great many desirable investments are not made at all.

One may ask here why the government itself does not aim at maximizing its income and deal with this matter by having a single payment. The explanation appears to be mostly simple inefficiency, in that the government does not recognize the situation that exists, but it is partly an innate characteristic of the use of illegal payments for the activity. These illegal payments are, almost of necessity, not appropriately recorded, and therefore no one knows exactly what the total is. Further, it is not necessarily obvious to a high-level official whether some particular delay he observes at a lower level is genuinely technical (as his inferior tells him) or is an effort to hold out for some additional payments.

The inefficiency is complicated by the fact that normally all the different agencies dealt with by the person attempting to establish a new factory are not even parts of the same ministry; hence, coordination is very difficult. The result of all of this is a set of payments markedly higher than would be desirable, even if we assume simply that the government's sole objective is to maximize its own revenue. This means that the rate of growth, living standards, and the like, are markedly lower than they would be if the purely exploitative but efficient government were in charge of matters.

I have discussed this process in terms of establishing a new manufacturing enterprise, but it is obvious that it fits many other situations. Simply living in the country may involve fairly high payments, particularly if the person who is living in the country has a higher-than-average living standard. The officials are rather apt to follow a policy Ludwig von Mises called "egalitarianism," but which I think would better be described as "private egalitarianism." They do not attempt to equalize incomes throughout society, since that would involve a reduction in their own incomes, but they do tend to equalize incomes in the private sector. It seems likely that the reason for this is not a desire for equality, although the officials may well rationalize it in that sense, but simply that this is the easiest way to collect their fees.

Plucking $10,000 from one wealthy man is much easier than plucking $100 from a hundred poor men. Thus, people who are in the private sector face what amounts to a very highly graduated income tax, and one that may effectively penalize productive labor much more severely than the type of progressive income tax with which we are familiar in Western countries. This is particularly so, since the wealthy man whose assets are relatively immobile and hard to conceal (for example, the builder of a steel plant) is an obvious target, whereas a wealthy man whose wealth is largely in Switzerland, who lives in comparative moderation while he is in Ghana and spends large amounts only when he is elsewhere, is much harder to tax. Thus, the system not only penalizes progress by lowering the incentives for hard work and intelligent investment, but in particular it penalizes those kinds of activities which tend to produce conspicuous assets.

There is another, very large cost imposed by the rent-seeking society of the type we are discussing, and this one is becoming important in the United States, too, although I think the previous ones I have mentioned are not yet significant. Let me begin by telling a story about Korea. In the years after the Korean war, President Rhee drove around the streets of Seoul in an old Packard automobile originally imported into Korea as the personal car of the American ambassador; it was sold to Rhee when the American ambassador got a newer car. The most important single businessman in Korea visited the United States and then returned to Korea, not by air or by passenger ship, but on a freighter. The freighter docked at Inchon, about twenty miles from Seoul, and there were on the deck of the freighter two Buicks, one green and one blue. Also, in the hold of the freighter there was a very large quantity of various things the businessman wanted to bring into Korea. When he arrived at Inchon, the customs inspectors promptly informed him that substantially everything he had with him was illegal for import.

The businessman, however, was a very good businessman, and he had planned for this contingency in advance. There was no reason why *he* could not land, and he went from the ship directly to the Kyung mu Dai (the Korean White House). There he told President Rhee that he had been concerned about the Korean president's driving around in an elderly car and had brought back a Buick for the president. In fact, he said that he had brought back two Buicks, so that the president could have his choice; he himself would use whichever one the president did not want. President Rhee was pleased and asked where the Buicks were. The businessman said, "Well, all my personal effects are currently being held up in customs in Inchon, but if you would like to see them immediately, I'm sure that you can arrange to get them released." President Rhee accordingly ordered that the businessman's personal luggage, including large items, be released. The businessman arrived the following day at Kyung mu Dai with two Buicks, and President Rhee chose the blue one.

Note that this very ingenious operation resulted in the businessman's getting a very large amount of material into Korea for payment of only about $5,000 or $6,000 in the prices of the time. Surely, if he had negotiated with the customs inspectors, the cost would have been on the order of $75,000 to $100,000. This is what I call rent-avoidance activity, and it is a major source of inefficiency in rent-seeking economies.

In these societies, a very major cost, and clearly a cost that varies a good deal from enterprise to enterprise, is the interference of the government. In most of the rent-seeking societies government officials want bribes, but in the United States the government makes specific administrative rules. Minimizing the cost of these bribes or regulations is a major activity of the higher management and, indeed, may become the *sole* activity. Some friends of mine visiting a factory on the outskirts of Seoul began their visit by talking to the president of the company. They asked whether his equipment was mainly Japanese or imported from Europe. He replied that it was mostly imported from Europe. They then went to visit the plant and discovered that almost every machine in it was in fact Japanese.

This issue is unimportant on its face; there was no reason why the plant should have one type of machinery rather than another, although it was true that it was during Rhee's tenure as president and that President Rhee was violently anti-Japanese. The impressive feature, however, is that the president of the company did not know enough about his own capital stock even to realize where it had been originated. He could not possibly have been engaging in a deliberate lie, because he knew that the visitors were going to go look at the machinery. He had to have been in ignorance.

This does not imply in any sense that he was inefficient. He had been devoting his time and attention to the area where he had the highest comparative advantage and the area with the highest payoff—greasing the wheels of government. He was asked a question about what, from his standpoint, was clearly a minor aspect of the company (production) and answered to the best of his ability. He normally left such matters to inferiors, who probably did at least a moderately good job, just as most American corporate presidents really pay very little attention to the janitorial staff in their factories.

The activity to which this corporate president was devoting himself is what I would like to call "rent avoidance." He was attempting to minimize the total rents that would be imposed on his company by direct bribe solicitation by higher officials and/or unfortunate administrative decision. The job is a difficult one. From the cost-benefit standpoint, is it better to invite the provincial governor to an elaborate dinner with *kisang* girls than to make a direct payment to the local magistrate? Perhaps the corporate president should visit the capital and spend several months there in general socializing.[9]

Further, many of these decisions are long-term investments. The

[9] The refugees from Communist China sometimes involve reasonably high-level officials. One of them has revealed that the governor of the province of Shantung characteristically spends nine of the twelve months of the year in Peking rather than in Shantung. This was no doubt sensible from his standpoint and may even be sensible from the standpoint of Shantung, but it surely does not lead to what Niskanen would call "process efficiency" in the Shantung government.

careful cultivation over a period of years of individual officials develops a very real type of human capital in the form of friendly relations that can be utilized. In the American context, Tommy the Cork, Clark Clifford, and Abe Fortas are all examples of people whose main stock-in-trade is this kind of connection.

No doubt such people are in fact invaluable to their companies or, for that matter, their branches of government, if it is a government enterprise. In the socialist economy, a man who has good contacts in the planning bureau is probably of more use to his particular enterprise than a good engineer. Probably also his personal income is a good deal higher than that of a good engineer.

The problem with this, although it is efficient from the standpoint of the individual enterprises, is that it involves a tremendous waste from the standpoint of the society as a whole. Large resources in terms of human capacity are diverted to the rent-seeking part of the government and the rent-avoidance activity in the private sector. In a way, the two activities tend to cancel each other. In these rent-seeking societies—such as traditional (or Communist) China, Korea, or India—they are, in a real sense, the major sources of income and wealth. In a way, there is a vast negative-sum game in which people with high natural talents who are willing to work hard can get very large returns while generating a social loss.

This illustrates a very old point in economics. Competition is not always a good thing. In a well-organized market, the individuals aiming solely at benefiting themselves end up benefiting other people. In a sufficiently badly organized market, and the market I am now describing is an example, they simply generate waste. Further, in most of the rent-seeking societies, the sum total of the activities of the rent seekers and the specialists in rent avoidance is not really zero-sum. They do not simply waste their own talents; in the course of their maneuvering, they impose costs on the rest of society that retard development.

The provincial governor who promulgates a new regulation with the intent of increasing the number of fees he gets for permitting people to avoid it not only increases his own income and the potential income of the specialists in rent avoidance, but he also imposes a real burden on society, for the regulation, in at least some areas, will be enforced. Further, he may, as a result of concentrating on this kind of activity, have this time distracted from such necessary functions of government as maintaining public order. He may not be supervising his junior officials, with the result that the kind of multiple exaction I have described above occurs. Altogether, one would expect poverty from this system, and, if we turn to the parts of the world where it is dominant, that is what we see.

If we examine the United States and most modern European countries, we find relatively little direct bribing of government officials. Note that I say relatively little, not zero, and I should also add that in my opinion the amount is increasing; unless changes are made, it will become quite a large amount in a generation or so. Still, in a direct sense the phenomenon of rent seeking does not exist.

In an indirect sense, rent seeking does exist to some extent, and the bureaucrats tend to be paid a good deal more than is actually necessary for the performance of their services, although the very highest officials are normally paid less than would be needed in order to attract people capable of managing these immense organizations. This conflict between fairly high pay for the lower officials and fairly low pay for the higher officials may be one of the reasons why in most Western countries the lower-level bureaucracy tends to be relatively uncontrolled from the top. The salaries offered to the upper administrators simply cannot attract people who have the personal ability necessary to control such a large apparatus.[10]

The bureaucrats and other government officials, however, if they do not do very much in the way of soliciting bribes, do in fact issue a very large number of regulations and laws that directly affect many private businessmen. Further, the actual administration of these laws is invariably subject to a good deal of discretion. I should say in passing that the highest level of discretion of this sort is in fact exercised not by what we think of as bureaucrats, but by an older bureaucracy, that is, the courts. The judges are far more likely to make decisions on their own without being deeply bound by the law than are the regular bureaucrats. This is concealed from view to some extent by the fact that the judge's decision is defined as the law, and we do not generally

---

[10] This assumes that there are people with this kind of ability. No private company is anywhere near as large as, let us say, the Department of Health, Education, and Welfare.

notice how little it is controlled by the law that existed before he pronounced it.

This matter aside, what we observe is the development of very large-scale rent-avoidance activities. The DuPont Corporation for many generations was headed by chemical engineers. In the early days, these engineers were members of the DuPont family, but after two generations in which the president was a young man who had married the daughter of the previous president, rather than a direct DuPont, it slipped into the control of people who are not members of the family. It is notable that the current president, Irving S. Shapiro, is not a chemical engineer but an attorney who is a specialist on public relations and government influence. I do not wish to criticize DuPont for this decision, which I think under the circumstances was very sensible, and I certainly do not wish to criticize Shapiro, who I think is an extremely competent, intelligent, and well-motivated man. However, I do criticize the social order that made it necessary for this company to switch to a manipulator for its chief executive. Surely our medicines and plastics will be poorer in the future than they would be had the company retained its concentration on essentially technological matters.

Note that all this is a sharp change in emphasis, not an absolute change in nature of the world. Private businessmen do a good deal of rent seeking and rent avoidance, too, but it is a relatively minor factor. As a bachelor, I normally spend Christmas with my sister and brother-in-law. About nine years ago, my brother-in-law went to a small town in Iowa to take over the management of a very small company founded by his father. It had been operated until that time by a very pleasant man who was essentially a salesman with little interest in the formal details of management. I well remember the first Christmas and the deluge of expensive gifts my brother-in-law received from the suppliers of various raw materials used by the company. My brother-in-law, as head of the company, was intensely interested in the quality and price of the products he bought and less interested in the personal relations with the companies that generated them. As a result, although the company today purchases something like ten times as much in the way of raw materials, he now gets Christmas cards.

It will be seen from this example that the sales vice-presidents of the various companies with which he dealt made the same kind of calculations to which I have been referring in my rent-avoidance discussion. What happened when my brother-in-law replaced his predecessor was simply that the relative cost-benefit calculations of an expensive gift, compared with very slight reduction in price, changed. Therefore, these vice-presidents switched their approach. This is characteristic of the market. Salesmen, like the one from whom I bought my house, do cultivate the personal arts that would characterize the rent-avoidance expert in a rent-seeking economy. There is a payoff to it, but it is a relatively modest payoff, and this particular type of personality and type of activity have a reasonable but not gigantic return.

As we move to more and more government activity, however, and as this government activity becomes more and more a matter that various individual officials can change at their discretion, we move to higher and higher investments in rent avoidance on the part of private individuals and companies. This is not inefficient from their standpoint. They are, indeed, behaving in an appropriate manner. From the standpoint of society as a whole, however, this activity is almost total waste. Today the small company of which my brother-in-law is president invests a fair amount of executive time in worrying about, and in some cases attempting to influence, government regulations. When he first took over ten years ago, this was a very small-scale activity. Now it is quite significant. Surely this use of time means (1) that the executive staff is larger than it was before and (2) that it devotes less attention to problems of production, product design, and distribution. The economy as a whole is less efficient, even though the adjustment by this little company to the present reality is an efficient one.

When I first went into the diplomatic service, there were two of us from the University of Chicago Law School in the same class. I ran into the second again about twenty years later. Like me, he had left the diplomatic service, but he had gone into jointly writing novels and rent avoidance. Specifically, he was vice-president of the Bank of America in Washington, although the Bank of America at that time had no branches east of the Mississippi. The job, which left him enough leisure so that he could write novels, involved serving on several government commissions, acting as a representative to some of the international banking organizations with headquarters in Washington, and, of course, developing friends. He was also much interested in public relations activities and apparently passed on almost all press releases by the Bank of America, although I am not sure that is so. I am sure that Bank of America was getting its money's worth from his activities, but it is very doubtful that the United States was.

He was only one representative of a very widespread phenomena. I would anticipate that, with time, the problems of New York will be complicated by more and more companies moving to the Washington area. As the principal economic activity of high officials becomes more and more concentrated on rent avoidance, we can anticipate steady growth of the Virginia and Maryland suburbs.

However, in the United States rent avoidance is not the only thing that absorbs resources. Private companies may be interested in influencing the government not to reduce their costs, but to increase the costs of their competitors or, perhaps, in getting a government-sponsored cartel organized. This would be a case of rent seeking by government activity. Further, the civil servants frequently feel that promotion can be achieved through expanding the scope of their bureau. This, again, involves rent seeking. It is likely, however, that under present circumstances in the United States and in most western European countries, this rent seeking is of much lower importance than rent avoidance. Once again, I doubt that this will continue to be true in the future.

Thus, the problem in the United States, although real and growing, is very modest compared with what we observe in the less developed parts of the world. Indeed, it seems to me that this difference is, to a large extent, the explanation for the backwardness of these areas or, perhaps more accurately, the advance of the West. The situation in which there was a relatively open economy and governments that had relatively little influence over the details of economic life was, historically, highly exceptional. The rent-seeking, rent-avoiding economy had been the historic norm and is today the world norm. The exceptions to it have been rare. In a way, what has been happening here in the United States and in Europe is a return to a more normal form of government from an extraordinarily unusual form. This more normal form of government apparently carries with it that other phenomenon that has been normal both in history and in the world today—poverty.

If we look around the world, then, the United States still seems to be a rather favorable place to live, both from the standpoint of existing capital assets and the prospect of producing more. Perhaps the Common Market in Europe, where individual governments are highly interventionist but where freedom of trade in the Common Market as a whole puts severe limits on their powers, may, with time, overtake and surpass the United States in real wealth. Still, we are well off. We have far less rent seeking and rent avoidance than most countries. We have far more rent seeking and rent avoidance, however, than we had a hundred years ago, and I fear that in another hundred years we will be a relatively normal country in this regard.

II.

Three Basic Papers on the Theory
and Measurement of Rent Seeking

3

The Welfare Costs of Tariffs, Monopolies, and Theft

by

GORDON TULLOCK

IN recent years a considerable number of studies have been published that purport to measure the welfare costs of monopolies and tariffs.[1] The results have uniformly shown very small costs for practices that economists normally deplore. This led R. A. Mundell to comment in 1962 that "unless there is a thorough theoretical re-examination of the validity of the tools upon which these studies are founded . . . someone will inevitably draw the conclusion that economics has ceased to be important."[2] If one can judge from conversations with graduate students, a number of younger economists are in fact drawing the conclusion that tariffs and monopolies are not of much importance. This view is now beginning to appear in the literature. On the basis of these measurements Professor Harvey Leibenstein has argued, "Microeconomic theory focuses on allocative efficiency to the exclusion of other types of efficiencies that, in fact, are much more significant in many instances."[3]

It is my purpose to take the other route suggested by Mundell and to demonstrate that the "tools on which these studies are founded" produce an underestimation of the welfare costs of tariffs and monopo-

[1] These studies are conveniently listed with a useful table of the welfare losses computed in each in Harvey Leibenstein, "Allocative Efficiency vs. 'X-Efficiency'," *American Economic Review* 56 (June, 1966): 392–415.

[2] R. A. Mundell, "Review of L. H. Janssen, *Free Trade, Protection and Customs Union*," *American Economic Review* 52 (June, 1962): 622.

[3] Leibenstein, "Allocative Efficiency," p. 392. In this article Leibenstein consistently uses the phrase *allocative efficiency* to refer solely to the absence of tariffs and monopolies.

lies. The classical economists were not concerning themselves with trifles when they argued against tariffs, and the Department of Justice is not dealing with a miniscule problem in its attacks on monopoly.

Statics

The present method for measuring these costs was pioneered by Professor A. C. Harberger.[4] Let us, therefore, begin with a very simple use of his diagram to analyze a tariff. Figure 3.1 shows a commodity that can be produced domestically at the constant cost of P_1 and imported at P_0. With the given demand and no tariff, Q_0 units will be purchased at a price of P_0. If a prohibitive tariff is imposed, Q_1 units will be bought at a price of P_1. The increase in price, it is argued, is merely a transfer from some members of the community to others, and the only welfare loss is consequently the shaded triangle. The studies purporting to measure the welfare costs of tariffs have simply computed the value of this triangle. From the geometry it is fairly obvious that the amount would normally be small.

There are a considerable number of costs that are ignored by this procedure. As a starter, collection of a tariff involves expenditure on customs inspectors and others who do the actual collection and on coast guards who prevent smuggling. Further, customs brokers are normally hired by the shipper to expedite the movement of their goods through customs.[5] Normally we pay little attention to collection costs because they are small, but in this case they may well be larger than the welfare triangle, which is also small. Thus, by simply adding in collection costs, we significantly increase the "social cost" of the tariff.

[4] A. C. Harberger, "Using the Resources at Hand More Effectively," *American Economic Review* 49 (May, 1959): 134–146. It should be noted that Harberger suggested the method for the measurement of the welfare costs of monopoly, but its extension to cover tariffs was the work of other scholars. The more careful scholars who have measured the welfare costs of tariffs have not all used this very simple application of Harberger's method, but a method such as illustrated in figure 3.2. I have chosen to begin with this method of measurement partly because it simplifies the exposition and partly because this procedure is the conventional wisdom on the matter. (Also see Leibenstein, "Allocative Efficiency.")

[5] Strictly speaking, the customs brokerage should be added on to the tax, thus producing a larger welfare triangle.

FIGURE 3.1

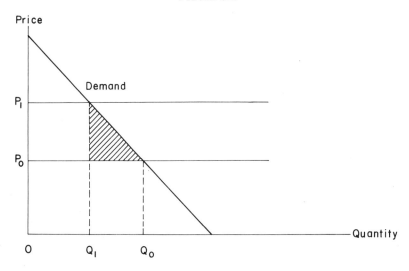

For a more significant criticism of this method of measuring the welfare cost, let us apply the procedure to a standard excise tax instead of a tariff. Assume that figure 3.1 shows a constant supply cost and a declining demand for some commodity in some country. Q_0 units are bought at a price, P_0. Now suppose that a tax is imposed, raising the price to P_1, and reducing sales to Q_1. The welfare cost of this tax is measured by the shaded triangle. But suppose further that the revenues raised by this tax are completely wasted—on building tunnels, for example, that go nowhere. Now the social cost of the total package of tax and wasteful expenditure is the welfare triangle plus the total tax revenue, or the trapezoid bounded by the lines showing cost, the cost-plus-tax, and the demand function. The people buying the product pay more than the cost, but no one benefits from the expenditure.[6] The funds are not transferred because no one benefits from the existence of the tax. The whole economy is poorer not just by the triangle, but by the whole amount of wasted resources.

The tariff involves a similar waste of resources, and consequently

[6] The government action might slightly increase the rents on the resources used to build the tunnel, and thus the owners of specialized resources might benefit slightly, but clearly this is a very trivial effect.

its social cost cannot be measured simply by the welfare triangle. Figure 3.1 can also be used to show the foreign and domestic costs of some type of good and the national demand for it. Since domestic cost is higher than the (delivered) cost of the foreign good, none would be produced domestically in the absence of a tariff. Q_0 units would be imported and consumed at a price shown by P_0. The country now puts on a prohibitive tariff, and the higher-cost domestic production takes over the complete market. Q_1 units are sold at P_1. The welfare triangle has been used to measure the welfare cost of this operation.[7] The argument for this procedure is, essentially, that the higher prices paid by the consumers represent a transfer payment, not a real loss to the economy. But who receives this transfer? The owners of the resources now engaged in inefficiently producing the commodity receive no more than they would have received had the tariff never been introduced and had they been employed in other industries.[8] These resources, however, are being inefficiently utilized, and the rectangle between P_1 and P_0 and bounded by the vertical axis and Q_1 measures the social cost of this waste. Thus the total welfare cost of the tariff is the triangle plus the much larger rectangle to its left.

The situation is identical to that which would arise if the government required an established domestic industry to abandon an efficient method of production and adopt an inefficient one. This could be graphed on the same diagram, and it would be generally agreed that the welfare loss would not be just the welfare triangle, but would also include the inefficient use of resources required by the governmental regulation shown in the rectangle to the left of the triangle. Since a tariff shifting production from export goods to import-replacement goods where the country has a comparative disadvantage is, in fact, a governmental requirement that the goods be obtained in an inefficient manner, the cases are identical. The cost of a protective tariff is the triangle plus the difference between domestic cost of production and the price at which the goods could be purchased abroad.

Let us, however, consider the situation in which there is some domestic production before the imposition of a tariff. Figure 3.2 shows

[7] Tibor Scitovsky, *Economic Theory and Western European Integration* (Palo Alto: Stanford University Press, 1958).

[8] There might be sizable but temporary rents to the firstcomers when the industry was first established.

FIGURE 3.2

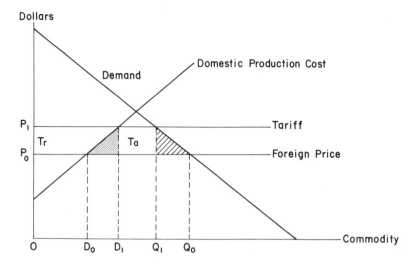

a commodity, part of which is imported and part produced domestically. The supply elasticity of the commodity from foreign sources is assumed infinite, but domestic production is carried on in conditions of increasing costs. Without the tariff, the price is P_0, domestic producers turn out D_0 units and $Q_0 - D_0$ units are imported to make up the total consumption of Q_0. Suppose, now, that Mr. Gladstone is prime minister and imposes a tariff on imports and an excise tax of the same amount on domestic production. With the new price, P_1, consumers will want only Q_1 units, and the shaded triangle measures the excess burden. Domestic production will remain D_0, but imports will shrink from $Q_0 - D_0$ to $Q_1 - D_0$. The government will receive a tax revenue equivalent to the entire rectangle bounded by the two price lines, the vertical axis, and Q_1.

Let us now change our example by assuming that the domestic excise tax is repealed, so that we have only a protective tariff. Domestic consumption and price would remain the same, but domestic production would expand to D_1 and imports would shrink accordingly. There would be an inefficient use of resources in producing things better imported, represented by the dotted triangle. Governmental revenues would shrink to the rectangle marked T_a and the owners of the resources in the domestic industry would receive an amount of resources equal to the area of the trapezoid T_r.[9] Clearly the social cost of the tariff is not just the shaded triangle, but also the dotted triangle, which shows a net waste of resources in inefficient production.

Dynamics: The Cost of Transfers

The trapezoid T_r, however, would appear to be a pure transfer and hence not to be included in the computation of the cost of the tariff. Strictly speaking this is so, but if we look at the matter dynamically, there is another social cost involved, and its magnitude is a function of the size of this transfer trapezoid. Generally governments do not impose protective tariffs on their own. They have to be lobbied or pressured into doing so by the expenditure of resources in political activity. One would anticipate that the domestic producers would invest resources in lobbying for the tariff until the marginal return on the last dollar so spent was equal to its likely return, which would produce the transfer. There might also be other interests trying to prevent the transfer and putting resources into influencing the government in the other direction. These expenditures, which may simply offset each other to some extent, are purely wasteful from the standpoint of society as a whole; they are spent not in increasing wealth, but in attempting to transfer or resist transfer of wealth. I can suggest no way of measuring these expenditures, but the potential returns are large, and it would be quite surprising if the investment was not also sizable.

Monopolies involve costs of a somewhat similar nature, and it follows that I will not be able to produce a method to measure their social costs. I will, however, be able to demonstrate that the welfare triangle method greatly underestimates these costs. The argument is customarily explained with the aid of a figure like figure 3.1. The monopolist charges the monopoly price P_1 instead of the cost P_0 for the commodity, and consumption is reduced from Q_0 to Q_1. The welfare triangle is a clear loss to the community, but the rectangle to its left is merely a transfer from the consumers to the owners of the monopoly. We may object to the monopolist's getting rich at the expense of the rest of us, but this is not a reduction in the national product.

In order to demonstrate that this line of reasoning ignores impor-

[9] See J. Wemelsfelder, "The Short-Term Effect of the Lowering of Import Duties in Germany," *Economic Journal* 70 (March, 1960): 94–104.

FIGURE 3.3

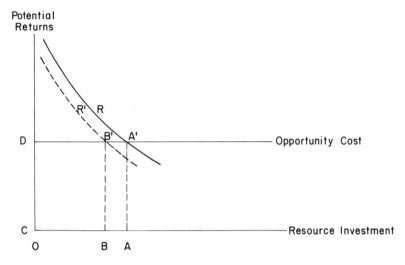

tant costs, I should like to take a detour through the economics of theft.[10] Theft, of course, is a pure transfer and therefore might be assumed to have no welfare effects at all. Like a lump-sum tax, it produces no welfare triangle and hence would show a zero social cost if measured by the Harberger method. This would, of course, be incorrect. In spite of the fact that it involves only transfers, the existence of theft has very substantial welfare costs. Our laws against theft do not deal with a trivial problem any more than do our laws against monopoly.

Figure 3.3 shows the situation confronting the potential thief. On the horizontal axis is shown the quantity of effort and capital (burglars' tools, etc.) he might invest in a career of crime. On the vertical axis are shown potential returns. The "opportunity cost" line shows the returns he could get for the same investment of work and material in

[10] The economics of illegal activities is an underdeveloped area, but Harold Demsetz discusses the subject briefly in "The Exchange and Enforcement of Property Rights," *Journal of Law and Economics* 7 (October, 1964) 11–26. J. Randolph Norsworthy's doctoral dissertation, "A Theory of Tax Evasion and Collection" (University of Virginia, 1966), is a more comprehensive examination of one type of illegal activity. Two unpublished items have been circulated among a few scholars: Gary Becker's "A Theory of Government Punishments and Rewards" and my own "Law and Morals," the unfinished manuscript of a book I began four years ago that has languished in draft form for almost all of those four years.

other occupations. It is assumed to be constant. Let us begin by assuming that taking another's property is not illegal. Under these circumstances the returns on various amounts of investment in the activity are shown by line R. The potential thief would invest the quantity of resources shown at A in theft, the cost to him would be the rectangle $AA'DC$, and his net return on the investment would be the triangular area above $A'D$.

The situation of a person who wished to guard his own assets, who might, of course, be the thief hoping to hold onto his loot, may also be shown on figure 3.3. On the horizontal axis are shown the resources invested in loss-minimizing activities.[11] The cost of each unit of resources put to this use is shown by the horizontal opportunity line, and the savings are on the vertical axis. The line R now shows the returns in the form of savings for each unit of "theft prevention." The total amount of resources invested would again be A.

The two situations are interrelated by more than the fact that they can be shown on the same diagram. The height of the R curve for the thief would depend upon the amount of resources invested by other members of the community in locks and other protections. Similarly, the individual in considering how many locks to buy would find that his R curve depended upon the resources being invested in attempts at theft by the rest of the population. When a potential thief invests money, say, in an improved lock pick, the R curve for people trying to protect their property moves downward. Similarly, hiring an armed guard to watch one's valuables moves the R curve for potential thieves down. Putting a new lock on my door reduces the chance that I will be robbed, but whether the gain will be worth the cost will depend upon the effort the thieves are willing to put into getting in. Over time the interaction between the investment in locks, the payoff on lock picks, and the investment in nitroglycerine and safes would come to equilibrium.

This equilibrium, however, would be extremely costly to the society in spite of the fact that the activity of theft involves only transfers. The cost to society would be the investments of capital and labor in the activity of theft and in protection against theft. If we consider

[11] The word *activities* may be misleading. One way of minimizing loss by theft is to have little or nothing to steal. In a world in which theft was legal, we could expect this fact to lead to a reduction in productive activities and a great expansion in leisure.

figure 3.3 as representing the entire society instead of individuals, then the social costs would be the area covered by the rectangle $AA'DC$. Transfers themselves cost society nothing, but for the people engaging in them they are just like any other activity, and this means that large resources may be invested in attempting to make or prevent transfers. These largely offsetting commitments of resources are totally wasted from the standpoint of society as a whole.

This lesson has been learned by almost all societies that have adopted a collective method of reducing this sort of income transfer. This collective procedure, laws against theft and police and courts to enforce them, can also be shown on figure 3.3. On the horizontal axis we now have resources invested by police and courts, with their opportunity cost shown as a horizontal line. The "protection" given by each unit of resources invested in these activities is shown by the R line. The society would purchase A amount of protective services, and the total cost would be the usual rectangle. The effect of this would be to reduce the expected returns on theft and the savings to be made by private investment in locks and safes. The new returns are shown by R' on figure 3.3, and there is a corresponding reduction in the resources invested in each of these fields to B'. Whether the establishment of a police force is wise or not depends upon an essentially technological question. If police activities are, for a range, more efficient than private provision of protection, then the R line will have the shape shown, and the police and court rectangle will have an area smaller than the sum of the two "savings" rectangles for theft and locks.[12] This is, of course, what we normally find in the real world.

Note, however, that we do not carry investment in police protection to the extent that it totally replaces private protection expenditures. Clearly it is more efficient to have some protective expenditures by the owners of property. Automobiles are equipped with locks and keys, presumably because the expansion of the police force that could be paid for from the cost of leaving them off would be less effective in preventing theft than locks and keys are.[13] The total social cost of theft

[12] It may be suggested that society should not be interested in saving the resources of thieves and, hence, that the value of the protection afforded by the police should be measured by the lock rectangle only. This, however, would be correct only to the extent that the resources would not be reallocated to socially acceptable production.

[13] James Buchanan and Gordon Tullock, "Public and Private Interaction under Re-

is the sum of the efforts invested in the activity of theft, private protection against theft, and the public investment in police protection. The theft itself is a pure transfer and has no welfare cost, but the existence of theft as a potential activity results in very substantial diversion of resources to fields where they essentially offset each other and produce no positive product. The problem with income transfers is not that they directly inflict welfare losses, but that they lead people to employ resources in attempting to obtain or prevent such transfers. A successful bank robbery will inspire potential thieves to greater efforts, lead to the installation of improved protective equipment in other banks, and perhaps result in the hiring of additional policemen. These are its social costs, and they can be very sizable.

But this has been a detour through the criminal law, and our major subject is monopoly. To return to figure 3.1, the rectangle to the left of the welfare triangle is the income transfer that a successful monopolist can extort from the customers. Surely we should expect that with so large a prize dangling before us, potential monopolists would be willing to invest large resources in the activity of monopolizing. In fact the investment that could be profitably made in forming a monopoly would be larger than this rectangle, since it represents merely the income transfer. The capital value, properly discounted for risk, would be worth much more. Entrepreneurs should be willing to invest resources in attempts to form a monopoly until the marginal cost equals the properly discounted return.[14] The potential customers would also be interested in preventing the transfer and should be willing to make large investments to that end. Once the monopoly is formed, continual efforts either to break the monopoly or to muscle into it would be predictable. Here again considerable resources might be invested. The holders of the monopoly, on the other hand, would be willing to put quite sizable sums into the defense of their power to receive these transfers.

As a successful theft will stimulate other thieves to greater indus-

---

ciprocal Externality," in *The Public Economy of Urban Communities*, ed. Julius Margolis (Baltimore: Johns Hopkins University Press, 1964), pp. 52–73.

[14] The margin here is a rather unusual one. Additional units of resources invested in attempting to get a monopoly do not increase the value of the potential monopoly, but only the likelihood of getting it. Thus they change the discount rate rather than the payoff.

try and require greater investment in protective measures, so each successful establishment of a monopoly or creation of a tariff will stimulate greater diversion of resources to attempts to organize further transfers of income. In Gladstone's England few resources were put into attempts to get favorable tariff treatment. In the United States today large and well-financed lobbies exist for this purpose. The welfare cost in the first case was very low; in the second it must be quite sizable. An efficient police force reduces the resources put into the activity of theft, and free trade or an active antitrust policy will reduce the resources invested in lobbying or attempting to organize monopolies.

The problem of identifying and measuring these resources is a difficult one, partly because the activity of monopolizing is illegal. The budget of the antitrust division and the large legal staffs maintained by companies in danger of prosecution would be clear examples of the social cost of monopoly, but presumably they are only a small part of the total. That very scarce resource, skilled management, may be invested to considerable extent in attempting to build, break, or muscle into a monopoly. Lengthy negotiations may be in real terms very expensive, but we have no measure of their cost. Similarly, a physical plant may be designed not for maximum efficiency in direct production, but for its threat potential. Again, no measure is possible. As a further problem, probably much of the cost of monopoly is spread through companies that do not have a monopoly but have gambled resources on the hopes of one. The cost of a football pool is not measured by the cost of the winner's ticket, but by the cost of all tickets.[15] Similarly the total costs of monopoly should be measured in terms of the efforts to get a monopoly by the unsuccessful as well as the successful. Surely more American businessmen know that the odds are against their establishing a paying monopoly, and they therefore discount the potential gain when investing resources in attempting to get one. The successful monopolist finds that his gamble has paid off, and the unsuccessful "bettor" in this particular lottery will lose, but the resources put into the "pool" would be hard to find by economic techniques. But regardless of the measurement problem, it is clear that the resources put into monopolization and defense against monopolization would be a func-

---

[15] This helpful analogy was suggested to me by Dr. William Niskanen.

tion of the size of the prospective transfer. Since this would be normally large, we can expect that this particular socially wasteful type of "investment" would also be large. The welfare triangle method of measurement ignores this important cost, and hence greatly understates the welfare loss of monopoly.

4

The Political Economy of the Rent-Seeking Society

by

ANNE O. KRUEGER

IN many market-oriented economies, government restrictions upon economic activity are pervasive facts of life. These restrictions give rise to rents in a variety of forms, and people often compete for the rents. Sometimes such competition is perfectly legal. In other instances, rent seeking takes other forms, such as bribery, corruption, smuggling and black markets.

It is the purpose of this paper to show some of the ways in which rent seeking is competitive and to develop a simple model of competitive rent seeking for the important case when rents originate from quantitative restrictions upon international trade. In such a case (1) competitive rent seeking leads to the operation of the economy inside its transformation curve; (2) the welfare loss associated with quantitative restrictions is unequivocally greater than the loss from the tariff equivalent of those quantitative restrictions; and (3) competitive rent seeking results in a divergence between the private and social costs of certain activities. Although the analysis is general, the model has particular applicability for developing countries, where government interventions are frequently all-embracing.

A preliminary section of the paper is concerned with the competitive nature of rent seeking and the quantitative importance of rents for two countries, India and Turkey. In the second section, a formal model of rent seeking under quantitative restrictions on trade is developed

NOTE: I am indebted to James M. Henderson for invaluable advice and discussion on successive drafts. Jagdish Bhagwati and John C. Hause made helpful comments on earlier drafts of this paper.

and the propositions indicated above are established. A final section outlines some other forms of rent seeking and suggests some implications of the analysis.

Competitive Rent Seeking

MEANS OF COMPETITION

When quantitative restrictions are imposed upon and effectively constrain imports, an import license is a valuable commodity. It is well known that under some circumstances one can estimate the tariff equivalents of a set of quantitative restrictions and analyze the effects of those restrictions in the same manner as one would the tariff equivalents. In other circumstances, the resource-allocational effects of import licensing will vary, depending upon who receives the license.[1]

It has always been recognized that there are some costs associated with licensing: paperwork, the time spent by entrepreneurs in obtaining their licenses, the cost of administrative apparatus necessary to issue licenses, and so on. Here, the argument is carried one step further: in many circumstances resources are devoted to competing for those licenses.

The consequences of that rent seeking are examined below. First, however, it will be argued that rent-seeking activities are often competitive and resources are devoted to competing for rents. It is difficult, if not impossible to find empirically observable measures of the degree to which rent seeking is competitive. Instead, some mechanisms under which rent seeking is almost certain to be competitive are examined. Then other cases are considered in which it is less obvious, but perhaps equally plausible, that competition results.

Consider first the results of an import-licensing mechanism when licenses for imports of intermediate goods are allocated in proportion to firms' capacities. That system is frequently used, and has been analyzed for the Indian case by Jagdish Bhagwati and Padma Desai.[2] When licenses are allocated in proportion to firms' capacities, invest-

[1] This phenomenon is explored in detail in Jagdish Bhagwati and Anne O. Krueger, *Foreign Trade Regimes and Economic Development: Experience and Analysis* (New York: Columbia University Press, forthcoming).

[2] Jagdish Bhagwati and Padma Desai, *Planning for Industrialization: A Study of India's Trade and Industrial Policies since 1950* (Cambridge: Cambridge University Press, 1970).

ment in additional physical plant confers upon the investor a higher
expected receipt of import licenses. Even with initial excess capacity
(due to quantitative restrictions upon imports of intermediate goods),
a rational entrepreneur may still expand his plant if the expected gains
from the additional import licenses he will receive, divided by the cost
of the investment, equal the returns on investment in other activities.[3]
This behavior could be perfectly rational even if, for all entrepreneurs,
the total number of import licenses remains fixed. In fact, if imports
are held constant as domestic income grows, one would expect the domestic value of a constant quantity of imports to increase over time,
and hence installed capacity would increase while output remained
constant. By investing in additional capacity, entrepreneurs devote resources to compete for import licenses.

A second sort of licensing mechanism frequently found in developing countries is used for imports of consumer goods. There, licenses
are allocated pro rata in proportion to the applications for those licenses from importers-wholesalers. Entry is generally free into im-
porting-wholesaling and firms usually have U-shaped cost curves. The
result is a larger-than-optimal number of firms operating on the down-
ward-sloping portion of their cost curves yet earning a "normal" rate of
return. Each importer-wholesaler receives fewer imports than he
would buy at existing prices in the absence of licensing but realizes a
sufficient return on those licenses he does receive to make it profitable
to stay in business. In this case, competition for rents occurs through
entry into the industry with smaller-than-optimal firms, and resources
are used in that the same volume of imports could be efficiently distributed with fewer inputs if firms were of optimal size.

A third sort of licensing mechanism is less systematic in that government officials decide on license allocations. Competition occurs to
some extent through both mechanisms already mentioned as businessmen base their decisions on expected values. But, in addition, competition can also occur through allocating resources to influencing the
probability, or expected size, of license allocations. Some means of influencing the expected allocation—trips to the capital city, locating

---

[3] Note that (1) one would expect to find greater excess capacity in those industries
where rents are higher, and (2) within an industry, more efficient firms will have greater
excess capacity than less efficient firms, since the return on a given amount of investment will be higher with greater efficiency.

the firm in the capital, and so on—are straightforward. Others, including bribery, hiring relatives of officials, or employing the officials themselves upon retirement, are less so. In the former case, competition occurs through choice of location, expenditure of resources upon travel, and so on. In the latter case, government officials themselves receive part of the rents.

Bribery has often been treated as a transfer payment. However, there is competition for government jobs, and it is reasonable to believe that expected total remuneration is the relevant decision variable for persons deciding upon careers. Generally, entry into government service requires above-average educational attainments. The literature on human capital provides evidence that choices as to how much to invest in human capital are strongly influenced by rates of return upon the investment. For a given level of educational attainment, one would expect the rate of return to be approximately equated among various lines of endeavor. Thus, if there appear to be high official-plus-unofficial incomes accruing to government officials and higher education is a prerequisite for seeking a government job, more individuals will invest in higher education. It is not necessary that government officials earn the same total income as other college graduates. All that is necessary is that there be an excess supply of persons seeking government employment or that highly educated persons make sustained efforts to enter government services. Competition takes place through attaining the appropriate credentials for entry into government service and through accepting unemployment while making efforts to obtain appointments. Efforts to influence those in charge of making appointments, of course, just carry the argument one step further back.

To argue that competition for entry into government service is, in part, a competition for rents does not imply that all government servants accept bribes or that they would leave government service were bribes not available. Successful competitors for government jobs might experience large windfall gains even at their official salaries. However, if the possibility of those gains induces others to expend time, energy, and resources in seeking entry into government services, the activity is competitive for present purposes.

In all these license-allocation cases, there are means, legal and illegal, of competing for rents. If individuals choose their activities on the basis of expected returns, rates of return on alternative activities will be equated and, in that sense, markets will be competitive.[4] In most cases, people do not perceive themselves to be rent seekers and, generally speaking, individuals and firms do not specialize in rent seeking. Rather, rent seeking is one part of an economic activity, such as distribution or production, and part of the firm's resources are devoted to the activity (including, of course, the hiring of expediters). The fact that rent seeking and other economic activities are not generally conducted by separate economic entities provides the motivation for the form of the model developed below.

ARE RENTS QUANTITATIVELY IMPORTANT?

Granted that rent seeking may be highly competitive, the question remains whether rents are important. Data from two countries, India and Turkey, suggest that they are. Gunnar Myrdal believes India may "on the balance, be judged to have somewhat less corruption than any other country in South Asia."[5] Nonetheless, it is generally believed that "corruption" has been increasing, and that much of the blame lies with the proliferation of economic controls following independence.[6]

Table 4.1 presents crude estimates, based on fairly conservative assumptions of the value of rents of all sorts in 1964. One important source of rents, investment licensing, is not included, for lack of any valid basis on which to estimate its value. Many smaller controls are also excluded. Nonetheless, it is apparent from table 4.1 that import licenses provided the largest source of rents. The total value of rents of Rs. 14.6 billion contrasts with Indian national income of Rs. 201 billion in 1964. At 7.3 percent of national income, rents must be judged large

[4] It may be objected that illegal means of competition may be sufficiently distasteful that perfect competition will not result. Three comments are called for. First, it requires only that enough people at the margin do not incur disutility from engaging in these activities. Second, most lines of economic activity in many countries cannot be entered without some rent-seeking activity. Third, risks of detection (especially when bribery is expected) and the value judgments associated with illegal activities differ from society to society. See Ronald Wraith and Edgar Simpkins, *Corruption in Developing Countries* (London: Allen and Unwin, 1963).

[5] Gunnar Myrdal, *Asian Drama: An Inquiry into the Poverty of Nations*, 3 vols. (New York: Pantheon Books, 1968), I, 943.

[6] Santhanam Committee, *Report of the Committee on Prevention of Corruption* (New Delhi: Ministry of Home Affairs, 1964), pp. 7–8.

TABLE 4.1
Estimates of Value of Rents, India, 1964

Source of Rent	Amount of Rent (billion rupees)
Public investment	0.365
Imports	10.271
Controlled commodities	3.000
Credit rationing	0.407
Railways	0.602
TOTAL	14.645

SOURCES:

Public investment: The Santhanam Committee, *Report*, pp. 11–12, placed the loss in public investment at *at least* 5 percent of investment. That figure was multiplied by the average annual public investment in the *Third Five Year Plan* (New Delhi: Planning Commission, 1961).

Imports: The Santhanam Committee, *Report*, p. 18, stated that import licenses were worth 100 to 500 percent of their face value. Seventy-five percent of the value of 1964 imports was used here as a conservative estimate.

Controlled commodities: These commodities include steel, cement, coal, passenger cars, scooters, food, and other price- and/or distribution-controlled commodities, as well as foreign exchange used for illegal imports and other unrecorded transactions. The figure is the lower bound estimate given by John Monteiro, *Corruption* (Bombay: Manaktalos, 1966), p. 60. Monteiro puts the upper bound estimate at Rs. 30,000 billion, although he rejects the figure on the (dubious) ground that notes in circulation are less than that sum.

Credit rationing: The bank rate in 1964 was 6 percent; Rs. 20.3 billion of loans were outstanding. It is assumed that *at least* an 8 percent interest rate would have been required to clear the market, and that 3 percent of bank loans outstanding would be equivalent to the present value of new loans at 5 percent. Data source: Reserve Bank of India, *Report on Currency and Finance, 1967–68* (New Delhi: Reserve Bank of India), tables 534 and 554.

Railways: Monteiro, *Corruption*, p. 45, cites commissions of 20 percent on railway purchases, and extra-official fees of Rs. 0.15 per wagon and Rs. 1.4 per 100 maunds loaded. These figures were multiplied by the 1964 traffic volume; 203 million tons of revenue-paying traffic originated in that year. Third plan expenditure on railroads was Rs. 13,260 million. There were 350,000 railroad goods wagons in 1964–65. If a wagon was loaded once a week, there were 17,500,000 wagons of freight. At Rs. 0.15 per load, this would be Rs. 2.6 million; 100 maunds equal 8,228 pounds, so at 1.4 Rs. per 100 maunds, Rs. 69 million changed hands; if one-fifth of railroad expenditures were made in 1964–1965, Rs. 2652 million was spent in 1964; at 20 percent, this would be Rs. 530 million, for a total of Rs. 602 million.

relative to India's problems in attempting to raise her savings rate.

For Turkey, excellent detailed estimates of the value of import licenses in 1968 are available.[7] Data on the c.i.f. prices of individual imports, their landed cost (c.i.f. price plus all duties, taxes, and landing charges), and wholesale prices were collected for a sizable sample of commodities representing about 10 percent of total imports in 1968. The c.i.f. value of imports in the sample was TL 547 million and the landed cost of the imports was TL 1,443 million. The value at the wholesale level of these same imports was TL 3,568 million. Of course, wholesalers incur some handling, storage, and transport costs. The question, therefore, is the amount that can be attributed to normal wholesaling costs. If one assumes that a 50 percent markup would be adequate, then the value of import licenses was TL 1,404 million, or almost three times the c.i.f. value of imports. Imports in 1968 were recorded (c.i.f.) as 6 percent of national income. On the basis of Aker's data, this would imply that rents from import licenses in Turkey in 1968 were about 15 percent of GNP.

Both the Indian and the Turkish estimates are necessarily somewhat rough. But they clearly indicate that the value of import licenses to the recipients was sizable. Since means were available of competing for the licenses, it would be surprising if competition did not occur for prizes that large. We turn, therefore, to an examination of the consequences of competitive rent seeking.

The Effects of Competitive Rent Seeking

The major proposition of this paper is that competitive rent seeking for import licenses entails a welfare cost in addition to the welfare cost that would be incurred if the same level of imports were achieved through tariffs. The effects of tariffs upon production, trade, and welfare are well known, and attention is focused here upon the additional cost of competitive rent seeking. A simple model is used to develop the argument. Initially, free trade is assumed. Then, a tariff or equivalent import restriction is introduced. Finally, an equal import restriction with competitive rent seeking is examined.

[7] I am indebted to Ahmet Aker of Robert College, who kindly made his data available to me. Details and a description of the data can be found in my forthcoming book.

THE BASIC MODEL

Two commodities are consumed by the country under investigation: food and consumption goods. Food is produced domestically and exported. Consumption goods are imported. Distribution is a productive activity whereby food is purchased from the agricultural sector, exported, and the proceeds used to import consumption goods that are sold in the domestic market. Labor is assumed to be the only domestic factor of production.[8] It is assumed that the country under consideration is small and cannot affect its international terms of trade. Physical units are selected so that the fixed international prices of both goods are unity.

The agricultural production function is

$$A = A(L_A), \; A' > 0, \; A'' < 0 \qquad (1)$$

where A is the output of food and L_A is the quantity of labor employed in agriculture. The sign of the second derivative reflects a diminishing marginal physical product of labor in agriculture, due, presumably, to fixity in the supply of land.

The level of distribution output, D, is defined to equal the level of consumption goods imports, M:

$$D = M. \qquad (2)$$

One unit of distributive services entails exchanging one unit of imports for food with the agricultural sector at the domestic terms of trade and exporting the food in exchange for imports at the international terms of trade. Constant returns to scale are assumed for the distribution activity; one unit of distribution requires k units of labor. Total labor employed in distribution, L_D, is

$$L_D = kD. \qquad (3)$$

A distribution charge of p_D per unit is added to the international price of imports:

$$p_M = 1 + p_D \qquad (4)$$

where p_M is the domestic price of imports. The domestic price of food is assumed to equal its unit international price.[9]

---

[8] Labor could be regarded as a composite domestic factor of production. Extensions to two or more factors would complicate the analysis but would not alter its basic results.

[9] These assumptions establish a domestic numeraire. The real analysis would be unaffected by proportional changes in the domestic prices.

Society's demand for imports depends upon the domestic price of imports and total income generated in agriculture.[10]

$$M = M(p_M, A) \tag{5}$$

where $\partial M/\partial p_M < 0$ and $\partial M/\partial A > 0$. Demand decreases with increases in the price of imports, and increases with increases in agricultural output (income). Equation (5) is derived from micro utility maximization with the assumption that farmers, distributors, and rent seekers all have the same consumption behavior. Domestic food consumption, F, is simply the quantity not exported:

$$F = A - M. \tag{6}$$

Since the fixed international terms of trade equal unity, food exports equal consumption goods imports.

Finally, it is assumed that the economy under consideration has a fixed labor supply, $\bar{L}$:

$$\bar{L} = L_A + L_D + L_R \tag{7}$$

where L_R is the quantity of labor engaged in rent seeking.

FREE TRADE

Under free trade, there is free entry into both agriculture and distribution and competition equates the wage in the two activities:

$$A' = p_D/k. \tag{8}$$

Equations (1) to (8) constitute the free-trade system. These eight equations contain the eight variables A, M, D, F, L_A, L_D, p_M, and p_D. Since there is no rent seeking under free trade, $L_R \equiv 0$.

It is easily established that free trade is optimal in the sense that the domestic price ratio under free trade equals the marginal rate of transformation between food consumption and imports. The consumption possibility locus is obtained by substituting into (6) from (1) and (7):

$$F = A(\bar{L} - kM) - M.$$

The locus has a marginal rate of transformation greater than one:

$$\frac{-dF}{dM} = kA' + 1 > 1, \tag{9}$$

---

[10] Food and imports are consumed. But, by choice of food as the numeraire (see equation [6]) and the assumed constancy of international prices, agricultural output serves as a measure of income.

which reflects the positive distribution cost of substituting imports for food consumption. The locus is concave:

$$\frac{d^2F}{dm^2} = k^2 A'' < 0,$$

since $A'' < 0$, which follows from diminishing returns in food production. Substituting from (8) into (9),

$$\frac{-dF}{dM} = 1 + p_D,$$

which establishes the aforementioned equality.

A free-trade solution is depicted in figure 4.1. Domestic food consumption and import consumption are measured along OF and OM, respectively. The consumption possibility locus is $\hat{F}\hat{M}$. At the point $\hat{F}$ no imports are consumed and hence there is no distribution. If distribution were costless, society could choose its consumption point from the line $\hat{F}A$. However, to consume one unit of import requires exchanging one unit of food and withdrawing k workers from agriculture to provide the requisite distributive services. With diminishing marginal product of labor in agriculture, the cost of additional imports in terms of forgone food production rises. Thus, the price of distribution, and hence the domestic price of imports, increases in moving

FIGURE 4.1

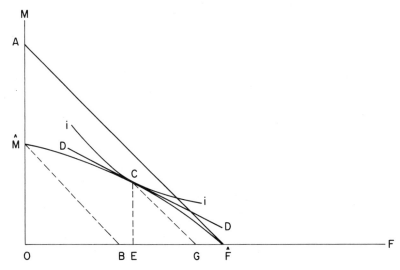

northwest from $\hat{F}$. The consumption point $\hat{M}$ has OB food exchanged for $O\hat{M}$ of imports. The distance $\hat{F}B$ is the agricultural output forgone to distribute $O\hat{M}$ imports.

If society's preferences are given by the indifference curve ii, point C is optimal. The price of distribution is reflected in the difference between the slope of $\hat{F}A$ and the slope of DD at C. At the point C, OG food would be produced, with EG ($=EC$) exported, and the rest domestically consumed.

A TARIFF OR AN IMPORT RESTRICTION WITHOUT RENT SEEKING

Consider now a case in which there is a restriction upon the quantity of imports

$$M = \overline{M} \tag{10}$$

where $\overline{M}$ is less than the import quantity that would be realized under free trade. Since entry into distribution is now limited, the competitive wage equality (8) will no longer hold. The relevant system contains (1) to (7) and (10). The variables are the same as in the free-trade case, and again $L_R = 0$. The system may be solved sequentially: given (10), D follows from (2), L_D from (3), L_A from (7), A from (1), F from (6), p_M from (5), and p_D from (4). Since equations (1), (6), and (7) remain intact, the solution for this case is also on the consumption possibility locus.

It is useful to establish the directions of change for the variables following a switch from free trade to import restriction. The reduced import level will reduce the labor employed in distribution and increase the labor force in agriculture. Diminishing returns will reduce the agricultural wage. The domestic price of imports, the distributive margin, and the wage of distributors will increase. Distributors will earn a rent in the sense that their wage will exceed the wage of those engaged in agriculture.

In the absence of rent seeking, a tariff and a quantitative restriction are equivalent[11] aside from the resultant income distribution. Under a quantitative restriction the distributive wage is higher than the agricultural. If, instead, there were an equivalent tariff with distribu-

---

[11] The change in the price of the import from the free-trade solution is the tariff equivalent of the quantitative restriction described here.

FIGURE 4.2

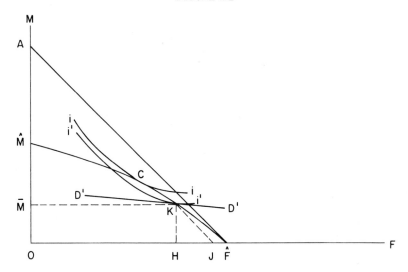

tion of the proceeds, the marginal produce of labor in agriculture would be unchanged, but agricultural workers would benefit by the amount of tariff proceeds redistributed to them, whereas traders' income would be lower. Since the allocation of labor under a tariff and quantitative restriction without rent seeking is the same and domestic prices are the same, the only difference between the two situations lies in income distribution.

The solution under a quantitative restriction is illustrated in figure 4.2, where $\hat{F}\hat{M}$ is again the consumption possibility locus and C the free-trade solution. With a quantitative restriction on imports in the amount $O\overline{M}$, the domestic prices of imports, and hence of distribution, rise from free trade to import restriction. Food output (OJ) and domestic consumption of food increase, and exports decline to HJ ($= O\overline{M}$). The indifference curve $i'i'$ lies below ii (and the point C), and the welfare loss may be described by the consumption and production cost measure given by Harry Johnson.[12]

The wage rate in distribution unequivocally rises for a movement from free trade to a quantitative restriction. The total income of dis-

[12] H. G. Johnson, "The Cost of Protection and the Scientific Tariff," *Journal of Political Economy* 68 (August, 1960): 327–345.

tributors will increase, decrease, or remain unchanged depending upon whether the proportionate increase in p_D is greater than, less than, or equal to the absolute value of the proportionate decrease of imports. For the moment, let p_D, p_M, and M represent free-trade solution values, and let p_D^*, p_M^*, and $\overline{M}$ represent import-restriction solution values. The total arc elasticity of demand for imports for the interval under consideration, η, is

$$\eta = \frac{-(\overline{M} - M)}{\overline{M} + M} \cdot \frac{p_M^* + p_M}{p_M^* - p_M} . \tag{11}$$

Total expenditure on imports will increase, decrease, or remain unchanged as η is less than one, greater than one, or equal to one. The total income of distributors will increase if

$$p_D^*\overline{M} > p_D M.$$

Multiplying both sides of this inequality by $(p_M^* + p_M)/(p_M^* - p_M)$, substituting from (11), and using (4),

$$1 + 2/(p_D^* + p_D) > \eta . \tag{12}$$

Hence, distributors' total income can increase even if the demand for imports is price elastic.[13] The smaller the free-trade distributive markup, the more likely it is that the distributors' total income will increase with a curtailment of imports. The reason is that an increase in the domestic price of imports results in a proportionately greater increase in the price of distribution.

AN IMPORT RESTRICTION WITH COMPETITIVE RENT SEEKING

In the import-restriction model just presented, the wage in distribution p_D/k exceeds the wage in agriculture A'. Under this circumstance, it would be surprising if people did not endeavor to enter distribution in response to its higher return. Resources can be devoted to rent seeking in all the ways indicated at the beginning of this discussion. This rent-seeking activity can be specified in a number of different ways. A simple and intuitively plausible specification is that people will seek distributive rents until the average wage in distribution and rent seeking equals the agricultural wage:[14]

---

[13] Proof of (12) uses the step that $p_D^*\overline{M} > p_D M$ implies $(p_D^* - p_D)/(p_D^* + p_D) > -(\overline{M} - M)/(\overline{M} + M)$. Note that in the continuous case, (12) reduces to $1 + 1/p_D > \eta$.

[14] As an alternative, the distributive production function (3) can be altered to treat all persons competing for import licenses as distributors so that L_D also encompasses L_R

$$A' = \frac{p_D \overline{M}}{L_D + L_R} . \tag{13}$$

One can regard all distributors and rent seekers as being partially engaged in each activity, or one can think of rent seekers as entering in the expectation of receiving import licenses. In the latter case, the final solution classifies the successful seekers in L_D and the unsuccessful ones in L_R. Equation (13) implies risk neutrality in this circumstance.

The model for import restriction with rent seeking contains the same equations, (1) and (7) and (10), and the same variables as the model for import restrictions without rent seeking. In addition, the new model contains (13) and the introduction of L_R as a variable. The essential factor of rent seeking is that L_R becomes positive.

Let us start with a solution for an import restriction without rent seeking and ask what happens to the values of the variables when rent seeking is introduced. By assumption $M = \overline{M}$ is unchanged, so that L_D is unchanged. Therefore, $dL_A = -dL_R$, because the labor that enters rent seeking can come only from agriculture. Substituting into the total differential of (1) and using (6),

$$dF = dA = -A' dL_R < 0 . \tag{14}$$

Agricultural production and food consumption are reduced by the introduction of rent seeking. Since the import level remains unchanged, rent seeking entails a welfare loss beyond that for an import restriction without rent seeking. The concavity of the agricultural production function results in a food loss that is less than proportional to decreases in L_A. Differentiating (5) totally,

$$0 = M_1 dp_M + M_2 dA \tag{15}$$

where M_1 and M_2 are the partial derivatives of (5) with respect to p_M and A, respectively. Solving (15) for dp_M, and substituting from (4) and (14),

$$dp_D = dp_M = \frac{M_2}{M_1} A' dL_R < 0 \tag{16}$$

since $M_1 < 0$ and $M_2 > 0$. The domestic cost of imports will be lower

---

and $A' = p_D \overline{M}/L_D$. Another alternative is to introduce a rent-seeking activity distinct from distribution with a wage determined from total rents $(p_D - A'k) \overline{M}/L_R$ and require that this wage equal the wages in distribution and agriculture. These specifications give results equivalent to those that follow from (13).

FIGURE 4.3

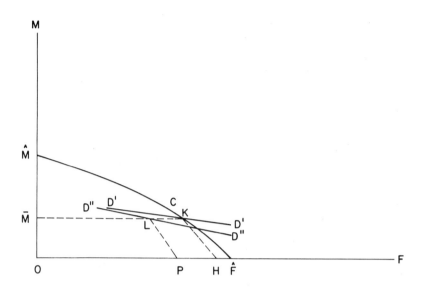

under rent-seeking competition. This follows from the decrease in the consumption of food relative to imports.

The results of (14) and (16) are not dependent upon the particular form of the equilibrium of the labor market. They hold for any specification of competitive rent seeking. Equation (13) serves to determine particular values for L_R and other variables of the system. The mere existence of competitive rent seeking is enough to determine the directions of change of the variables.

The above results are sufficient to indicate that, for any given level of import restrictions, competition among rent seekers is clearly inferior to the tariff equivalent of the restrictions, in that there could be more food consumed with no fewer imports under the latter case than under the former. To the extent that rent seeking is competitive, the welfare cost of import restrictions is equal to the welfare cost of the tariff equivalent plus the additional cost of rent-seeking activities. Measurement of that excess cost is considered below.

The tariff-equivalent and rent-seeking equilibria are contrasted in figure 4.3. Equilibrium under rent seeking will be at some point such as L, with the same consumption of imports but with smaller production and consumption of food than occurs under a tariff. The points K

and C are the tariff-equivalent and free-trade equilibria, respectively. The line $D'D'$ corresponds to the domestic price of imports in figure 4.2, and the steeper line $D''D''$ corresponds to the lower domestic price of imports under competitive rent seeking.

So far, it has been shown that for any given level of import restriction, a tariff is Pareto-superior to competitive rent seeking, and the properties of rent-seeking equilibrium have been contrasted with those of the tariff-equivalent case in the absence of competition for the rents. A natural question is whether anything can be said about the properties of rent-seeking equilibrium in contrast with those of a free-trade equilibrium, which is, after all, the optimal solution. It has been seen that the number of persons engaged in distribution declines from free trade to import restriction without rent seeking and increases as one goes from that situation to competition for import licenses. Likewise, agricultural output increases between free trade and the tariff-equivalent case and declines between that and rent seeking. The question is whether any unambiguous signs can be placed on the direction of these changes between free trade and rent seeking and, in particular, whether society can produce and consume less of both goods under rent seeking than under free trade.

The answer is that if inequality (12) is satisfied, the absolute number of persons $(L_D + L_R)$ in distribution will increase going from a free-trade to a rent-seeking equilibrium. If import demand is more elastic, the number of persons in distribution will decline. Contrasted with a free-trade equilibrium, there would be less agricultural output and fewer imports when inequality (12) holds. If, with import restriction, the income from distribution $p_D^* \overline{M}$ is greater than distributors' income at free trade, more persons will be employed in distribution-cum-rent seeking with import restriction than are employed under free trade.

MEASURING THE WELFARE LOSS FROM RENT SEEKING

A tariff has both production and consumption costs, and it has already been shown that rent seeking entails costs in addition to those of a tariff. Many forms of competition for rents, however, are by their nature difficult to observe and quantify, and one might therefore question the empirical content of the result so far obtained.

Fortunately, there is a way to estimate the production cost of rent seeking. That cost, in fact, is equal to the value of the rents. This can be shown as follows. The rent per import license, r, is:

$$r = p_D - kA'. \tag{17}$$

This follows because the labor required to distribute one unit of imports is k, which could be used in agriculture with a return A'. Note that at free trade r equals zero. A distributor could efficiently distribute an import and earn his opportunity cost in agriculture with zero rent. The total value of rents, R, with competitive rent seeking is thus the rent per unit of imports times the amount imported.

$$R = r\bar{M} = (p_D - kA')\bar{M}. \tag{18}$$

Using (3) and (13),

$$R = \left(p_D - \frac{kp_D\bar{M}}{L_D + L_R}\right)\bar{M} \tag{19}$$

$$= p_D\left(1 - \frac{L_D}{L_D + L_R}\right)\bar{M}$$

$$= \frac{p_D\bar{M}L_R}{L_D + L_R}$$

Thus the total value of rents reflects the agricultural wage (A') times the number of rent seekers.

The value of rents reflects the value (at current prices) of the domestic factors of production that could be extracted from the economy with no change in the final goods and services available for society's use. Thus, if the value of rents is known, it indicates the volume of resources that could be transferred out of distribution and into other activities with no loss of distributive services from an initial position of rent-seeking activity. The estimates of rents in India and Turkey, therefore, may be interpreted as the deadweight loss from quantitative restrictions in addition to the welfare cost of their associated tariff equivalents if one believes that there is competition for the rents.

The value of the rents overstates the increase in food output and consumption that could be attained with a tariff to the extent that the marginal product of labor in agriculture is diminishing, since the equilibrium wage will rise between the tariff and the competitive rent-seeking situation. In the case of a constant marginal product of labor in alternative uses, the value of rents will exactly measure forgone output.

THE IMPLICATIONS OF RENT SEEKING FOR TRADE THEORY

Recognition of the fact of rent-seeking alters a variety of conclusions normally obtained in the trade literature, and examination of such cases is well beyond the scope of this paper. A few immediately derivable results are worth brief mention, however.

First, an import prohibition might be preferable to a nonprohibitive quota if there is competition for licenses under the quota. This follows immediately from the fact that a prohibition would release resources from rent seeking, and the excess cost of domestic production might be less than the value of the rents. Second, one could not, in general, rank the tariff equivalents of two (or more) quotas, since the value of rents is a function of both the amount of rent per unit (the tariff equivalent) and the volume of imports of each item.[15] Third, it has generally been accepted that the more inelastic the domestic demand, the less the welfare cost of a given tariff is likely to be. For the quota-cum-rents case, the opposite is true: the more price inelastic the demand, the greater the value of rents and the greater, therefore, the deadweight loss associated with rent seeking. Fourth, it is usually believed that competition among importers will result in a better allocation of resources than will a monopoly. If rent seeking is a possibility, however, creating a monopoly position for one importer will generally result in a higher real income, if not in a preferable income distribution for society. Finally, devaluation under quantitative restrictions may have important allocation effects because it diminishes the value of import licenses, and hence the amount of rent-seeking activity, in addition to its effects upon exports.

Conclusions and Implications

In this paper, focus has been on the effects of competition for import licenses under a quantitative restriction of imports. Empirical evidence suggests that the value of rents associated with import licenses can be relatively large, and it has been shown that the welfare cost of quantitative restrictions equals that of their tariff equivalents plus the value of the rents.

[15] I am indebted to Bhagwati for pointing out this implication.

While import licenses constitute a large and visible rent resulting from government intervention, the phenomenon of rent seeking is far more general. Fair trade laws result in firms of less-than-optimal size. Minimum wage legislation generates equilibrium levels of unemployment above the optimum with associated deadweight losses, as shown by John Harris and Michael Todaro.[16] Ceilings on interest rates and consequent credit rationing lead to competition for loans and deposits and/or high-cost banking operations. Regulating taxi fares affects the average waiting time for a taxi and the percentage of time taxis are idle, but probably not their owners' incomes, unless taxis are also licensed. Capital gains tax treatment results in overbuilding of apartments and uneconomic oil exploration. And so on.

Each of these and other interventions lead people to compete for the rents, although the competitors often do not perceive themselves as competing in this way. In each case there is a deadweight loss associated with that competition over and above the traditional triangle. In general, prevention of that loss can be achieved only by restricting entry into the activity for which a rent has been created.

That, in turn, has political implications. First, even if they can limit competition for the rents, governments that consider they must impose restrictions are caught on the horns of a dilemma. If they do restrict entry, they are clearly "showing favoritism" to one group in society and choosing an unequal distribution of income. If, instead, competition for the rents is allowed (or cannot be prevented), income distribution may be less unequal, and certainly there will be less appearance of favoring special groups, although the economic costs associated with quantitative restrictions will be higher.

Second, the existence of rent seeking surely affects people's perception of the economic system. If income distribution is viewed as the outcome of a lottery where wealthy individuals are successful (or lucky) rent seekers, whereas the poor are those precluded from or unsuccessful in rent seeking, the market mechanism is bound to be suspect. In the United States, rightly or wrongly, societal consensus has been that high incomes reflect, at least to some degree, high social

---

[16] J. R. Harris and M. P. Todaro, "Migration, Unemployment, and Development: A Two-Sector Analysis," *American Economic Review* 60 (March, 1970): 126–142; M. P. Todaro, "A Model of Labor Migration and Urban Employment in Less Developed Countries," *American Economic Review* 59 (March, 1969): 138–148.

product. As such, the high American per capita income is seen as a result of a relatively free market mechanism and an unequal distribution is tolerated as a by-product. If, instead, it is believed that few businesses would survive without exerting "influence," even if only to bribe government officials to do what they ought in any event to do, it is difficult to associate pecuniary rewards with social product. The perception of the price system as a mechanism rewarding the rich and well-connected may also be important in influencing political decisions about economic policy. If the market mechanism is suspect, the inevitable temptation is to resort to greater and greater intervention, thereby increasing the amount of economic activity devoted to rent seeking. As such, a political vicious circle may develop. People perceive that because of competitive rent seeking the market mechanism does not function in a way compatible with socially approved goals. A political consensus therefore emerges to intervene further in the market, rent seeking increases, and further intervention results. While it is beyond the competence of an economist to evaluate the political impact of rent seeking, the suspicion of the market mechanism so frequently voiced in some developing countries may result from it.

Finally, all market economies have some rent-generating restrictions. One can conceive of a continuum between a system of no restrictions and a perfectly restricted system. With no restrictions, entrepreneurs would seek to achieve windfall gains by adopting new technology, anticipating market shifts correctly, and so on. With perfect restrictions, regulations would be so all-pervasive that rent seeking would be the only route to gain. In such a system, entrepreneurs would devote all their time and resources to capturing windfall rents. Although neither of these extreme types could ever exist, one can perhaps ask whether there might be some point along the continuum beyond which the market fails to perform its allocative function to any satisfactory degree. It will remain for further work to formalize these conjectures and to test their significance. It is hoped, however, that enough has been said to stimulate interest and research on the subject.

5

The Social Costs of Monopoly
and Regulation

by

RICHARD A. POSNER

WHEN market price rises above the competitive level, consumers who continue to purchase the sellers' product at the new, higher price suffer a loss, L (figure 5.1), exactly offset by the additional revenue that the sellers obtain at the higher price. Those who stop buying the product suffer a loss, (D), not offset by any gain to the sellers. This is the "deadweight loss" from supracompetitive pricing, and in traditional analysis its only social cost, L being regarded merely as a transfer from consumers to producers. Loss D, however, underestimates the social costs of monopoly. The existence of an opportunity to obtain monopoly profits will attract resources into efforts to obtain monopolies, and the opportunity costs of those resources are social costs of monopoly, too.[1] Theft provides an instructive analogy. The transfer of wealth from victim to thief involves no artificial limitation of output,[2] but it does not follow that the social cost of theft is zero. The opportunity for such transfers draws resources into thieving and in turn into protection

NOTE: Research on this paper was supported by a grant from the National Science Foundation to the National Bureau of Economic Research for research in law and economics. The paper is not an official National Bureau publication, since it has not yet undergone the full critical review accorded Bureau publications, including approval by the Bureau's Board of Directors. I am grateful to William F. Baxter, Gary S. Becker, Harold Demsetz, Victor R. Fuchs, William M. Landes, Sam Peltzman, and George J. Stigler for helpful comments on previous drafts of the paper.

[1] Gordon Tullock, "The Welfare Costs of Tariffs, Monopolies, and Theft," chapter 3 in this volume.

[2] If a thief took three radios from a home and on the way out dropped one, which broke, the resulting loss would correspond to the deadweight loss of monopoly.

FIGURE 5.1

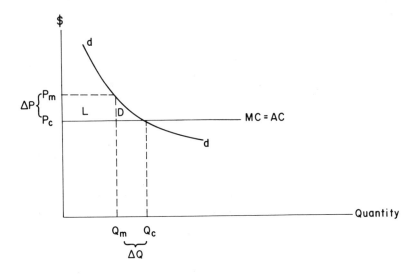

against theft, and the opportunity costs of the resources consumed are social costs of theft.[3]

This sort of analysis has long been familiar in a few special contexts. Arnold Plant's criticism of the patent system, made more than a generation ago, was based on the effect of the patent monopoly in drawing greater resources into invention than into activities that yield only competitive returns. Lester Telser's theory of resale price maintenance is in the same vein, as is the literature on nonprice competition among members of a cartel.[4] But, although the tendency of monopoly rents to be transformed into costs is no longer a novel insight, its implications both for the measurement of the aggregate social costs of monopoly and for a variety of other important issues relating to mo-

[3] Tullock, "The Welfare Costs of Tariffs, Monopolies, and Theft;" Gary S. Becker, "Crime and Punishment: An Economic Approach," *Journal of Political Economy* 76 (March–April, 1968): 169–217.

[4] Arnold Plant, "The Economic Theory Concerning Patents, *Economica* 1 (n.s.) (February, 1934): 30–51; Lester Telser, "Why Should Manufacturers Want Fair Trade?" *Journal of Law and Economics* 3 (October, 1960): 86–105; George J. Stigler, *The Organization of Industry* (Homewood, Ill.: Irwin, 1968), pp. 23–28; George W. Douglas and James C. Miller III, "The CAB's Domestic Passenger Fare Investigation," *Bell Journal of Economics and Management Science* 5 (Spring, 1974): 204–222.

nopoly and public regulation (including tax policy) continue for the most part to be ignored. The present paper is an effort to rectify this neglect.[5]

The first section presents a simple model of the social costs of monopoly, conceived as the sum of the deadweight loss and the additional loss resulting from the competition to become a monopolist. The second section uses the model to estimate the social costs of monopoly in the United States and the social benefits of antitrust enforcement. The estimates are crude; their primary value may simply be to induce skepticism about the existing empirical literature on the social costs of monopoly. The third section considers the implications of the analysis for several qualitative issues relating to monopoly and public regulation.

A Model of the Social Costs of Monopoly

ASSUMPTIONS

The critical assumptions underlying the model are the following:

1. Obtaining a monopoly is itself a competitive activity, so that, at the margin, the cost of obtaining a monopoly is exactly equal to the expected profit of being a monopolist. An important corollary of this assumption is that there are no intramarginal monopolies—no cases, that is, where the expected profits of monopoly exceed the total supply price of the inputs used to obtain the monopoly. If there were such an excess, competition in the activity of obtaining the monopoly would induce the competing firms (or new entrants) to hire additional inputs in an effort to engross the additional monopoly profits.

2. The long-run supply of all inputs used in obtaining monopolies is perfectly elastic. Hence, the total supply price of these inputs includes no rents.

3. The costs incurred in obtaining a monopoly have no socially valuable by-products.

The first two assumptions assure that all expected monopoly rents are transformed into social costs, and the third that these costs

[5] See Anne Krueger, "The Political Economy of the Rent-Seeking Society" (chapter 4 in this volume), for a parallel approach to the measurement of the social costs of import licenses in India and Turkey.

FIGURE 5.2

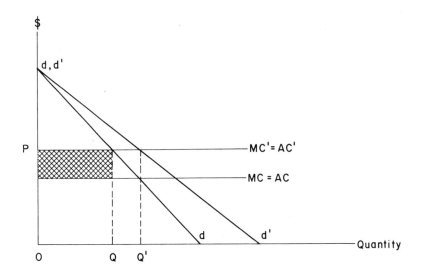

do not generate any social benefits.[6] But how reasonable are such assumptions?

1. The first is a standard assumption of economics and, pending better evidence than we have, seems a reasonable one in the present context. Anyone can try to obtain a patent, a certificate of public convenience and necessity, a television license, a tariff, an import quota, or a minimum-wage law, and anyone can try to form a cartel with his competitors or, if he is a member of a cartelized industry, to engross a greater share of the monopoly profits of the industry.[7] Nonprice competition in the airline industry illustrates the last point. If the Civil Aeronautics Board (CAB) places a floor under airline prices that exceeds the marginal cost of providing air transportation under competitive conditions, the situation initially is as depicted in figure 5.2 and is unstable. Since nonprice competition is not constrained, the airlines will expend resources on such competition (better service, etc.) until the marginal costs of air transportation rise to the level (*P* in figure 5.2)

---

[6] Another assumption, but one that does not affect the analysis, is that the monopoly is enjoyed for one period only; otherwise the optimum expenditures on obtaining a monopoly could not be compared directly with *L* in figure 5.1.

[7] Other than by reducing price, a method of obtaining a larger share of the cartel's profits that would not involve a socially wasteful use of resources.

where the industry is earning only a normal return.[8] The result will be the transformation of the monopoly profits initially generated by the regulatory price floor—the shaded rectangle—into higher costs for the industry. The demand curve shifts to the right because the increased expenditures on service improve the product from the standpoint of the consumer. But the additional consumer surplus is not great enough to offset the higher costs; otherwise the higher level of service would have been provided without the spur of monopoly pricing.

If nonprice competition were forbidden (say, at zero cost) or were somehow not feasible, it would not follow that our assumption that monopolizing as a competitive activity would be overthrown. It would mean simply that the expected profits of the airline business would be greater than if the airlines could expect those profits to be dissipated in nonprice competition. Hence, more resources would be devoted to obtaining a license from the CAB in the first place. The expected profits from monopoly pricing of air transportation would still be zero.

2. Although the assumption that obtaining monopolies involves constant costs seems plausible as a first approximation—there seems little reason to think that it involves using resources whose long-run supply is inelastic—a more important point is that the assumption may not be a crucial one. Assume that suppliers of inputs into monopolizing do obtain rents. In the long run, the availability of such rents will attract additional resources into the production of those inputs, and these resources will be wasted from a social standpoint. Some possible exceptions are considered below under "Other Applications," point 7. Clearly, however, the production function of monopolies requires greater attention than I give it in this paper. The assumption of a perfectly elastic long-run supply may fail for an input as foreign to conventional economic analysis as political power.

3. In the airline example, the expenditures on monopolizing had a socially valuable by-product (improved service), although the value was less than its cost. However, the possibility that expenditures on monopolizing will yield such by-products will be ignored in the development of the model, and its principal relevance, therefore, is to methods of monopolizing that have little or no social value. The forma-

---

[8] See Douglas and Miller, "The CAB's Domestic Passenger Fare Investigation."

tion of a cartel, the procuring of a tariff or other protective legislation, and the merging of competing firms in a market to produce a monopoly (where the merger does not enable economies of scale or other efficiencies to be realized) are examples of such methods. (Even in these cases, there will be some socially valuable by-products [e.g., information] if, for example, the cartel agreement fails to limit nonprice competition.) At the opposite extreme, obtaining a monopoly by cutting costs or prices or by innovation will normally yield social benefits greater than the expenditures on monopolizing.

Several more preliminary points should be noted briefly.

1. Legal and illegal monopolies must be distinguished. The threat of punishment can be used to increase the expected costs of monopolizing and thereby reduce the amount of resources invested in the activity. To the extent that enforcers' resources are merely substituted for monopolizers', there will be no social savings,[9] but the literature on punishment suggests that activities such as monopolizing can be deterred at low social cost by combining heavy monetary penalties (i.e., transfer payments) with modest resources devoted to apprehending and convicting offenders.[10] Hence, under an optimum system of penalties, the social costs of illegal monopolies might be quite low.

2. As an extension of the last point, note that the observed monopoly profits in an industry may actually underestimate the social costs of monopoly in that industry. Considerable resources may have been expended by consumers or enforcers to reduce those profits. Monopoly profits in an industry could be zero, yet the social costs of monopoly in that industry very high, if enforcement of antimonopoly measures were both expensive and effective.

3. Given uncertainty, the expected monopoly profits of any firm seeking a monopoly may be much smaller than the actual monopoly profits, and so will its expenditures. If ten firms are vying for a monopoly having a present value of $1 million and each of them has an equal chance of obtaining it and is risk neutral, each will spend $100,000 (as-

---

[9] Gary S. Becker, *Economic Theory* (New York: Alfred A. Knopf, 1971), p. 101.

[10] Becker, "Crime and Punishment: An Economic Approach." This could, to be sure, merely shift the problem to a new level: the opportunity to obtain substantial rents from apprehending and convicting monopolists will induce enforcers to pour resources into enforcement activities. This problem is analyzed in William M. Landes and Richard A. Posner, "The Private Enforcement of Law," *Journal of Legal Studies* 5 (January, 1975): 1–46.

suming constant costs) on trying to obtain the monopoly. Only one will succeed, and his costs will be much smaller than the monopoly profits, but the total costs of obtaining the monopoly—counting losers' expenditures as well as winners—will be the same as under certainty. If the market for monopoly is in fact characterized by a high degree of uncertainty, this would explain why the costs of obtaining monopoly have largely eluded detection. Most of the costs are incurred in unsuccessful efforts to obtain a monopoly: the lobbying campaign that fails, the unsuccessful attempt to obtain a bank charter or form a cartel.

4. It might seem that where monopoly is obtained by bribery of government officials, the additional loss of monopoly with which this paper is concerned would be eliminated, since a bribe is a pure transfer. In fact, however, bribery merely shifts the monopoly profits from the monopolist to the officials receiving the bribe and draws real resources into the activity of becoming an official who is in a position to receive these bribes.[11]

THE MODEL

Given the assumptions explained above, the total social costs of monopoly prices in figure 5.1 are simply $D + L$, and since $D \simeq$ $\frac{1}{2}\Delta P\Delta Q$ and $L = \Delta P(Q_c - \Delta Q)$, the relative sizes of D and L are given by

$$\frac{D}{L} \simeq \frac{\Delta Q}{2(Q_c - \Delta Q)} . \tag{1}$$

This ratio can also be expressed in terms of the elasticity of demand for the product in question at the competitive price and the percentage increase in price brought about by monopolization (p):

$$\frac{D}{L} \simeq \frac{p}{2(1/\epsilon - p)} . \tag{2}$$

The partial derivatives are

$$\frac{\partial(D/L)}{\partial \epsilon} \simeq \frac{2p}{(2 - 2p\epsilon)^2} > 0;$$

$$\frac{\partial(D/L)}{\partial p} \simeq \frac{2\epsilon}{(2 - 2p\epsilon)^2} > 0. \tag{3}$$

In words, the ratio of D to L is smaller, the less elastic the demand for

[11] See Krueger, "The Political Economy of the Rent-Seeking Society."

the industry's product at the competitive price and the smaller the percentage price increase over the competitive level. At moderate elasticities and percentage price increases, D is only a small fraction of L (and hence of the total costs of monopoly). For example, at an elasticity of one[12] and a price increase over the competitive level of 10 percent, D is only 5.6 percent of L.

Observe that the model does not assume that the actual supracompetitive price being charged (P_m in figure 5.1) is the optimum monopoly price for the industry (otherwise the supracompetitive price increase would not be determined independently of the elasticity of demand, as in [2]). The rationale of this procedure is that perfect monopoly is presumably rare; it will, however, be considered as a special case later.

Using R_c to denote total sales revenues at the competitive price, C, we can approximate the total social costs of monopoly by

$$D + L = pR_c - \tfrac{1}{2}\Delta P \Delta Q \qquad (4a)$$

$$= R_c(p - \tfrac{1}{2}\epsilon p^2). \qquad (4b)$$

The partial derivatives of C are (approximately):

$$\frac{\partial C}{\partial R_c} = p - \tfrac{1}{2}\epsilon p^2 > 0 \text{ iff } \epsilon p < 2;$$

$$\frac{\partial C}{\partial p} = R_c(1 - \epsilon p) > 0 \text{ iff } \epsilon p < 1; \qquad (5)$$

$$\frac{\partial C}{\partial \epsilon} = -\tfrac{1}{2}p^2 R_c < 0.$$

In words, the social costs of monopoly will usually—not always—be higher, the larger the industry's sales revenues at the competitive price and output and the greater the percentage price increase over the competitive level. And they will always be higher, the less elastic the demand for the product at the competitive price, the costs of monopoly being greatest when demand is totally inelastic at the competitive price.

Formulas (2) and (4b) are accurate only for small changes in the

---

[12] Throughout this paper, ΔQ is treated as a positive number. Therefore, $\epsilon = [(\Delta Q/\Delta P)(Q/P)]$ is also positive.

price level. Yet monopolization might result in large price increases. Hence (1) and (4a) remain useful. For purposes of empirical estimation, it is helpful to derive two additional formulas: one for the case where data on the deadweight loss, the elasticity of demand, and the monopoly price increase are available and the elasticity of demand is assumed to be constant, and the other for the case where data on the monopoly increase, the monopoly output, and the elasticity of demand at the monopoly price are available and the demand curve is assumed to be linear.

1. For the case of constant elasticity, let $k \equiv P_c/P_m$ and $R_m \equiv$ total sales revenue at the monopoly price and output. Then, since $Q_c = \alpha P_c^{-\epsilon}$ and $Q_m = \alpha P_m^{-\epsilon}$, and therefore $\Delta Q = \alpha(P_c^{-\epsilon} - P_m^{-\epsilon})$, D/L and C are approximately

$$\frac{D}{L} = \frac{(kP_m)^{-\epsilon} - P_m^{-\epsilon}}{2P_m^{-\epsilon}} = \frac{k^{-\epsilon} - 1}{2}; \tag{6}$$

$$C = D + L = D\left(1 + \frac{2}{k^{-\epsilon} - 1}\right) = R_m\left(1 - k\right)\left(\frac{k^{-\epsilon} + 1}{2}\right).^{13} \tag{7}$$

The partial derivatives of D/L are (approximately):

$$\frac{\partial(D/L)}{\partial k} = \frac{-\epsilon}{2k^{\epsilon+1}} < 0;$$

$$\frac{\partial(D/L)}{\partial \epsilon} = \frac{-k^{-\epsilon}\ln k}{2} > 0. \tag{8}$$

In words, the ratio of the deadweight loss of monopoly to the additional loss is smaller, the smaller the monopoly price increase, and greater, the more elastic the demand (k, the ratio of the competitive to the monopoly price, is larger, the smaller the relative price increase).

2. For the case where the elasticity of demand at the monopoly price (as well as the monopoly price increase and the quantity sold at the monopoly price) is known or can be computed, and the demand curve can be approximated by a straight line, we begin by determining the slope of the demand curve at the monopoly price:

$$\frac{\Delta Q}{\Delta P} = \frac{\epsilon Q_m}{P_m}. \tag{9}$$

---

[13] For the special case where the firm is able to charge the optimum monopoly price for the industry, see appendix at end of chapter.

FIGURE 5.3

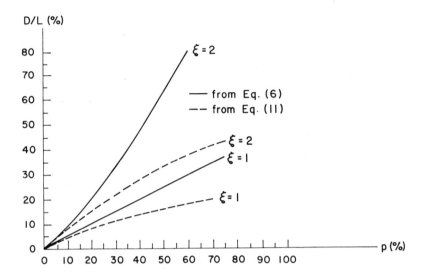

Since the slope of the linear demand curve is constant, this equation can be used to find ΔQ and hence C and D/L:

$$C = R_m(1 - k)\left[1 + \tfrac{1}{2}\epsilon\,(1 - k)\right]; \tag{10}$$

$$\frac{D}{L} = \frac{\epsilon(1 - k)}{2}.^{14} \tag{11}$$

The estimates produced by our two formulas for the ratio of the deadweight to the additional loss from monopoly—equations (6) and (11)—turn out not to be very different for price increases of less than 25 percent, and even for much larger price increases if the elasticity of demand is no greater than one (see figure 5.3).

Empirical Estimates

The formulas developed in the preceding part can be used to derive, from the estimates of the deadweight loss of monopoly made by Ar-

---

[14] In the special case where the firm is able to charge the optimum monopoly price,

$$C = \frac{3}{2}\frac{R_m}{\epsilon}, \tag{10'}$$

$$\frac{D}{L} = \frac{1}{2}. \tag{11'}$$

nold Harberger and others, an estimate of the total social cost of monopoly. Harberger,[15] estimating an average monopoly price increase of
about 6 percent and assuming that the elasticity of demand was constant and equal to unity, found the deadweight loss from monopoly in
the manufacturing sector to be equal to (at most) 0.1 percent of GNP.
Harberger's (implicit) k is 0.9434, and from equation (6) the ratio of D
to L in Harberger's analysis is, therefore, 0.03. Hence, if D is 0.1 percent of GNP, L is about 3.3 percent and C about 3.4 percent of GNP.
David Schwartzman used similar methods and found D equal to about
0.1 percent of GNP too.[16] But he assumed a price increase of 8.3 percent and an elasticity of demand of 1.5. Plugging these values into
equation (6) yields $D/L = 0.06$. Hence, if $D = 0.1$ percent of GNP,
$L = 1.7$ percent and $C = 1.8$ percent.

Neither estimate can be given much credance, however, because
of the method both Harberger and Schwartzman employed to determine the monopoly price increase. Persistently above-average rates of
return were used both (1) to identify the monopolized industries and
(2) to calculate the monopoly price increase. If the approach of this paper is correct, such a procedure is improper, especially the second
step. Because of uncertainty, many monopolists may enjoy supernor-
mal rates of return ex post, but those rates will understate the percentage of the monopolist's revenues that is attributable to monopoly pricing, unless no cost whatever was incurred in obtaining (or maintaining)
the monopoly.[17]

A better method of calculating the social costs of monopoly (deadweight plus additional loss) is to obtain from industry studies estimates
of the monopoly price increase and of the elasticity of demand at the
relevant points along the demand curve. An independent estimate of
the elasticity of demand would be unnecessary if we could assume
that, after the price increase, the price charged was the optimum mo-

[15] Arnold C. Harberger, "Monopoly and Resource Allocation," *American Economic Review* 44 (May, 1954): 77–87.

[16] David Schwartzman, "The Burden of Monopoly," *Journal of Political Economy* 68 (November–December, 1960): 627–630.

[17] This point is distinct from the (also valid) objections to Harberger's procedure raised in George J. Stigler, "The Statistics of Monopoly and Mergers," *Journal of Political Economy* 64 (January–February, 1956): 33–40—that monopoly profits are often capitalized into the valuation of a firm's assets and that some of the profits may be received as rents by suppliers of the firm's inputs.

nopoly price; where an independent estimate of ϵ is available, it can serve as a check on that assumption. To illustrate, there have been a number of estimates of the percentage by which CAB regulation has increased the price of airline travel. The simple average of these estimates is 0.66.[18] If a 66 percent price increase over competitive levels is assumed to raise the price of air travel to the optimum monopoly level, then the elasticity of demand at the monopoly price can be calculated, from the formula that equates marginal cost to marginal revenue,[19] to be 2.5 at the monopoly price. An independent estimate of the long-run elasticity of demand for air travel made by H. S. Houthakker and Lester D. Taylor is 2.36,[20] which is virtually identical to my calculation.

If we assume a constant elasticity of 2.5 and solve for D/L using equation (6′) from the appendix, $D = 1.29L$, and (from equation [7′]) it is readily calculable that the total social cost of the airline monopoly is equal to 92 percent of the total revenue of the industry at the monopoly price. However, the assumption of a linear demand curve seems more plausible than the assumption of constant elasticity, especially for large relative price increases, which one expects to find associated with a rising elasticity of demand as substitutes become increasingly attractive. If, therefore, equations (10′) and (11′) are used instead of (6′) and (7′), $D = 0.5L$ and $C = 0.6R_m$, still a very large social loss from the regulation-induced airline monopoly. (These esti-

[18] Computed from Richard E. Caves, *Air Transport and Its Regulators* (Cambridge, Mass.: Harvard University Press, 1962), p. 372; William A. Jordon, *Airline Regulation in America* (Baltimore: Johns Hopkins University Press, 1970), pp. 110–111, 124–125; and Yale Law Journal, "Is Regulation Necessary? California Air Transportation and National Regulatory Policy," *Yale Law Journal* 74 (July, 1965): 1416–47.

[19] This was essentially the procedure used by David Kamerschen, "Estimation of the Welfare Losses from Monopoly in the American Economy," *Western Economic Journal* 4 (Summer, 1966): 221–236, to estimate the deadweight loss from monopoly in manufacturing. He has been criticized, rightly, for assuming that firms in concentrated industries subject to the Sherman Act's prohibition of collusive pricing are typically able to charge the profit-maximizing monopoly price. The assumption is more plausible with regard to a regulated industry in which entry and price competition are limited by the regulatory agency, and the Sherman Act is inapplicable.

[20] H. S. Houthakker and Lester D. Taylor, *Consumer Demand in the United States, 1929–1970* (Cambridge, Mass.: Harvard University Press, 1966), p. 124. This is presumably the elasticity of demand at the regulated price, since only a small part of the airline industry is exempt from CAB regulation.

mates ignore, however, the partially offsetting benefits of excessive nonprice competition in the airline industry.)

All previous studies of the cost of monopoly to the economy have been based on supposed monopoly pricing in manufacturing alone. Yet the ability of firms to maintain supracompetitive prices must be greater in industries in which a regulatory agency limits entry and price competition than in the manufacturing sector, where express collusion is forbidden by the Sherman Act. Table 5.1 collects estimates of the regulation-induced price increase and the elasticity of demand at the current price for several industries for which these data are available. Two estimates of elasticity are given: one (ϵ_1) is derived from the price-increase data, on the assumption that the industry is charging the optimum monopoly price; the other (ϵ_2) is an independent estimate of elasticity. The estimates of the total social costs of the regulation in question (C_1, where ϵ_1 is the estimate of elasticity used, and C_2, where ϵ_2 is used) are based on the assumption that the industry's demand curve is linear in the relevant region and are expressed as a percentage of the total revenues of the industry.

These estimates are, of course, very crude, but they do suggest that the total costs of regulation may be extremely high, given that about 17 percent of GNP originates in industries—for example, agriculture, transportation, communications, power, banking, insurance, and medical services—that contain the sorts of controls over competition that might be expected to lead to supracompetitive prices.[21] Indeed, the costs of regulation probably exceed the costs of private monopoly. To be sure, a higher percentage of GNP—30 percent—originates in manufacturing and mining, a highly concentrated sector of the economy, and the conventional wisdom associates high concentration with supracompetitive pricing. But only about one-fifth of the output of this sector comes from industries in which four firms account for 60 percent or more of sales, and there is little theoretical basis for believing that the sellers in less concentrated industries could

[21] Of course, not all markets in the regulated industries are in fact subject to the relevant regulatory controls (almost half the trucking industry, for example, is exempt from regulation by the Interstate Commerce Commission). On the other hand, tariffs and similar restrictions (e.g., the oil import quota) are excluded from the estimate of the percentage of GNP affected by regulation.

TABLE 5.1
Social Costs of Regulation

	Regulatory Price Increase (%)	Elasticity		Costs (as % of industry's sales)	
		ϵ_1	ϵ_2	C_1	C_2
Physicians's services	.40[a]	3.500	0.575[b]	.42	.31
Eyeglasses	.34[c]	0.394	0.450[c]	.39	.24
Milk	.11[a]	10.000	0.339[d]	.15	.10
Motor carriers	.62[c]	2.630	1.140[f]	.57	.30
Oil	.65[g]	2.500	0.900[g]	.60	.32
Airlines	.66	2.500	2.360	.60	.19

SOURCES:

[a] Reuben A. Kessel, "Higher Education and the Nation's Health: A Review of the Carnegie Commission Report on Medical Education," *Journal of Law and Economics* 15 (April, 1972): 119, 73.

[b] H. S. Houthakker and Lester D. Taylor, *Consumer Demand in the United States, 1929–1970* (Cambridge, Mass.: Harvard University Press, 1966), p. 99 (short run).

[c] Lee Benham, "Price Structure and Professional Control of Information," University of Chicago Graduate School of Business, mimeographed, March, 1973, pp. 19, 30 (simple average).

[d] H. S. Houthakker, "New Evidence on Demand Elasticities," *Econometrica* 33 (April, 1965): 286. This estimate is for all goods; an estimate limited to dairy products in the Netherlands was not significantly different (Robert Ayaynian, "A Comparison of Barten's Estimated Demand Elasticities with Those Obtained Using Grisch's Method," *Econometrica* 37 [January, 1969]: 79–94).

[e] Average estimates in Department of Agriculture studies cited in Thomas Gale Moore, *Freight Transportation Regulation* (Washington, D.C.: American Enterprise Institute, 1972); and Richard N. Farmer, "The Case of Unregulated Truck Transportation," *Journal of Farm Economics* 46 (May, 1964): 398–409.

[f] Simple averages of various estimates for transportation in Scandinavia (see Ragnar Frisch, "A Complete Scheme for Computing All Direct Costs and Cross Demand Elasticities in a Market with Many Sectors," *Econometrica* 27 [October, 1969]: 649).

[g] Cabinet Task Force on Oil Import Control, *The Oil Import Question* (Washington, D.C.: Government Printing Office, 1970).
NOTE: C_1 based on ϵ_1; C_2 based on ϵ_2.

collude effectively without engaging in behavior prohibited by the Sherman Act.[22] Not all violations of the Sherman Act are detected and punished, but the secret conspiracies that escape detection are probably not very effective—even the great electrical conspiracy, an elabo-

[22] Reuben A. Kessel, "A Study of the Effects of Competition in the Tax-exempt Bond Market," *Journal of Political Economy* 79 (July–August, 1971): 706–738. Kessel's

rate and relatively durable conspiracy among a very small group of firms, apparently succeeded in raising prices by less than 10 percent on average.[23] It would be surprising if the price level of the manufacturing and mining sector as a whole were more than about 2 percent above the competitive level.[24] Assume that it is 2 percent, and that the average elasticity of demand for the products of this sector, at current prices, is 1.1607.[25] Then the total social costs of monopoly in this sector are 1.9 percent of the total revenues generated in the sector (from equation [10]). This amounts to a total dollar loss substantially smaller than that generated in the regulated sector.[26] And this is true even if we assume that prices in the manufacturing and mining sector are, on average, 4 percent rather than 2 percent, above the competitive level.[27]

This comparison excludes, of course, both the relative costs of regulation and of antitrust enforcement and the relative benefits of monopoly in the two sectors.[28] Were these additional factors included,

---

study of underwriting costs shows that an increase beyond eight in the number of bids does not reduce those costs substantially. An industry where the four largest firms have less than 60 percent of the market is apt to contain at least eight significant competitors.

[23] U.S. Congress, Joint Committee on Internal Revenue Taxation, *Staff Study of Income Tax Treatment of Treble Damage Payments under the Antitrust Laws* (Washington, D.C.: Government Printing Office, 1965), p. 39.

[24] If we assume that only in industries where the four-firm concentration ratio exceeds 60 percent is undetected collusion likely, and that collusion allows these industries to maintain prices, on average, 5 percent above the competitive level, whereas in the rest of the manufacturing and mining sector the average price level is only 1 percent above the competitive level, then average prices for the entire sector would be only 1.83 percent above the competitive price level. (Statistics on the distribution of output among industries in different four-firm concentration ratio groups are from the 1963 Census of Manufactures.)

[25] This figure is a simple average of the long-run price elasticities for nine product groups within the manufacturing and mining sector estimated in Houthakker and Taylor, *Consumer Demand in the United States*, pp. 72, 74, 83, 112–114, 116, 128–131.

[26] The simple average of the social-cost estimates presented in table 5.1 is 34.9 percent of the total revenues of the regulated industry. Assuming that 50 percent of the output of that sector is produced in markets that are regulated in a manner similar to the industries in table 5.1 and that the average social cost of regulation in each such market is 34.9 percent of total revenue, the social costs of regulation would be equal to 3 percent of GNP, whereas the social costs of monopoly in manufacturing and mining would be equal to 0.6 percent of GNP.

[27] In which event the social costs of monopoly in that sector would be about 1.2 percent of GNP.

[28] To return to an earlier point, the assumed monopoly price increase in the man-

TABLE 5.2
Social Costs of Cartelization

Industry	Cartel Price Increase (%)	Elasticity		Costs (as % of industry's sales)	
		ϵ_1	ϵ_2	C_1	C_2
Nitrogen	0.75[a]	2.3256	1.4493[a]	.62	.30
Sugar	0.30[a]	4.3276	0.3390[b]	.36	.22
Aluminum	1.00[c]	2.000	—	.75	—
Aluminum	0.38[c]	3.6311	—	.42	—
Rubber	1.00[c]	2.0000	—	.75	—
Electric bulbs	0.37[c]	3.7023	—	.42	—
Copper	0.31[c]	4.2499	—	.36	—
Cast-iron pipe	0.39[d]	3.5641	—	.42	—

SOURCES:
[a] George W. Stocking and Myron W. Watkins, *Cartels in Action* (New York: Twentieth Century Fund, 1946), pp. 163, 166, 46.
[b] Houthakker, "New Evidence on Demand Elasticities," p. 286; obviously a much too low estimate for one food product sold at a cartel price!
[c] Stocking and Watkins, *Cartels in Action*, pp. 228, 251, 64–65, 343, 127.
[d] *United States Pipe* v. *Addyston Pipe and Steel Co.*, 85 F. 271 (6th Cir. 1898).

however, it is doubtful that the comparison would become more favorable to the regulated sector. In particular, while there are theoretical reasons for believing that concentration in unregulated markets is associated with economies of scale and other efficiencies,[29] there is no accepted theory or body of evidence that ascribes social benefits to regulation limiting entry and price competition.

The analysis developed here can also be used to estimate the social benefits of the antitrust laws. Table 5.2, which is constructed on the same basis as table 5.1, presents estimates of the social costs of several well-organized (mainly international) private cartels.[30]

---

ufacturing and mining sector may underestimate the social costs of monopoly in that sector. Those costs may be reflected in expenditures by consumers and enforcers in preventing monopoly pricing.

[29] Harold Demsetz, "Industry Structure, Market Rivalry, and Public Policy," *Journal of Law and Economics* 16 (April, 1973): 1–9.

[30] As distinct from the sorts of covert conspiracies that might escape detection under present enforcement of the Sherman Act (see Stigler, *The Organization of Industry*, pp. 268–270).

Presumably, collusive price increases of this magnitude and the attendant very substantial social costs are deterred by current enforcement of the American antitrust laws. A complete cost-benefit analysis of the antitrust laws would, however, also require estimation of (1) the costs of administering those laws,[31] and (2) the large social costs imposed by the many perverse applications of antitrust laws that are, perhaps, an inevitable by-product of having such laws.

A very large disclaimer concerning the accuracy of the estimates presented in this part of the paper needs to be entered at this point. Quite apart from any reservations about the realism of the assumptions on which the model used to generate these estimates is based, the crudeness of the data on price increases and elasticities of demand precludes treating the estimates of the costs of the monopoly and regulation as anything more than suggestive. The suggestions are, however, interesting ones: (1) previous studies of the costs of monopoly may have grossly underestimated those costs, and (2) the costs of monopoly are quite probably much greater in the regulated than in the unregulated sector of the economy, despite the greater size of the latter sector.

Other Applications

1. In a recent paper William S. Comanor and Robert H. Smiley attempt to show that a large part of the inequality in the distribution of wealth in contemporary America is attributable to monopoly.[32] They use studies such as Harberger's[33] to determine the aggregate wealth transfer from consumers to the owners of monopoly firms and, by a series of additional assumptions concerning the incomes of consumers and shareholders, family size, the savings rate, and so on, derive an estimate of the distributive impact of monopoly. Many of the assumptions are questionable, but even if their correctness were conceded

[31] A point to be kept in mind is that, while these costs are incurred annually, private, unlike governmentally protected, cartels eventually collapse (although they often re-form later). Hence, table 5.2 gives an exaggerated picture of the average annual costs of cartelization as it would exist in the absence of the Sherman Act.

[32] William S. Comanor and Robert H. Smiley, "Monopoly and the Distribution of Wealth," *Quarterly Journal of Economics* 89 (May, 1975): 177–194.

[33] Harberger, "Monopoly and Resource Allocation."

the conclusion would be highly doubtful. There is no reason to think that monopoly has a significant distributive effect. Consumers' wealth is not transferred to the shareholders of monopoly firms; it is dissipated in the purchase of inputs into the activity of becoming a monopolist.

2. Oliver Williamson[34] has argued that the refusal of the courts to recognize a defense of economies of scale in merger cases under the Clayton Act is questionable because, under plausible assumptions concerning the elasticity of demand, only a small reduction in the merging firms' costs is necessary to offset any deadweight loss created by the price increase that the merger enables the firms to make (see figure 5.4).

This analysis is incomplete, however. The expected profits of the merger ($ABEF$) will generate an equivalent amount of costs as the firms vie to make such mergers or, after they are made, to engross the profits generated by the higher postmerger price through service competition or whatever. As a first approximation, the total social cost of the merger is $ABEF + BCD$ and exceeds the cost savings ($GDEF$) made possible by it. The curves could, of course, be drawn in such a way that the merger would generate net cost savings; the point is only that there is no presumption that anticompetitive mergers generate net savings. This consideration, together with the high cost of litigating issues of cost savings, may provide a justification for refusing to recognize a defense of efficiencies in merger cases where the merger is likely to produce a substantial increase in monopoly power.

3. It has been argued[35] that the antitrust laws should not concern themselves with practices that are merely methods of price discrimination, since there is no basis for thinking that discrimination increases the deadweight loss of monopoly, and it may reduce it (it will reduce it to zero if discrimination is perfect). The conclusion may be justifiable by reference to the costs of administering anti-discrimination rules, but the basis on which it has been defended by its proponents is incorrect. Even when price discrimination is perfect, so that the deadweight loss of monopoly is zero, the total social costs of a dis-

---

[34] Oliver E. Williamson, "Economics as an Antitrust Defense: The Welfare Trade-offs," *American Economic Review* 58 (March, 1968): 18–36.

[35] For example, Ward S. Bowman, Jr., *Patent and Antitrust Law: A Legal and Economic Appraisal* (Chicago: University of Chicago Press, 1973).

FIGURE 5.4

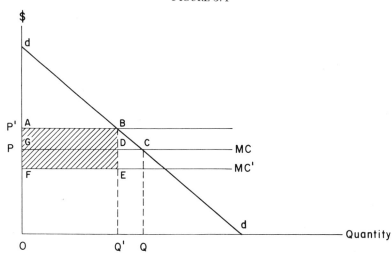

criminating monopoly are greater than those of a single-price monopoly.[36] Under perfect price discrimination, C is the entire area between the demand curve and the marginal (= average) cost curve, and it is greater than $D + L$ at any single price (see figure 5.1).

4. It is occasionally suggested that the case for antitrust enforcement has been gravely weakened by the theory of the second best. Since the elimination of one monopoly in an economy containing other monopolies (or other sources of divergence between price and marginal cost, such as taxation) may reduce the efficiency of resource allocation, antitrust enforcement may increase, rather than reduce, D. The true economic basis for antitrust enforcement, however, is not D but $D + L$, and we have seen that, under plausible assumptions as to the elasticity of demand, D is only a small fraction of $D + L$, at least for moderate increases in price above the competitive level. The social costs measured by L, like the social costs of theft (i.e., the opportunity costs of thieves' and policemen's time and of the labor and capital inputs into locks, burglar tools, etc.), are unaffected by the existence of second-best problems.[37]

[36] I abstract from the costs of administering the price-discrimination scheme; these increase the costs of discriminating monopoly relative to those of nondiscriminating monopoly.

[37] Cf. Richard S. Markovits, "Fixed Inputs (Investment) Competition and the Vari-

5. The analysis in this paper suggests a possible explanation for the positive correlation that has been found between concentration and advertising.[38] It may be easier to collude on price than on the amount of advertising. Although there is no great trick to establishing an agreed-upon level of advertising and detecting departures from it, the incentives to violate any such agreement are strong because the gains from a successful advertising campaign may be difficult to offset immediately and hence offer promise of a more durable advantage than a price cut would. In that event the situation is similar to non-price competition in the airline industry. If price is fixed by the cartel but the level of advertising is not, or at least not effectively, the monopoly profits generated by the cartel price will be transformed into additional expenditures on advertising. Cartelization is presumably more common in concentrated industries.

This analysis suggests, incidentally, a possible difficulty in distinguishing empirically between Telser's theory of resale price maintenance[39] and an alternative explanation that stresses cartelization by dealers. In Telser's theory, manufacturers impose resale price maintenance in order to induce dealers to provide services in connection with the resale of the manufacturer's brand. If Telser's theory is correct, we would expect to find resale price maintenance imposed where the efficient merchandising of a product involved the provision of extensive point-of-sale services. However, a dealer's cartel might also result in the dealers' competing away the cartel profits through service competition.

6. Discussions of the "social responsibility" of large corporations generally assume that a firm (or group of firms) having some monopoly power could, without courting bankruptcy, decide to incur somewhat higher costs in order to discharge its social responsibilities. Thus, in figure 5.1, even if MC rose to P_m, the firm would still be covering its costs. However, if the analysis in this paper is correct and the expected profits of monopolizing are zero, it follows that the entire area L in

---

ability of Fixed Inputs (Investment): Their Nature, Determinants, and Significance," *Stanford Law Review* 24 (February, 1972): 507–530.

[38] This finding has been questioned, however, (e.g., Robert B. Ekelund, Jr., and William P. Gramm, "Advertising and Concentration: Some New Evidence," *Antitrust Bulletin* 15 (Summer, 1970): 243–249).

[39] Telser, "Why Should Manufacturers Want Fair Trade?"

figure 5.1 will represent fixed costs to the firm unless the monopoly was obtained under conditions of uncertainty. In the latter case the fixed costs will be somewhat lower, but in the former any increase in MC will jeopardize the firm's solvency.

7. Assuming that the decision to create or tolerate a monopoly has been made, it may still be possible to prevent the expected monopoly profits from being completely transformed into social costs. The basic technique is to reduce the elasticity of supply of the inputs into monopolizing. (Thus, the present discussion modifies my original assumption of perfect supply elasticity.) Consider, for example, a market that is a natural monopoly. If the monopolist is permitted to charge a monopoly price—and suppose that he is—he may set a price that exceeds the average costs of new entrants, albeit those costs are higher than his, and new entry will presumably occur. The resulting increase in the average costs of serving the market is an example of the social costs of monopoly (independent of the welfare triangle). These costs can be reduced, however, by a rule limiting entry. Such a rule will reduce the responsiveness of a key input into monopolizing—capacity to produce the monopolized product—to increases in the expected value of the monopoly. But the rule is not very satisfactory. Prospective entrants will have an incentive to expend resources on persuading the agency to change or waive the rule, and the monopolist to expend them on dissuasion. Moreover, the more efficient the rule is at keeping out new entrants at low cost to the monopolist, the greater will be the expected value of having a natural monopoly, and, hence, the greater will be the resources that firms expend on trying to become the first to occupy a natural-monopoly market.[40]

As another example, consider the recurrent proposal to replace the present method of assigning television licenses (now awarded to the applicant who convinces the Federal Communication Commission in a formal hearing of his superior ability to serve the public interest) by an auction system. This proposal is frequently supported on distributive grounds: why should the licensee, rather than the public, receive the rents generated by the limited allocation of electromagnetic spectrum for broadcasting? But there is also an efficiency justification

[40] This is the obverse of the situation discussed in Harold Demsetz, "Why Regulate Utilities?" *Journal of Law and Economics* 11 (April, 1968): 55–65, where competition to become a monopolist results in a competitive price level.

for the proposal. The auction would substitute a transfer payment for a real cost, the expenditures on the hearing process by competing applicants. To be sure, these expenditures might simply be redirected into rigging the bidding. But this could be discouraged, possibly at low cost, by appropriate legal penalties. The objective would be to increase the expected costs of obtaining the license (other than by an honest bid), which include any expected punishment costs, to the point where the applicants are induced to make the costless transfer rather than to expend real resources on trying to obtain the license outside the auction process. As mentioned earlier, in an optimum system of penalties the resources expended on enforcement would be slight.

The patent laws embody a somewhat similar economizing technique. In their absence inventors would expend substantial resources on preserving the secrecy of their inventions. Their efforts in this direction would generate indirect as well as direct social costs by retarding the spread of knowledge. By providing a legal remedy against "stealing" inventions, the patent laws reduce the level of such expenditures in much the same way as the existence of legal penalties for theft reduces the level of resources that people devote to protecting their property from thieves.

An interesting method of reducing the social costs of monopoly is used by labor unions. The existence of a monopoly wage might be expected to induce the expenditure of more and more resources by workers seeking entry into the union, until the expected benefits of union membership were reduced to zero. However, unions traditionally have rationed membership in a way that greatly reduces the marginal benefits of expenditures on obtaining membership, and hence the resources expended in that pursuit, by conditioning membership on a status difficult or impossible for the job seeker to buy at any price, such as being white or the son of a union member.[41] In the limit, this method of rationing would reduce the elasticity of the supply of inputs into obtaining union membership, and hence the social costs of labor monopolies (excluding the welfare triangle), to zero, disregarding the costs resulting from the exclusion of possibly better-qualified workers who do not meet the membership criterion. Yet

[41] The use of such methods by unions is being increasingly limited by government regulations designed to eliminate racial discrimination.

even this method may not be ultimately effective in preventing the transformation of monopoly rents into social costs. The more profitable union membership is, the greater are the resources that workers will be willing to invest (e.g., in forgone earnings due to being on strike) in union-organizing activities.

8. One reason why most students of tax policy prefer income taxes to excise taxes is that the misallocative effect of an income tax is believed to be less than that of an excise tax: the cross-elasticity of demand between work and leisure is assumed to be lower than that between a commodity and its substitutes. Even if correct, this does not mean that the total costs of collecting a given amount of revenue by means of an income tax are lower than those of collecting an excise tax. The amount of the tax transfer represents potential gain to the taxpayer, and he will expend real resources on trying to avoid the tax until, at the margin, cost and gain are equated. A critical question in comparing the costs of income and excise taxation is therefore the shape and location of the supply curves for avoiding income tax liability and excise tax liability, respectively. In the case of a highly progressive income tax system in which expenses for the production of income are deductible, the comparison is likely to be unfavorable to income taxation. Were the marginal income tax rate in the highest bracket 90 percent (as it once was in this country), the taxpayer would continue expending resources on tax avoidance until the expected value of a dollar so expended fell below ten cents. Thus, he might spend as much as ten times his marginal tax liability in order to reduce that liability to zero. (How much he would actually spend would depend on the location and shape of the supply curve for avoidance and on his resources and attitude toward risk.) This analysis is not conclusive against the income tax. It might be possible to increase the private marginal costs of avoidance by punishment or by disallowing the deduction of expenses on avoidance. The main problem would be to distinguish legitimate from illegitimate avoidance efforts.[42] Still, no general presumption that excise taxation is less costly than income taxation can be derived from an analysis limited to the allocative costs of taxation, corresponding to the deadweight loss of monopoly.

---

[42] It would make no sense to punish everyone who believed that some provision of the Internal Revenue Code was not intended to apply to his activity.

APPENDIX TO CHAPTER 5

In the special case where the firm is able to charge the optimum monopoly price for the industry, so that $P_c = MC = P_m(1 - 1/\epsilon)$, equation (6) becomes

$$\frac{D}{L} = \frac{(1 - 1/\epsilon)^{-\epsilon} - 1}{2} \tag{6'}$$

and equation (7) becomes

$$C = \frac{R_m[(1 - 1/\epsilon)^{-\epsilon} + 1]}{2\epsilon}. \tag{7'}$$

Since a demand curve of constant elasticity is nonlinear, the question arises whether the linear approximation of the deadweight loss used in equations (6) and (7) (and [6'] and [7']) introduces a source of serious inaccuracy. It appears not to, at least in the simple case where $\epsilon = 1$, and therefore

$$\frac{D}{L} = \frac{\int_{Q_m}^{Q_c} P \, dQ - P_c \, \Delta Q}{(P_m - P_c)Q_m} = \frac{ln \, (1/k) - 1 + k}{1 - k}. \tag{6''}$$

The appendix table, which compares D/L as calculated from equation (6) (with $\epsilon = 1$) and from equation (6''), shows that the linear approximation overestimates the deadweight loss, but not seriously.

Appendix Table

		D/L	
p (%)		Eq. (6)	Eq. (6'')
5		.025	.025
10		.050	.049
15		.075	.072
20		.100	.094
50		.250	.216

NOTE: p = Monopoly price increase.
D/L = Ratio of deadweight to additional loss.

III.

Some Subsequent Contributions
to Theory and Measurement

6

Efficient Rent Seeking

by

GORDON TULLOCK

MOST of the papers in this volume implicitly or explicitly assume that rent-seeking activity discounts the entire rent to be derived. Unfortunately, this is not necessarily true; the reality is much more complicated. The problem here is that the average cost and marginal cost are not necessarily identical.

This is surprising because in competitive equilibrium the average cost and marginal cost are equal and rent seeking is usually a competitive industry. If marginal cost is continuously rising, then marginal and average cost will be different.[1] In the ordinary industry the average cost curve of an individual enterprise is usually U-shaped, with economies of scale in the early range and diseconomies of scale in the latter range. In equilibrium, the companies will be operating at the bottom of this cost curve, and therefore average and marginal costs will be equated.

A second and much more important reason for the equality of marginal and average cost is that if there is some resource used in production of anything produced under continuously rising costs, then the owners of that resource will charge the marginal cost. People engaged in manufacturing (or whatever activity with which we are dealing) will face a cost that incorporates these rents of the original factor owners. Thus, the assumption that the costs are constant over scale is suitable for practical use.

Unfortunately, both these reasons are of dubious validity in the case of rent seeking. First, there seem to be no particular economies of scale. As far as we can see, for example, such monster industries as big

---

[1] This is obviously also true if marginal cost is continuously falling.

oil and the natural gas producers do not do as well in dealing with the government as do little oil or, in the gas case, householders. In general, it would appear that there is no range of increasing returns in rent seeking. However, this is admittedly an empirical problem and one for which, at the moment, we have little data. It is, in any event, dangerous to assume that the curves are all U-shaped and competition will adjust us to the minimum point of these curves. This is particularly so, since there is no obvious reason why all rent seekers should have identical efficiencies.

The second and more important reason why we can normally assume that supply curves are, in the long run, flat is that if they are continuously rising, factory owners can generally achieve the full rent by selling their factors at their marginal value; hence, the enterprises face essentially flat supply prices. Unfortunately, this has only a limited application in rent seeking. Suppose, for example, that we organize a lobby in Washington for the purpose of raising the price of milk and are unsuccessful. We cannot simply transfer our collection of contacts, influences, past bribes, and so forth to the steel manufacturers' lobby. In general, our investments are too specialized, and, in many cases, they are matters of very particular and detailed good will to a specific organization. It is true that we could sell the steel lobby our lobbyists with their connections and perhaps our mailing list. But presumably all these things have been bought by us at their proper cost. Our investment has not paid, but there is nothing left to transfer.

Similarly, the individual lobbyist spends much time cultivating congressmen and government officials and learning the ins and outs of government regulations. There is no way he can simply transfer these contacts, connections, and knowledge to a younger colleague if he wishes to change his line of business. The younger colleague must start at the bottom and work his way up. Thus, it seems likely that in most rent-seeking cases, the supply curve slants up and to the right from its very beginning. This means that rent-seeking activities are very likely to have different marginal and average costs, even if we can find an equilibrium.

It might seem that with continuously upward sloping supply curves and a competitive industry, there would be no equilibrium. This turns out not to be true, although the equilibrium is of a somewhat unusual nature. The analytical tools required to deal with it are drawn more from game theory than from classical economics.

In my article, "On the Efficient Organization of Trials,"[2] I introduced a game that I thought had much resemblance to a court trial or, indeed, to any other two-party conflict. In its simplest form, we assume two parties who are participating in a lottery under somewhat unusual rules. Each is permitted to buy as many lottery tickets as he wishes at one dollar each, the lottery tickets are put in a drum, one is pulled out, and whoever owns that ticket wins the prize. Thus, the probability of success for A is shown in equation (1), because the number of lottery tickets he holds is amount A and the total number in the drum is $A + B$.

$$P_A = \frac{A}{A + B} \tag{1}$$

In the previously cited article, I pointed out that this model could be generalized by making various modifications in it, and it is my purpose now to generalize it radically.[3]

Let us assume, then, that a wealthy eccentric has put up \$100 as a prize for the special lottery between A and B. Note that the amount spent on lottery tickets is retained by the lottery, not added onto the prize. This makes the game equivalent to rent seeking, where resources are also wasted.

How much should each invest? It is obvious that the answer to this question, from the standpoint of each party, depends on what he thinks the other will do. Here, and throughout the rest of this paper, I am going to use a rather special assumption about individual knowledge. I am going to assume that if there is a correct solution for individual strategy, then each player will assume that the other parties can also figure out what that correct solution is. In other words, if the correct strategy in this game were to play \$50, each party would assume that the other was playing \$50 and would only buy fifty tickets for himself, if that were the optimal amount under those circumstances.

---

[2] Gordon Tullock, "On the Efficient Organization of Trials," *Kyklos* 28 (1975): 745–762.

[3] For a previous generalization of the model and an application to arms races, see Gordon Tullock, *The Social Dilemma: The Economics of War and Revolution* (Blacksburg, Va.: Center for Study of Public Choice, 1974), pp. 87–125.

As a matter of fact, the optimal strategy in this game is not to buy $50.00 worth of tickets but to buy $25.00. As a very simple explanation, suppose that I have bought $25.00 and you have bought $50.00. I have a one in three chance of getting the $100.00 and you have a two in three chance. Thus, the present value of my investment is $33.33 and the present value of yours is $66.66, or, for this particular case, an equal percentage gain. Suppose, however, that you decided to reduce your purchases to $40.00 and I stayed at $25.00. This saves you $10.00 on your investment, but it lowers your present value of expectancy to only $61.53 and you are about $5.00 better off. Of course, I have gained from your reduction, too.

You could continue reducing your bet with profit until you also reached $25.00. For example, if you lowered your purchase from $26.00 to $25.00, the present value of your investment would fall from $50.98 to $50.00, and you would save $1.00 in investment. Going beyond $25.00, however, would cost you money. If you lowered it to $24.00, you would reduce the value of your investment by $1.02 and only save $1.00. It is assumed, of course, that I keep my purchase at $25.00.

I suppose it is obvious from what I have said already that $25.00 is equilibrium for both, that is, departure from it costs either one something. It is not true, however, that if the other party has made a mistake, I maximize my returns by paying $25.00. For example, if the other party has put up $50.00 and I pay $24.00 instead of $25.00, I save $1.00 in my investment but reduce my expectancy by only $0.90. My optimal investment, in fact, is $17.00. However, if we assume a game in which each party knows what the other party has invested and then adjusts his investment accordingly, the ultimate outcome must be at approximately $25.00 for each party.[4] The game is clearly a profitable one to play, and, in fact, it will impress the average economist as rather improbable. However, it is a case in which inframarginal profits are made, although we are in marginal balance. At first glance, most people feel that the appropriate bet is $50.00, but that is bringing the

---

[4] It would make no difference in the reasoning here, or in any of the following work, if there were an insurance company always willing to buy a bid at its true actuarial value. For example, if you had put in $25.00 and the other party had also put in $25.00, it would give you $50.00 for it, and if you had put in $26.00 and the other party $25.00, it would give you $50.98. But rent seeking normally involves risk, and hence I have kept the examples in the risky form.

total return into equality with the total cost rather than equating the margins.

To repeat, this line of reasoning depends on the assumption that the individuals can figure out the correct strategy, if there is a correct strategy, and that they assume that the other people will be able to figure it out, also. It is similar to the problem that started John von Neumann on the invention of game theory, and I think it is not too irrational a set of assumptions if we assume the kind of problem that rent seeking raises.

But there is no reason why the odds in our game should be a simple linear function of contributions. For example, they could be an exponential function, as in equation (2):

$$P_A = \frac{A^r}{A^r + B^r}. \tag{2}$$

There are, of course, many other functions that could be substituted, but in this paper we will stick to exponentials.

It is also possible for more than two people to play, in which case we would have equation (3):

$$P_A = \frac{A^r}{A^r + B^r, \ldots, n^r}. \tag{3}$$

The individuals need not receive the same return on their investment. Indeed, in many cases we would hope that the situation is biased. For example, we hope that the likelihood of passing a civil service examination is not simply a function of the amount of time spent cramming, but that other types of merit are also important. This would be shown in our equations by some kind of bias in which one party receives more lottery tickets for his money than another.

We will begin by changing the shape of the marginal cost curve and the number of people playing, and leave bias until later. Table 6.1 shows the individual equilibrium payments by players of the game, with varying exponents (which means varying marginal cost structures) and varying numbers of players. Table 6.2 shows the total amount paid by all of the players, if they all play the equilibrium strategy.

I have drawn lines dividing these two tables into zones I, II, and III. Let us temporarily confine ourselves to discussing zone I. This is the zone in which the equilibrium price summed over all players leads

TABLE 6.1
Individual Investments
(N–person, No Bias, with Exponent)

	Number of Players				
Exponent	2	4	10		15
1/3	8.33	6.25	3.00		2.07
1/2	12.50	9.37	4.50	I	3.11
1	25.00	18.75	9.00		6.22
2	50.00	37.50	18.00		12.44
3	75.00	56.25	27.00		18.67
5	125.00	93.75	45.00	II	31.11
8	200.00	150.00	72.00		49.78
12	300.00	225.00	108.00	III	74.67

TABLE 6.2
Sum of Investments
(N–Person, No Bias, with Exponent)

	Number of Players					
Exponent	2	4	10	15		Limit
1/3	16.66	25.00	30.00	31.05		33.30
1/2	25.00	37.40	45.00	46.65	I	50.00
1	50.00	75.00	90.00	93.30		100.00
2	100.00	150.00	180.00	186.60		200.00
3	150.00	225.00	270.00	280.05		300.00
5	250.00	375.00	450.00	466.65	II	500.00
8	400.00	600.00	720.00	746.70		800.00
12	600.00	900.00	1,080.00	1,120.05	III	1,200.00

to a payment equal to or less than the total price. In other words, these are the games in which expectancy of the players, if they all play, would be positive. Although we will start with these games, as we shall see below there are cases in which we may be compelled to play games in zones II and III where the expectancy is negative.

If we look at zone I, it is immediately obvious that the individual payments go down as the number of players rises, but the total amount paid rises. In a way, what is happening here is that a monopoly profit is being competed away. Note, however, when the exponent is one-third or one-half, even in the limit there is profit of $66.66 or $50.00 to the players taken as a whole. Thus, some profit remains. With the cost curve slanting steeply upward, these results are to some extent counterintuitive. One might assume that with a positive return on investment, it will always be sensible for more players to enter, thereby driving down the profits. In this case, however, each additional player lowers the payments of all the preceding players and his own, and the limit as the number of players goes to infinity turns out to be one where that infinity of players has, at least in expectancy terms, sizable profits.

Throughout the table, in zones I, II, and III, individual payments go down as we move from left to right, and total payments rise. We can deduce a policy implication from this, although it is a policy implication to which many people may object on moral grounds. It would appear that if one is going to distribute rents, nepotism is a good thing because it reduces the number of players and, therefore, the total investment. This is one of the classical arguments for hereditary monarchies. By reducing the number of candidates for an extremely rent-rich job to one, you eliminate such rent-seeking activities as civil war, assassination, and so forth. Of course, there are costs here. If we reduce the number of people who may compete for a given job, you may eliminate the best candidate or even the best two thousand candidates. This cost must be offset against the reduction in rent-seeking costs.

On the other hand, many cases of rent seeking are not ones in which we care particularly who gets the rent. In such matters as government appointments where there are large incomes from illegal sources, pressure groups obtaining special aid from the government, and so on, we would prefer that there be no rent at all, and, if there must be rent, it does not make much difference to whom it goes. In these cases, clearly measures to reduce rent seeking are unambiguous gains. Thus, if Mayor Richard Daley had confined all of the more lucrative appointments to his close relatives, the social savings might have been considerable.

If we go down the table, the numbers also steadily rise. Looking at two players, for example, from an exponent of one-third, which represents an extremely steeply rising cost curve, to an exponent of two, which is much flatter, we get a sixfold increase in the individual and total payments. This also suggests a policy conclusion. On the whole, it would be desirable to establish institutions so that the marginal cost is very steeply rising. For example, civil servants' examinations should be, as far as possible, designed so that the return on cramming is low, or, putting it another way, so that the marginal cost of improving one's grade is rapidly rising. Similarly, it is better if the political appointments of the corrupt governments are made quickly and rather arbitrarily, so that not so many resources are invested in rent seeking.

Once again, however, there is a cost. It may be hard to design civil service examinations so that they are difficult to prepare for and yet make efficient selections.[5] Here again, if we are dealing with appointments to jobs that we would rather not have exist, the achievement of profits through political manipulations and the like, there is no particular loss in moving down our table. Thus, laws that make it more expensive or more difficult to influence the government—such as the campaign contribution laws—may have considerable net gain by making the rise in marginal cost steeper. There is a considerable expense involved, however. The actual restrictions placed on campaign contributions are designed in a highly asymmetrical manner, so that they increase the cost for some potential lobbyists and not for others. Whether there is a net social gain from this process is hard to say.

So much for zone I; let us now turn to zones II and III. In zone II, the sum of the payments made by the individual players is greater than the prize; in other words, it is a negative-sum game instead of a positive-sum game as in zone I. In zone III, the individual players make payments that are higher than the prize. It might seem obvious that no one would play games of this sort, but, unfortunately, this is not true.

Before von Neumann began his work on the theory of games, students of probability divided gambling situations into two categories: pure chance and games of strategy. We may take two simple examples. If Smith flips a coin and Jones calls the outcome, we have a game of pure chance, provided only that Smith does not have enough skill ac-

---

[5] There is another solution, which is to put the civil service salary at the same level as equivalent private salaries. Under these circumstances, there would be no rent seeking. Given the political power of civil servants, however, I doubt that this would be possible.

tually to control the coin. This is so even if the coin is not a fair one, although Jones might not properly calculate the odds under those circumstances. In this game, the properly calculated, but mathematical, odds are fifty-fifty, and there is no great problem.

Consider, however, a very similar game, in which Smith chooses which side of the coin will be up and covers it with his hand until Jones calls either heads or tails. The coin is then uncovered, and if Jones has properly called the bet, Smith pays him; if he has not, Jones pays Smith. This is a game of strategy. The early writers in this case reasoned that there was no proper solution to the game, because if there were a proper solution, both parties could figure it out. Thus, for example, if the proper thing for Smith to do was to play heads, he would know that Jones would know that this was the proper thing to do; hence, the proper thing for Smith to do would be to play tails. Of course, if the proper thing is to play tails, then Jones will also know that; therefore, the proper thing to do is to play heads. It will be seen that this is an example of the paradox of the liar.

The early students of probability argued that in circumstances like these there was no proper solution and referred to it as a game of strategy, which was roughly equivalent to throwing up their hands. In games of this sort, von Neumann discovered that there might be (not necessarily was, but might be) a solution. In the particular case of coin matching, there is no simple solution, but in many real-world situations there could be a strategy for Smith that he would still retain even though Jones could figure it out and make the best reply.

If there was such a strategy, it was called a saddle point. Von Neumann also pointed out that one should consider not only pure strategies but also mixed strategies. Further, in zero-sum games there is always some mixed strategy that has a saddle point. This proof can also be extended to differential games, which are the kind of games we are now discussing, but, unfortunately, it applies only to zero-sum games, and our games are not zero-sum.[6]

A broader concept of equilibrium was developed by Nash, but unfortunately the games in zones II and III have a very pronounced discontinuity at 0. In consequence, there is no Nash equilibrium. These games have neither dominant pure strategies, saddle points, nor domi-

---

[6] Except, of course, for those games which lie along the boundary between zone I and zone II.

nant mixed strategies. They are games of strategy in the older sense of the word, games for which we can offer no solution.

Let us here reexamine the idea of a solution in order to make this clear. If there is such a solution, anyone can compute it. Thus, Smith must choose his strategy knowing that Jones will know what he is going to do. Similarly, Jones must choose knowing that Smith will be able to predict accurately what he will do. There is no law of nature that says all games will have solutions of this sort, and these, unfortunately, are in a category that do not.

For a simple example, consider the game shown on table 6.1 in which there are two players, Smith and Jones again, and assume that the exponent on the cost function is 3. The individual payment is shown as $75, and the result of the two players putting up $75 is that they will jointly pay $150 for $100. Each is paying $75 for a fifty-fifty chance on $50, which appears to be stupid.

However, let us run through the line of reasoning that may lead the two parties to a $75 investment. Suppose, for example, that we start with both parties at $50. Smith raises to $51. With the exponent of three, the increase in the probability that he will win is worth more than $1—in fact, considerably more. If Jones counters, he also gains more than $1 by his investment. By a series of small steps of this sort, each one of which is a profitable investment, the two parties will eventually reach $75, at which point there is no motive for either one to raise or lower his bid by any small amount. They are in marginal adjustment, even though the total conditions are very obviously not satisfied.

But what of the total conditions? For example, suppose that Jones decides not to play. Obviously, his withdrawal means that Smith is guaranteed success, and, indeed, he will probably regret that he has $75 down rather than $1, but, still, he is going to make a fairly good profit on his investment.

Here we are back in the trap of the coin-matching games. If the best thing to do, the rational strategy, in this game is not to play, then obviously the sensible thing to do is to put in $1. On the other hand, if the rational strategy is to play, and one can anticipate the other party will figure that out, too, so that he will invest, then the rational thing to do is to stay out, because you are going to end up with parties investing at $75. There is no stable solution.

Games like this occur many times in the real world. Poker, as it is actually played, is an example, and most real-world negotiations are also examples of this sort of thing; in the case of poker, there is no social waste, because the parties are presumably deriving entertainment from the game. Negotiations, although they always involve at least some waste, may involve fairly small amounts because the waste involved in strategic maneuvering may be more than compensated by the transfer of information that may permit achievement of a superior outcome. But in our game this is not possible. In the real world there may be some such effect that partially offsets the waste of the rent seeking. In most rent-seeking cases, however, it is clear that this offset is only partial, and in many cases of rent seeking the activity from which the rent will be derived is, in and of itself, of negative social value. Under these circumstances, not only do we have the waste of rent seeking, we also have the net social waste imposed by the rent itself.

In the real world, the solution to rent seeking is rather apt to end up at $75 in our particular case instead of at zero, because normally the game does not permit bets, once placed, to be withdrawn. In other words, the sunk costs are truly sunk; you cannot withdraw your bid. For example, if I decide to cram for an examination or invest a certain amount of money in a lobby in Washington that is intended to increase the salaries of people studying public choice, once the money is spent, I cannot get it back. If it turns out that I am in this kind of competitive game, the sunk-cost aspect of the existing investment means that I will continue making further investments in competition with other people studying for the examination or in hiring lobbyists. In a way, the fact that there is an optimal amount—that even with the previous costs all sunk we will not go beyond $75 in the particular example we are now using—is encouraging. Although sunk costs are truly sunk, there is still a limit to the amount that will be invested in the game.

Note that this game has a possible precommitment strategy.[7] If one of the parties can get his $75 in first and make it clear that it will not be withdrawn, the sensible policy for the second party is to play zero; hence, the party who precommits makes, on this particular game, a profit of $25.

[7] Thomas C. Schelling, *The Strategy of Conflict* (Cambridge, Mass.: Harvard University Press, 1960).

Unfortunately, this analysis, although true, is not very helpful. It simply means that there is another precommitment game played. We would have to investigate the parameters of that game, as well as the parameters of the game shown in tables 6.1 and 6.2, and determine the sum of the resources invested in both. Offhand, it would appear that most precommitment games would be extremely expensive because it is necessary to make large investments on very little information. You must be willing to move before other people, and this means moving when you are badly informed.[8] But, in any event, this precommitment game would have some set of parameters, and, if we investigate them and then combine them with the parameters of the game that you precommit, we would obtain the total cost. I doubt that this would turn out to be a low amount of social waste.

The situation is even more bizarre in zone III. Here the equilibrium involves each of the players' investing more than the total prize offered. It is perhaps sensible to reemphasize the meaning of the payments shown in table 6.1. They are the payments that would be reached if all parties, properly calculating what the others would do, made minor adjustments in their bids and finally reached the situation where they stopped in proper marginal adjustment. They are not in total equilibrium, of course.

Once again, the simple rule—do not play such games—is not correct, because if it were the correct rule, then anyone who violated it could make large profits. Consider a particular game invented by Geoffrey Brennan, which is the limit of table 6.1 as the exponent is raised to infinity. In this game, $100 is put up and will be sold to the highest bidder, but all the bids are retained, that is, when you put in a bid, you cannot reduce it. Under these circumstances, no one would put in an initial bid of more than $100, but it is not at all obvious what one *should* put in. Further, assume that the bids, once made, cannot be withdrawn but can be raised. Under these circumstances, there is no equilibrium maximum bid. In other words, it is always sensible to increase your bid above its present level if less than $100 will make

---

[8] As an amusing sidelight on this problem, a referee of an earlier draft of this paper objected to my above paragraph on the ground that the first party should not put in $75 but some smaller number closer to $55 that would be enough to bar the other party. Note, however, that if one paused to figure out the actual optimal number, the other party would get in first with his $75.

you the highest bidder. The dangers are obvious, but it is also obvious that refusal to play the game is not an equilibrium strategy, because of the paradox of the liar mentioned above.

In games in zones II and III, formal theory can say little. Clearly, these are areas where the ability to guess what other people will do, interpret facial expressions, and so on, pays off very highly. They are also areas where it is particularly likely that very large wastes will be incurred by society as a whole. Unfortunately, it seems likely that rent seeking is apt to lead to these areas in some cases.

Obviously, as a good social policy, we should try to avoid having games that are likely to lead to this kind of waste. Again, we should try to arrange that the payoff to further investment in resources is comparatively low, or, in other words, that the cost curve points sharply upward.

One way to lower the social costs is to introduce bias into the selection process. Note that we normally refer to bias as a bad thing, but one could be biased in the direction of the correct decision. For example, a civil service exam might be so designed that it is very likely to pick out people who have the necessary natural traits and is very hard to prepare for. This would be bias in favor of the appropriate traits, but it would be a desirable thing. Similarly, we would like to have court proceedings biased in such a way that whoever is on the right side need not make very large investments in order to win, and if this is true, the people on the wrong side will not make very large investments either, because they do not pay.

On the other hand, bias can be something which, at least morally, is incorrect. We referred above to Mayor Daley's appointments of his relatives, and this would be a kind of bias. In that particular case, presumably bias would reduce total rent seeking and not lower the functional efficiency of the government of Chicago, but there are many cases where this kind of bias *would* lower efficiency.

Bias, it will be seen, is rather similar to the restriction on the number of players we have discussed above. Instead of totally cutting off some players, we differentially weigh the players. For example, assume that player A is given five times as many coupons for his one-dollar investment as are the other players. This would bias the game in his favor, although not to the extreme of prohibiting others from buying tickets. This kind of bias, once again, is rather similar to designing

TABLE 6.3
Individual Investments
(2-Party, Bias, Exponent)

Exponent	Bias			
	2	4	10	15
1	22.22	16.00	8.30	5.90
2	44.44	32.00	16.53	11.72
3	66.67	48.00	24.79	17.58
5	111.11	80.00	41.32	29.30
8	177.78	128.00	66.12	46.88
12	266.67	192.00	99.17	70.31

your examination to select natural traits. If player A can, with one hour of cramming, incréase his probable score on a civil service exam as much as can player B with five hours of cramming, then the system is biased in favor of A, and we would anticipate that the total cost of rent seeking would go down.

Let us now turn to table 6.3. In this table, we have only two parties competing because the situation is mathematically complex and, in any event, having more than two parties would require a three-dimensional diagram. Along the top is the degree of bias toward one player, which is measured here simply in the number of tickets he gets per dollar, it being assumed that the less-advantaged player gets one ticket per dollar. We have omitted the lower exponents of table 6.1, because it is immediately obvious that bias very sharply reduces total rent seeking.

Table 6.4 is the sum over both players of all the payments shown in table 6.3, and, in this case, they always just double the figures in table 6.3.

It turns out that, using our simple mathematical apparatus, both players—the one who is favored by the bias and the one who is not—make the same investment. This is a little counterintuitive, but not very, since most of us do not have very strong intuitions on these matters. In any event, it may simply be an artifact of the particular mathematical formalism we have chosen.

It will be noted immediately that zone I is much larger in this case than in the unbiased cases of tables 6.1 and 6.2. Indeed, even with an

TABLE 6.4
Sum of Investments
(2-Party, Bias, Exponent)

Exponent	Bias			
	2	4	10	15
1	44.44	32.00	16.60	11.80
2	88.88	64.00	30.06	23.44
3	133.34	96.00	49.58	35.16
5	222.22	160.00	82.64	58.60
8	355.56	256.00	132.24	93.76
12	533.34	384.00	198.34	140.62

exponent of 8—which means an extremely flat cost curve—a bias of 15 leads to the game still being in zone I. Thus, such bias does pay off heavily in reducing rent seeking.

It is also true that this kind of bias, in general, is easier to arrange by socially desirable techniques than the earlier suggestions made to reduce rent seeking. Once again, designing personnel selection procedures so that they select the best man at relatively low cost to him is an example. Another would be some kind of policy selection process that was heavily biased in favor of efficient, or "right," policies. Both these techniques, if we could design them, would have large payoffs, not only in reducing rent-seeking activity but also in increasing efficiency of government in general. Thus, it seems to me that introducing this rather special kind of bias into rent seeking would be desirable in many areas, even if we ignore the rent-seeking savings.

However, for many rent-seeking activities, it is admittedly very hard to find a way to introduce bias at all or to introduce bias in a way that leads to better outcomes. Once again, if we assume that Mayor Daley does not restrict his appointments to his relatives but simply gives relatives a differential advantage, depending on how close they are to him, we have a bias system that will reduce rent seeking. However, it will not lead to outcomes in any way superior. Similarly, the restrictions placed on campaign contributions and other methods of attempting to influence government policy are biased in the sense that they are heavier burdens for some people than for others, and it is not clear whether this bias will lead to policy choices superior to those obtained without it. Thus, the only gain is the possibility of reduction in total rent seeking.

Thus ends our preliminary investigation of rent seeking and ways to reduce its social cost. When I have discussed the problem with colleagues, I have found that the intellectually fascinating problem of zones II and III tends to dominate the discussion. This is, indeed, intellectually very interesting, but the real problem we face is the attempt to lower the cost of rent seeking, and this will normally move us into zone I. Thus, I hope that the result of this paper is not mathematical examination of the admittedly fascinating intellectual problems of zones II and III, but practical investigation of methods to lower the cost of rent seeking.

APPENDIX TO CHAPTER 6
Mathematical Appendix, or Labor Saving Calculation Methods

When I first began working on this paper, I discovered that the equations that would have to be solved were higher-order equations, and therefore simply assigned to my graduate assistant, William J. Hunter, the job of approximating the results by using a pocket calculator. He promptly discovered the rather astonishing regularity of column 1, which implied that it would not be all that difficult to solve the equations even if they were higher order. Before I had had time to do anything other than shudder vaguely about the problem, however, I went to lunch with my colleague, Nicolaus Tideman, told him the problem, and he solved it on a napkin. This gave us the equation for tables 6.1 and 6.2. Having discovered this simple algorithm, when we wanted to prepare tables 6.3 and 6.4, once again we asked Tideman, and he obliged with equal speed. The equations used are:

$$P_A = R\frac{N - 1}{N^2} \qquad \text{(Tables 6.1, 6.2)}$$

$$P_A = R\frac{b}{(b + 1)^2} \qquad \text{(Tables 6.3, 6.4)}$$

where

P_A = equilibrium investment,
R = exponent, or the determinant of steepness of the supply curve,
N = number of players, and
b = bias weight.

7

Two Laws of Survival for Ascriptive Government Policies

by

DWIGHT R. LEE AND DANIEL ORR

ASCRIPTIVE allocation is a system in which resource use rights are allocated or proscribed on the basis of membership or nonmembership in a group or class. Examples range in time from the laws on gleaning in the Book of Deuteronomy (to glean one must be widowed, an orphan, or an outsider) to modern programs of affirmative action (to be hired one must be a member of à disadvantaged group). Ascriptive allocation, contrary to the suggestion of those examples, need not be a leveling force: the laws of primogeniture and entail were intended to preserve an aristocracy, much of our contemporary labor law effectively bars occupational mobility, and such institutions as academic tenure and the civil service certainly protect the relatively well-off. Ascriptive rules can originate in custom or widely practiced habit, and they may be directed to the service of some widely shared social objective. On the other hand, they may originate in legislation passed in response to the political pressures of a self-serving group. Two objectives of special-interest pressure are of particularly great importance: programs that provide cash or in-kind transfers, and laws creating, assigning, and protecting monopoly power. Petitioning for these has been given the vivid title "rent seeking" by Anne Krueger.[1]

Elsewhere, Gordon Tullock expresses concern that rent seeking, which he discerns as a traditional and widespread method of allocation and distribution, is again on the rise in Western economies, where it is

---

[1] Anne O. Krueger, "The Political Economy of the Rent-Seeking Society," chapter 4 in this volume.

gradually constricting the scope and sphere of market allocation.[2] In this paper, we will develop theoretical analyses of several examples taken from two classes or types of government program, those which fix prices and those which control market entry. Our analysis can be taken to support Tullock's pessimistic appraisal. Governmental ascription does indeed appear to be crowding voluntary exchange aside in numerous ways, both crude and subtle, and there seems to be no abatement in sight. Our analysis suggests the possible presence of another troubling element in the picture, too: the graver and more persistent the misallocations caused by various programs in response to rent seeking, the more likely those programs are to survive—the more difficult they will be to repeal or eliminate.

Why does a government policy acquire sacred-cow status, so that politicians find it virtually impossible to cut society's losses? The optimistic theory of government-as-omniscient-benefactor would explain policy persistence in terms of some near-unanimous perception of golden benefits for all: policies survive because they are good. (For two decades or more, two examples sustained and nurtured that perception: the Social Security Act and the Employment Act of 1946.) It now appears more likely, however, that the greater the waste and inefficiency induced by a government program, the more difficult it is to modify or repeal the program. There is a ready explanation for this perverse effect. Any government policy can affect the opportunities and constraints faced by individuals as they decide how to employ their resources. A policy is undesirable if it discourages efficiency in the use of resources (through either monetary incentives or outright restrictions), and many policies do cause resources to be transferred from more valuable to less valuable uses. Commitments private individuals make in response to the undesirable policy would end in losses to those people who have privately misallocated, should the policy be removed. For some time now, we have been aware that the political pressure to institute an inefficient policy that yields benefits to a group can impose a cost that is diffused over the entire population. Having succeeded in imposing such a cost, the beneficiary group is directly affected by the policy and would suffer a loss if the policy were to be discarded. Diffused losses and focused gains explain the initial success

[2] Gordon Tullock, "Rent Seeking as a Negative-Sum Game," chapter 2 in this volume.

in securing the adoption of such policies, whereas the diffused gains and concentrated losses serve to explain the failure of efforts to repeal. If repeal is initiated, political resistance can be expected to be stronger, the more pronounced the induced inefficiencies.

A second and perhaps more remarkable finding emerges from our analysis. Efforts to cartelize or control markets even with the support of governmental sanction frequently may be thwarted by a variety of ingenious rent-sharing responses initiated by parties who were never intended to be beneficiaries of the rent-creating legislation. A commonly observed pattern is for rent-collecting opportunities to be created, then to be eroded by the entry of rent sharers. The diffusion of benefits does not eliminate the inefficiencies initiated by the programs, but it does tend to diminish the basis of support for the program. Thus, for a program to be perpetual, its benefits must remain concentrated in an identifiable, politically active interest. The establishment of fixed prices turns out to be an important monopolizing device, which does not preserve the concentration of benefits through time.

Thus, we offer two tentative findings: the ability of a rent-transferring government policy to survive is directly related (1) to the magnitude of the inefficiency it induces and (2) to the ability of the beneficiary group to resist the efforts of others to share in the rents. Such tentative findings have in the past been called "laws" by economists.

Barriers to Entry Imposed by Government

Examples can readily be found to illustrate the survival power of policies that induce inefficiency while simultaneously preserving concentrated benefits. Particularly obvious instances involve the control of entry into an industry: the first one we consider is the Interstate Commerce Commission's (ICC) control of entry into interstate trucking. A person who wishes to establish an interstate trucking firm first needs a "certificate of public convenience and necessity." These certificates specify the product to be transported and the route. The prospective trucker can either petition the ICC for the required certificate or purchase an existing certificate from an owner. However, unless he is interested in a product and a route for which no other trucking firm owns a certificate, he is unlikely to obtain one from the ICC. Existing trucking firms have substantial influence on ICC decisions, and they are sensitive to the dangers of "excessive" competition. The surest way to start a trucking firm, then, is to purchase the necessary certificate on the open market.

The higher the price of certificates on the open market, the greater the inefficiency caused by the ICC's regulations. The certificate's price provides a measure of the monopoly rents created by the regulatory process. In a fully efficient allocation, such as would tend to arise under unrestricted competition, resource owners would perceive the same return in trucking as elsewhere, and the value of certificates would be zero. The waste induced by the policy may be considerable. The certificates of one bankrupt trucking firm were recently auctioned off for $21 million. The market value of all certificates has been estimated to be in the neighborhood of $2 billion.[3] This figure also provides a measure of the opposition an attempt to deregulate trucking would encounter from the trucking industry. By eliminating the value of the certificates, deregulation would impose a tremendous loss on their owners. To avoid this loss, the trucking industry exerts political pressure against deregulation. The greater the inefficiency of ICC regulation, the larger the loss to the trucking industry from deregulation and the more we can expect the firms to mobilize against deregulation. The issuance of certificates, meanwhile, can be restricted to assure that the rents created by trucking regulation will remain intact.

It is true that consumers would gain more from deregulation than the trucking industry would lose, but this gain, even if consumers could be made aware of it, is spread over so many that it provides no effective motive for organizing politically.

A similar control-of-entry example is the licensing of taxicabs. Most major cities issue a limited number of operating permits, one being required for each taxi operated. As in the trucking example, the market price of these permits reflects the value of additional resources in the taxi business over their value in alternative pursuits, and therefore the inefficiency caused by the licensing policy. In New York City a permit for a single cab currently sells for around $50,000. Obviously any attempt to eliminate this inefficiency by allowing free entry into

---

[3] Thomas Moore, "The Beneficiaries of Trucking Regulation," *Journal of Law and Economics* 21 (October, 1978): 327–343.

taxi service would meet strong resistance from those with substantial wealth in the form of taxi permits. The greater the inefficiency, the higher the market value of the permits and the more political resistance an attempt at deregulation would encounter.

Restriction of entry and maintenance of price are very similar devices for market control, of course. In a simple *static* model of monopoly, with an invertible demand curve for the monopolized good, it does not matter whether the firm sets price and allows quantity demand to adjust or sets output and allows price to adjust. In actual markets, with potential entrants anxious to share in the monopoly returns, there is a crucial advantage in being able to fix output rather than price. This is especially true in cases involving the sharing of markets by cartels: output quotas simultaneously provide a mechanism for profit maintenance and profit sharing.

Other Price-Fixing Programs

A couple of examples are offered that support our hypotheses that greater inefficiency breeds deeper entrenchment, and that price fixing is a less-than-perfect form of market control compared with full control over supply quantity when viewed from the perspective of the rent-seeking would-be monopolist.

First, consider price supports in agriculture. Price supports create rents that are captured by those who happen to be owners of farmland at the time when supports are instituted: farmland prices rise in reflection of expected greater profitability from crops. The immediate removal of price supports would cause a perceptible destruction of capital values in farmland and hence would be politically unacceptable. However, with inflation and changes in relative price, support levels that are denominated in dollar terms can be allowed to diminish in real terms with the consequence that farmland does not appreciate as rapidly as other productive assets. Predictably, the more vigorous the activity in governmental purchase-and-storage programs, the harder it would be for politicians to repudiate those programs because the greater and more visible would be the drop in the prices of agricultural land. Also predictably, if farmers could by some means establish effective output quotas in all crops (as they have in tobacco), there

FIGURE 7.1

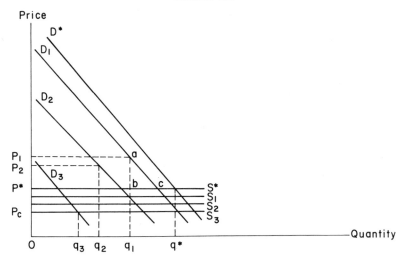

would be a major increase in the rents captured in land values and an enormous application of resources to the protection of those quotas through political action.

A second instructive type of price fixing is in housing rent-control laws. Most price-control actions directed at single markets originate at the initiative of producers, as we would expect, for wealth increases to individual producers who succeed in establishing price floors under their products will usually exceed the wealth increases that individual consumers could hope to realize through establishment of a price ceiling in the same market.

Housing rental rates, however, are an exception to the usual pattern. This is best explained by the fact that the interest of consumers in this commodity is quite large because it accounts for a large budget share, and there are typically a large number of unorganized suppliers. The act of mobilizing consumer interests in this market is a very simple, appealing, and direct one, whereas the producer interest against rent control is less easy to mobilize. Rent control also illustrates our two propositions: price controls are an imperfect substitute for full control over conditions of market supply, and inefficiency breeds tenacity of policy.

Figure 7.1 illustrates the basis for these arguments in the housing rental market. Demand curve D^* represents the demand for housing with the distribution of quality found in an uncontrolled market, and curves D_1, D_2, and D_3 represent demands for housing space that reflect diminishing shifts in the distribution of quality. S^* represents the marginal cost of supplying a unit of housing space that has the quality index associated with demand D^*. S_1, S_2, and S_3 similarly are the marginal cost curves for housing of the quality reflected in the demand curves D_1, D_2, and D_3, respectively.[4]

Assume an initial equilibrium at price P^* and quantity q^*, with D^* and S^* being the relevant demand and supply curves. Next assume that a rent ceiling on housing is set at P_c in response to political pressure from tenants. The short-run gains motivating this political pressure are given by $(P^* - P_c)q^*$, since in the market period quantity and quality will be unaffected by the rent control. This implies, of course, that in the market period there are no inefficiencies associated with the rent-control policy; the effects are purely redistributive. In the process of adjustment, however, both the quantity and the quality of rental housing will decline in response to the control. Quality reductions are accomplished quite simply by the reduction of maintenance or elimination of "free" services previously provided by the landlord. Quantity reductions come about through conversion to condominium or cooperative ownership or, in later stages with lower-quality properties, by abandonment. Suppose, as in figure 7.1, a quantity decline to q_1 is accompanied by a quality decline sufficient to make D_1 the market-period demand curve. The rental rate that clears q_1 units from the market is P_1. Hence, the adjustment response increases both the marginal value of housing space[5] and the market-period gains conveyed to tenants by the rent ceiling at P_c. Those gains, at the time when q_1 is the effective quality and D_1 is the effective demand, are given by $(P_1 - P_c)q_1$, the market-period supply curve being of zero elastic-

---

[4] Figure 7.1 is constructed via this conceptual process: (1) select a particular level (index, distribution) of quality; (2) let the market equilibrate, determining a rental rate and housing stock of that quality which clears; (3) vary the rental rate and "observe" what happens to supply and demand; (4) reduce the quality level and repeat.

[5] This increase will occur only if the marginal value (MV) of housing space is greater than the long-run marginal cost ($LRMC$) of supplying it, but we can expect $MV > LRMC$ until the long-run equilibrium is reached at the rent ceiling P_c.

ity through q_1. Note that the gains are larger than at the program's inception.

So it appears likely that political support for rent controls will increase, at least for a time, after the controls are imposed, and this increase in political support will be accompanied by an increase in the inefficiency the control policy induces.[6]

With the further passage of time, quantity will continue to adjust downward. At the quantity q_2, the accompanying decline in quality will make D_2 the relevant demand curve. At this point the gains to tenants from continued rent controls have declined to $(P_2 - P_c)q_2$, which is roughly comparable with the gains received when they were initially imposed. We expect at this stage that political support for a continuation of the policy, though weakening, will still be adequate to offset opposing political influences.

Eventually, however, quantity and quality adjustments will equilibrate the housing market at the price ceiling P_c. Quantity will have declined to q_3, and the decline in quality will be such that D_3 is the relevant demand curve. The marginal value of housing of that quality is equal to its marginal cost; gains no longer accrue to tenants because of the rent-control policy, and the short-run inefficiencies resulting from the policy have been eliminated.[7] If the rent controls remain in force long enough for this equilibrium to be established, the motivation for their support will have vanished; as the short-run inefficiency of the policy disappears, so does the basis of its support. In rent control, gains that tenants receive are dissipated over time through quality and quantity reductions. The adjustment process will, if continued for a sufficient time, diminish tenant gains from rent controls sufficiently to permit the policy's repeal.

By contrast, suppose it had been possible at the outset for a "ten-

[6] At the initiation of the adjustment process, the market period misallocation is zero. At the time of (q_1, D_1), it is measured by the triangle *abc*.

[7] Clearly the long-run inefficiencies have grown through time and may be very large by the time the price-control equilibrium has been reached. However, given sufficient adjustment time for D_3 and S_3 to become relevant, the costs of making alternative housing commitments will probably make D^* an overstatement of value, even in the long run. (For example, transactions costs in ownership markets may diminish through competition and political pressure.) Therefore, the long-run inefficiencies associated with the rent-control policy, after all adjustments have occurred, will be less than figure 7.1 would indicate.

ant league" to control the flow of resources into housing services. The quantity and quality adjustments that eventually re-equilibrated the market could never have occurred, and the tenant gain would have been a permanent rent, captured by forcibly diverting resources from more highly valued uses.

Recent Experience in Air Transportation

The spectacular consequences of airline deregulation also lend support to our two theses. The Civil Aeronautics Board (CAB) allocated service routes and set fares for the interstate carriers, which may have been intended to be sufficient to assure an orderly monopoly market but was not. The monopoly rents resulting from restriction of routes and fares prompted more subtle forms of entry (some of it encouraged by the CAB). Airlines competed with more spacious seating, more in-flight service, and, most important, more frequent flights for greater passenger convenience.[8] Cost competition on the input side, in conjunction with fixed prices on the output side, predictably was carried to the point at which excess profits were dissipated; in fact, because quality competition frequently was pursued to a point where fixed costs were not covered, the return on capital in the airline industry was reduced below the level in the economy at large.

This is not to say that all rents from airline regulation were dissipated. Many of those rents continued to be captured as salaries and wages to employees of the airline industry, and they generated substantial political support for the continuation of regulation.

Figure 7.2 suggests what has happened in the airline industry. The curve D_1 represents the demand for service (measured in passenger miles) and AC_1 represents the industry's average cost in the early profitable stages of regulated operation. Let P_1 be the profit-maximizing price enforced by the CAB, and q_1 the service volume de-

[8] See George W. Douglas and James C. Miller, "Quality Competition, Industry Equilibrium, and Efficiency in the Price-Constrained Airline Market," *American Economic Review* 64 (September, 1974): 657–670, for a theoretical discussion of the relationship between price and quality in regulated markets, accompanied by empirical evidence from the airline industry. For an analysis of differences between price and nonprice competition, see George J. Stigler, "Price and Nonprice Competition," *Journal of Political Economy* 76 (February, 1968): 149–154.

FIGURE 7.2

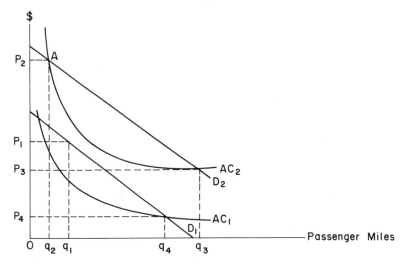

manded. Economic profits are realized by the industry. Without price competition this profit motivates adjustments such as larger aircraft fleets to operate more frequent service. These adjustments shift the average cost curve outward. They also shift the demand curve out as the quality of the service improves. This quality competition continues until D_2 and AC_2 are the relevant demand and average cost curves, respectively, and economic profits have been driven to zero, with equilibrium being reached at price P_2 and quantity q_2.[9]

Once the zero-profit equilibrium is reached, the rents generated by the restrictions on entry and price will accrue to suppliers of inputs specialized to the airline industry. Deregulation will reduce or eliminate those rents, and those who receive them can be expected to oppose deregulation. But from the perspective of investors directly concerned with the rate of return on their investment, deregulation can be an attractive possibility. As seen in figure 7.2, the reduction in prices below P_2 that is sure to follow deregulation will, between P_2 and P_3, result in positive profits. Competition may eventually drive price

[9] Assuming the horizontal segment of AC_1 lies below the initial price P_1, the absence of price competition assures that the zero-profit equilibrium will not occur at the intersection q_3. It is interesting to note that for a given shift in the average cost curve, the less consumers value the accompanying increase in quality (the smaller the outward shift in the demand), the more that will be demanded in this zero-profit equilibrium.

down to P_3 and eliminate profits once more, but at q_3 investors reap normal returns, and the profitable period of adjustment may be long in duration.[10]

What happened in air transport that never happened in the regulation of trucking? Much has been made of the charm, vigor, and panache of Alfred Kahn, but would he have been (or will he be) as successful in his attempts to deregulate highway freight? We are pessimistic that trucking deregulation will be politically acceptable, because in that industry the adjustment to regulation has been completed, and the regulation-induced rents have not diminished relative to the gains to owners in the industry that would be generated by deregulation. To elaborate on that point, the device that drives average cost up to the level of average revenue in the trucking industry is the certificate of public convenience and necessity. By reducing to zero the value of this capital asset, deregulation would destroy the existing firms' capital rather than enhance it as in the case of the airlines.

Moreover, suppose that the trucking industry, through nonprice competition, has reached a zero-profit position such as A in figure 7.2. The short-run profits resulting from deregulation would probably be much smaller than has been observed in the airlines. This follows so long as the price elasticity of demand for airline travel is greater than the price elasticity of demand for trucking services at an equilibrium like A, which seems likely.[11] As is easily seen from figure 7.2, the less price elastic the demand, the smaller the profit potential from price competition at position A. So, from the perspective of the trucking industry, there is little to gain from the elimination of ICC regulation.

The important difference, then, between trucking regulation and airline regulation is that in the environment created by the CAB it was optimal to install excess capacity that created the potential for substantial profits from deregulation. The politically influential special-interest group (the owners of the airline industry) was in a position to

[10] The long-run adjustment to the new equilibrium may include quality reductions that shift both the demand curve and average cost curve downward, with the new equilibrium being at a position such as (P_4, q_4) in figure 7.2. This type of adjustment permits large profits to be made before the new equilibrium is reached but does not permit factor owners to maintain their regulation-based rents.

[11] Airline travel is, for a large part of the traveling public, a "luxury good"; truck transport is an essential productive input that usually accounts for a relatively small part of total production cost.

capture much of the gain from deregulation. Given that possibility, an inefficient policy can lose its political viability despite its inefficiencies.

However, even when such a policy is eliminated, we cannot rule out the possibility of resurrection. Once the postderegulation competitive adjustment has been completed, the airlines will stand to gain anew from price and entry restriction, and, once again, the greater the monopoly burden that can be imposed and captured, the greater the political pressure for a new round of regulatory policy. If regulation is reimposed, however, the airlines may take the precaution of imposing restrictions on the capacity they may acquire, thereby reducing the probability that renewed pressure for deregulation will be effective.

Conclusion

It is no surprise that government intervention on behalf of economic interest can cause inefficiency of resource use in particular markets, or that the larger the rents transferred by those policies, the more tenacious the defense of them will be. What is surprising is the vigor of the market process itself and the extent to which it can compete away ascribed advantages, even when operating under as grave a burden as imposed prices. The "policy implication" of this paper, then, is: if one seeks a governmentally chartered cartel and aspires that it shall be perpetually effective, it is necessary to obtain complete control over all terms of market supply—price, quality (including all terms of servicing and maintenance), output rates, and delivery schedules. Otherwise, loopholes will gradually be found through which rents will be transferred to other recipients.

This paper offers several examples of the process whereby rents initially concentrated in one beneficiary group become dispersed. After that dispersion occurs, the residual inefficiencies the policy causes provide a greater impetus to its abolition, since the dispersion of benefits has weakened its support base.

8

The Social Costs of
Monopoly Power

by

Keith Cowling and Dennis C. Mueller

IN 1954, Arnold Harberger[1] estimated the welfare losses from monopoly for the United States at 0.1 of 1 percent of the gross national product. Several studies using different assumptions have appeared since, reconfirming Harberger's early low estimates.[2] These papers have firmly established as part of the conventional wisdom the idea that welfare losses from monopoly are insignificant.

The Harberger position has been, almost from the start, subject to attack, however.[3] D. R. Kamerschen essentially followed the Harberger methodology but assumed an elasticity of demand consistent with monopoly pricing behavior at the industry level and obtained welfare loss estimates as high as 6 percent. Richard Posner made some rough estimates of the social costs of acquiring monopoly power but,

NOTE: This paper was started during the summer of 1975 when Keith Cowling visited the International Institute of Management and completed during the summer of 1976 when Dennis Mueller participated in the University of Warwick's Summer Workshop. Thanks are extended to both these institutions for their support. In addition, special thanks are due Gerald Nelson, who made the welfare loss calculations for the United States, and Clive Hicks for making the estimates for the United Kingdom.

[1] Arnold C. Harberger, "Monopoly and Resource Allocation," *American Economic Review* 44 (May, 1954): 77–87.

[2] E.g., David Schwartzman, "The Burden of Monopoly," *Journal of Political Economy* 68 (November–December, 1960): 627–630; F. M. Scherer, *Industrial Market Structure and Market Performance* (Chicago: Rand McNally, 1970); and D. A. Worcester, Jr., "New Estimates of the Welfare Loss to Monopoly: U.S. 1956–69," *Southern Economic Journal* 40 (October, 1973): 234–246.

[3] E.g., George J. Stigler, "The Statistics of Monopoly and Merger," *Journal of Political Economy* 64 (February, 1956): 33–40.

using Harberger's calculations, concluded that the real problem was the social cost of regulation rather than of private market power.[4]

The most sophisticated critique of Harberger's approach has been offered by Abram Bergson.[5] Bergson criticizes the partial equilibrium framework employed by Harberger and all previous studies and puts forward a general equilibrium model as an alternative. He then produces a series of hypothetical estimates of the welfare losses from monopoly, some of them quite large, for various combinations of the two key parameters in this model, the elasticity of substitution in consumption and the difference between monopoly and competitive price. Not surprisingly, Bergson's estimates, which suggest that monopoly can be a matter of some consequence, have induced a sharp reaction.[6]

We shall level several objections against the Harberger approach. We then calculate estimates of the welfare loss from monopoly, using procedures derived to meet these objections, and obtain estimates significantly greater than those of previous studies. Although several of our objections have been made by others, none has systematically adjusted the basic Harberger technique to take them into account. Thus all previous estimates of monopoly welfare losses suffer in varying degrees from the same biases incorporated in Harberger's original estimates.

We do, however, employ a partial equilibrium framework as followed by Harberger and all subsequent empirical studies. Although a general equilibrium framework would be preferable, such an approach requires simplifying assumptions, which, to our mind, are just as restrictive as those needed to justify the partial equilibrium approach. For example, Bergson must assume that social welfare can be captured

---

[4] D. R. Kamerschen, "An Estimation of the Welfare Losses from Monopoly in the American Economy," *Western Economic Journal* 4 (Summer, 1966): 221–236; Richard A. Posner, "The Social Costs of Monopoly and Regulation," chapter 5 in this volume.

[5] Abram Bergson, "On Monopoly Welfare Losses," *American Economic Review* 63 (December, 1973): 853–870.

[6] See R. Carson, "On Monopoly Welfare Losses: Comment," *American Economic Review* 65 (December, 1975): 1008–14, and D. A. Worcester, Jr., "On Monopoly Welfare Losses: Comment," *American Economic Review* 65 (December, 1975): 1015–23. In addition to the points Bergson raises in his own defense, we have serious objections to the arguments made by Carson and Worcester. Some of these are presented below in our critique of previous studies.

via a social indifference curve and, further, that this indifference curve is the *CES* variety. The assumption that the elasticity of substitution (σ) is constant further implies, for a disaggregated analysis, that the elasticity of demand for each product (η_i) is the same, since $\eta_i \rightarrow \sigma$ as the share of the ith product in total output approaches zero. But the assumption that η_i is the same for all i is the same assumption made by Harberger and most other studies. It introduces a basic inconsistency between the observed variations in price-cost margins and the assumed constant elasticities in demand, which our study seeks to avoid. Given such problems, we have adopted the partial equilibrium framework, with all the necessary assumptions it requires.[7]

We present estimates for both the United States and the United Kingdom based on data gathered at the firm level.

Theoretical Analysis

We have four substantive criticisms of the Harberger approach:

1. In the partial equilibrium formula for welfare loss, $(dp \cdot dq)/2$ where dp is the change in price from competition to monopoly and dq is the change in quantity, dp and dq were considered to be independent of each other. Generally low values of dp were *observed* and low values of dq were *assumed*. Harberger assumed that price elasticities of demand in all industries were unitary. This must inevitably lead to small estimates of welfare loss.

2. The competitive profit rate was identified with the mean profit rate and thus automatically incorporated an element of monopoly. In fact, the underlying approach was a "constant degree of monopoly," in which distortions in output were associated with deviations of profit rate from the mean rather than from the competitive return on capital.

3. The use of industry profit rates introduces an immediate aggregation bias into the calculation by allowing the high monopoly profits of those firms with the most market power to be offset by the losses of other firms in the same industry. Given assumption (1), a further aggregation bias is introduced, which can easily be shown to result in additional downward bias in the estimates.

4. The entire social loss due to monopoly was assumed to arise

---

[7] Bergson, "On Monopoly Welfare Losses."

from the deviation of monopoly output from competitive levels. To this should be added the social cost of attempts to acquire monopoly positions, existing or potential.

We now seek to justify each of these four criticisms.

INTERDEPENDENCE OF dp_i AND dq_i

Assuming profit maximizing behavior, we can define the implied price elasticity of demand ($\hat{\eta}_i$) for a specific firm by observing the mark-up of price on marginal cost:

$$\hat{\eta}_i = \frac{p_i}{p_i - mc_i} \qquad (1)$$

For a pure monopolist or perfectly colluding oligopolist, $\hat{\eta}_i$ is the industry elasticity of demand. In other cases $\hat{\eta}_i$ reflects both the industry demand elasticity and the degree of rivals' response to a change in price the ith firm perceives.[8] Using (1), we shall obtain welfare loss estimates by individual firms from their price-cost margins. These estimates indicate the amount of welfare loss accompanying a single firm's decision to set price above marginal cost, given the change in its output implied by $\hat{\eta}_i$.[9] To the extent other firms also charge higher prices because firm i sets its price above marginal cost, the total welfare loss associated with firm i's market power exceeds the welfare loss we estimate. To the extent a simultaneous reduction to zero of all price-cost margins is contemplated, however, $\hat{\eta}_i$ overestimates the net effect of the reduction in p_i on the ith firm's output. What the latter effect on output and welfare would be is a matter for general equilibrium analysis and is not the focus here. Rather, we attempt an estimate of the relative importance of the distortions in individual firm outputs, on a firm by firm basis, on the assumption that each does possess some monopoly power, as implied by the price-cost margin it chooses, and that each does use it.

This approach emphasizing the interdependence of observed price distortions and changes in output contrasts with the methodology of Harberger, Schwartzman, Worcester, and Bergson, who ob-

---

[8] J. Cubbin, "Apparent Collusion, Price-Cost Margins, and Advertising in Oligopoly," mimeographed, University of Warwick.

[9] We need here an assumption of perfect competition everywhere else, of course. We shall ignore problems of the second best, along with the general equilibrium issue more generally throughout the paper.

serve (or, in Bergson's case, assume) $(p_i - mc_i)/p_i$ and then *assume* a value of η_i.[10] Harberger observed generally low values of dp_i and yet chose to assume that $\eta_i = 1$ and therefore that dq_i was also very small. But it is inconsistent to observe low values of dp_i and infer low elasticities unless one has assumed that the firm or industry cannot price as a monopolist—that is, unless one has already assumed the monopoly problem away.[11] Assuming interdependence, we obtain the following definition of welfare loss:

$$dW_i = \frac{1}{2} \cdot \frac{dp_i}{p_i} \cdot \frac{dq_i}{q_i} \cdot p_i q_i \qquad (2)$$

where $\dfrac{dp_i}{p_i} = \dfrac{1}{\hat{\eta}_i}$ and $\dfrac{dq_i}{q_i} = \hat{\eta}_i \dfrac{dp_i}{p_i} = 1$ [12]

$$\therefore \quad dW_i = \frac{dp_i}{p_i} \cdot \frac{p_i q_i}{2} . \qquad (3)$$

Assuming constant costs, we can rewrite (3) in terms of profits:

$$dW_i = \frac{\Pi_i}{p_i q_i} \cdot \frac{p_i q_i}{2} = \frac{\Pi_i}{2} . \qquad (4)$$

This formulation obviously contrasts sharply with Harberger's:

$$dW_i = \frac{p_i \cdot q_i \cdot \eta_i \cdot t_i^2}{2} \qquad (5)$$

where $t_i = dp_i/p_i$, $\eta_i = 1$.

It is obvious that if t_i is small, the welfare loss is going to be insignificant. If t_i were a price increase due to tariff or tax, then it might be

[10] Harberger, "Monopoly and Resource Allocation"; Schwartzman, "The Burden of Monopoly"; Worcester, "New Estimates of the Welfare Loss to Monopoly"; and Bergson, "On Monopoly Welfare Losses." The Harberger and Schwartzman estimates are at the industry level.

[11] This position is questioned by J. L. Wenders, "Entry and Monopoly Pricing," *Journal of Political Economy* 75 (October, 1967): 755–760, and others who attempt to show how implausible the implied η_i's are. However, their calculations are erroneous because they fail to recognize (1) that the degree of collusion is a variable—we need not assume perfect joint profit maximization—and (2) that entry is conditional on the same variables (plus others) that determine $(p_i - mc_i)/p_i$—for example, η, the degree of concentration, and, for differentiated products, advertising also.

[12] This is true so long as the firm is in equilibrium, that is, if the firms' expectations about the behavior of rivals are actually borne out. If this were not the case, then the elasticity on which the pricing decision was made would not correspond to the elasticity implied by the change in output. We assume firm equilibrium in our calculations.

assumed to be independent of η_i, and equation (5) would give a reasonable estimate of welfare loss.[13] But where t_i is a firm decision variable, η_i and t_i must be interdependent, and formulas for calculating welfare losses should take this interdependence into account. Worcester criticizes Bergson for doing essentially this with his hypothetical general equilibrium calculations, but Worcester himself followed the Harberger line without demure.[14] In contrast with Harberger and Worcester, Bergson allowed himself to pick some combinations of t_i and η_i which implied high values of welfare loss.[15]

Harberger defended his choice of a demand elasticity of 1.0 across all products on the grounds that what was "envisage[d was] not the substitution of one industry's product against all other products, but rather the substitution of one great aggregate of products (those yielding high rates of return) for another aggregate (those yielding low rates of return)."[16] Thus, the use of $\eta = 1.0$ was an attempt to compensate for the disadvantages of employing a partial equilibrium measure of welfare loss to examine a general equilibrium structural change. But this is not only awkward; it answers neither the criticisms raised by Bergson against the partial equilibrium approach nor those we have just presented.[17] For this reason, we will define the partial equilibrium methodology properly and obtain the best estimates we can, recognizing that the issues raised by general equilibrium analysis and the theory of second best regarding the net effect of a simultaneous elimination of all monopoly power will remain unanswered. We return to this point below.

THE MEASUREMENT OF MONOPOLY PROFITS

The obvious measure of monopoly profit is the excess of actual profits over long-run competitive returns. For an economy in equi-

---

[13] But not necessarily so. Taxes and tariffs may be applied according to elasticity expectations.

[14] Worcester, "New Estimates of the Welfare Loss to Monopoly," and "On Monopoly Welfare Losses: Comment." The latter of these also offers some empirical support. His collection of industry price elasticities is either irrelevant (including many agricultural products and few manufacturing ones) or suspect (no allowance having been made in the studies quoted for quality change over time) and is certainly not comprehensive.

[15] Bergson, "On Monopoly Welfare Losses."

[16] Harberger, "Monopoly and Resource Allocation," p. 79.

[17] Bergson, "On Monopoly Welfare Losses."

librium, the competitive profit rate is the minimum compatible with long-run survival, given appropriate allowances for risk. Monopoly profit is thus the difference between actual profits and profits consistent with this minimum rate.

Harberger and all subsequent studies have based their monopoly profit estimates on the size of the deviation between actual profit rates and the mean rate.[18] To the extent that observed profits contain elements of monopoly rent, the mean profit rate exceeds the minimum long-run survival rate. The deviations between profit rates above the mean and the mean rate underestimate the level of monopoly returns, and the estimate of monopoly welfare is biased downward.[19] Indeed, if all firms and industries were in long-run equilibria, all would earn profits equal to or greater than the minimum, and the use of deviations from the mean would minimize the size of the measured monopoly profits. But it is unreasonable to assume that the time periods investigated in Harberger's study, the others that followed, or our own, are long enough or stable enough for all firms and industries to be in equilibrium. The presence of firms earning profits less than the competitive norm creates a methodological problem for a study of monopoly welfare losses. All studies to date have implicitly assumed that a monopolist's costs are the same as those of a firm in competitive equilibrium, and that all welfare loss is from the loss of consumers' surplus caused by a monopoly price above marginal cost. But what is the appropriate assumption to make for a firm experiencing losses? It seems unrealistic to assume that its costs are at competitive levels and its prices below them. A reasonable assumption is that these firms are in disequilibrium, probably with costs currently above competitive levels. When calculating monopoly welfare losses, therefore, we simply drop all firms (or industries where relevant) with profits below the competitive return on capital, in effect assuming that they will eventually either return to a position where they are earning normal profits or disappear. In either case, they represent no long-run loss to society. (Some of these losses may represent expenditures by firms hoping to secure monopoly positions from other firms in the industry, as

---

[18] Harberger, "Monopoly and Resource Allocation."

[19] Worcester, "New Estimates on the Welfare Loss to Monopoly," makes some allowance for this bias by using 90 percent of the median profit rate, but this adjustment is obviously rather ad hoc.

discussed below. These losses are then part of the social costs of monopoly. We attempt to account for them in one of our welfare loss formulas.)

Previous studies, as far as we can tell, have followed Harberger and treated deviations in profits below and above the mean symmetrically. That is, an industry whose profit rate was 5 percent below the mean profit rate was considered to have created as large a welfare loss as an industry whose profits are 5 percent above the mean.[20] Thus, these studies have not actually estimated welfare loss under monopoly with perfect competition as the standard of comparison but have effectively compared welfare loss under the present regime with what would exist were the degree of monopoly equalized across all firms and industries. Under such procedures, a constant degree of monopoly power, however high, would result in no welfare loss. Despite some theoretical support, this approach raises practical difficulties. How does one measure or define this elusive concept of a constant degree of monopoly? How is such a world created without an omniscient planner or regulator? In addition, monopoly in product markets could be expected to induce distortions in factor markets. Finally, as developed below, the existence of monopoly power in product markets attracts resources to its acquisition and protection, which are part of the social cost of monopoly beyond the accompanying distortions in output. For these reasons, and because it appears to be most directly in the spirit of the analysis, we have compared monopoly profits with competitive returns and considered only deviations above the competitive rate when estimating welfare losses.

Following Harberger and other previous studies, we have attempted to minimize the transitory component in our estimates by using averages of firm profits over several years.[21] Nevertheless, some

---

[20] One might believe that the losses by firms earning profits below the norm represent a form of *factor surplus loss* that must be added to the consumer surplus loss to obtain the full losses from monopoly. But as Worcester, "New Estimates of the Welfare Loss to Monopoly," has shown, these factor surplus losses, if properly measured, are an alternative way of estimating the consumer surplus losses and should be used instead of the consumer surplus measure, rather than in addition to it, if used at all.

[21] Harberger, "Monopoly and Resource Allocation," uses five years of "normal" business activity in the twenties for his original study of the United States. Following his lead, we have chosen four years in the sixties, between a recession and the Vietnam War boom, for the U.S. estimates. The results reported below for the United Kingdom are for

of the companies earning profits above competitive levels in our samples are in temporary disequilibrium, and the welfare losses associated with these firms can be expected to disappear over time. Thus, our estimates of monopoly profits combine both long-run monopoly profits and short-run disequilibrium profits. To the extent our time periods are representative of the U.K. and U.S. economies under "normal" conditions, our calculations are accurate estimates of the annual losses from monopoly, both permanent and transitory, that can be expected in these countries. A further effort to eliminate the transitory monopoly components from the data would require a specification of what is meant by "permanent" and "transitory" monopolies. Many economists would take it for granted that in the long run all monopolies are dead, and thus monopoly, like unemployment, is a short-run phenomenon. As with unemployment, the questions are how serious the problem is when it exists, and how long it lasts. We address the first of these questions, but a full answer to the second is clearly beyond the scope of our essentially cross-section analysis.

AGGREGATION BIASES FROM USING INDUSTRY DATA

Previous studies of monopoly welfare losses, with the exception of Worcester, have used industry data at a fairly high level of aggregation.[22] At any given time some firms in an industry are likely to be earning profits below the competitive level. We have already discussed the methodological issues raised in a study of monopoly welfare losses by firms earning negative economic profits. If it is true that these firms are in short-run disequilibrium, then they should be dropped from an industry before calculating the industry's profit rate. Previous studies with calculations based solely on industry data have effectively combined the negative profits of some firms with the positive profits of others in estimating the welfare losses from monopoly. Thus, they have implicitly assumed that the monopoly profits earned by the most profitable firms in the industry are somehow offset or mitigated by those experiencing transitory losses. But if there is a monopoly problem in an industry, it is represented by the positive rents earned by those firms with profits above the norm, and the losses of

---

only two years, 1968–1969. The U.K. results for 1970–1974 indicate that averaging profits over five years does not change the nature of the outcome.

[22] Worcester, "New Estimates of the Welfare Loss to Monopoly."

firms temporarily unable to compete successfully in no way alleviates the social costs arising from the monopoly positions of the other firms. The present study therefore measures monopoly welfare losses by using firm-level monopoly profit estimates.

A second aggregation bias is introduced into the estimates of all previous studies other than Kamerschen's through the assumption of a constant elasticity of demand across all industries.[23] This results in the profit margin's appearance as a squared term in the welfare loss formula. The use of average firm profit margins (including firms with negative profits) implicit in the use of industry data further biases the welfare loss estimates downward. The extent of this bias is measured below.

WELFARE LOSS IN THE ACQUISITION OF MONOPOLY POWER

Gordon Tullock and Richard Posner have argued that previous studies understate the social costs of monopoly by failing to recognize the costs involved in attempts to gain and retain monopoly power.[24] These costs could take the form of investment in excess production capacity, excessive accumulation of advertising goodwill stocks, and excessive product differentiation through research and development.[25] Efforts to obtain tariff protection, patent protection, and other types of preferential government treatment through campaign contributions, lobbying, or bribery are parts of the social costs of monopoly as defined by Tullock and Posner. To the extent that these expenditures enter reported costs in the form of higher payments to factor owners and legitimate business expenses, firm costs in the presence of monopoly exceed costs under perfect competition. Estimates of welfare loss based on those profits remaining, *net* of these expenditures, under-

---

[23] Kamerschen, "An Estimation of the Welfare Losses from Monopoly."

[24] Gordon Tullock, "The Welfare Costs of Tariffs, Monopolies and Theft," chapter 3 in this volume; Posner, "The Social Costs of Monopoly and Regulation."

[25] See Michael Spence, "Entry, Capacity, Investment, and Oligopolistic Pricing," Technical Report 131, Institute for Mathematical Studies in the Social Sciences, Stanford University. It is interesting to note that this type of activity generally dominates the entry-limiting pricing response. Entry-limiting pricing can be thought of as having extra capacity because of potential entry and actual use to produce output. Thus the profits associated with restricting output are lost. From this viewpoint we cannot accept Posner's position that the elimination of entry regulation would eliminate waste. As the probability of entry increases, so would the optimal degree of excess capacity. Monopoly pricing would be maintained but social waste would still occur.

estimate the social cost of monopoly in two ways: (1) by understating monopoly rents and so understating the distortions in output monopoly produces, and (2) by failing to include these additional expenditures as part of the costs of monopoly.

Three adjustments to the usual welfare triangle measure of monopoly welfare loss are made to account for the additional expenditures to redistribute monopoly rents that monopoly power induces. First, advertising is added to monopoly profit in calculating the welfare triangle loss to allow for the understatement of monopoly profit that expenditures of this type produce. Second, all advertising is added to the welfare loss. This takes the extreme view of advertising as merely an instrument for securing market power. To the extent advertising provides useful information to consumers, this measure overstates the cost of monopoly.[26] Third, all measured, after-tax profits above the competitive cost of capital are used as the estimate of the expenditures incurred by others to obtain control of these monopoly rents. Obviously this estimate is but a first approximation. It is an underestimate if the firm has, in the acquisition and maintenance of its monopoly position, incurred expenditures that are included in current costs. It is an overstatement if actual and potential competitors can successfully collude to avoid these wasteful outlays. This argument can always be rebutted, however, by carrying the Tullock-Posner analysis one stage back and including expenditures of resources to enter the potential competitor's position, and so on. The arguments that after-tax profits underestimate the additional costs associated with monopoly seem at least as reasonable as those suggesting overestimation.

AN OBJECTION AND ALTERNATIVE ESTIMATING TECHNIQUE

The assumption that demand elasticity equals the reciprocal of the price-cost margin, equation (1), can give rise, when price-cost margins are small, to firm-level elasticity estimates much greater than existing industry-level estimates and imply large increases in output from the elimination of monopoly. This has led several observers to

---

[26] Given the interests of the agent doing the advertising, there will always be an inherent bias in the information provided, so the argument for advertising as a provider of information should not be taken too seriously. Even if we base our welfare measures on postadvertising preferences, it is still possible to demonstrate that monopolies (and a fortiori oligopolies) invest in too much advertising. See Avinash Dixit and Vincent Norman, "Advertising and Welfare," *Bell Journal of Economics* 9 (Spring, 1978): 1–17.

FIGURE 8.1

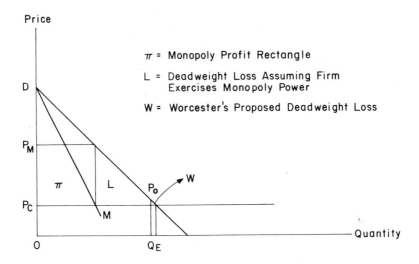

Price

π = Monopoly Profit Rectangle

L = Deadweight Loss Assuming Firm
  Exercises Monopoly Power

W = Worcester's Proposed Deadweight Loss

criticize the use of the Lerner formula and the underlying assumption
that firms set price as if they possess and utilize market power. Worcester has made the argument most forcefully: "Serious error . . . .
arise[s] if the 'monopolist' is only an oligopolist who fears entry, unfavorable publicity, government regulation or a weaker position at the
bargaining table should profits be too high, and for such reasons prices
at P_o [figure 8.1] and sells output Q_E in spite of the fact that the marginal revenue is far below zero at that point."[27] The elasticity of demand
is lower at P_o than at P_M, and the expansion in output following a reduction in price to competitive price P_c is obviously much smaller if we
assume the "monopolist" sets price equal to P_o. Thus Worcester's depic-
tion of the problem does meet the objections many have raised against
the use of the Lerner formula to estimate demand elasticities. We observe only that if one assumes from the start that "monopolists" are so
constrained in their behavior that they must set price so low that marginal revenue is negative, it can be no surprise that calculations incor-
porating this assumption indicate insignificant welfare losses. But any
estimates of welfare losses within a partial equilibrium framework that
impose demand elasticities significantly below those implied via the

---

[27] D. A. Worcester, Jr., "Innovations in the Calculations of the Welfare Loss to Monopoly," *Western Economic Journal* 7 (September, 1969): 234–246, 236–237. Note that
our figure 8.1 and Worcester's are drawn to scale.

FIGURE 8.2

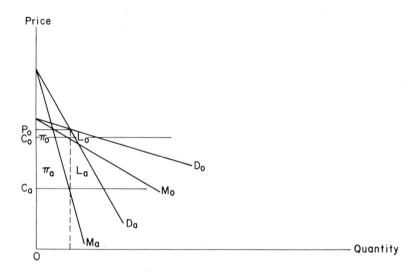

Lerner formula must implicitly be assuming that firms set price in such an environment, if the data on price-cost margins are accepted at face value.

The latter assumption may not be valid, however, and its abandonment allows a reconciliation of existing profit margin data with lower demand elasticity figures without also introducing the assumption that monopolists are either irrational or impotent. The preceding section discusses several business outlays made to maintain or preserve monopoly positions. Conceptually these are better treated as *investments* out of current profits made to secure future monopoly rents than as current production costs, as is done for accounting purposes and carried through into the economist's calculations based on accounting data. A rational monopolist will not take these into account in making his short-run pricing decision. We can thus reconcile the monopoly pricing assumption with small demand elasticity estimates by assuming that average costs contain much investment expenditure and that marginal production costs are below these.

In figure 8.2 let C_0 be observed costs, including investment outlays, and P_0 observed price. For such price and cost figures to be consistent with monopoly pricing behavior, the firm's demand schedule would have to be D_0. Price P_0 would be consistent with a much more inelastic demand schedule, D_a say, if actual production costs were at C_a. Note that both profits (π), and the welfare triangle losses (L) are much larger under the more inelastic demand schedule assumption.

Thus, an alternative procedure for calculating the welfare losses from monopoly to the one described above would be to estimate price-cost margins from data on demand elasticities, where now we estimate demand elasticities from data on price-cost margins. We do not pursue these calculations here. First, because we do not have demand elasticity data applicable to firms, and the imposition of any constant η across all firms is obviously ad hoc. Second, the choice of any η in line with existing industry estimates would lead to welfare loss estimates far greater than those calculated here. The highest of the elasticities used in previous studies has been $\eta = 2.0$. This implies a profit margin of 50 percent and a welfare triangle loss equal to one-quarter of sales. These estimates exceed those reported here whenever the firm's profits are *less* than one-half of sales. Since this is true for all our firms, our welfare loss estimates are all smaller than under the alternative procedure.

We believe that reported costs do contain large amounts of investment expenditures beyond the advertising we allow for, that production costs are lower therefore, and that individual-firm demand elasticities are typically lower than we implicitly estimate. We emphasize, however, that any attempt to take these costs into account and adjust demand elasticities accordingly, while maintaining the assumption that companies do possess and exercise market power, will lead to larger estimates of welfare loss, underlining again the conservative nature of our calculations.

Empirical Estimates

Empirical estimates of the social cost of monopoly power were obtained for both the United States and United Kingdom. We provide two sets of estimates, one based on our assumptions (ΔW_{CM}^k), the other based on Harbergerian assumptions (ΔW_H^k), both measured at the firm level. For each approach we give a range of four estimates defined in table 8.1.

Thus for $k = 1$ we define two alternative estimates of the welfare

TABLE 8.1
Alternative Definitions of Social Cost

k	ΔW^k_{CM}	ΔW^k_{H}
1	$\Pi/2$	$(R/2).(\Pi/R)^2$
2	$(\Pi + A)/2$	$(R/2)[(\Pi + A)/R]^2$
3	$A + [(\Pi + A)/2]$	$(R/2)[(\Pi + A)/R]^2 + A$
4	$\Pi' + A + (\Pi + A)/2$	$R/2[(\Pi + A)/R]^2 + A + \Pi'$

NOTE:

Π = before-tax profit
Π' = after-tax profit
A = advertising
R = total revenue.

triangle, the one (ΔW^1_{CM}) based on interdependence of dp_i and dq_i, the other (ΔW^1_H) based on the Harberger methodology. This latter estimate is included for comparison with previous results, especially from the viewpoint of bias due to aggregation. For $k = 2$ the same calculations are performed, but in calculating dp_i advertising expenditure (A_i) is deducted from cost. For $k = 3$ we add in advertising expenditure as a social cost, and for $k = 4$ we also add in monopoly profits *after tax* as a further element of social cost. It should be noted at this point that in calculating dp_i the appropriate profit measure is *before-tax* profit, since the price and quantity choice of a monopolist should not be affected by a tax on profits. Thus, in contrast with most previous studies, we use before-tax profits to measure the distortion between price and costs under monopoly (the ΔW's for $k = 1,2,3$). However, it is *after-tax* monopoly profits that invite additional expenditures to gain monopoly, and these are added in to obtain our fourth measure of welfare loss.

To estimate monopoly profits, an estimate of the return on capital of a firm in a competitive industry is needed. Any estimates based on actual returns earned in existing industries run the danger of including monopoly rents. The stock market might be regarded as coming fairly close to satisfying the free entry and exit requirement of a competitive industry, however. The returns on corporate stock will include monopoly rents to the extent that they become capitalized over the period for which the rate is estimated. The use of these returns for the United

States is, therefore, equivalent to assuming (1) that all existing monopoly rents are fully capitalized at the beginning of the period, and (2) that changes in monopoly rents over the period are accurately anticipated.

For the United States, we use as our estimate of competitive return on capital the Fisher-Lorie index of returns on a fully diversified portfolio of listed stocks for 1963–1966. This estimate was 0.12 percent, which might be compared with the average return on capital earned by the firms in our sample (0.14%).

For the United Kingdom, we use the pre-tax real cost of capital as calculated by J. S. Flemming, L. D. D. Price, and S. A. Byers.[28] These estimates avoid entirely the newly capitalized monopoly rent problem mentioned above. For the 1968–1969 period, they yield an estimate of the cost of capital of 8.15 percent.[29]

The firms in our samples include companies operating in both intermediate and final goods markets. To justify adding triangular measures of welfare loss for final and intermediate products, we must assume that the demand schedule for intermediate products represents a derived demand schedule, as in traditional Marshallian analysis. Under this assumption, triangular measures of welfare loss calculated

---

[28] J. S. Flemming, L. D. D. Price, and S. A. Byers, "The Cost of Capital, Finance, and Investment," *Bank of England Quarterly Bulletin* 16 (June, 1976): 193–205.

[29] It may be argued that because of inflation we are undervaluing land or capital. This should not be a serious problem for the United States, since our data follow a period of quite modest price increases. Given that inflation in the United Kingdom in 1968–1969 was substantial, though very much less than in the seventies, we have corrected our data at the company level. Using data from J. S. Walker, "Estimating Companies' Rate of Return on Capital Employed," *Economic Trends* (November, 1974): pp. xx–xxix; we multiplied the profit figure derived from the company accounts by the ratio of the average rate of return at replacement cost to the average rate of return at historical cost and subtracted from this the estimated book value of assets times the cost of capital. The ratio of rates of return used was 9.4 : 13.4 in 1968 and 8.2 : 12.4 in 1969. We should in fact be using the ratio of the rate of return at replacement cost to the rate of return at book value, but the latter rate was not available on a comparable basis (see Walker's table 3). This means that our measure of excess profits and therefore of welfare loss will tend to be biased down, given that (1) asset revaluations generally take place at merger, when acquired assets are given a current market valuation, and (2) revaluations, of land and buildings especially, do take place periodically, their frequency being related to the rate of inflation. The cost of capital measure used was the forward-looking, pre-tax measure that was estimated at 8.15 percent for the period 1968–1969 by Flemming, Price, and Byers, "The Cost of Capital."

from intermediate product demand schedules fully capture the loss in consumer welfare monopoly caused by distortions in the intermediate markets, as Daniel Wisecarver has recently demonstrated.[30] If we assume that advertising and other efforts to obtain monopoly power are as wasteful when undertaken in intermediate markets as in final goods markets, the formulas presented in table 8.1 can be applied for both intermediate and final good producers.

U.S. ESTIMATES

The range of welfare loss estimates for the United States are presented in table 8.2. They refer to the 1963–1966 period, and the sample comprises the 734 firms on the COMPUSTAT tape with usable information.[31] The firms are ranked according to the size of welfare loss as measured by ΔW_{CM}^4. General Motors leads the list with an annual welfare loss of over \$1.75 billion, which alone is over one-quarter of 1 percent of average GNP during the period and exceeds Harberger's original welfare loss estimate for the entire economy. Most of the other members of the top twenty are names one also might have expected. One possible exception is AT&T. AT&T's gross profit rate was, in fact, less than our estimate of the cost of capital (≈ 0.12). Its advertising entry on the COMPUSTAT tape (and in this case we did have a COMPUSTAT figure; see chapter appendix) was \$0.75 billion, and it is AT&T's advertising that leads to the high ΔW_{CM} estimate we have for it. Advertising also weighs heavily in the ΔW_{CM}^4 estimates for Unilever, Proctor and Gamble, Sears Roebuck, Genesco, Colgate-Palmolive, Pan Am, and Pacific Tel. At first sight this might seem surprising, particularly with respect to regulated firms like AT&T and Pacific Tel. But, as Posner has argued, this is precisely what one expects to find in industries with high market power, and, as Posner himself stresses, firms under regulatory constraint can be expected to engage, if anything, in more wasteful dissipation of their monopoly rents through expenditures like advertising than nonregulated firms.[32] It is interest-

[30] Daniel Wisecarver, "The Social Costs of Input-Market Distortions," *American Economic Review* 64 (June, 1974): 359–372.

[31] The COMPUSTAT tape contains data on a sample of large firms, mostly in manufacturing, listed on U.S. stock exchanges. The data definitions used in making the estimates are discussed in the appendix.

[32] Posner, "The Social Costs of Monopoly and Regulation."

TABLE 8.2

Monopoly Welfare Losses by Firm: United States, 1963–1966 (yearly averages in $ millions)

Company and Rank	ΔW^1_{CM}	ΔW^2_{CM}	ΔW^3_{CM}	ΔW^4_{CM}	ΔW^1_H	ΔW^2_H	ΔW^3_H	ΔW^4_H
1. General Motors	1060.5	1156.3	1347.8	1780.3	123.4	146.2	337.8	770.2
2. AT&T	0.0	257.3	1025.0	1025.0	0.0	13.4	781.1	781.1
3. Unilever	0.0	160.0	490.5	490.5	0.0	19.5	350.0	350.0
4. Procter & Gamble	56.7	180.1	427.0	427.0	3.3	33.0	279.9	279.2
5. DuPont	225.1	241.9	275.4	375.3	36.3	41.7	75.2	175.2
6. Ford Motor	160.4	217.5	331.7	331.7	5.2	9.3	123.5	123.5
7. IBM	251.7	264.0	288.7	319.8	36.8	40.5	65.2	96.3
8. Reynolds, R. J.	73.1	138.5	269.3	278.8	10.8	38.5	169.3	178.8
9. Sears Roebuck	36.2	115.0	272.5	272.5	0.5	4.4	162.0	162.0
10. Eastman Kodak	136.3	157.9	201.1	258.5	27.7	36.8	80.0	137.4
11. American Cyanamid Co.	27.6	98.7	240.8	240.8	1.9	23.6	165.8	165.8
12. Genesco, Inc.	0.0	67.5	202.6	292.6	0.0	14.9	150.0	150.0
13. Exxon Corp.	115.6	143.0	197.8	197.8	2.4	3.7	58.5	58.5
14. Colgate-Palmolive Co.	3.9	56.7	160.3	160.3	0.0	7.6	111.8	111.8
15. Chrysler Corp.	39.8	78.4	155.5	155.5	1.1	3.0	80.1	80.1
16. General Electric Co.	83.4	105.2	148.8	148.8	2.6	4.0	47.6	47.6
17. Pan Am Airways	1.1	49.8	147.2	147.2	0.1	7.5	104.9	104.9
18. Pacific Tel. & Tel.	0.0	18.4	138.1	138.1	0.0	0.8	128.5	128.5
19. Gillette Co.	27.8	56.0	112.3	129.2	4.7	18.9	75.3	92.2
20. Minnesota Mining & Mfg.	62.5	77.4	107.1	129.1	8.2	12.6	42.3	64.3
TOTALS, ALL FIRMS[a]	4527.1	7454.9	14005.4	14997.6[b]	448.2	897.8	7448.3	8440.1[b]
TOTAL ÷ GCP[c]	0.0396	0.0652	0.1227	0.13137	0.0040	0.0079	0.0652	0.0739

[a] The ΔW^1's for all firms having monopoly profits (II) less than zero, were set equal to zero. The ΔW^2, ΔW^3 and ΔW^4's for firms with (II + A) < 0 were set equal to zero. The latter was one on the assumption that these firms would not survive in the long run and hence represent no *long-run* welfare loss to society. There are 421 firms with II > 0 and 525 firms with (II + A) > 0 in the sample of 734 firms.

[b] When profits, after deducting taxes and the cost of capital (II') are less than zero, $\Delta W^4 = \Delta W^3$.

[c] The total welfare loss for all firms by each ΔW measure is first divided by the total sales of the 734 firms in the sample and then multiplied by the ratio of corporate sales to gross corporate product over all industries (2.873) as given in Arthur B. Laffer, "Vertical Integration by Corporations, 1929–65," *Review of Economics and Statistics* 51 (February, 1965): 91–93.

ing that six of the forty largest welfare losses are accounted for by regulated firms (three telephone companies and three airlines) in which advertising made up all or most of the losses.

At the bottom of table 8.2 the losses are summed over the firms,
with positive profit margins as defined for the ΔW^1 and ΔW^2 measures
(see table notes) and then expressed as a proportion of our estimate of
the gross corporate product (GCP) originating in the 734 firms in the
sample. It should be stressed, again, that the totals do not represent
the estimated gains from the simultaneous elimination of all monopoly
power. Such estimates could be obtained only via general equilibrium
analysis. What we estimate via our partial equilibrium analysis is the
relative cost of monopoly for each firm, and the column totals present
average estimates of these costs for our sample of firms. Note, however, that the *additions* to our cost estimates that occur in moving from
the W^2_{CM} to the W^3_{CM} and W^4_{CM} columns do sum across all firms, since
these are estimates of the wasted expenditures made in pursuit of monopoly. If we see product market power as a ubiquitous characteristic
of the economy, then it might be reasonable to assume that this estimate of monopoly welfare loss could be generalized to the entire economy. To the extent one believes monopoly power is more or less pervasive in other sectors, our estimates must be raised or lowered.[33]
Assuming the social costs of monopoly are the same across all sectors,
we obtain estimates for our preferred model (ΔW^k_{CM}) ranging between
4 and 13 percent of GCP. Thus, all losses are significant, but the range
is considerable, depending on what components of social cost one includes. For the Harberger approach, the range is between 0.4 and 7
percent. The lowest of these follows the Harberger assumptions most
closely, but nevertheless we estimate a welfare loss four times as big as
he did. This difference is explained largely by the aggregation bias incorporated into the industry level estimates.

The extent of this bias can be seen by considering table 8.3. Each
firm was assigned to an industry at the appropriate level of aggregation, and we aggregated over the firms in each industry. Just as negative profit firms were excluded in calculating welfare losses at the firm
level, negative profit industries are excluded here in calculating welfare losses across industries. For the ΔW^k_{CM} measures, aggregation bias

[33] Ibid.

TABLE 8.3
Comparison of Firm and Industry Welfare Loss Estimates, United States, 1963–1966.

	ΔW_{CM}^1	ΔW_{CM}^2	ΔW_{CM}^3	ΔW_{CM}^4	ΔW_{II}^1	ΔW_{II}^2	ΔW_{II}^3	ΔW_{II}^4
Summation over firms	4527.1	7454.9	14,005.4	14,997.6	448.2	897.8	7448.3	8440.1
Summation over 4-digit industries	3767.8	6902.5	13,752.6	14,052.8	276.9	628.8	7478.9	7790.2
Summation over 3-digit industries	3619.0	6680.5	13,355.4	13,512.8	237.4	577.7	7252.5	7410.4
Summation over 2-digit industries	3515.2	6634.5	13,262.7	13,287.9	178.9	485.3	7113.5	7148.8
4-Digit industry estimate Sum firms estimate	.832	.926	.982	.937	.618	.700	1.004	.923
3-Digit industry estimate Sum firms estimate	.799	.896	.954	.901	.530	.643	.974	.878
2-Digit industry estimate Sum firms estimate	.776	.890	.947	.886	.399	.541	.955	.847

is due simply to the inclusion of losses by some firms in the calculation of each industry's profits. Table 8.3 shows how this bias varies with the level of aggregation and with the choice of measure. Industry estimates are between 78 and 98 percent of the firm level estimates in aggregate. For the ΔW_H^k estimates, a further course of bias is introduced by the squared term, $(\Pi/R)^2$, in the formula. It can be seen from table 8.3 that for the $\Delta W^1{}_H$ measures, the two-digit industry estimates aggregate to only 40 percent of the firm-level estimates.[34] Note, however, that the biases are much smaller for the ΔW^3 and ΔW^4 measures, and that in the case of the $\Delta W^3{}_H$ measure at the four-digit level, the bias goes slightly the other way. This comes about because the industry estimates include advertising for firms earning less than normal profits. Thus in future work along these lines, when data are limited to industry level observations, the ΔW^3 and ΔW^4 measures have an additional advantage over the other two measures.

UNITED KINGDOM ESTIMATES

These estimates have been calculated on the same basis as the U.S. estimates, but since no convenient computer tape was available, we contented ourselves with an analysis of the top 103 firms in the United Kingdom for the periods 1968–1969 and 1970–1974.[35] Over these periods the firms were responsible for roughly one-third of GNP and were therefore proportionately more important than the 734-firm samples from the COMPUSTAT tape for the United States. The time periods used have been dictated by the availability of data. The basic source was EXTEL cards, but advertising expenditure was estimated by aggregating up from the brand level, using estimates of press and television advertising contained in MEAL. We can therefore expect that our advertising expenditure figures will be biased down by the amount of nonmedia advertising, as is true also for the United States. Table 8.4 gives the results for 1968–1969, with firms again being ranked by

---

[34] Worcester, "New Estimates of the Welfare Loss to Monopoly," plays down the extent of the bias by focusing on the *absolute* differences between the measures. Given that the absolute values of losses are small using ΔW_H^1, even very large relative biases result in small absolute distortions, as one would expect. For additional evidence on the importance of aggregation bias in previous studies, see J. J. Siegfried and T. K. Tiemann, "The Welfare Cost of Monopoly: An Inter-Industry Analysis," *Economic Inquiry* 12 (June, 1974): 190–202.

[35] The top one hundred varies somewhat over time.

TABLE 8.4
Monopoly Welfare Losses by Firm: United Kingdom 1968–1969 (£ million)

Company and Rank	ΔW_{CM}^1	ΔW_{CM}^2	ΔW_{CM}^3	ΔW_{CM}^4	ΔW_{Π}^1	ΔW_{Π}^2	ΔW_{Π}^3	ΔW_{Π}^4
1. British Petroleum	74.1	74.4	75.1	82.7	5.1	5.1	5.8	13.4
2. Shell Transport & Trading	49.4	50.8	53.6	53.6	2.2	2.3	5.1	5.1
3. British-American Tobacco	26.8	27.0	27.5	49.1	1.0	1.1	1.6	23.1
4. Unilever	2.8	11.3	28.2	29.0	0.0	0.2	17.2	18.0
5. I.C.I.	17.6	18.8	21.1	27.9	0.5	0.5	2.9	9.6
6. Rank Xerox	13.9	14.0	14.2	27.5	3.4	3.4	3.5	16.9
7. I.M.B. (U.K.)	11.1	11.2	11.3	21.9	2.2	2.2	2.4	12.9
8. Great Universal Stores	9.6	10.0	11.0	21.6	0.5	0.5	1.5	12.1
9. Beecham	6.2	8.9	14.3	20.4	0.6	1.3	6.7	12.8
10. Imperial Group	2.8	8.6	20.1	20.1	0.0	0.1	11.7	11.7
11. Marks & Spencer	9.8	9.8	9.8	18.6	0.6	0.6	0.6	9.5
12. Ford	7.2	7.8	8.8	16.6	0.2	0.2	1.3	9.1
13. F. W. Woolworth	7.3	7.4	7.8	15.9	0.3	0.4	0.7	8.9
14. J. Lyon	0.0	0.7	2.8	14.2	0.0	0.0	2.1	13.4
15. Burmah	5.3	5.5	5.9	13.9	0.2	0.3	0.7	8.7
16. Distillers	5.6	6.1	7.1	13.4	0.2	0.2	1.2	7.5
17. Rank Organisation	11.5	11.7	12.1	12.5	1.2	1.2	1.7	2.1
18. Thorn	5.6	6.1	7.1	12.5	0.3	0.3	1.4	6.7
19. Cadbury Schweppes	1.8	5.0	11.4	12.3	0.0	0.3	6.7	7.6
20. Reckitt & Coleman	2.9	4.7	8.3	10.4	0.1	0.3	3.9	6.0
TOTAL, ALL FIRMS (102)	385.8	435.0	537.4	719.3	21.4	24.2	118.8	304.4
TOTAL ÷ GCP	0.0386	0.0436	0.0539	0.0720	0.0021	0.0024	0.0119	0.0305

NOTE:
Number of firms with $\Pi > 0 = 82$.
Number of firms with $\Pi + A > 0 = 86$.

ΔW_{CM}^4. The two major oil companies, British Petroleum and Shell, dominate the table. The social cost associated with British Petroleum alone is roughly a quarter of 1 percent of GNP. The other members of the top ten are industry leaders plus British-American Tobacco. Two interesting features of the top twenty are the high ranking of Rank Xerox despite its size (explained presumably by its U.K. patent rights) and, in contrast with the United States, the low ranking of automobile manufacturers (absent from the top twenty in 1970–1974). We have computed estimates of welfare loss for 1970–1974, but we have not reported them here. It is well known that the early seventies was a period of very rapid inflation in the United Kingdom, and this undoubtedly raises problems—for example, how to account adequately for stock appreciation and the revaluation of capital. Despite these difficulties, it is somewhat reassuring to note that the 1970–1974 results look very much like the 1968–1969 results, except that the oil companies have become even more dominant.[36]

The aggregate estimates of welfare loss for ΔW_{CM}^k range between 3.9 and 7.2 percent of GCP for 1968–1969. The estimate for ΔW_{CM}^1 is almost identical with that for the United States, but in each of the other cases the value for the United Kingdom is well below that for the United States. The obvious and important difference between the two sets of results is the apparently greater expenditure on advertising in the United States. Taking direct account of advertising quadruples the welfare loss estimate for the United States, but in the case of the United Kingdom welfare loss goes up by only about 40 percent (compare ΔW_{MC}^1 with ΔW_{MC}^3).[37] When the Harberger approach is used, estimates of welfare loss vary between 0.2 and 3 percent of GCP for the United Kingdom in the same period.

Again our evidence suggests significant welfare loss due to monopoly power. One other point is especially notable in the United

[36] Indeed, comparing the results for the two periods indicates the large extent to which oil companies have benefited from the recent "oil crisis." However, this inference has to be qualified by the problems raised for the measurement of profit by stock appreciation during a period of rapid inflation of oil prices.

[37] This does not, of course, mean that advertising implies no additional social costs, since profit margins and the level of excess profits may both be partly determined by advertising insofar as elasticities of demand and entry barriers are influenced by the level of advertising in monopolistic industries. We should also note that in some cases our direct adjustment for advertising is very significant (e.g. Unilever, Imperial Group and Beecham Group).

Kingdom results (e.g., in the case of the oil companies): the international distribution of these social costs. Monopoly power held by United Kingdom companies in foreign markets may be advantageous to the United Kingdom economy while being disadvantageous in the global sense. Thus the issue is distributional and adds an international dimension to the distributional issues already implicit in our analysis. In any national evaluation of the social costs imposed by the actions of a particular company, the international distribution of these costs would presumably gain some prominence.

Implications and Conclusions

Previous studies of the social costs of monopoly have generally (and often unconsciously) assumed that "monopolies" set prices as if they possessed no market power, that the only important distortions in output are brought about through deviations in one firm's market power from the average level of market power, that the losses of some firms (perhaps incurred in unsuccessful attempts to obtain monopoly power) legitimately offset the monopoly rents of others, and that all expenditures made to create and preserve monopoly positions are part of the normal costs that would exist in a world without monopolies. With the problem so defined, it is not surprising that most of these studies have found welfare losses from monopoly to be small.

Since we know from general equilibrium analysis that monopoly allocation distortions may be offsetting, the conclusion that partial equilibrium analysis yields small welfare loss estimates has seemed all the more impressive. Yet each of the studies that has come up with low estimates has done so largely because it has made assumptions (e.g., demand elasticities equal to 1.0; monopoly profits are deviations from mean profits) that can be rationalized only as ad hoc attempts to answer the general equilibrium question. In contrast, the present study defines a procedure for estimating the costs of monopoly consistent with a partial equilibrium analysis that assumes market power does (or may) exist. Our results reveal that the costs of monopoly power, calculated on an individual firm basis, are, on average, large. The conclusion that "even" a partial equilibrium analysis of monopoly indicates that its costs are insignificant no longer seems warranted.

This conclusion has potentially important policy implications.

Antitrust policy consists typically not of a frontal attack on all existing market power, but of selective assaults on the most flagrant offenders. Our partial equilibrium estimates of monopoly welfare losses indicate the most significant contributors to these losses. The tops of our lists of the largest welfare losses by firm are logical starting points for intensified enforcement of antitrust policy. Our figures and supporting analysis further demonstrate that the "monopoly problem" is broader than traditionally suggested. A large part of this problem lies not in the height of monopoly prices and profits per se, but in the resources wasted creating and protecting them. These costs of monopoly should be considered when selecting targets for antitrust enforcement.

One might argue that the high profits of some firms reflect economies of scale, and therefore that these firms should not be the victims of antitrust policy. This argument points to some form of regulatory or public enterprise solution to the monopoly problem. But our estimates of the losses from monopoly represent a still further understatement of their potential magnitude. Should a policy forcing the most efficient size or organizational structure upon the entire industry be adopted, the welfare loss under the existing structure would have to be calculated by using the profit margin of the most efficient firm and the output of the entire industry rather than the profit margins of the individual firms and their outputs.

These considerations suggest the difficulty in estimating the social gains from eliminating all monopoly power, since one has almost to know what form of policy is to be used (antitrust, regulation) and what the underlying cause of monopoly power is before answering this question. Nevertheless, this is the question traditionally asked in studies of monopoly welfare losses, and the reader who has persisted to this point can justifiably ask what light our figures cast on it. By their very nature, partial equilibrium calculations cannot give very precise estimates of these gains, but they may establish orders of magnitude. As stressed above, we regard the Harbergerian calculations based on uniform demand elasticities of 1.0 as essentially efforts to solve the general equilibrium problem inherent in this question. As such, we regard them as the most conservative estimates of what eliminating all monopoly would produce. Thus, we would expect eliminating all monopoly to yield gains at least as large as the 7 and 3 percent of gross corporate product we estimate for the United States and United

Kingdom, respectively, using ΔW_H^4. To the extent that firms sell differentiated products and operate in separate markets—that is, to the extent that they have and utilize market power—these gains are pushed in the direction of our ΔW_{CM}^4 estimates of 13 and 7 percent. Further upward pressure on these estimates is created by considering some of the other factors ignored in our calculations. We have already emphasized that reported profits understate true profits to the extent that firms compete for monopoly power by investing in excess plant capacity, advertising, patent lawyers, and so on. But much of the competition for *control* over monopoly rents may take place within the firm itself among the factor owners. Such competition will lead to an understatement of actual monopoly rents both through the inflation of costs caused by wasteful competition among factors owners and through the inclusion of part of the winning factor owners' shares of monopoly rents as reported costs. A large literature now exists on the variety of objectives managers have and the ways in which these objectives are satisfied through discretionary control over company revenues. To the extent that managerial control over firm revenues is the reward for successfully competing against other factor groups and potential managers, reported profits understate the true profitability. By ignoring these possibilities, we have erred in being conservative when estimating the social cost of monopoly. It is our reasoned guess that these additional costs would at least equal the "washing out" effect of the simultaneous elimination of all monopoly power on our partial equilibrium estimates and, therefore, that these latter figures are, if anything, underestimates of the true social costs of monopoly.

There is an alternative, aggregative approach to the question. Joseph Phillips, in an appendix to Paul Baran and Paul Sweezy,[38] isolated several categories of expenditure, dependent on the existence of "monopoly capitalism" (e.g., advertising, corporate profits, lawyers' fees). Their sum came to over 50 percent of U.S. GNP. Although the assumptions upon which these calculations were made are rather extreme, they do suggest both an alternative method of analysis and the potential magnitude of the problem. Here too it should be noted that our approach has been essentially micro-oriented and neoclassical; we have taken the returns on corporate stocks as our cost of capital. A

[38] Paul Baran and Paul Sweezy, *Monopoly Capital* (New York: Monthly Review Press, 1966).

more aggregative view might argue that profits are not at all necessary to generate the savings required to sustain a given rate of growth, since alternative macro policies are available. From this perspective, all profits are excess profits, and our estimates of social cost are too conservative. Still further weight would be added against the position that monopoly power is unimportant, if the link with the distribution of political power were considered.

Of course, any public policy has its own sets of costs and inefficiencies. For Tullock-Posner reasons, a concerted effort to apply or strengthen the antitrust laws induces large, defensive expenditures on the part of business. Price and profit regulation leads to efforts to change, influence, or circumvent the rules. The public enterprise solution raises the same sort of problems, with members of the bureaucracy participating in the competition for monopoly rents. Thus any alternative for dealing with existing monopoly power may involve higher costs than the monopolies themselves create. The present study does not answer this question, but it does dispel the notion that it need not even be asked, since the costs of monopoly within the present environment are necessarily small. The question of what the costs and benefits from alternative antimonopoly policies are still seems worth asking.

APPENDIX TO CHAPTER 8

Data: Definitions and Sources

UNITED STATES

All data on individual firms, with one exception, were taken from the COMPUSTAT tape of 1969, and all definitions conform therefore to those given in the COMPUSTAT manual. The numbers in brackets { } refer to the variable numbers assigned on the COMPUSTAT annual industrial file.

The competitive return on capital used in calculating monopoly profits was .1197, the geometric mean of the monthly Fisher-Lorie index of returns on the market portfolio between January, 1963, and December, 1967. The firm's capital was measured as total assets/liabilities and net worth less intangibles (goodwill, patents, etc.). The latter were deducted on the grounds that they largely represent capitalized monopoly rents.[39] Thus, the firm's opportunity cost of capital was estimated as:

$$CC = .1197 \, (DATA \, \{6\} - DATA \, \{33\}).$$

[39] See Stigler, "The Statistics of Monopoly and Merger"; and Kamerschen, "An Estimation of the Welfare Losses from Monopoly."

Two estimates of monopoly profits were formed to compute the triangle measures. The first is gross profit flow (net income + interest expense + income taxes) less the cost of capital (CC).

$$\Pi = DATA \{18\} + DATA \{15\} + DATA \{16\} - CC.$$

The second is the first plus advertising ($A = DATA \{45\}$). For roughly 85 percent of the sample firms, the COMPUSTAT entry for advertising was missing, however. The product of the firm's sales ($DATA \{12\}$) and the industry-advertising-to-sales ratio for the firm's industry as given in *Advertising Age* was substituted for this entry in these cases.[40]

To calculate the ΔW^4 measures, income taxes ($DATA \{16\}$) were subtracted from Π to obtain Π'.

UNITED KINGDOM

All data on individual firms, with the exception of advertising, originated in the data tabulations of the Exchange Telegraph Statistics Service (EXTEL). Most of the relevant data in a summarized form was available in various issues of the *Times Review of Industry and Technology*. In the case of advertising, the firm data had to be estimated by aggregating estimates of press and TV advertising of the various products produced by each firm. These data were extracted from various issues of MEAL (*Advertisers Annual Analysis of Media Expenditure*) and, in the case of 1968, from the *Statistical Review of Press and T.V. Advertising* (Legion Publishing Company). *Who Owns Whom* was used in the process of aggregation.

Each firm's capital was measured as total tangible assets less current liabilities (excluding bank loans, overdrafts, and future tax). Profit was measured before interest and tax and then adjusted for the estimated cost of capital.[41]

---

[40] *Advertising Age*, June 7, 1965, pp. 101–103.

[41] Flemming, Price, and Byers, "The Cost of Capital, Finance, and Investment."

9

Competitive Process, Competitive Waste, and Institutions

by

ROGER CONGLETON

"The activity which we call economic, whether of production or of consumption or of the two together, is also, if we look below the surface, to be interpreted largely by the motives of the competitive contest or game, rather than those of mechanical utility functions to be maximized."[1]

ECONOMIC models have by and large focused on the cooperative aspect of economic activity: that of mutually beneficial exchange in a world of scarcity. In so doing, economic theory has sought to illuminate the principle of "spontaneous coordination" by which the multifarious ends of individuals are woven into a network of transactions that benefit everyone involved. In the world normally modeled by economists, there is no explicit conflict or resource devoted to games of conflict. Property rights are enforced without cost and clearly defined areas of individual autonomy (opportunity sets) specify the range of individual endeavor. The ingredients that determine an individual's opportunity set are essentially unalterable features of the world: human and nonhuman wealth legitimately possessed and exchange possibilities defined by externally provided prices. The clear definition of property rights is such that within them no attempt to transfer another's wealth can be successful unless it is the result of voluntary ex-

NOTE: I wish to thank Charles Breedon who made several helpful comments on an earlier draft of this paper.

[1] F. H. Knight, *The Ethics of Competition and Other Essays* (New York: Harper and Brothers, 1935), p. 301.

change. In such a world the cost of conflict is effectively infinite, and thus no resources are devoted specifically to the conflicts or competitive processes of normal economic activity. No resources are devoted to bargaining, to monopolizing, toward increasing one's market share, or to political wheeling and dealing. It is a world of complete rule of law, natural and social. One's opportunities in society are rigorously defined and clearly understood by all in such economic models.

However, if the world is not clearly understood by all, or if one's opportunity set is not entirely determined externally by forces beyond the influence of an individual actor, situations are very likely to arise in which an economically rational individual will use the resources at his disposal to influence his range of options at the expense of others. Resources will be devoted to activities that are purely redistributional, at best, and voluntary only in the sense that affected individuals (may) have voluntarily accepted the rules of the competitive arena, rules that may be very limited indeed. The mutual advantage of voluntary exchange is often tied to the conflict of bargaining, to real efforts to protect one's property, and to attempts at misleading, if not defrauding, one's potential trading "partner." Property rights, as they exist, are social products that can be and are influenced by the actions of individuals to the benefit or detriment of other members of the affected society. Indeed, the right to alter rights seems to be one of the most enduring, though the methods that must be used vary greatly from place to place and time to time. Attempts to model the disposition of economic resources that ignore these important uses of economic wealth will miss important aspects of the process of resource allocation and distribution. It is within this world that the rent-seeking literature attempts to shed light. The focus of this literature has been primarily instances of what might be called bureaucratic rent seeking: seeking favors of or positions in important bureaus. A general theme of this approach has been that monopoly power is socially inefficient, not only because of its static welfare properties, but also because individuals will waste resources attempting to establish positions where monopoly rents can be earned (or avoided).

A paradox of this line of reasoning seems to have gone largely unnoticed. The dominant source of the waste associated with rent-seeking activity arises because not all of the would-be rent acquirers will be successful in their attempts to acquire monopoly power—that is to say, because of the competitive nature of rent seeking itself. The essential difference between rent-seeking activity and competition in ordinary markets is not whether resources are "wasted" in the process, but rather that successful monopolization *ends* competition (or at least lessens it to a large extent) and the competition that takes place in competitive markets does not. Thus, one cannot arrive at antitrust policy simply by pointing to the costs associated with monopolization; the costs of monopolization will tend to be less than the costs of competitive markets if they are measured strictly in terms of the resources utilized for strictly competitive purposes. For in the case of successful monopolization, one has these costs only until the monopoly position is successfully established, while in a competitive market these costs continue to be borne ad infinitum. With the creation of a monopoly position, it would seem, the costs of competing are avoided, and thus the strictly competitive use of resources may be greatly reduced.

This is not to say that the general line of argument offered in this literature is incorrect, but rather that this particular inference should not be made in the language used above. A proper statement of the general thrust of the rent-seeking literature would be that *some kinds of competition are preferable to others*. As this wording suggests, the importance of what might be called the rent-seeking approach extends far beyond the narrow, but important, confines of bureaucratic rent seeking. The rent-seeking approach seems to be a natural device to examine and compare competitive processes that differ in the nature of the rivalry and/or the institutional setting under which the competitive process takes place.

In this paper, two general types of rivalry are examined under three institutional arrangements for determining the dispensation of the rewards of competition.[2] It is hoped that analysis of highly simplified models will add to the theory of competitive process in general and that some light will be shed upon features of competitive incentives that affect the extent of competitive efforts and the degree to which such efforts may be wasteful. The settings examined, though ad-

[2] This use of the word *competition* is more like its use in biology than in ordinary sports or games, for it includes arenas of conflict in which the strategic possibilities of competing parties are not approximately the same. Games often include both aggressive (offensive) and defensive strategies, though in practice a competing party may be circumstantially constrained to use one or the other of these possibilities. In the normal use of the word *competition*, there is an assumed parity that may be lacking in the cases

mittedly a caricature of real-world settings, seem to be relevant to many issues of interest to both political scientists and economists.

Competitive activities are, for our purposes, characterized by the possibility of using resources to alter one's share of some sought reward in a way that is at least partly at the expense of other competitors. There are thus two necessary preconditions of competitive activities: (1) the reward must be scarce, and (2) there must be the possibility of affecting one's share of that reward by the use of resources at one's disposal. Scarcity alone creates the incentive and environment necessary for competition to take place.

In order to focus clearly on the competitive use of resources, our primary concern will be a world that has only a single, homogeneous, all-purpose commodity that we shall call "wealth." This restriction will later be relaxed to allow consideration of competitive games in which strategies take the form of indirect bribes to third parties controlling the dispensation game rewards. Our analysis will use much of the jargon of game theory and focus on the types of pure strategies that individuals may be expected to adopt in a variety of institutional circumstances. Although single-good worlds have been used before in economic analysis, there has not been, to my knowledge, an exploration of the conflict that must naturally follow from such circumstances. It may well be due to the conceptual subtlety of mutually beneficial exchange that economists spend their efforts there, for people without economic training seem intuitively aware of the great potential for conflict. So much so that in the absence of economic training, most individuals seem hard pressed to grasp the very idea of a mutually advantageous transaction; the jargon and concepts of force and conflict seem much more natural to them.

"Winner Take All That Remains" Games in a State of Nature

The first type of rivalry to be examined will be games that are characterized by a "winner take all that remains" distribution of the game

considered here. It is the use of resources in an arena of conflict that demarcates competitive activities in the sense used here from noncompetitive activities, games in which there are scarce rewards, struggled for by those directly involved in the game. Relative success comes at the expense of other competitors in the game settings of interest here. Note that this does not in principle limit our discussion to negative-sum or zero-sum games, since positive-sum games can also be competitive in the sense used here.

rewards. This game form loosely characterizes all games of establishing monopoly power, including the preponderance of work done in the rent-seeking literature. The game is, as any competitive game must be, characterized by a scarce (hence finite) reward to be distributed to the "winners" of the game while alloting nothing to the "losers." The activity of competing in this game is itself *not* a costless activity. The winner of the game is he who devotes the greater resources to the competitive activity.

To illustrate this kind of game in the simplest terms, consider the familiar island of Crusoe and Friday, where a finite quantity of "wealth" exists, insufficient to satisfy both Friday and Crusoe simultaneously. Imagine Friday and Crusoe engaged in a game of conquest for the privilege of winning all the wealth that exists on the island. Since wealth is an all-purpose good, it may be used to attack or defend wealth as well as for consumption, consumption being the only direct source of utility that wealth provides. If neither Friday nor Crusoe has a particular advantage in the initial distribution of wealth or in ability to deploy wealth for attack or defense, then the victor will be that individual who devotes most of his wealth to "attack" (or who vanquishes the attack through superior defense). If the game limited strategies to nearly all-out attack (or defense), one would have a familiar "prisoner's dilemma" situation with the equally familiar Nash equilibrium of full attack–full attack shown in figure 9.1. Effectively all resources would be wasted in competitive activity with essentially no wealth left for consumption.

A somewhat more interesting game, and a more "realistic" one, would be the similar game in which each competitor can choose to employ as much wealth for attack as he wishes, saving the remainder to be consumed along with the hoped-for spoils of victory. The consumption payoff to Crusoe of devoting X units of wealth to attack-defense in this game would be $R - Y - X$ if X is greater than Y, and zero if X is less than Y; where Y is the extent of the resources that Friday devotes to attack-defense and R is the total level of wealth present on the island at the disposal of the two game players. Friday's payoff is zero if Crusoe's level of investment is greater than his $(X > Y)$ and equals $R - Y - X$ if his level of attack-defense is greater than that of Crusoe $(Y > X)$. In the event that $X = Y$, each player receives $(R - Y - X)/2$, the remainder of his own resources after the standoff. To maxi-

FIGURE 9.1

Friday

Crusoe	Full Attack-Defense (less one unit)	Inaction
Full Attack-Defense (less one unit)	1, 1	16, 0
Inaction	0, 16	15, 15

mize one's consumption payoff in this game, a player should devote "one more" unit of wealth to attack-defense than does his competitor. By minimizing the cost of victory, one maximizes the amount of wealth left to be consumed by the victor.

Of course, the problem is that each competitor will be attempting to maximize the size of his consumption payoff according to this rule, and in order to use the rule one must know the other's strategy. If a single choice of strategy must be made simultaneously by both parties, the selections can be based only upon judgment and not upon assuredness of mathematical optimization. There exist no dominant strategies, no level of competitive investment that will prove optimal regardless of one's competitor's decision. One's best course of action depends ultimately upon the course of action chosen by one's competitor. However, if strategies may be revised in light of evidence about one's competitor's intent, use of the payoff-maximizing rule leads each competitor to revise continuously upward the level of resources that should be devoted to the competitive process. Friday may choose to use half his resources, Crusoe would rationally counter with a bit more than half his own, and Friday with a bit more than that. In the absence of scarcity this process can continue ad infinitum, but in the presence of resource constraints the process of escalation is limited by the resources at the disposal of the competitors. Since we have assumed that Friday and Crusoe initially each command half the island's wealth, this process would continue until each invests all the resources at his disposal, effectively duplicating the game solution of the simpler game developed above. The possibility of escalation may, in this way, tend to generate outcomes in which all the competitors' resources are wasted on competitive activity.

"Winner Take All That Remains" Games and Arbitrators Open to Influence

Not all games that seem totally wasteful from the competitors' perspective are necessarily socially wasteful in the Paretian sense. Often third parties benefit from the competitive efforts of those directly involved in rivalrous conduct, lessening the waste associated with competitive processes. Such third parties may be divided into two categories: those who can affect the game outcome and those who cannot. The first group will be, of course, the primary interest of competitors and is the first to be included in our analysis.

The extreme case of third-party influence is the case where some individual outside the competitive arena can actually determine the outcome. If the opinion of an arbitrator, judge, superior, or other authority is beyond the influence of the would-be competitors, or if the division is in a sense already determined by some rule that uses criteria beyond the influence of the affected parties—such as race, consanguinity, or the occurrence of some truly random event—then there can be no fruitful competitive use of resources. The reward may still be scarce, but the possibility of efficacious competitive action is ruled out. However, this situation is unlikely to be the case. If even the facts of the situation matter, there will be an opportunity for each affected party to attempt to provide "facts" in the quantity and detail that seem most likely to add effectively to his expected share of the reward. Matters other than the "facts" often enter in as well. Demonstrations of loyalty, trustworthiness, or other influencing merits often affect decisions of binding arbitrators. More direct means of influence are also sometimes available. For our purposes, influences can be divided into two categories: direct and indirect transfers of wealth. A direct transfer involves a simple transfer of ownership from one of the competitors to the arbitrator. An indirect transfer is one in which a competitor uses some of his resources to provide some "service" to the arbitrator.

The possibility of either or both kinds of influence being used by two or more parties returns the allocation of resources to the competitive arena. The competitive means have changed from guns to buttering up the relevant authority, but if the prize is to be awarded to some winning party at the expense of the losing party, the game format remains. However, preserving the game format does not mean that the game will necessarily be as wasteful as it was under different institutional arrangements. To illustrate the effect of institutions on the extent of social waste, even in cases where the game format is not or cannot be changed, let us modify the circumstances facing Crusoe and Friday on the island.

Suppose that the chief of the neighboring island hears that both Friday and Crusoe have arrived and are about to be involved in the game of conquest outlined above. Suppose further that, being an imaginative and industrious politician, he sees that the game of conquest will be disastrously wasteful and sets sail for the island to impose some kind of settlement on the new islanders. Assume that the chief is willing and able to accept bribes and will reward the high bidder with all the wealth that has not been turned over to him in the form of bribes. This is, of course, one familiar version of the rent-seeking game. Note that, given this decision rule, Friday and Crusoe face the same game format as before the chief's arrival, with the one difference that competitive efforts are now devoted to bribing the chief rather than to battle in the literal sense.

The strategic use of resources is the same as before so far as Crusoe and Friday are concerned. The optimal strategy is to invest just a bit more than the other invests in competitive activity. In this case, each should try just barely to outbribe the other. If a period of escalation is allowed (as at an open auction), there will be a tendency for each competitor to devote all his resources to the competitive bidding process. As far as the individual competitors are concerned, there will once again be complete waste of the island's resources. However, because wealth is not exhausted in battle but merely transferred to the chief, there is no waste in the usual economic sense. The result would be Pareto-optimal, since any distribution of wealth in a single-good world is Pareto-efficient. A comparison between the earlier game and this game of competitive bribing reveals that this shift of institutions is a Pareto-superior move (assuming that the wealth of the island is valued over the chief's opportunity cost at home). The chief is better off and Crusoe and Friday are no worse off under the new arrangements. (Of course, competitive efforts to become chief may be intensified, that is to say, this competitive game may be imbedded in others, but these other levels of competitive activity are beyond the scope of interest here.)

There are many situations in which the arbitrator is prevented from taking direct bribes: perhaps the factors of concern are not merely wealth; perhaps it is feared that there would be more wasteful competition to become arbitrator if his income were to be increased or partially dependent upon direct bribes; or perhaps allowing bribes would lead to a change in the role of arbitration itself. Thus it is common to find competitive games similar to the one faced above in which the chief cannot accept direct bribes (at least as an ordinary aspect of his entitlements) but may be indirectly influenced.

If, in our example, the chief were constrained by law, custom, or fear of the gods to accept only indirect emoluments, the payoffs to being the arbitrator are changed. But if these indirect payments utilize wealth and the quality or quantity of the influence remains an increasing function of the level of resource investment, the game will not be changed markedly from the viewpoint of the competitors so long as the reward is to be allocated in the same manner as before, that is, to the victor go the spoils. The game remains a game of judgment in the absence of escalation, and again the optimal strategy would be to employ just the barest minimum of resources beyond that of one's competitor. The same tendency for risk aversion and escalation to lead to the total employment of the wealth for competitive purposes would be present. The primary difference is that the value of the transfers to the chief may, in his eyes, be below that of the wealth used to effect the transfers. The competitive activity remains wasteful in the eyes of the competitors and a transfer of wealth is made to the chief, but the value of the resources or performance actually received by the chief will tend to be less than before. It cannot be greater, since he could have used the all-purpose commodity, wealth, to recreate his indirect payments. Thus, in his eyes, resources will be wasted relative to the case of direct bribes, although this case would still be Pareto-superior to the case of direct conquest in a state of nature. The inefficiency of indirect transfers is a primary source of rent-seeking waste.

There are two senses of waste involved here, waste to the society of three, including the arbitrator, and waste in so far as the competitors are concerned. In some cases, the second of these wastes may be more relevant. A person is not usually considered obligated to purchase unproductive services from another in the normal course of economic transactions, although, strictly speaking, under the Pareto criteria such transactions may be required if no net harm was incurred by the "purchasers."

The inefficiency of indirect transfers to an arbitrator or group with such powers may be lessened (or enlarged) if the preferred method generates positive benefits to individuals not directly involved in the competitive activity, third parties who may be called "innocent bystanders." The judge may, for example, choose to make his decision based upon evidence of greater altruism, or he may organize the competition so that it has some public-good character deemed useful, such as a competitive foot race or the display of some other socially appreciated skill or process. These considerations can increase the social efficiency of indirect payments. Indirect influence may in this way be Pareto-superior to direct payments if the recipients collectively would be willing to offer greater wealth for their treatment than the chief otherwise would have received. Of course, increased efficiency is not guaranteed simply by the existence of "bystander" effects. The chief could have created competitive incentives leading to competitive activity with effects outside the competitive game but imposing costs rather than benefits on nonparticipants. "Scalps" or their conceptual equivalents are often used as evidence of merit, particularly the "scalps" of the chief's own competitors at a different game level. Thus indirect transfer schemes could be even less efficient than the usual rent-seeking analysis of situations would seem to indicate. The efficiency of indirect transfers depends entirely upon the nature of competitive incentives and the indirect instruments used in the process of competition. The normal conclusion of the rent-seeking literature is thus by no means guaranteed simply because of the indirect nature of transfers. It is true that in the cases usually examined, the uninvolved "by-stander" effects are negative or small and as a first approximation may be ignored. However, generally in discussions of competitive institutions, they cannot be so easily discounted.

Competitive Games in a Majority-Rule State

A simple modification of the institutional setting developed above is the case where the game outcome is determined by the majority of some arbitrating group of individuals. In modern democratic states this is often the case for legislative matters, to some extent for trials by jury, and common when a ruling board of one sort or another will be the deciding factor. For most questions of policy, promotion, or the dispensation of badges of merit, only a limited number of the would-be candidates will be successful. In many cases there will be but a single winner, particularly in the case of policy. The "winner takes all that remains" format thus remains an appropriate game form under majority-rule institutions.

To continue with our illustration, suppose that the neighboring tribe is ruled by a triumvirate of a form where two of the three leaders (triumvirs) have by custom or law the power to decide, in more or less the same manner as the chief in our previous examples, the fate of the distribution of wealth between Crusoe and Friday. Once again, if the decisions of the triumvirate are beyond the possible influence of both Friday and Crusoe, no resources would be devoted to competitive activities. However, for reasons touched on before, this is unlikely to be the case. To the extent that the game format remains "winner take all that remains," Friday and Crusoe will continue to devote wealth to the competitive activity of influence. However, in this institutional setting there is no parallel tendency for all of the island resources to be devoted to the competitive activities.

Let us again begin with the case of direct bribes. If the island resources are to be distributed between the competitors according to a single majority vote so that the competitor who gets a majority gets all the reward and the loser(s) none, then it will clearly be in the interests of the competing parties to influence the way voters cast their ballots. In the case of direct bribery, one should attempt to offer larger bribes than one's competitor(s) to a majority of the voting agents. However, one need not always increase the level of one's own bribes in response to increases by one's competitor. One can gain the same advantage by *changing the distribution* of bribes across voters, and do so at lesser expense. In fact, there is no pattern of bribes that can be dominated only with the full use of one's resources, if competitors begin on more or less even ground.

Suppose that Crusoe were reckless enough to devote his full share of the island's wealth to competitive bribery and then announce his intentions to Friday. Would Friday be forced to reciprocate with a similar level of competitive effort? Let us consider two possible bribing patterns for Crusoe under these circumstances. First, suppose that Crusoe had announced that he was going to distribute his wealth equally across the voters, that is, a bribing pattern of (5, 5, 5). It is clear that Friday could successfully respond to this extreme effort by devoting just slightly more than the amount spent by Crusoe to a bare majority of the voters. For example, he might use a pattern of (5.5, 5.5, 0) which yields a two-to-one majority among the triumvirs and requires only eleven units of wealth to oppose Crusoe's use of fifteen. One might ask whether Crusoe's strategy was a reasonable one under the circumstances. A better strategy might appear to have been allocating his wealth equally between a bare majority of the voters, for example (7.5, 7.5, 0). Were such the announced pattern of Crusoe, Friday could have responded with bribes of (0, 8, 1) which yields an even more economical majority for Friday requiring only nine units of wealth.

If Crusoe were similarly able to revise his bribing pattern in light of Friday's intentions, he may counter any pattern of bribes offered or intended with a distribution of bribes requiring fewer resources. For example, Crusoe might respond to Friday's pattern of (5.5, 5.5, 0) with a pattern of (6, 0, 1), and Friday to this new pattern with (0, 1, 2), and so forth. Each iteration uses fewer resources for competitive purposes than the round before it.[3] Thus we have the rather surprising result

[3] To determine the least-cost majority: (1) order the bribes of one's competitor from lowest to highest bribe; (2) offer a bit more, d, than is currently being received to a bare majority drawn from the low end of the spectrum determined under (1); (3) offer nothing to all others. If the sum of these bits, d, can be less than the sum of the bribes received by the new minority, then the new majority can be formed using fewer resources than those of one's competitor (if this amount is greater than zero). If d can be arbitrarily small, this will always be possible.

that under majority-rule arbitration a series of response and counter-response *de-escalates*. In the limit virtually no resources will be devoted to the competitive activity. However, since the strategy (0, 0, 0) is never a winning pattern of bribes, no equilibrium level of competitive activity will be reached. Although there is no dominant distribution of bribes or even level of bribes that will ultimately be received by the triumvirs, there is a clear tendency for the level of bribes to be small (indeed vanishingly small) if time is available for competitor interaction to occur. (If e is the minimum effective bribe, there is a tendency for equilibrium strategies to converge toward patterns resembling $(e, e + d, 0)$, where d is the smallest amount that can be added to e so that a triumvir perceives $e + d$ to be greater than e.)

Majority-rule arbitration changes the nature of the game faced by competitors. Although wealth is still to be allocated on a "winner take all that remains" basis, the winner is no longer simply the one who devotes the larger amount of resources to the game of influence. Instead, he is the one who successfully brings a majority coalition to vote, an activity that requires resources, yet is not determined by sheer level of competitive effort. Had competitors been constrained to offer equal bribes to all triumvirs, or had the triumvirate used a unanimous-decision rule instead of majority rule, the original format could have been preserved, and so would the tendency for competitors to exhaust their resources in the process of competition. However, the tendency for majority-rule arbitration to defuse competitive games of influence seems to accord well with the observations of Gordon Tullock and Anne Krueger regarding the relatively larger amounts of rent seeking that occurs in the third world vis-à-vis the western democracies,[4] and so remains an important variant of "winner take all that remains" games.

The efficiency characteristics of majority-rule arbitration parallel those of single-man arbitration. Because of the single-good character of the situation analyzed, any outcome will be Pareto-optimal given the existing institutional arrangements. Comparing the majority-rule outcomes with those under anarchy reveals that majority-rule arbitration is Pareto-superior to the game of dominion under anarchy. Both competitors are better off since comparative efforts tend to de-esca-

---

[4] Gordon Tullock, "Rent Seeking as a Negative-Sum Game"; Anne O. Krueger, "The Political Economy of the Rent-Seeking Society," chapters 2 and 4 in this volume.

late, which allows more wealth to be used for consumptive purposes. The triumvirs may be assumed better off, although this inference depends upon their unmentioned alternatives at home. A comparison between single-man arbitration and majority-rule arbitration cannot be made without much additional detail, except to point out the obvious, that the competitors are better off under majority-rule arbitration. Analysis of indirect means of influence and the existence of external benefits and/or costs of the process of competition is as before. If sufficient external benefits are generated to more than offset the inherent losses of indirect transfers, indirect means of competition may be Pareto-superior to direct forms of influence. If not, indirect means of influence will be Pareto-inferior to competition utilizing direct means of influence.

"Proportional Share" Games under Nature

At this point we would like to move from changing the institutional setting of the game to a change in the format of the game itself. Clearly not all competitive games are of the "winner take all that remains" variety, nor even all important games, though clearly they are an accurate description of a great many important areas of competitive activity. A second general type of game, what might be called the "proportional share" game, is equally important and often an alternative game form to the "winner take all" variety. In a "proportional share" game, competition takes place over the division of a scarce reward, where the share of the prize received depends upon the relative size of individual competitive efforts. One who has expended more resources than another wins not all the reward, as in the previous game format, but a proportionately *larger share* according to the extent of his efforts relative to others. The particular form of interest here is the case where an individual who devotes twice as much "effort" as another receives a share of the reward twice as large as the others. In an N-person version of such games, the jth person's reward can be written as $(E_j / \Sigma \ E_i)R$, where R is the total reward available and E_j is the level of resource investment devoted to this competitive activity. The important new feature of this format is that a non-zero investment in competitive resources guarantees one a non-zero share of the reward.

FIGURE 9.2

Friday

Crusoe	Full Attack	Half Attack	Inaction
Full Attack	0,0	7.5,0	15,0
Half Attack	0,7.5	7.5, 7.5	22.5,0
Inaction	0,15	0,22.5	15,15

No level of competitive investment would assure this in the "winner take all that remains" format developed above.

Consider the changed circumstances that Crusoe and Friday would face in the original island setting if the game is changed from one of all-or-nothing dominance to a "proportional share" version. Suppose that the wealth may be used as before to attack or defend but that this time the circumstances allow one to influence the size of one's share of the island's wealth vis-à-vis the other's rather than to establish island-wide dominance. The game form analogous to the two-by-two matrix of the game of conquest is a three-by-three matrix. Such a matrix is shown in figure 9.2. Note that in this game there is a dominant strategy for each and hence a Nash equilibrium. The dominant strategy for each is to employ half the resources at his disposal to competitive activity. Thus, in this discrete form of the "proportional share" game, only half the island's resources are wasted by strictly competitive uses. The game outcome in effect ratifies the individual's decision to save half his resources for consumption. Because fewer resources are wasted in this game than in the anarchistic version of the "winner take all that remains" games discussed previously, a move to the former from the latter would be a Pareto-superior move.

The three-strategy game, however, is not as natural a game as one in which the competitors can vary their competitive efforts nearly continuously between no effort and complete commitment. A player's task in such games is, of course, to maximize his return to competitive investment $P(X)$, which in this game format may be written as:

$$P(X) = \frac{X}{X + Y} (R - X - Y) \tag{1}$$

where X is the competitive effort of player X, Y is the level of effort of other players, and R is the resource base of the game. In our illustration X may be thought of as Crusoe's competitive use of wealth, Y as Friday's, and R as the total wealth of the island to be allocated by the game outcomes and strategies. Differentiating with respect to X and setting the partial derivative obtained equal to zero yields:

$$0 = \frac{-X^2 - 2XY - Y^2 + YR}{(X + Y)^2} . \tag{2}$$

Solving this for X yields:

$$X = -Y \pm \sqrt{YR} . \tag{3}$$

Since X, R, and Y must be real and greater than or equal to zero, one of the possible solutions is eliminated, leaving as our result

$$X = -Y + \sqrt{YR} . \tag{4}$$

To determine whether or not this function represents maxima rather than minima of the payoff function, one must establish that the second derivative with respect to X over the relevant range is negative.

$$\frac{\partial^2 R}{\partial X^2} = \frac{-2X - 2Y}{(X + Y)^2} - 2 \frac{(-X^2 - 2YX - Y^2 + YR)}{(X + Y)^3} . \tag{5}$$

Placing over the common denominator and collecting terms yields:

$$\frac{\partial^2 R}{\partial X^2} = \frac{-2YR}{(X + Y)^3} \tag{6}$$

Since X, Y, and R must be positive, $- 2YR/(X + Y)^3$ will be negative. Hence $X = -Y + \sqrt{YR}$ represents maxima of the payoff function over the range of game strategies allowed. It specifies Crusoe's optimal level of competitive investment for a level of Friday's competitive effort, Y. There is no dominant strategy for Crusoe, since his best strategy depends upon the level of Y chosen by Friday. However, the lack of a dominant strategy does not preclude the existence of equilibrium strategies, strategies that, once chosen, cannot be improved upon without a change in strategy on the part of one's competitor(s). To determine whether such strategies exist, one must see if there is a strategy pair that simultaneously maximizes the competitive reward to each.

Since the game's reward structure is symmetrical with respect to Friday and Crusoe, Friday's reward-maximizing strategy can be determined, as was Crusoe's, and would be described by the following equation:

$$Y = -X + \sqrt{XR} . \tag{7}$$

Substituting this representation of Friday's strategy into Crusoe's optimal strategy function yields:

$$X = -(-X + \sqrt{XR}) + \sqrt{(-X + \sqrt{XR})R} . \tag{8}$$

Solving this for X yields:

$$X = R/4 , \tag{9}$$

Crusoe's half of the equilibrium strategy pair. Substituting this value into Friday's optimal strategy function yields $Y = R/4$, the same strategy investment in competitive activity chosen by Crusoe. Recall that R in this game refers to the total amount of resources available. If R were distributed equally at the start of the game, as assumed in our illustration, an $R/4$ investment in competitive effort means that each individual will invest half the resources at his disposal. This was of course the dominant strategy and equilibrium in the discrete three-by-three version of the game developed above. However, the lack of a dominant strategy means that in a one-time run of this game, strategy must be a matter of judgment rather than optimization alone. The proper strategy depends upon both the optimal strategy function and one's judgment of the likely strategic choice of one's competitor(s).

However, if there is a chance for this game to escalate—that is, for one to gather information about one's competitor and he about one's reaction to this information and so on—this game has a tendency to escalate and to converge toward the equilibrium developed above. The illustration of the optimal strategy functions for Crusoe and Friday

FIGURE 9.3

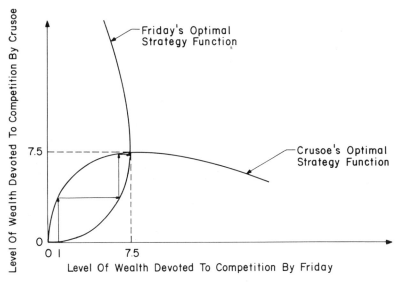

Level Of Wealth Devoted To Competition By Friday

in figure 9.1 allows us to make this point clear with the help of an illustrating converging series. The general shapes of these curves will be the same regardless of the size of R, rising from zero to $R/4$ and falling thereafter back to zero at R. In our example, R is thirty, and feasible strategies for each participant are limited to half the resources of the game, though this does not really matter so long as each competitor has at least one-quarter of the resource total. Selection of any strategy will, if naively reacted to by adopting the optimal strategy called for, lead to a series of strategic adjustments that converge to the strategy where each invests half his own resources (one-quarter of the game total).[5]

Referring to figure 9.3, or to the two optimal strategy functions, one should notice that an optimal strategy never calls for a level of competitive investment greater than 7.5 ($R/4$ in general). Suppose Friday begins or plans to begin with a single unit level of competitive investment. Upon learning Friday's intention, Crusoe would respond

[5] Notice that if $Y = 0$, the optimal strategy function is not defined. However, it is apparent that some non-zero level of competitive effort by X will, according to the payoff function (equation [1]), be better than similar inaction. Note that the payoffs to mutual inaction is $R/2$. Given inaction on the part of one's competition ($Y = 0$), $X > 0$ would yield $R - X$, which is greater than $R/2$ if X is less than $R/2$.

with an investment of approximately 4.5 units. Friday, learning of Crusoe's intentions, would respond with approximately 7.2 units, whereupon Crusoe would counter with about 7.5 units. Friday would reciprocate with 7.5 units. This being an equilibrium strategy pair, no further movement would occur. Both Friday and Crusoe invest half their initial wealth in the purely competitive activity. Regardless of the initial choice (so long as it is less than R), the strategies will converge smoothly to the equilibrium strategies of $R/4$, $R/4$ (7.5, 7.5 in this case).

Thus, while the "proportional share" game is one whose properties are not as intuitively obvious as those of the other game format, the two formats do have some similar properties. They are both games of judgment that, in the simple recurring adjustment to one's competitors' competitive play or intentions, lead one to an equilibrium situation captured by their respective simpler discrete versions. The important difference is the extent to which the island's resources are wasted in competitive activity. The wasted resources of the "proportional share" game amount to only half those of the "winner take all" game (in the two person cases examined). Clearly Friday and Crusoe, offered a choice of games, would prefer the second with its less competitive environment.

Proportional Sharing with an Arbitrator Open to Influence

As in the "winner take all that remains" games developed earlier, "proportional share" games are often influenced by third parties and/or generate effects affecting third parties who are not directly involved in the competitive arena. In this section of the paper we are primarily concerned with the effects of "influencers," since other third-party effects will tend to have properties mirroring those of our earlier discussion. The first case examined will once again be the extreme case in which a single individual has the power and/or authority to allocate completely the resources of the competing parties. As before, our interest lies in games with formats similar to the one developed under the anarchy setting.

Suppose, once again, that a neighboring chief becomes aware of the wasteful nature of Crusoe and Friday's competitive system of allocation and comes to the island to distribute them by other means.

Once again, if his judgment is beyond the influence of both Crusoe and Friday, there will be little value gained by attempting to affect the chief's decision. For example, a commitment to distribute the wealth of the island equally might nearly accomplish this, though efforts to obscure the extent of the island's wealth (in effect competing with the chief) would, of course, follow to some extent. However, most societies recognize that some individuals merit a greater share of the pie than others, though there is a wide range of variation in the nature of merits considered relevant for the allocative decision. If the chief decides to allocate wealth proportionate to demonstrable merit, the game format faced by Friday and Crusoe at the onset remains unchanged, though the competitive means change from weaponry to demonstrations of the relevant category of merit. If merit is simply a matter of "gifts" rendered to the chief, the competitive game becomes a game of transferring wealth to the chief. The resources devoted to strictly competitive activity would be simply transferred to the chief, who, in view of the resulting demonstration of equal "merit" by Friday and Crusoe, would distribute the remaining wealth equally. The result so far as Crusoe and Friday are concerned is unchanged; each has wasted half his resources on competitive activity. However, since these resources have been transferred to the chief intact, there is no social waste to this competitive process. The result is Pareto-optimal and Pareto-superior to the results under anarchy if the wealth received by the chief exceeds the value of his opportunity cost.

However, considerations of merit are rarely such that direct transfers are allowed to carry all the weight of evidence. Indirect transfers, as before, may create value for the chief below that possible by direct transfers. Hence they tend, other things being equal, to generate a social loss when viewed from the direct transfer alternative. As before, the ingredients of merit may demand that Crusoe and Friday bestow benefits to individuals other than the chief, which may in total moderate or overcome the inherent inefficiencies of indirect means of influencing the chief. One might require that wealth be used effectively to generate more wealth (inventiveness) for the chief's tribe or to demonstrate benevolence or altruism, which might lead to an alternative Pareto-efficient outcome, or, in the extreme case, even one that is Pareto-superior to the case of direct bribes (for example, a successful innovation may dramatically improve techniques of creating or using wealth). As developed before, indirect means of payment or influence may generate outcomes worse or better than the apparent inefficiency found by focusing upon the chief's loss of welfare. It should be noted that, whereas the competitors are each better off in this competitive format, the chief was much better off under the other. His transfers within a "proportional share" game between two people are only half what they were under the "winner take all" format. Thus, if allowed to pick the game format played by those under his authority, he would naturally prefer the "winner take all that remains" format over "proportional share" games, other things being equal.

"Proportional Share" Games and Majority Rule

"Proportional share" games are not easily adapted to majority-rule allocation. As was true of "winner take all" games, this format cannot be maintained intact in a shift to majority-rule arbitration. However, this feature of majority-rule institutions is itself of interest and will be examined next. The most straightforward way of establishing something approximating a majority-rule version of the "proportional share" game is to allow voting on the same issue of the proportion of the reward due each competitor. In the two-person case of Friday and Crusoe on the island, this amounts to determining the ratio of rewards received by Friday to those received by Crusoe, a single number greater than zero. When a single number is to be chosen from a continuum by using a majority-rule decision-making procedure, the number chosen will be that preferred by the median voter (if the preferences of the voters are single peaked over the domain voted upon). For this reason, the attentions of the competitors will be directed toward generating a favorable median voter "opinion" on the matter of their relative merit. If the distribution of voters is stable, so that the same individual would continue to be the median voter during any election count, this voter would receive virtually all the attention of the competitors. His position would be very much like that of the single arbitrator developed above. However, if influence is possible at all, it is likely that more than one person's vote can be influenced. In the extreme case where voter preferences are, in effect, determined by the relative "bribes" received from Crusoe and Friday, *every distribution of bribes will have a voter distribution associated with it.* The median voter is, in such instances, *entirely* determined by the strategic use of wealth employed by the competing parties.

In this game, the payoff received by Crusoe if he allocates M_x units of wealth to the median voter and S_x to the other voters is:

$$P(M_x) = \frac{M_x}{M_x + M_y} (R - M_x - M_y - S_x - S_y) \tag{10}$$

where M_y is Friday's expenditure on the median voter, R is the total resource base of the game, and S_y is the total expenditure by Friday on members other than the median voter. The distribution of M_y, M_x, S_y, S_x across voters establishes a particular median voter. Since transfers to voters other than the median voter subtract from the size of the reward to be distributed but do not add to the size of one's share (apart from helping to determine a particular median voter), both competitors will make these auxiliary payments as small as possible consistent with generating the sought median voter. As a first step, these auxiliary payments should be limited to just half the voters (the half receiving the smallest sum from one's competitor). If this strategy is adopted by both parties, then S_x and S_y can be very small indeed, approaching zero. All but the median voter will, under this scheme, receive nothing from one competitor and some vanishingly small bribe from the other. Their votes would thus tend to favor granting all the remaining reward to the competitor offering the non-zero bribe. The proper allocation of effort toward the median voter can be determined by maximizing one's payoff with respect to M_x. Taking the partial derivative of the payoff function given above with respect to M_x and setting the result equal to zero yields:

$$0 = \frac{R - 2M_x - M_y - S_x - S_y}{(M_x + M_y)} - \frac{M_x(R - M_x - M_y - S_x - S_y)}{(M_x + M_y)^2}. \tag{11}$$

Solving for M_x yields:

$$M_x = -M_y \pm \sqrt{M_y (R - S_x - S_y)} . \tag{12}$$

Since M_x must be no less than zero, this eliminates one of the possible descriptions of M_x, leaving:

$$M_x = -M_y + \sqrt{M_y (R - S_x - S_y)} . \tag{13}$$

Notice that this formula is very similar to the optimal strategy function developed in the original "proportional share" games (equation [4]). However, this strategy function establishes the proper level of resources to devote to a median voter, given (1) a particular voter distribution resulting in a particular median voter and (2) values for S_x, S_y, and M_y. Like the earlier function, this optimal median voter bribe formula depends critically upon the level offered by one's competitor, here Friday. Like the earlier function, this function has a maximum, a maximum that approaches $R/4$ as S_x and S_y approach zero. Thus the largest bribe that it is rational to offer the median voter will tend to be less than half Crusoe's initial endowment. However, there is no tendency for strategic revision to generate convergence to that maximum, as was the case in the other two institutional settings. In this setting a competitor can often achieve better results and use fewer resources by generating a new voter distribution and a new median voter.

Although it is not possible to determine any particular equilibrium distribution of bribes between the voting arbitrators, since every such distribution can be beaten by an alternative, it is possible to characterize the equilibrium levels of competitive effort. An optimal strategy will entail giving the minimum effective bribe, e, to half the arbitrators, zero to the other half, and some amount to the median voter dictated by equation (13). In the case of a triumvirate, one triumvir will get 0, one will get M_x, and one will get e. Given such a strategy announcement by Crusoe, $(0, M_x, e)$, Friday could respond with a strategy of $(e, 0, M_y)$, which makes the bribing ratio of the third triumvir the median apportionment of the remaining wealth, namely M_y/e (the others being all to Crusoe or all to Friday). Crusoe could respond with $(M_x, e, 0)$, which makes the first triumvir the median voter, Friday with $(0, M_y, e)$, and so on. If M_y and M_x eventually reach stable levels, then there will be a constant distribution of effort or intended effort across triumvirs. It should be clear from this discussion that such an equilibrium will depend upon the resource base of the game, R, and the minimum resource level required to influence a voter's decision, e.

Notice that the series of bribing strategy adjustments entails choosing the other competitor's e level of effort as the most promising candidate for median voter and relegating the former median voter to an extreme. Since e is the median voter effort of Y, and M_y, the level paid to the former median, becomes S_y, and S_x is e, the new median voter bribe for Crusoe becomes:

$$M_x = -e + \sqrt{e(R - M_y - e)} . \tag{14}$$

Because this game is symmetric, a similar function describes the median voter strategies of Y, namely:

$$M_y = -e + \sqrt{e(R - M_x - e)} .\qquad(15)$$

Stable levels of competitive effort are implied if both equations (14) and (15) are simultaneously satisfied, as is the case in

$$M_x = -e + \sqrt{e(R - [-e + \sqrt{e(R - M_x - e)}] - e)} .\qquad(16)$$

Squaring, collecting terms, squaring again, and collecting terms yields:

$$0 = M_x^4 + 4eM_x^3 + (6e^2 - 2eR)M_x^2$$
$$+ (5e^3 - 4e^2R)M_x + 2e^4 - 3e^3R + e^2R^2 .\qquad(17)$$

Equation (17) can be factored into a product of quadratics and the four roots then established using the quadratic formula:

$$0 = (M_x^2 + 3eM_x + 2e^2 - eR)(M_x^2 + eM_x + e^2 - eR) ,\qquad(18)$$

the roots of which are:

$$M_x = \frac{-3e \pm \sqrt{e^2 + 4eR}}{2} ,\qquad(19a)$$

$$M_x = \frac{-e \pm \sqrt{4eR - 3e^2}}{2} .\qquad(19b)$$

Although all these roots will satisfy the conditions of equation (17), not all will satisfy those of equation (16), nor will those roots that satisfy (16) necessarily satisfy the constraint that M_x be greater than or equal to zero. The single root that does satisfy these conditions characterizes equilibrium strategies in terms of e and R.

$$M_x = \frac{-3e + \sqrt{e^2 + 4eR}}{2}\qquad(20)$$

This equation indicates that as the minimal effective bribe approaches zero, so does the equilibrium level of competitive investment. Contrariwise, as it gets relatively large, so does the total resource commitment to the competitive process. A similar equation can be found for M_y implying that M_y will equal M_x at the resource equilibrium.

Given a period for iterative adjustment of status, equation (20) implies that the competitive effort generated under majority-rule arbitration may be substantially larger or smaller than that which occurs under a single arbitrator. However, our tacit assumption that e is relatively small suggests that the total competitive efforts will be smaller than those which would occur under a single arbitrator. For example, if R is 30 units of wealth and e is 0.1 unit of wealth, then M_x and M_y are each approximately 1.58 units of wealth. In addition to expenditures on the median voter, there are the resources devoted to establishing a particular median voter, in this case 0.1 units of wealth each. The total competitive effort of both competitors is twice 1.68 units of wealth, or 3.38 units of wealth, which is, of course, far less than the 15 units of wealth used in our illustration under a single arbitrator. (Had e been 4 units instead, this total would have been approximately 18.27 units of wealth.)

Recall that in similar circumstances, a "winner take all that remains" format under majority-rule arbitration tended toward greater de-escalation. That is, levels of competitive effort tended toward a smaller limit. Under a triumvirate government and where the minimum effective bribe is e, the bribes tended in the limit toward $4e$, 0.4 units of wealth, if e is 0.1. Thus majority-rule arbitrators may tend to receive, *on average*, higher transfers if the game format is "proportional share" rather than "winner take all that remains" (if a period is allowed for interaction and adjustment), and arbitrators may be expected to prefer the former game format to the latter, even in the complete absence of any concerns for equity.

Conclusion and Summary

This paper has explored some of the effects that institutions and rules governing the disposition of competitive rewards can have on both the quantity of resources used for competitive purposes and the extent to which such uses may be wasteful or beneficial. While it is not news that institutions matter, it is useful to know how institutions may affect levels of competitive effort and, more importantly, the kind of competitive efforts engaged in. Further, the extent to which competitive effort may be socially wasteful is clearly another important concern. Light has been shed on this issue by our efforts to trace the course of competitive resources: are resources merely transferred, are they transformed to less valuable assets, and, if so, does the process of transformation generate any spillover benefits or costs? Answers to these questions will, by and large, determine whether some particular *competitive instrument* is efficient or not. It has been shown that institutions can, at least in highly simplified circumstances, create incentives for individuals to use less wasteful or even productive competitive means. Under both game formats, it proved possible to shift from competitive methods that consumed resources to ones that merely transferred them (e.g., the shift from anarchy to a single arbitrator changed the competitive means from warfare to bribery and generated a Pareto-superior state).

A second possible institutional device was also illustrated: changing the dispensation of the game reward. One can change the level of competitive effort that will be called forth by changing the way in which that effort increases one's share of the reward. A shift from a "winner take all that remains" rule to a "proportional share" rule decreased the level of competitive effort under both anarchy and single-man arbitration, and, though the results of such a shift under democratic arbitration are less clear, there seems to be a tendency for such a shift to increase the level of competition effort. Although changes in distributive rules are not always possible—that is, some game outcomes are mutually exclusive and so necessarily of the "winner take all that remains" variety—it is clear from the cases developed that, when possible, such changes can have substantial results on the level of competitive effort called forth. Thus one can affect both the level and kind of competitive effort that will take place through institutional measures.

However, it has *not* been shown that *any* "refinement" will be to the advantage of either the competitors or society as a whole. In general the interests of arbitrators and those of the competitors are juxtaposed. In each of the circumstances examined arbitrators benefit from additional competition whereas competitors emerge poorer from additional competitive requirements. Thus arbitrators have an incentive to increase the level of competition, even when such competition may be judged inefficient from a Paretian standpoint. In the case of a single arbitrator it proves to his advantage to shift from the proportional-sharing rule to a "winner take all that remains" rule of distributing game rewards, regardless of whether the competitive means being used are socially efficient or not. Greater levels of indirect transfers surely are to such an arbitrator's advantage. It seems apparent that contriving circumstances to promote competition, even where none is inherent in the problem at hand, would be advantageous to would-be arbitrators. Policies that artificially limit the number of possible "winners" clearly will be in the interest of those with the power to decide who will be among the victorious. Further, arbitrators have an interest in avoiding situations that prevent affected parties from influencing their judgment.

While it is clear that institutions play an important role in generating the kind and level of competitive effort that will exist, it should also be clear that transforming institutions is itself a competitive game. Both scarcity (only one institution can be adopted) and efficacy (the ability to transform or adopt institutions) are clearly present. No particular facet of behavior can be both illegal and legal in the same sense at the same instant. Nor can there be but one collective decision-making rule, however complex, embodied in explicit or implicit constitutions. This is not to say that Pareto-superior changes in institutions are impossible, but that such changes, even if possible, will tend to be accompanied by at least the normal conflict of any bargaining process. Our analysis of such games suggests that there may be less competitive waste under democratic institutions than under anarchy or single-man rule, though there may be on similar grounds more "improvements" forthcoming.

Constitutional revision represents but one extreme of the competitive arena. In principle, competitive incentives exist at all levels from the household to the firm to the political and judicial levels of action, and competitive efforts should be expected to accompany these incentives. Because the process of competition may be expected to utilize resources at every level, economic welfare analyses clearly require an examination of these processes as well as the end states generated. The costs (or benefits) of "getting there" are bound to have an effect upon the desirability of the destination. The possibility of adopting rules or customs at each level that affect both the costs and the directions taken clearly represents one essential way of improving the voyage.

IV.
Applications of Rent-Seeking Theory

10

Rent Seeking under External Diseconomies

by

JAMES M. BUCHANAN

THE papers in part II of this book were the first efforts to extend economic analysis to allow for rent-seeking or profit-seeking behavior in the *creation* of monopoly positions, whether this behavior takes place within a dynamic model of market interaction or within a political-governmental decision structure. Several important principles have emerged from this discussion, despite the early stage of development of what remains essentially a new extension of economic theory. First of all, as Tullock demonstrates, the orthodox measure of the welfare costs of monopoly, which is concentrated on estimates of value of the familiar Harberger welfare triangles, tends to be far too low. Second, as Kreuger shows convincingly, any arbitrary restrictions on market freedom created through governmental auspices will attract investment in rent seeking, setting off a process that will tend to dissipate the potential rents available ex ante to those investors who succeed in securing the scarce permits.

My purpose in this paper is to develop a further application, one that has not, to my knowledge, been made. I shall demonstrate that when profit- or rent-seeking behavior is fully incorporated into familiar situations where external diseconomies exist, serious questions are raised concerning the efficacy of the efficiency-generating policy steps almost universally recommended by economists. A second but equally important aspect of the analysis demonstrates that, quite apart from the questions that might be raised about the net welfare effects of policy actions, the prospects for securing agreement among politically decisive members of the community depend critically on the precise manner in which efficiency-producing institutional reforms are proposed. These public-choice implications suggest the policy efficacy of narrowing the range of policy options that should be seriously discussed.

External Diseconomies with Nonspecialized Resources

Consider a situation where there exist genuine Pareto-relevant external diseconomies. Further, we explicitly define this to be a setting where the absence of private ownership rights is acknowledged to be the underlying structural or institutional defect. We have a "tragedy of the commons," where separate decision-takers, persons or firms, utilize a commonly available, unowned and hence unpriced resource. Examples can be the familiar ones—pollution of a stream, traffic on a freeway, despoliation of a public beach. The familiar welfare results emerge: independent action produces an overutilization of the common facility. Efficiency criteria dictate that usage be restricted, and, in this case, the assignment of private ownership rights can be predicted to accomplish the results required by standard efficiency criteria.

In the common-usage setting, the average product of resources employed in utilizing the facility will be equated to the marginal product (in value terms) of resources employed elsewhere in the economy. The initial situation may be depicted in figure 10.1. The assignment of ownership rights will cause owners to reduce the application of resources to the facility; the previously existing externalities will be internalized.[1] Usage will be cut back to the point where the marginal product from resources applied to the facility is equal to the marginal product of resources applied elsewhere in the economy. The owners will, by reducing application of resources to the facility, be able to secure the marginal product of the facility itself, measured by the triangle R in figure 10.1. This is (with linear functions) equivalent to the triangle G in the construction, which measures the social wastage under the common usage situation. The potential value of the facility, measured by its potential marginal product when efficiently utilized, is "destroyed" by the overusage.

[1] The classic paper on this is F. H. Knight, "Some Fallacies in the Interpretation of Social Cost," *Quarterly Journal of Economics* 38 (1924): 582–606.

FIGURE 10.1

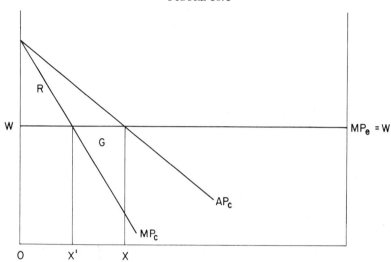

In this initial model, we assume that resources applied to the facility are not specialized. Hence, resource owners who shift to other employments neither gain nor lose by the institutional change toward private ownership. The net wealth of the community increases by the marginal product of the optimally used facility, and this increase in social product accrues exclusively to those who secure the ownership rights.

To this point, the analysis has not jumped outside the bounds of elementary textbook discussion. Let us now apply the theory of rent seeking. Suppose that the external diseconomies are recognized to exist in the initial situation, and further suppose that it is generally predicted that the government will, in fact, step in and create private ownership rights as a means of ensuring efficient facility usage. This prediction on the part of rent- or profit-seeking entrepreneurs will prompt investment in efforts to secure the scarcity rents that ownership rights will offer. Such investment will vary in form, depending on accompanying predictions concerning the manner in which rights are to be created. We may examine several possible cases.

If the scarce ownership rights are to be auctioned off, prospective purchasers need do little more than estimate the discounted value of the facility. The successful bid will be approximately equal to this value, as viewed ex ante, and the proceeds of the auction sale of ownership rights may be shared among members of the general public. In this case, the wealth increment generated by the change in institutional structure is channeled from the new owners of the rights to the members of the community at large.

Suppose, however, that ownership rights are not to be auctioned off, but are instead to be "assigned" by politician-bureaucrats to "deserving" citizens. Let us suppose further that these politician-bureaucrats are totally "incorruptible," and furthermore that they are totally immune to influence of any sort. In this case, the wealth generated by the institutional shift to private ownership accrues exclusively to those who are differentially favored in the allocation. This is the model that accords most closely with the textbook discussion, where the manner of assignment is not discussed and where rent-seeking behavior in anticipation of favorable treatment is implicitly assumed not to take place.

Suppose now, however, that the politician-bureaucrats are totally corruptible, and that explicit bribes in money are widely observed. In this third case, those who have the power to assign property rights can secure the full value of the facility. The net wealth increase that is due to the efficient use of the facility through time is fully captured by the politician-bureaucrats.

Note that the differences among the three models of assignment discussed to this point are purely distributional. These differences involve the sharing of the present value equivalents of the net gains that the efficient use of the facility will generate for the community. In each case, the presumption is that the facility will henceforward be operated efficiently and that overall there will be a clear "social gain" in making the initial institutional shift from common to private ownership. In none of the cases examined is there social waste involved in rent-seeking activity.

Let us now, however, introduce a rent-seeking model with quite different results. Suppose that politician-bureaucrats are totally incorruptible in money, but that they are subject to influence by indirect means of persuasion, familiar in pressure-group or lobbying discussion. Prospective bidders for ownership rights will be prompted to invest in methods of persuasion, in influence, in lobbying of all forms. To the extent that entry into such activity is not itself restricted, the expected returns from such investment may be predicted to approximate

the rate of return on investment in the economy generally. But if such
rent-seeking activity is not directly beneficial to the politician-
bureaucrats whose behavior is the target of the efforts, there may be
no net wealth increase in the community. Rent seeking may fully dissipate the "social gains" anticipated from the institutional shift. In such
a case, there may be no efficiency-related argument for trying to make
the institutional shift to ensure that the facility will be operated efficiently. To be sure, efficient operation will characterize the facility
after the change, but the efficiency gains will have been fully offset by
the "inefficient" rent-seeking efforts of prospective owners. In the net,
the community will be no better off with than without the institutional
change from common usage to private ownership.

This is, of course, a limiting case, and the complete dissipation of
efficiency gains through rent seeking may occur only in particular circumstances. Some net increments to wealth might be expected to accrue to successful bidders for the new ownership rights, some to the
politician-bureaucrats who make the assignments, and possibly some
gains would be expected to spill over to the public generally in most
settings. But the argument does indicate that the promised gains implicit in the familiar welfare-economics applications may be much less
significant than they are often made to appear. When this is recognized and when we acknowledge further that the existence of genuine
external diseconomies cannot be observed readily, the whole "internalization of externalities" analysis must be treated with considerable
skepticism.

External Diseconomies with
Specialized Resources

This general result may be strengthened and extended when we modify the example in only one way. We now assume that the persons or
firms who are initially applying resource bundles to the commonly
used facility must suffer some reduction in direct resource return from
a shift to alternative employments. This situation may arise for any one
of several reasons. The facility may be large relative to the total area of
the economy within which resources are applied. Resources may have
become specialized for usage on the common facility. The costs of shift
themselves may be significant. All these may be depicted generally in

FIGURE 10.2

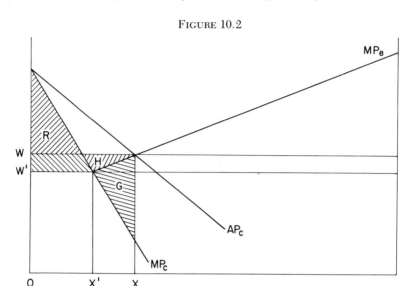

figure 10.2, which differs from figure 10.1 only by the downward slope of the marginal product curve for the economy external to the facility.

The necessary conditions for attaining efficient usage remain unchanged. Resource employment on the common facility should be reduced from OX to OX', where the values of marginal product for like units of resources are equalized as between the usage of the facility and other employments. Private ownership will, as before, effectively internalize the external diseconomy in usage that previously existed. The difference between this and the model depicted in figure 10.1 lies in the impact of internalization through ownership on those persons and firms who are initially applying resources to the common-usage facility. The equalization of marginal product required by efficiency criteria here involves a reduction in the marginal products of the resource units that can be shifted. The direct payments per unit of mobile resource that would be generated by a competitive process will be less after the institutional change than before.

One way of stating this is to say that the resource owners applying mobile units of resource to the common-usage facility before the assignment of ownership secure some share of the marginal product of the facility itself, and that this share will accrue to the new owner of the facility after the institutional change that assigns private ownership rights. This may be shown readily in terms of the geometry of figure 10.2. The marginal product of the facility under private ownership arrangements is shown by the shaded triangle, R, in figure 10.2. In market equilibrium, all of this product would be earned by the assigned owners of the facility. The "social wastage" generated by the usage of the facility as if it were a free good is shown by the shaded triangle, G, which is smaller than R ($G < R$). That is to say, a shift to efficient operation through the restriction of usage resulting from the assignment of private ownership rights will generate scarcity rents to owners in excess of the "social wastage." The difference is owing to the fact that some share of the facility's marginal product is secured by those who apply mobile resource units in facility usage before the ownership assignment. All owners of mobile resources will find their direct resource returns reduced, from W to W' in figure 10.2. Most of this reduction in resource returns to owners of mobile resources will be offset by increases in payments to rent recipients in other sectors of the economy. The sum of these offsetting increases is not, however, sufficient to offset fully the decline in net "wages" to the owners of mobile resource units. The difference is shown in figure 10.2 by the small shaded triangle, H, which must be subtracted from the scarcity rentals on the facility to secure a measure of the net "social gains."

Let us now apply the several rent-seeking cases introduced in the first section to this setting. Consider first the case where private ownership rights are simply auctioned off among bidders. The successful bids will sum to approximately the marginal product of the facility that has been commonly used before the change, that is, to R, in discounted value terms. The general public may in this way secure an increment to net wealth. The sum of the successful bids will, however, exceed the net efficiency gains (in discounted value) that the efficient operation of the facility guarantees. The net wealth of owners of mobile resource units (call this "labor" for simplicity in analysis) will be reduced, whether such resource units be employed on the particular facility under efficient operation or elsewhere in the economy. The net wealth of rent recipients elsewhere in the economy will be increased because of the increase in the supply of complementary resource inputs.

If the politician-bureaucrats are totally incorruptible and are known to be immune to any influence, our second case considered above, the institutional change to private ownership will increase the wealth of the successful applicants straightforwardly. The subsequent reallocation of mobile resources will also increase the net wealth of rent recipients elsewhere in the economy. Offsetting these increases will be some reduction in the net wealth of all owners of mobile resources. In the net, however, the total gains will be larger than the total losses.

If the politician-bureaucrats are totally corruptible, our third case, the only change is that the members of this decision-making group, rather than those who are successful in securing the new ownership rights, will acquire the value of the marginal product of the facility under efficient operation.

As in the first section, the differences among these first three cases considered are exclusively distributional; these differences involve only the sharing of the net increment to wealth that the efficient operation of the facility will guarantee, along with the sharing of the gains and losses that the subsequent resource reallocation will generate.

Let us now examine, however, the rent-dissipation case, in which prospective facility owners are prompted to invest resources in indirect efforts to influence political decision makers. In the limiting case, all the potential scarcity rents will be dissipated as before, but note here that there will arise a *net efficiency loss* for the community as a whole as a result of the shift from common usage to private ownership, despite the fact that such arrangements are guaranteed to produce an efficient operation of the facility through time. The net loss arises here because the returns to the owners of mobile resources are reduced in the process of shifting to an efficient usage of the facility, while at the same time the full marginal product of the facility itself is competed away in wholly wasteful rent seeking.

As we move away from the limiting case in which all potential scarcity rents are dissipated and as we allow for some differential rents to be secured by successful seekers of ownership rights, by politician-bureaucrats through explicit payments or through the enjoyment of perquisites, and by the public generally, these conclusions about net efficiency losses to the community must be modified. However, these residual rents must remain equal to or higher than the difference between the initial "social wastage" and the marginal product of the facility under efficient operation if a "social gain" to the community is to be generated by the shift to private ownership. This finding once again suggests that the possible external diseconomies must be reckoned to be considerably more serious than the orthodox analysis might indicate before any restriction of common-usage arrangements can be justified.

Public Choice Implications

To this point, the analysis has been confined to the rent-seeking activity of prospective private owners as this might possibly affect the net welfare gains or welfare costs of institutional attempts to internalize external diseconomies. I have deliberately refrained from introducing the obvious questions raised concerning the effects of rent-seeking behavior, and the predictability of this behavior, on the acceptability of institutional rearrangements to members of the community, to the voting constituency, and through this to the potential decision makers. These public-choice questions may be easily answered in the separate cases discussed in both the first two sections.

In the basic model described in the first section, where non-specialized resources are applied to the common usage of the facility, there is no net transfer of wealth between rent recipients and the owners of mobile resources. By construction here, the scarcity rentals made possible by the internalization of the externality are the only rental prospects anywhere in the economy. Owners of mobile resource units will, therefore, remain indifferent as to the proposals that will either allocate the net increments to wealth to the successful applicants for ownership rights, as new owners, or to the politician-bureaucrats themselves (envy considerations aside). These owners of mobile resource units will also tend to look indifferently on the rent-dissipating activity under the free-entry, indirect-influencing case. By dramatic contrast, the owners of mobile resources, as members of the voting-taxpaying-beneficiary public, should positively support the assignment of ownership rights through the auctioning process, since this can ensure that the net efficiency gains are neither dissipated by unproductive rent seeking nor distributed exclusively to others in the community. To the extent that citizens make the required connection between governmental receipt of the bid monies and the return of these monies in the form of tax reduction, public expenditure increases, or direct transfers, we should predict that the auction method of assigning new ownership rights would tend to dominate alternative schemes in some political sense when we recognize that mobile resource owners make up a larger voting group than those who might secure rents.

The second basic model is more interesting in terms of its public-choice implications. As I have shown, any restriction on common usage by newly assigned owners will reduce the directly imputed payments to the owners of the mobile resources. Insofar as this effect is recognized in advance, owners of mobile resources, who would have been indifferent in the first model, will tend to oppose any and all arrangements predicted to generate some shift of resources away from the common-usage facility unless, of course, appropriate compensations are included. To the extent that the incremental rents promised by the efficient usage of the facility attract rent-seeking investment that tends to be dissipated in wasteful influence-affecting activity, the scope for possible compensations to those adversely affected will be reduced. If the scarcity rents are not "used up" in rent seeking, compensations are conceptually possible; the institutional shift to private ownership is, potentially, Pareto-superior to the common-usage status quo ante. The compensations required here would, however, be quite complex; transfers would have to be made between rent recipients, generally, and owners of mobile resource units, generally, and not just those directly involved in the reallocation away from the facility itself.

The public-choice aspects of the institutional adjustment in both this model and in the setting of the second section suggest that the auction method of assigning ownership rights may dominate other methods, in terms of both welfare gains and political acceptability. The auction method tends to ensure, first of all, that rent-seeking investment be directed productively in the bids made for the scarcity rights, rather than wastefully in attempts to influence decision makers. Second, the method ensures that there are no opportunities for political corruption, either directly or indirectly through the perquisites of lobbying activity. Third, and perhaps most important, the auction method tends to make possible a *distribution* of these social gains among members of the public in such a way as to generate widespread political support.

Somewhat interestingly, those economists who have been most closely associated with the proposals for auctioning off scarce rights in the usage of inherently crowdable facilities have not, to my knowledge, stressed the advantages that this analysis emphasizes. Ronald Coase, John Dales, and others who have advocated the auction method have done so largely, if not exclusively, on allocative efficiency grounds, as means of ensuring that those best able to utilize scarce facilities effectively secure access to these facilities. This orthodox efficiency-based argument is relevant, especially in situations where resale of assigned rights is either prohibited by law or strongly discouraged. The more important efficiency argument may, however, be that analyzed in this paper, that of ensuring that gains will not be dissipated in rent seeking and that these gains will be distributed in such a way as to benefit the public generally, not just the successful rent-seekers.[2]

We do observe the assignment of ownership rights through auctioning, the most familiar example being perhaps the assignments of rights to drill for offshore oil and gas. We do not, however, observe the auction method in use in many circumstances where it might seem to be applicable. We do not observe auctioning in the assignment of rights to use radio spectrums, in the assignment of rights to pollute, in the assignment of airline routes, in the assignment of franchises to bus and trucking companies, in the assignment of local and regional utility franchises. In all these examples and many others we observe direct political-bureaucratic regulation through the assignment of franchises, permits, and licenses.[3] The analysis of this paper suggests that these

---

[2] The argument in favor of the auctioning method must be tempered when we recognize that the target for rent-seeking activity may be shifted "upward" to the level of the politician-bureaucrat who has the power to dispose of the auction receipts, the second stage discussed in chapter 1.

[3] This listing is not to be taken to imply that all regulated activities are necessarily inefficient in a totally unregulated setting. Regulation may, of course, be initially justified on common-usage arguments similar to those assumed in the analysis of this paper. Or comparable regulation may be justified on "natural monopoly" arguments. However, many industries may be subjected to regulation on wholly specious arguments unrelated to the efficiency properties of the unregulated setting. Much of the argument developed in this paper may be applied, however, regardless of the initial causes for regulation. The auctioning of bids to franchises may be compared with more direct regulation independently of whether the restricted licenses of franchises are warranted in the first place. Interestingly, the common-usage facility has been discussed in the literature independently of the discussion of natural monopoly. Yet these clearly reduce to the same thing. For a recent treatment of some of the historical development of ideas on natural monop-

noncontract or nonauction methods of regulation are institutionally more viable than the auction alternative. Simple public-choice analysis suggests that the political support for such noncontract or nonauction methods is likely to arise directly from those who are successful in the assignment process, along with those who occupy decision-making positions in the political-bureaucratic structure. The fact that these groups do seem to support direct regulation suggests empirically that the scarcity rents are not fully dissipated.[4] The acquiescence of the public in the distributional results of direct regulation, as opposed to the alternative distribution that might be available under the contract or auction alternative, suggests empirically that the differential effects are probably not fully recognized.

---

oly, especially as applied to the contracting of franchises, see Mark Crain and Robert Ekelund, "Chadwick and Demsetz on Competition and Regulation," *Journal of Law and Economics* 19 (April, 1976): 149–162.

[4] The basis for the support of direct regulation by those who are regulated is analyzed in James M. Buchanan and Gordon Tullock, "Polluters' Profits and Political Response: Direct Controls versus Taxes," *American Economic Review* 65 (March, 1975): 139–147.

11

Economics as a Guide to Antitrust Regulation

by

HAROLD DEMSETZ

IT is too soon, perhaps too late, to be confident that the currently fashionable criticism of regulation will result in reform. If reform does materialize, there can be no doubt that George Stigler's work will have had an impact on policy. However, should reform fail, Stigler will have assessed correctly the minuscule role of academicians in political affairs, his theory of regulation being partly an explanation of why academic notions of the general interest will seldom prevail over the political power of the special interests. Either way he is a winner.

The general interest presumably can be determined by looking to analysis, best of all to economic analysis. This assumes that academicians have much to say to policy makers that would be worthy of their attention if only they could neglect their desire to be elected. That article of faith is not completely unsupportable, at least not for a believer such as myself. Economics has much to say about this life, and, according to Gary Becker, about any other life also. We know what to expect from price control, from the minimum wage, from an increase in money supply, and from the imposition of a tariff—some basic, if not always simple, truths of economics.

When we turn to antitrust policy, the guidance economics can offer is much less clear or is, at least, unevenly clear. This inadequacy is examined here, first in general terms, then in regard to the current ambiguity about market concentration and monopoly, and finally with respect to some issues raised by monopolization.

Antitrust economics is at its weakest when addressing broad issues of normative policy and at its strongest when explaining particular pricing and marketing practices, an example of which is Aaron Director's insight into tie-in sales. The strength of economics in specific applications derives from our willingness to accept that the monopoly model is or is not applicable to a particular situation. Nonetheless, on broad issues, such as the identification of *excessive* degrees of monopoly and the problem of monopolization, economics does not yet offer a coherent message to antitrusters.

This state of affairs is somewhat different in several other areas of economics, where consistent messages about the benefits of free trade and the causes of inflation can be voiced, though they may go unheeded. Again, the explanation is the willingness of economists in these areas to assume for their purposes that the well-worked-out models of competition and monopoly are applicable. Broad policy judgments are easier if one can use a standard economic mode.

For antitrust problems, however, the primary issue *is* the assessment of the competitiveness of industrial behavior, with a view toward increasing competition where it is found inadequate. It is a problem to which relatively little theoretical attention has been given. Determining the degree of competitiveness is a very different problem from applying either the competitive or monopoly model to a particular situation.

Economics during the course of its development certainly did address the problem of monopoly, perhaps more frequently than any other problem. But it is safe to state as a general proposition that economic theory concentrated on the problem of examining the implications of monopoly already assumed to exist or of competition already assumed to be effective; perhaps that is why economists have been so effective in analyzing particular business practices where a patent, copyright, or government regulation creates a recognized measure of monopoly. But this aspect of monopoly and competition hardly helps to assess the closeness of actual to realizable competition in unprotected markets. The causes, characteristics, sources, and measurement of competition are given little more theoretical attention than are the origins and nature of self-interest.

Classical writers mainly sought an explanation of equilibrium prices and of how resources would be allocated in a decentralized economy. To examine this, it was sufficient to assume that the relevant markets were known and that they could be characterized either by the designation of monopoly or by competition without regard to how one would actually determine the competitiveness of a market. There could be no confusion between diamonds and water. Their substitutability was assumed to be negligible, and the sizes of their markets were conceptually clear. Explanations for the multitude of goods, for the differentiating characteristics of these goods, or for the characterization of their markets as competitive or monopoly simply were not objectives of the theory.

In more recent times, the explicit formulation of the conditions necessary for instantaneous long-run competitive equilibrium—large numbers, perfect knowledge, and complete resource mobility—has nurtured a belief that competition as an ordering force is weaker where these assumptions are *descriptively* less well approximated. These assumptions, of course, aid in thinking about the implications of *assumed* monopoly and competition, but the modern use of these assumptions as measurement criteria for the presence or absence of *objective* monopoly extends their role considerably. Small numbers of market participants and lack of full knowledge have come to identify less competitive situations in modern work. These assumptions and their main implication, the horizontal firm demand curve, seem to offer to antitrusters guidance, in principle at least, as to where monopoly or competition is to be found. Concepts such as the Lerner index of monopoly, relating price to marginal cost, reflect the adoption of these criteria, criteria that have become widely adopted principles of antitrust economics. Nonetheless, these are incorrect criteria upon which to construct standards of antitrust policy.

Suppose it is more costly to be certain about the quality-adjusted price of commodity A than about that of commodity B. Should this violation of the assumption of perfect knowledge about prices lead us to believe that monopoly is a greater problem in industry A than in industry B? The greater information cost in A should give rise to a greater variability in price per quality-adjusted unit among firms selling A than among firms selling B, and, perhaps, even to more negatively sloped demands for firms producing A than for firms producing B. Although no difference in quality-adjusted prices can exist in the absence of imperfections, the greater price variance for A is consistent with a degree of competition that is as intensive and as complete as is economic in industry A, given the fact that it is more costly to resolve consumer (and producer) uncertainties about product quality. Competition yields the variance in price for A and for B that is warranted by the costs of reducing variance. The theory of competition may be useful for predicting in which case price variance will be greater, but it cannot be deployed easily to determine whether competition is adequate from the viewpoint of antitrust.

Similarly, the theory of competition may be used to understand whether existing industry structures are likely to have arisen as a result of highly effective competition, perhaps operating in a context of scale economies. But the assumption of large numbers in perfect competition cannot be used easily to judge whether existing structures yield the appropriate amount of competition, given the realities of underlying cost structures.

Differences in scale economies, in inherent capabilities of producers, or in the real costs of determining product quality create the theoretical possibility of wide varieties of industry structures and elasticities of demands facing firms, all of which are consistent with as full a measure of competition as is feasible from the viewpoint of antitrust, given that the costs of realizing "perfect" competition are not zero. When antitrusters examine an industry, they are dealing with a situation characterized by positive information cost, positive resource mobilization cost, and the heavy hand of chance. Conceptually it may be possible to consider the implications of a change from a situation of scale economies and positive information cost to one of diseconomies of scale and costless information, but what can be done on a blackboard cannot be done by a judge hearing an antitrust case, a fact fully exposed by the impossibility of perfect competition as a descriptive condition of the world. Neither the assumptions of the perfectly competitive model nor its implications of horizontal firm demand curves can be used as indexes of whether competition is as fully operative as is economically possible.

The amount by which a market diverges from the perfect competition model definitely is not the practical policy issue; the inelasticity of the firm's demand curve, or some derivative measure of monopoly, is not an index of the effectiveness with which competition is regulating the market. If in some situations information is more costly or less valuable to gather, then less of it will be secured; similarly, the more costly it is to duplicate the efforts of others, the smaller will be the elasticities of the demand curves facing innovative firms. What is required for competition to yield efficiency is for rivalry to tolerate no greater or lesser degree of demand inelasticities than is dictated by the real costs of becoming informed and of producing substitutes, that is, by the cost of competing. If it seems that firm demand is too inelastic, even after the real costs of competing are taken into account, then there is a possibility for improvement through sensible antitrust action. But a very high elasticity of firm demand also may reflect a situation in which competition is not working effectively. Some of the real costs of competing may be ignored, perhaps because of government subsidies to compete or because of uneconomic prohibitions against branding, quality differentiation, and advertising. The high firm elasticities of demand in such markets would be excessive, and a social policy interested in the efficient amount of competition would call for a cessation of subsidies and an end to such prohibitions.

The proper issue for antitrust, then, is not the degree to which a market descriptively diverges from perfect competition, but the degree to which it diverges in either direction from that intensity of competition which takes account of the real social costs of competing. No one yet has successfully tackled this problem, so central to antitrust policy, although the unsuccessful effort by Clark to define workable competition represents an important attempt to do so.

Economies of scale may make atomistic industry structures too costly to be worth bringing about. This widely recognized possibility has motivated many attempts to measure scale economies, but these studies probably are not as reliable as the concentration ratios themselves in detecting the efficiencies of large firms. If the theory of competition tells us anything about industry structure, it is that an organization of an industry that has persisted for a long period of time in the absence of legal restrictions on entry fundamentally reflects underlying cost conditions. This proposition, which I have argued elsewhere[1] and which must be considered to cover cases of superior firms that exhibit lower cost independently of scale economies, is consistent with

[1] Harold Demsetz, "Industry Structure, Market Rivalry, and Public Policy," *Journal of Law and Economics* 16 (April, 1973): 1. Also see Harold Demsetz, "Two Systems of Belief about Monopoly," in *Industrial Concentration: The New Learning*, ed. Harvey J. Goldschmid, H. Michael Mann, and J. Fred Weston (Boston: Little, Brown and Company, 1974), pp. 164–184.

and probably derives from Stigler's use of the survivor test in assessing scale economies.

A fairly clear message to antitrusters is implied by this use of the notion of competition in combination with what intraindustry profit-rate patterns seem to indicate. Proposals to deconcentrate industries whose structures (without government aid) have remained concentrated for long periods are likely to penalize consumers by constraining firms to uneconomical sizes and by removing incentives to grow through efficient performance, even if such deconcentration would increase collusion costs. Unfortunately, the vast literature relating market concentration and collusion has overshadowed the cost complications of restructuring industries, and the message actually received by antitrusters takes little account of the cost increases likely to result from deconcentration.

The message that seems to have come through most emphatically to antitrusters is the importance of market concentration as an index of the effectiveness of competitive forces. The market concentration doctrine is based primarily on the statistical correlation between concentration and profit rates. These studies have been defended and attacked elsewhere. There is no need to go over that ground. Even if the market concentration doctrine contains a measure of truth—that it is somewhat easier to collude in concentrated markets—there is no implied call for deconcentration, because the degree of competition already constraining the behavior of firms in concentrated industries may be the best that can be had, given the underlying cost structure of firms.

Here, using industry data similar to that employed by Stigler, I would like to re-examine two different tests due to Stigler. Stigler's results, which lend support to the belief that monopoly and concentration are correlated, are of special interest because they are less likely to suffer from the ambiguity that plagues studies of the correlation between concentrations and levels of profits. Because accounting techniques are very imperfect in producing measures appropriate to economic judgments, the positive correlations generally found may reflect monopoly or the fact that superior firms record high profits while they enlarge their share of the market. However, Stigler's tests rest on propositions about the variability of, rather than the level of,

profit rates, and because they do they inadvertently reduce the chance
of confusing superior performance with monopoly.

One of the tests that Stigler discusses in *Capital and Rates of Return in Manufacturing*[2] examines the cross-sectional variability of
rates of return within groupings of concentrated and unconcentrated
industries. Stigler reasons that if monopoly and concentration are correlated, some profit rates in concentrated industries will remain high,
being resistant to entry, while in other concentrated industries, because entry is easier or demand conditions are poorer, no better than
competitive rates will be earned; competitive industries will not experience the protection enjoyed by (some of) the concentrated industries, so high rates of return will not be observed as frequently. Hence
the market concentration doctrine implies that for cross-sectional observations made during a given time interval the dispersion of rates of
return among competitive industries will be smaller than among monopolistic industries. Stigler tests this implication by comparing the
standard deviation of rates of return within a group of concentrated
industries with that for a group of unconcentrated industries for selected time periods. His "unadjusted" data do not support the market
concentration doctrine; in fact, the standard deviation is greater for
unconcentrated industries. But when he adjusts the data for withdrawal of profits in small companies through excessive managerial salaries, Stigler finds evidence supporting the market concentration
doctrine.

Recognizing that correlations between *levels* of profit rates and
concentration may be due (in part) to the performance of superior
firms rather than to monopoly, one is led to ask whether superior performance would also confound attempts to measure the presence of
monopoly by examining the *variance* in profit rates. Competitive superiority of firms may raise profit rate levels as recorded by accountants at the same time that superiority of firms produces an increase in
concentration, but there is no compelling reason to expect that profit
rates will vary more among concentrated industries, all of which will
tend to have more superior firms, than among unconcentrated industries, all of which will tend to have fewer such firms. Stigler's test thus

[2] George J. Stigler, *Capital and Rates of Return in Manufacturing Industries*
(Princeton: Princeton University Press, 1963).

seems to support the market concentration doctrine less ambiguously than studies dealing with profit-rate levels.

There are, however, two problems with his test. We now know that larger firms tend to earn higher profit rates than smaller firms, so that if the size distribution of firms is different in concentrated industries than in unconcentrated industries, the Stigler test could be tracking the effect of firm size, not of concentration.[3] Second, Stigler's method of taking account of the profit withdrawal phenomenon may have overcorrected. Robert Kilpatrick,[4] when examining Stigler's work correlating profit-rate levels and concentration, found some evidence of overcorrection; hence the "confirmatory" evidence derived with the adjusted data also may reflect this overcorrection.

Both these problems can be mitigated by repeating Stigler's test while holding firm size "fixed" to correct for both the problem of varying mixes of firm sizes and the salary withdrawal problem. By holding firm size constant, we can more clearly isolate the impact of concentration, and, since profit withdrawal through inflated wages is thought to be peculiarly a problem of small firms, we can obviate any need to adjust for salary withdrawals; data for firms of a given size ought to suffer approximately equally from the salary withdrawal phenomenon, however concentrated the industries in which they compete. By taking specific size classes of firms, it is possible to improve the confidence that can be attached to any association that might be revealed between the standard deviation of profit rates and industry concentration.

Standard deviations of profit rates from four-digit IRS industries are compared with industry concentration (by linking three-digit census data) in table 11.1 for five size classes. The asset size classes of firms are (1) less than $500 million, (2) $500 million to $5,000 million, (3) $5,000 million to $50,000 million, (4) $50,000 million to $100,000 million, (5) above $100,000 million. The standard deviation of profit rates tends to be greater for very large and very small firms than for

[3] The share of industry output produced by firms of asset size over $100 million varies considerably more in unconcentrated industries than in concentrated industries. The coefficient of variation of the share of output of such firms in industries with four firm concentration ratios in excess of .50 is .290, whereas for less concentrated industries the coefficient is .866.

[4] Robert W. Kilpatrick, "Stigler on the Relationship between Industry Profit Rates and Market Concentration," *Journal of Political Economy* 76 (May–June, 1968): 479.

TABLE 11.1
Standard Deviations of Profit Rates

Four Firm Concentration	Asset Size Class of Firms						Number of Industries
	1	2	3	4	5	1 to 5	
Less than 50	.053	.022	.032	.047	.065	.034	61
Between 50 and 60	.439	.050	.025	.057	.048	.039	11
Above 60	.070	.022	.014	.027	.067	.053	6
Less than 35	.049	.024	.030	.054	.074	.034	37
Between 35 and 50	.060	.019	.035	.036	.048	.034	24
Above 50	.354	.042	.022	.052	.060	.048	17

SOURCE: Research Program on Competition and Public Policy, U.C.L.A. (computer data base directed by J. Fred Weston at U.C.L.A.).

NOTE: Profit rates are average profits for 1958–1961, 1963–1967. At the time of calculation, the data base for the excluded year, 1962, contained no breakdown of profit rates by firm size.

moderate-sized firms. If firm size is ignored, as it is in the last column of standard deviations, the standard deviation of profit rate for concentrated industries is larger than for unconcentrated. This is contrary to Stigler's result when he worked with data unadjusted for the salary withdrawal problem. Perhaps the difference in time period studies accounts for this reversal. However, once firm size is controlled, as it is in the remaining columns, no clear relationship between concentration and standard deviations emerges. The greater variance exhibited by large firms, regardless of industry concentration, creates a puzzle, but, nonetheless, by this test there is no evidence to support the market concentration doctrine.

The second test used by Stigler is to measure the persistence of profits over time. Stigler reasons that "competitive industries will have a volatile pattern of rates of return, for the movements into high-profit industries and out of low-profit industries will . . . lead to a constantly changing (over time) hierarchy of rates of return. In the monopolistic industries, on the other hand, the unusually profitable industries will be able to preserve their preferential position for considerable periods of time."[5]

The test suggested by Stigler's reasoning properly is concerned with stability in the time patterns of relative profit rates of different

[5] Stigler, *Capital and Rates of Return*, p. 70.

TABLE 11.2
Correlation of Rates of Return for Concentrated,
Unconcentrated, and Ambiguous Industries,
1938–1957

	1938–1947		1947–1957	
	Number of Comparisons	Average Correlations	Number of Comparisons	Average Correlations
	Rates of Return in Year t and $(t + 1)$			
Concentrated	9	.76	8	.74
Unconcentrated	9	.69	8	.72
Ambiguous	9	.82	8	.77
	Rates of Return in Year t and $(t + 7)$			
Concentrated	3	.60	4	.57
Unconcentrated	3	.04	4	.26
Ambiguous	3	.16	4	.38

SOURCE: Stigler, *Capital and Rates of Return*, p. 71.

industries, not with the stability over time of an industry's profit level. If concentration implies difficulty in entering an industry, the relative profit positions among concentrated industries should be subjected to less scrambling over time. The relative profit positions in unconcentrated industries, by virtue of easier entry, should be scrambled much more quickly.

Here again is a test that is less likely to confuse the impact of superior performance with that of monopoly. Concentrated industries may exhibit higher profit levels than unconcentrated industries because superior performance by some firms, measured by high accounting profits, will be associated with the acquisition of large market shares by these firms. However, there is the possibility of confusing the effects of product diversification with those of concentration. Hence, a showing of greater stability in the relative profits of concentrated industries provides less ambiguous support for the market concentration doctrine than earlier studies correlating concentration and profit-rate levels.

A sample of the results reported by Stigler is given in table 11.2. The pattern of coefficients strongly supports the market concentration doctrine. But here there is the possibility of the confusion mentioned above. The larger diversification of product mix produced by large firms will impart a stability to their relative profits not present among smaller, more specialized firms. Since large firms are more important in concentrated industries, concentration may be a proxy for diversification.[6]

Table 11.3 controls for firm size and re-examines the persistence of relative profit patterns by concentration of industry. The entries in this table are calculated as follows. Industries are placed in one of the three concentration categories, and rates of return are classified by asset size of company. For a particular intersection of these two classifications, rates of return are correlated for year t and year $t + n$. For small values of n there will be several and for larger values of n fewer such correlations, and these are averaged to calculate the entry in table 11.3.

The data, derived from the same base as table 11.1, indicate that large firms do exhibit greater persistence in relative profit positions, but industry concentration displays no significant or consistent relationship to the pattern of intertemporal stability of relative profit rates. These results, in combination with other evidence that has been gathered recently, cast suspicion on the message that antitrusters have most frequently heard from economists: that market concentration and monopoly are related in a way that lends propriety to a policy of deconcentration.

The use of profit rates as evidence of monopoly, usually in conjunction with market concentration studies, has been criticized by Tullock and more recently by Posner.[7] Their point is that the competition to become (and maintain) a monopoly requires resources, the employment of which can be expected to exhaust the return to monopolizing. Variations in profit rates thus are not likely to be correlated with variations in monopoly, and where monopoly does exist the real cost that it imposes on the economy, which includes resources expended to acquire the monopoly, will be underestimated if profit rates play an important role in the methodology of estimating that cost.

[6] The mean share of output produced by firms larger in asset size than $100 million is .284 for industries with concentration ratios less than .50 but .726 for more concentrated industries.

[7] Gordon Tullock, "The Welfare Costs of Tariffs, Monopolies, and Theft," chapter 3 in this volume; Richard A. Posner, "The Social Costs of Monopoly and Regulation," chapter 5 in this volume.

The acceptance of this reasoning removes much of the empirical support for the market concentration doctrine, since that support derives from correlations between market concentration and profit rates. However, acceptance also creates a puzzle. What is it that causes profit rates to be correlated with concentration? One possible answer is that systematic risk is correlated with both the profit and concentration. Or it may be that superior firms earn higher profit rates and also expand to make their industry more concentrated than it would otherwise be. This notion, which also is consistent with observed differences between large and small firm profit rates, depends on two preconditions, neither of which is implausible: imperfect substitutability between the

TABLE 11.3

Intertemporal Correlation of Rates of Return by Four Firm Concentration and Asset Size of Firm (1958–1967 Excluding 1962)

Industry Concentration	Asset Size Class					
	1	2	3	4	5	1 to 5
Average of Correlations between Years t and (t + 1)						
Less than 50	.072	.387	.763	.770	.906	.830
Between 50 and 60	.144	.605	.417	.804	.832	.890
Above 60	.204	.203	.519	.478	.917	.889
Average of Correlations between Years t and (t + 2)						
Less than 50	.038	.318	.631	.660	.861	.764
Between 50 and 60	.004	.661	.249	.710	.759	.795
Above 60	.041	.141	.315	.415	.853	.809
Average of Correlations between Years t and (t + 3)						
Less than 50	.116	.302	.548	.571	.811	.721
Between 50 and 60	.207	.519	.342	.655	.667	.727
Above 60	.559	.456	.210	.134	.858	.811
Average of Correlations between Years t and (t + 4)						
Less than 50	.019	.233	.508	.499	.799	.712
Between 50 and 60	.128	.399	.090	.680	.719	.744
Above 60	.211	.295	−.131	−.089	.851	.794
Average of Correlations between Years t and (t + 5)						
Less than 50	.061	.276	.484	.446	.742	.668
Between 50 and 60	.437	.532	.024	.693	.842	.816
Above 60	.064	.029	−.201	−.046	.816	.725
Average of Correlations between Years t and (t + 6)						
Less than 50	.189	.237	.453	.362	.688	.615

TABLE 11.3 (continued)

Industry Concentration	Asset Size Class					
	1	2	3	4	5	1 to 5
Between 50 and 60	.098	.569	.384	.613	.768	.844
Above 60	.322	.392	−.126	.132	.882	.797
Average of Correlations between Years *t* and (*t* + 7)						
Less than 50	.165	.242	.426	.327	.664	.571
Between 50 and 60	−.662	.545	.291	.444	.744	.826
Above 60	.218	.166	−.488	.199	.806	.710
Average of Correlations between Years *t* and (*t* + 8)						
Less than 50	.084	.275	.418	.241	.610	.522
Between 50 and 60	.069	.674	−.000	.232	.494	.758
Above 60	.246	−.396	−.735	.244	.829	.759

SOURCE: Research Program in Competition and Public Policy, U.C.L.A. (computer data base directed by J. Fred Weston at U.C.L.A.).

NOTE: Regional industries are excluded. At the time of calculation, the data base for the excluded year, 1962, contained some errors.

capabilities of firms and the inability of accountants to separate rent from profit.

Posner does not treat extensively the problem of how firms might invest in trying to become monopolists, but the question of monopolization (as distinct from the existence of monopoly) clearly is raised. Posner does point to the tactic of buying government protection, and it is easy to imagine how real resources can be expended either by firms to influence politicians or by politicians to get elected. But if we rule out this route to monopolization, in what does a firm invest? It is reasonable to suppose that a firm attempts to outdistance its rivals primarily by becoming more efficient. It invests in new techniques, new organizations, and in obtaining new and different answers to old questions. If it succeeds significantly, it moves into a dominant position, one that no doubt conveys some degree of control over its price. These investments hardly can be called social costs of monopolization. Rather, they are social benefits of competing. In situations where the government is not the source of monopoly power, calculations of the type made by Posner to measure the social cost of monopoly are likely to result in overestimates. Thus, if we measure the amount by which the price of aluminum exceeded its cost and combine this with estimates of the elasticity of demand in order to measure the social cost of monopoly, as does Posner, we fail to recognize that Alcoa's investments made cost lower than it would have been had Alcoa not tried to maintain a dominant position in the aluminum industry. That lower cost is a benefit of Alcoa's attempt to monopolize, whether or not it was successful. Faced with this very real Schumpeterian possibility, what guidance do we give to antitrusters?

Monopolization has two plausible routes. One follows a circuitous path through fifty state capitals and Washington, D.C. The other is to obtain very dominant control over resources "essential" to the production of a good. The acquisition by U.S. Steel through a series of mergers and purchases of about 90 percent of this nation's high-quality iron ore allowed it (behind a tariff barrier) to control domestic output for a decade after the corporation's formation (after which time high-quality ores began to be depleted). There may be a cost "justification" for centralizing such control, but the potential for monopolization created by an attempt to obtain a *dominant* ownership interest in an "essential" resource suggests that concern is proper. I refer here to the quantum of control exercised by U.S. Steel shortly after its formation and not to control of, say, 80 percent of an input by ten large companies. Such control, except through legal patent, I believe, is rare, and a decade for the market to eliminate or reduce substantially the abuse arising therefrom may not be long relative to what could be achieved through antitrust.

The point is that control over an "essential" technological input should not be confused with a dominant position in the product market, such as that obtained by Alcoa. When access to "essential" resources is open to existing and potential rivals, dominance in the product market generally will reflect the superior competitive performance of the dominant firm.

In a sense, such a firm does "control," or is controlled by, an input not so easily duplicated by its rivals: a superior team of people or a superior method of organizing such a team. But the putting together of such a team is the essence of socially productive rivalry, and one organization's success does not block others from attempting to do still better. It is what should be meant by competition among organizations.

To break up a superior team merely because it is successful surely is fraught with the danger of destroying the source of such productivity. To resist the securing of a dominant ownership interest in a resource such as high-grade iron ore is less likely to penalize such productivity and more likely to reduce unproductive sources of dominance.

Alleged barriers to entry, such as advertising, vertical integration, and capital requirements, all fall into the class of competitive tactics more likely to be associated with productive rivalry than with unproductive monopolization. Any firm can acquire advertising inputs, can alter its structure so as to become more integrated vertically, and can acquire capital. None of the inputs required to compete in these dimensions is available to only one or a few such firms. The skillful use of such inputs by some firms very likely reflects productive rivalry, not restrictive monopolization. The current flurry of concern over such "barriers to entry" reflects the poor guidance too often offered to antitrusters by economists.

In the main, the poor guidance given by economics to antitrust policy is caused by the great theoretical gap in our knowledge about the relationship between actual competition and efficient amounts of competition. However, there are two guidelines, in addition to keeping a watchful eye on ownership dominance of an important input, that, though not without risk of error, seem worth pursuing. Neither is very dramatic or imaginative.

One can see benefits in encouraging firms to seek to better their rivals, and so we ought to hesitate before penalizing success merely because it results in an increase in concentration. It is somewhat more difficult to see great gains flowing from price collusion, and a modest recommendation that antitrusters again pursue the collusive price agreements seems in order. However, the use of market concentration in the product market as a proxy for such an agreement not only courts the danger of discouraging beneficial competitive rivalry, but also admits to an absence of a scientific method for discerning collusion. If some concentrated industries are colluding, they should leave tracks in the data as well as in the letter file.[8] It may be useful to keep a judi-

---

[8] A good example of what can be done along this line is provided by Donald O. Parsons and Edward John Ray, "The United States Steel Consolidation: The Creation of Market Control," *Journal of Law and Economics* 18 (April, 1975): 181.

cious eye on concentrated industries, but there is no need to use concentration in the product market as a substitute for evidence of collusion.

In addition to private price collusion, it is difficult to see great gains flowing from government protection of industries from competition, although in some cases, as with patent protection, such a case can be made. Monopolization through government protection is likely to be as difficult to defend intellectually as it is to attack politically. There seems ample room in both dimensions for advising that such protection should be withdrawn.

Short of these general recommendations, and perhaps even including them, it seems that economists might well use antitrust problems as a guide for studies yet to be undertaken, and that this might be more desirable than that we should persist in giving policy guidance about matters we have not yet mastered.

Caution when advocating policy is especially important in the case of antitrust. Unlike most regulatory agencies, the Antitrust Division and the Federal Trade Commission are likely to take our suggestions seriously, partly because the theoretical vacuum encourages these regulatory agencies to rely more heavily than other agencies on any help they can find, and partly because these agencies, since they do not work persistently on the task of regulating a particular industry, are less likely to be "captured" by those they oversee. This combination of unsatisfactory theory and absence of "captors" encourages them to be overly influenced by the scribbling academics. The use of vague notions about "shared monopoly," "barriers to entry," "predatory behavior," as well as the heavy reliance on profit rates, are indicative. In addition, these agencies, more than most, are likely to be swept along by intellectuals into fashionable, popular attacks on this or that industry, since there is little else to guide their efforts.

Charged with the vague, perhaps impossible task of finding and reducing excessive degrees of monopoly, these agencies are adrift without rudder or guidance from persistent currents. They alter course frequently in response to insubstantial puffs of hot air, or they are driven before the sudden wind of popular opinion, harangued by politicians who also bend before these gusts, only to find that the storm has passed them by. Impatiently they wait for the next cloud on the horizon.

12

The Transitional Gains Trap

by

GORDON TULLOCK

ONE of the major activities of modern governments is the granting of special privileges to various groups of politically influential people. Air transportation, for example, has been cartelized by the Civil Aeronautics Board, surface transportation by the Interstate Commerce Commission, and we are prevented from receiving "too-high" interest rates on our bank accounts by the Federal Reserve Board and various other government agencies. On the whole, however, the profit record of these protected industries does not seem to differ systematically from that of the unprotected. This raises questions of why these special privileges do not seem to do much good.[1]

General Argument

The purpose of this article is to discuss this apparent long-run unprofitability of government aid programs. To give a preview of the general plot, it will be my thesis that there are only transitional gains to be made when the government establishes special privileges for a group of people. The successors to the original beneficiaries will not normally make exceptional profits, but, unfortunately, they usually will be injured by cancellation of the original gift.[2] Indeed, we will be on what, paradoxically, seems to be an inefficient portion of the Paretian frontier.

[1] All this has led David Friedman to propound what he calls "Friedman's Second Law" and what others call "Friedman II's Law," which is "the government can't even give anything away."

[2] See James M. Buchanan and Gordon Tullock, "The 'Dead Hand' of Monopoly," *Antitrust Law and Economic Review* 1 (Summer, 1968): 85–96, for a similar analysis of

Although some government restrictions are clearly designed to benefit specific groups of people, this is by no means the only way in which such special privileges can arise. The pharmaceuticals industry, for example, fought hard against the 1962 consumer protection legislation. Since it has come into effect, they have become, on the whole, satisfied with it because it turns out that it has reduced the vigor of competition and their profits are consequently about as big as they were before, without the risk involved in the introduction of new and improved drugs.[3] Even in those cases where the government regulation was fairly clearly motivated by a desire to help some particular group, it usually turns out that at least some features are not to the advantage of the benefited group. Apparently government moves in mysterious ways its wonders to perform and is not completely controlled even by the best-organized pressure group.

Taxi Medallions

Let us consider a very simple example of government monopoly creation. This example will be the taxi medallion system, although my simplified description will not correspond exactly to that in New York. On figure 12.1 we show the demand for taxicab services with the usual down-slanting line, labeled D, and their cost as a horizontal line, labeled P. In a competitive environment, the price charged would also be at cost and C units of taxi service would be purchased at a price, P. With supply of taxis restricted, the price rises to P', and, of course, there is now a significant monopoly profit, shown by the usual rectangle. We shall, for the moment, ignore the question of what happens to the taxis idled by this change and simply concern ourselves with the taxi owners and drivers who have the right to drive under the new dispensation (i.e., who have the taxi medallions). It is clear that they have gained a great deal.

Suppose, however, we wait for a number of years. By now, the

---

private monopoly. For an earlier analysis in somewhat the same spirit, see George J. Stigler, "Capitalism and Monopolistic Competition: I. The Theory of Oligopoly—Monopoly and Oligopoly by Merger," *American Economic Review* 40 (May, 1950): 23–34.

[3] See Sam Peltzman, "An Evaluation of Consumer Protection Legislation: The 1962 Drug Amendments," *Journal of Political Economy* 81 (September–October, 1973): 1049–91, especially 1086–89.

FIGURE 12.1

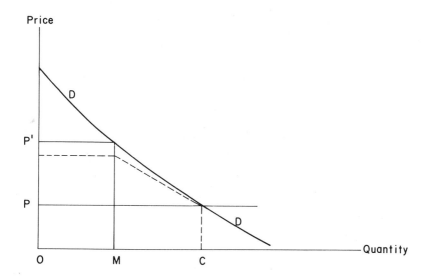

capital value of the monopoly profit has been fully taken into account in the industry. New entrants enter only by purchasing the medallion, with the result that they get only normal profits.[4] Further, the surviving original owners have opportunity costs equivalent to the value of the medallions upon which they receive normal returns. The customers, of course, are worse off.

Can we suggest a compensation scheme that would get us out of the mess? Normally, the answer to this question is no, because the implied transaction costs are excessive. If we could somehow identify those people who are now not using a cab but who would at a slightly lower price and tax *them* so that the distribution of the burden followed the dotted line on figure 12.1, it would be possible gradually to buy back the monopoly from its current owners and hence benefit everyone. Unfortunately, we have no way of doing it; hence my reference to the situation as being an "inefficient point on the Paretian frontier."

There is a possible way in which we might get out of the trap. It may be that the monopolistic organization of the industry is not effi-

---

[4] Richard D. Auster, "The GPITPC and Institutional Entropy," *Public Choice* 19 (Fall, 1974): 77–83.

cient for one reason or another. The number of taxicab medallions in New York has remained unchanged for a very long period of time. It seems unlikely that the demand and cost of taxicabs during that period of time has continuously been such that the unchanged number of cabs maximized the monopoly gains. A brief examination of the other regulated industries or specially privileged areas will usually lead to the same conclusion. The owners of the monopoly are not efficiently exploiting the consumer, not because they are stupid, but because the political problems involved in manipulating government are great. Any change in the number of cabs other than doubling or tripling them would require that the medallions be given fractional value, unless it were intended to change the proportionate ownership of different medallions. The problems of having the individual owner of a medallion suddenly find that he had the right to operate 1.07 cabs (or 0.93 cabs) would probably preclude any possibility of political success for such a move. Certainly the transactions cost for getting such a proposal approved by all the cab owners would be immense.

Note that frequently the gains obtained by the organizers or beneficiaries of this kind of cartel arrangement, even in the transitional period, are quite small. On figure 12.1, when the cartel was introduced, there was a sharp reduction in the total number of units produced. Clearly, the cost of reducing capacity in this way could be considerable and must be borne by someone. In the particular case of the New York medallions, they were actually provided for all existing cabs and, in the short run, had very little effect. Later, when the demand for cabs went up, they restricted the growth of the cab business. In order to achieve immediate profits, it would have been necessary to dispose of some producing assets in order to get the monopoly gains. This is, of course, not a special characteristic of this type of monopoly.

Blue Laws

To take an example of the way this kind of thing works, let me offer my own explanation for the reason that "blue laws" are frequently supported by the mercantile community. They are not, of course, the main force behind the blue laws. Suppose a community has a certain number of supermarkets that are open seven days a week. It is proposed that they be required by law to close all day Sunday. Merely

having the store open imposes certain costs that cannot be totally eliminated. There have to be a certain number of people on duty, the lights
have to be turned up to a certain level, heating and air-conditioning
have to be handled a little differently than when the store is closed,
and so on. Thus, a reduction in the number of hours the store is open
does reduce the total cost. In essence, each sale is accomplished with
somewhat less in the way of cost because the customers are compelled
to come more closely grouped, and various economies can be derived
from that. In a way, requiring that the stores close down on Sunday is
somewhat similar in its effect to destroying one-seventh of the stores.

If a private business acquired all the stores in order to extract monopoly rents, it would find it necessary to reduce its capacity. Presumably, it would do this in part by closing down stores and, to some extent, by reducing the time they are open. The private business could
seek the most profitable combination of these two methods of reducing
capacity. But this is not really a political opportunity available to the
mercantile supporters of blue laws; hence, their monopoly will be less
efficient than a private monopoly.

The result, then, of forcing the stores to close on Sunday should
be, temporarily, a rise in profits. If they are in a highly competitive
environment, this profit will be completely competed away; but many
retail stores are in monopolistic competitive environments, and this
will partially protect them from that contingency. Still, a good deal of
the cost-saving will inevitably pass on to the consumers, who presumably would prefer to pay a little more and have the greater convenience of having the stores open all week.

Once the blue laws have been enacted, however, the stores are
operating at somewhat above normal return on their assets, and the
customers find themselves a little more crowded in their shopping
than they really want to be. Under the circumstances, the construction of new stores is highly likely. Eventually, then, we will have the
situation in which there are more stores than there were before and
the return on all stores is, once again, normal. The customers are not
being served quite so well, so we have a social cost, but it is not practically possible to put a tax on the customers and use that tax to buy the
stores back to their original position. On the other hand, although the
store owners are now making normal profits, the repeal of the blue
laws would be quite inconvenient for them. With the blue laws re-

pealed, some of them would surely start opening on Sunday and the costs saved by going to a six-day week would be reimposed. They would suffer a considerable transitional loss.

Related Phenomena

For blue laws the transitional gain was extremely small. In other cases, there may be quite large initial gains. The organization of a new labor union, which raises wages by 15 percent for its current employees,[5] does bring a very large improvement in the well-being of the current laborers who remain employed. Essentially, however, this is simply a capital gift to the existing laborers; it does not significantly benefit the new laborers who will in the long run replace them in the industry. With wages in this industry averaging 15 percent above wages elsewhere, the number of people who want to become employees immediately becomes much larger than can be employed. Under the circumstances, some method of rationing jobs is necessary. If this method is a straight hereditary method—that is, in order to get in, you have to be children of the previous members of the union—then the gain is retained permanently within these families.

More normally, however, the method of rationing these high-wage jobs is through the seniority clause. Senior employees have a prescriptive right to their jobs.[6] Granted the work force is not entirely stable, this means that the entire burden of unemployment falls on the new workers. Since in the early years, in any event, the employer will be restricting employment and investing in labor-saving devices (because of the higher wages he is paying), this phenomenon may mean that the new entrant to the union spends a good deal of time as a very low-seniority worker with only intermittent employment.

Presumably, the situation is brought into equilibrium with the discounted lifetime income stream for becoming a union member (which means a long period of intermittent employment at first and

[5] Normally, of course, with some reduction in the total number of employees, so some people get hurt even at that time.

[6] In some of the lower-paid occupations, the opposite phenomenon is currently occurring. Unemployment insurance rates are now high enough so that there is a desire on the part of the senior employees to take paid vacations periodically, with the result of what is called "reverse seniority."

then high-wage employment later) equal to the return on taking a non-unionized job. When this equilibrium has been reached (and it surely has been for all the older unions), once again we are in a situation where no one is better off as a result of the existence of the union than he would be had the union never been organized. Unfortunately, there is a deadweight social loss, and there are a number of people, the members of the union, who will lose very considerably from the ending of the union. The transitional gain has been completely "sunk," but the possibility of large transitional losses remains.

A somewhat similar situation exists with respect to agriculture. The very large gains in value of farm products, as a result of the Agricultural Adjustment Administration's initial work, were quickly capitalized into the value of land. Whoever owned farmland at the time the program was instituted made immense gains, but these gains were fully capitalized. We are now stuck with the situation in which there are significant social losses, but a powerful political group would suffer transitional losses by the termination of the program. No one is gaining now in the sense that his income is higher than it would be had the institution never been established, except, of course, those people who have received larger inheritances from their parents than they otherwise would.

The higher-than-competitive wages now paid in much of the government sector are another example. They depend essentially on the fact that families of government employees now make up something on the order of one-third of all voters.[7] Government employees use a somewhat odd method of capitalizing the gains. Suppose some category of government employee is paid more than is necessary to attract an adequate number of suitably qualified personnel. There will be an excess of people who want the jobs. They must be rationed in some way, and the method used by the United States government (and, indeed, by many local governments) is the civil service examination. If the prices being paid are at the market level, then the civil service examination would be more or less unnecessary. The number of candi-

---

[7] This estimate is a little shaky, but government employees do make up about 19 percent of all employed persons. They appear to vote about 50 percent more frequently than do nongovernment employees, and hence the computation of one-third. For investigation of the evidence on this point, see Thomas E. Borcherding, ed., *Budgets and Bureaucrats* (Durham, N.C.: Duke University Press, 1977).

dates who would turn up for the jobs would be about what is needed, and the methods used in private industry to select suitable employees could be used.

On the other hand, if the pay is above that necessary to attract adequate labor, then the civil service exam takes the form of a rationing device. The exam is made harder than is necessary or it covers irrelevant matters such as knowledge of American history. As a result, the employees are actually overqualified for the job itself, although not for the examination. In equilibrium, individuals choosing to take a civil service job would expect about the same discounted lifetime earnings if they had taken a job in private industry that had an inherent requirement for higher quality labor than in the civil service job.

There is a significant social cost in the sense that the jobs are held by people whose native capacity is such that they could hold better jobs equally well. For example, the private post offices that are now so successfully competing with the government Postal Service, in those areas where they are legal, normally hire much lower quality labor and pay a much lower wage than does the Postal Service. It should be emphasized that, although this is true, they also get much more work from their employees. A custom of working only part of the day has developed in the Postal Service, and many letter carriers are done with their day's work in much less than an eight-hour stint.[8]

In the particular case of the civil service employees, the initial increase in their wages is essentially a pure transfer. It is only with time, as the higher wages attract higher quality labor, that a social cost not connected with the transfer itself is generated. With respect to most of the other activities we have discussed, however, the benefit received by beneficiaries comes by way of a change in the economy that is not, in and of itself, a pure transfer. They are given monopoly privileges of some sort in most cases.

Any economist will, of course, say that pure transfers are better as a way of transferring money than the establishment of monopoly privileges. Indeed, in the case of agricultural subsidy programs, it used to be quite common for economists to demonstrate that all the beneficiaries could be given the same benefit for a small fraction of the cost to the rest of the population.

[8] "Mail Carrier Likes His Job," *Washington Post*, June 14, 1974.

This argument is a little oversimple because it starts by assuming the total cost to the transfer is simply its tax rate. Of course, there is also an excess burden attached to each tax, and this excess burden, as in figure 12.1, can be almost identical with the excess burden of the monopoly. Nevertheless, it must be admitted that if one looks over the set of government institutions used to generate special benefits for special groups, it is usually true that a well-designed set of taxes could generate the same revenue for the beneficiaries at much lower cost to the victims.

Why, then, is the less-efficient technique adopted? So far as I know, there are only two explanations for this. The first, which is fairly old, is based on the information cost.[9] Not to repeat here the full details of the argument,[10] it is simply that the pushing through of such a benefit for a special class requires that the cost of the benefit not be obvious to the very much larger collection of voters who will be injured by it. This, in turn, requires a certain degree of complexity in the subsidy, and direct cash payment raised out of direct taxes would normally not meet that requirement.

In addition to this argument, Paul Rubin has recently suggested another.[11] He points out that budgetary allocations are reconsidered every year in almost all countries. On the other hand, once an institution has been set up, it is not automatically re-examined on a regular basis, nor does its continued existence require a positive affirmative vote in the legislature. Under the circumstances, then, if a program was set in hand to give me $1 million a year out of the Treasury, I would have to face a series of annual votes on that $1 million. If, on the other hand, the laws were rearranged in such a way that I got a monopoly worth $1 million a year, this monopoly would remain in existence (and probably largely unnoticed) until such time as positive effort was made to terminate it. In the first case, I would have to have returned to the lobbying effort every year, whereas in the second case, once I get it, I keep it until something untoward happens.

Rubin points out that under these circumstances pressure groups

[9] Gordon Tullock, *Toward a Mathematics of Politics* (Ann Arbor: University of Michigan Press, 1967).

[10] Ibid., pp. 103–106.

[11] Paul H. Rubin, "On the Form of Special Interest Legislation," *Public Choice* 21 (Spring, 1975): 79–90.

would prefer the type of preferential benefit that does not require continuous budgetary appropriations, simply because it is cheaper. They have to make only one lobbying effort and then perhaps a defense seven or eight years later if the issue comes up for further discussion. This is quite different from running a continuing lobby to raise the issue every single year as part of the budget process.

Whether one or the other (or both) of these explanations is correct, or whether there is a third that either replaces or supplements these, is not of vital importance to our present concerns. It is certainly true that this type of institution is very widely found in our society and that the social cost is great. It is also true that, in general, the benefits are now long in the past. They were transitional benefits at the time the institution was first founded. As of now, there is no one who is positively benefiting from the organization and there is a large deadweight loss. However, there are a large number of people who would suffer large transitional costs if the institution were terminated. These transitional costs in many cases are large enough so that compensation of the losers would impose upon society an excess burden of the same order of magnitude as the cost of the present institution.

Summary and Conclusion

It is hard for an economist to recommend any positive action to deal with this kind of situation. It is, as the title of this article suggests, a trap. I can recommend very strongly that we try to avoid getting into such traps in the future, but what about the ones into which we have already fallen? In those cases where there are efficiency gains from reorganizing the industry, we could presumably compensate the present beneficiaries, but the political possibilities seem to me to be very small. In those cases where the excess burden on the necessary tax for compensation would be as great as the deadweight loss, this alternative is not available even in theory. Granted the omnipresence of institutions of this sort and their very large deadweight loss, it is conceivable that simultaneously abolishing all of them would lead to a net gain for almost everyone. The individual would lose his particular privilege but would gain from the loss of privileges of other people. It is doubtful that such a change would be truly Pareto-optimal, but it might come close. As to its political practicality, I do not have to explain why I think it is low.

The moral of this on the whole depressing tale is that we should try to avoid getting into this kind of trap in the future. Our predecessors have made bad mistakes and we are stuck with them, but we can at least make efforts to prevent our descendants from having even more such deadweight losses inflicted upon them.

13

Rent Seeking in an

Aging Population

by

DANIEL ORR

A shift in the age distribution of the U.S. population is a clearly fore-seeable event that will have gradually increasing but profound effects on the economy. The effects of past birthrate changes have already been perceived and analyzed as they bear on the financial status of, and possible disincentive effects created by, the social security system.[1] The same kinds of effects, stemming from an increasingly large portion of the population having retired from productive work, will soon be observed elsewhere in the economy.

Table 13.1 shows past changes and projected future changes in the population age distribution. The increase through time in the number of people above age sixty-five and in the fraction of the population in that age group has been steady and is likely to continue through the next eight decades.[2] This paper offers a speculative analysis of the effects that increases in the number of elderly and in the average age of the population will have on rent-seeking behavior.

Rent seeking, as explained elsewhere in this volume, is the active pursuit, involving resource expenditure, of transfer payments or monopoly franchises from government. The reasons for rent seeking can be well understood from conventional maximization-of-expected-utility (or expected return) analysis. Rent seeking is rivalrous re-distributive activity that seldom conveys any gain in aggregate wealth;

[1] The large literature is listed in Alicia H. Munnell, *The Future of Social Security* (Washington, D.C.: The Brookings Institution, 1977).

[2] See the appendix to this chapter for a discussion of the methods employed in forecasting population levels.

TABLE 13.1

U.S. Population and Age Distribution and Projections,
by Decade, 1920–2050

Year	Total Population	Under 21	21 to 65 (%)	Over 65 (%)	Ratio of Workers to Retired*
1920	105,710	43,103	57,659 (54.5)	4,948 (4.7)	11.6:1
1930	122,775	47,669	68,468 (55.8)	6,638 (5.4)	10.3:1
1940	131,670	45,307	77,344 (58.8)	9,019 (6.8)	8.6:1
1950	150,698	51,100	87,328 (58.0)	12,270 (8.1)	7.2:1
1960	179,323	69,005	93,758 (52.3)	16,560 (9.2)	5.7:1
1970	203,211	76,970	106,175 (52.2)	20,066 (9.9)	5.3:1
Projection Series I: Fertility Rate 1.7					
1980	220,732	73,442	122,363 (55.4)	24,927 (11.3)	4.9:1
1990	236,264	68,477	137,963 (58.4)	29,824 (12.6)	4.6:1
2000	245,876	66,887	147,167 (59.9)	31,822 (12.9)	4.6:1
2010	250,892	61,963	154,092 (61.4)	34,837 (13.9)	4.4:1
2020	253,011	59,185	148,724 (58.8)	45,102 (17.8)	3.3:1
2030	249,315	56,823	137,468 (55.1)	55,024 (22.0)	2.5:1
2040	241,083	53,773	132,385 (54.9)	54,925 (22.8)	2.4:1
2050	230,998	51,755	126,931 (55.0)	52,312 (22.6)	2.4:1
Projection Series II: Fertility Rate 2.1					
1980	222,159	74,869	122,363 (55.1)	24,927 (11.2)	4.9:1
1990	243,513	75,726	137,963 (56.7)	29,824 (12.2)	4.6:1
2000	260,378	80,485	148,071 (56.9)	31,822 (12.2)	4.7:1
2010	275,335	79,974	160,524 (58.3)	34,837 (12.7)	4.6:1
2020	290,115	82,871	162,142 (55.9)	45,102 (15.5)	3.6:1
2030	300,349	85,176	160,149 (53.3)	55,024 (18.3)	2.9:1
2040	308,400	86,535	166,940 (54.1)	54,925 (22.8)	3.0:1
2050	315,622	89,330	170,798 (54.1)	55,494 (17.6)	3.0:1

SOURCES: 1920–1970: U.S. Bureau of the Census, *Historical Statistics of the United States, Colonial Times to 1970* (Washington, D.C., 1975), Data Series A 119–134, p. 15. 1970–2050 (both series): U.S. Bureau of the Census, Current Population Reports, Series P-25, Population Estimates and Projections, *Projections of the Population of the United States, 1977–2050*, No. 704, July 1977, tables 8, 9, 11, 12.

*Column 3 divided by column 4.

indeed, usually it can be expected to diminish aggregate wealth, first, because of the resources consumed directly in both pressing and resisting the activity, and second, because of the altered incentives that some programs impose on those from whom tribute is transferred. The "services" provided by government in response to the activity of rent seekers can take two forms: appropriation and transfer of wealth or creation and allocation of monopoly power.

Determinants and Measures of Rent-Seeking Activity

As with any economic activity, we expect rent seeking to be pursued most vigorously at times when its expected return is highest. Four factors, which vary in magnitude through time, combine to determine the rate of return on rent seeking to a particular individual.

First, there is the expected return to productive effort. Productive effort can be directed in various ways: taking a job, starting a business, accumulating human capital, or initiating professional practice. Returns to an individual from these pursuits will vary with aptitude and with the extent of competition and demand. If rent seeking and productive effort both are regarded purely as means to obtain goods for consumption, then the return to productive effort is the opportunity cost of rent seeking, and anything conducive to a higher value of return serves to diminish the likelihood that the individual will engage systematically in rent seeking. On the other hand, if rent seeking is itself viewed as a consumption activity,[3] though no consumption utility is derived from productive effort, then the analysis becomes more complicated; an increase in wages can leave more time free for the active pursuit of rent seeking.

The second factor affecting the extent and direction of an individual's rent seeking is the size and structure of government. Just as financial and contract enforcement systems and transportation and communication networks are the infrastructure of productive activity, so responsive legislators and ideologically committed administrators are the infrastructure of rent-seeking activity. Bankers and trucking firms increase their wealth by advertising, client visits, and other actions that stimulate demand for their services, and the same is true of legislators and bureaucrats. Thus it is not uncommon to observe that many

---

[3] That possibility initially seems bizarre, but clearly many activists enjoy the pastime of political manipulating, and it is no less plausible that consumption utility is derived from those efforts than that it is obtained from work. People with unattractive work opportunities should be expected to be found in pursuit of rents, in part because of the increases in satisfaction that derive from the activity itself.

programs of transfer are instigated by legislators, bureaucrats, and intellectuals who reap publicity and consulting fees, and such programs are more heavily publicized and promoted by those people than by the intended beneficiary groups. In many cases, individuals who are potential beneficiaries must be tutored regarding their opportunity to receive transfers and regarding the tacit and overt obligations created by the receipt of transfers.

The third factor affecting the level of an individual's rent-seeking activity is the perceived supply of accessible rents that can either be directly transferred or created and allocated by some monopoly-inducing government action. Bidding rents away in the form of direct income transfers is a low-income, large-group activity and seldom originates at the initiative of beneficiaries. Such programs as Medicare, food stamps, Head Start, and the like are simple transfers of wealth, and their acceptance is facilitated by a rapid growth of wealth in the society at large. Those engaged in wealth accumulation face a high opportunity cost of resisting taxation, so long as the marginal tax rate remains well below 100 percent. By contrast, the processes of creating and appropriating rent by monopoly charter are far more sophisticated activities, usually initiated by smaller and wealthier groups on their own behalf. Examples would include defense contracting, manipulating regulatory commissions, and bidding for research grants and contracts, all, of course, subsequent to securing passage of the enabling and funding legislation that must precede such opportunities. Rent seeking of this type is entrepreneurial activity and in some circumstances may accidentally lead to the creation of wealth and not just its transfer (as may have happened, for example, through the application of new metallurgical and electronic techniques developed in Mercury, Apollo, and subsequent space programs).

The fourth factor affecting individual participation in rent seeking, and one that is particularly important in considering pure transfer activity, is the numerical size of the group or interest that seeks to enlist the individual in pursuit of transfers. There is surely some optimal size and optimal electoral concentration of such groups. If the size is too small or too diffused or too concentrated geographically, the voting power of the group is reduced, prospects of success are diminished, and the incentive to join is decreased. If the size is too large, the benefit claims of the transferees may, unless individually negligible in magnitude, discourage the transferors sufficiently so that they either cease producing or become alarmed to the point of decisive counter-response. If the rent-seeking group is very large, an individual may perceive his role to be payer of tribute, even though he qualifies as a beneficiary. An individual's perception of his likely success in rent seeking and of the effort that will be required of him, then, will depend on the number of others enlisted in the same pursuit.

Thus, rent-seeking behavior on the part of the individual can be explained or analyzed in conventional supply-and-demand terms, with promotional and brokerage services provided by legislators and bureaucrats and with the transferred rents produced and consumed by individuals. Unlike conventional goods markets, there is no market-clearing, privately perceived price that rations among demanders or induces productive effort by suppliers. In this regard the market resembles the market for a governmentally supplied public good, but the crucial dimensions of public goods, nonexclusivity and nonrivalrous consumption, are missing in rent-seeking markets. This absence has led to some remarkable sophistry on the part of various proponents of redistribution, who, to rationalize the policy they espouse, have attempted to show that the income distribution is itself a public good and that the free rider problems that confront the provision of nonexclusive, nonrival goods and justify government provision of such goods also serve to justify the government provision of a more equal distribution of income.[4] Despite the manifest weakness of such a line of argument in *justification* of transfers, it does serve to illustrate the *working* of the process. The factors that proximately determine the volume of different kinds of rents that are transferred will be the same as those which govern the quantities of different public goods supplied: the politician-brokers will assess the impact of different levels of provision on voter behavior. Thus, as in the markets for public goods, there will be a range of possible amounts, with decisively negative voter response to quantities deemed too small or too large and voter tolerance or acclaim of amounts in the wide range of values in between. The absence of any continuously operative price adjustment in response to excess demand makes these markets far less likely to be near equilibrium or moving toward it than private goods markets are.

[4] See Lester Thurow, "The Income Distribution as a Pure Public Good," *Quarterly Journal of Economics* 85 (May, 1971): 327–336.

Despite the unconventional character of the market for governmentally transferred rents, empirical analysis of its scope is possible. At least two measures of activity in the market can be conceptualized: a conventional dollar measure of the volume of real purchasing power transferred, or the portion of the labor force engaged on a full-time equivalent basis in legislating, administering, soliciting, and resisting the processes of transfer. Neither measure can be obtained directly from any index or table; either will require judgmental manipulation to resolve the allocations of time by legislators, executive appointees, bureaucrats, lobbyists, and private activists between rent seeking and other activities that may be viewed as productive. (To what extent does the social worker, public utilities commissioner, or tax collector respond to demand that would be effective in private market arrangements? To what extent does the Corps of Engineers engage in the provision of public goods whose absence would diminish real social wealth?) Neither measure as described directly captures the welfare impact of rent seeking. They both fail to reflect the potentially important disincentive effects that can stem from the government's accommodation of rent seekers. The percentage of the labor force diverted into rent seeking and tribute avoidance, moreover, can be used as a rough measure of output forgone only if we assume that rent-seeking activity has negligible effect on the rate of employment,[5] as well as on the productivity of those individuals who are not rent seekers.

Rent Seeking among the Elderly

The previous list of factors that determine the level of rent-seeking activity engaged in by individuals can serve as a framework for analysis of rent seeking by the elderly. Senior citizens (to indulge in a loathsome cliché) have emerged during the past decade as an unusually vigorous ascriptive group. The central focus of their activity has been in the conversion of social security into a major program of income transfer and also into a major political issue.

It is typical of rent-seeking activity that resources are expended more or less constantly by both the proponents and the opponents of

[5] It was suggested earlier in the text that rent seeking could be stimulated by unemployment (via a diminution of opportunity costs). Rent seeking carried to excess can also induce unemployment (via disincentive effects on potential employers).

the enabling legislation. Once the legislation has been passed, efforts to revise or repeal it continue to operate. Beneficiaries seek to defend and enhance their gains, whereas those who pay tribute mount arguments for modification or repeal. Until very recently, before 1968, roughly, social security could not have been described as a program induced by rent seeking. At about that time, Congress began to change the social security law biennially and sometimes annually. The idea that social security was to be a retirement base, necessarily supplemented out of other income and wealth, was supplanted by the view that it should be sufficient to take care of all retirement needs. Medicaid inserted a new element into the program, that of conflict between beneficiaries and doctors. Terms and conditions governing the provision of care were under more or less constant scrutiny by Congress and the HEW bureaucrats and were an object of vigorous lobbying. Thus, in 1968, the carefully cultivated view of social security as an actuarially based, individually financed insurance program began to glimmer and fade. Increasingly since then it has been perceived as a full-scale scramble for transfers. This revision of image was a product of drastic escalation in both taxes and real benefits, changes engineered by political, academic,[6] and bureaucratic entrepreneurs, enthusiastically endorsed by a growing population of postretirement beneficiaries, and (until recently) accepted by a labor force lulled into passivity by prospective benefits that were escalating much more rapidly than taxes. Because it was credibly established in the beginning that benefits currently legislated would be maintained or even escalated into the future, resistance to rent-seeking manipulations of social security was weak.

Our experience with the social security program vividly illustrates a perplexing dimension of the issue of rent seeking by the elderly. The elderly are an ascriptive minority to which nearly everyone expects to belong: nearly everyone reaches a stage at which being old is the most desirable alternative available. Thus, in a system almost wholly free from ascriptive tendencies, provision for one's own old age is in the interest of everyone. Prior to social security, that provision

---

[6] The classic rationale for a nonfunded social security system is Paul Samuelson, "An Exact Consumption Loan Model of Interest with or without the Social Contrivance of Money," *Journal of Political Economy* 66 (December, 1958): 467–482.

was made through the family, through savings or private charity, or, as a last desperate alternative, through the county poorfarm. Nearly everywhere in the United States, public sentiment precluded any significant upgrading of the last. Private provision was simply too deeply entrenched as an ideological tenet to tolerate an attractive publicly provided alternative.

That ideological tenet had a decisive effect on the design of the social security system. In fact, it is probably the chief reason why social security was until very recently depicted as a kind of insurance program, and why the "contributions" (taxes) paid into the system still affect the level of benefits. Clearly, had it not been for that tradition of individually kept and separately budgeted tax and expenditure accounts in social security, there would be no "crisis" in the program today—at least, no visible crisis. Were benefits paid out of general tax revenues, it is certain that increased deficit financing and more rapid inflation would hide the imbalance. The maintenance of a pay-as-you-go system serves to publicize the extent of any excessive legislative generosity toward the old. In a time when the relative size of the elderly population is increasing, the current outlays needed to operate the pay-as-you-go system indicate the costs of promised future benefits, and although today's thirty-to-forty-year-olds are not being taxed an amount sufficient actuarially to defray the benefits they have been promised, they are being taxed an amount sufficient to make them wish they could abdicate those future benefits in exchange for tax relief. Thus, if social security's benefits were limited to income supplementation for the elderly, and if the program were kept on a balanced pay-as-you-go basis, there would be little danger that social security would lead to grotesque ascriptive misallocation.

However, optimism may be misplaced on confinement to income supplementation or maintenance of pay-as-you-go. As to the second, there is a more than remote possibility of general revenue funding for all of social security, including old age and survivors' insurance, which would make the elderly a formidable ascriptive force—they are numerous, easily identified, and easy to mobilize because the opportunity cost of their time is low. Insofar as confinement to income supplementation is concerned, a number of potential problems can be identified, not the least of which is the already crucial dependence of the health care industry on Medicare and Medicaid revenues. A number of other industries represented by powerful lobbies stand to lose significantly if they fail to find an adequate response to the foreseen changes in age distribution. The education industry is in a depression that will continue to deepen. The elderly are a group with abundant free time. Why not institute a federal program to send old folks to school? Local taxpayers would almost surely greet such an idea with derision, but a joint lobbying effort by the American Association of Retired Persons and the National Education Association in support of such a proposal would force congressmen to treat it seriously. The building industry will discover that demand has shifted away from suburban quarter-acre estates to locations closer to work, shopping, and entertainment; why not institute a program of interest-free loans to the elderly so they may rehabilitate urban housing? Lawyers, in respite from their current crushing load of divorce work, will doubtless seek to institute highly ramified tax laws governing inheritance, pensions, and gifts, which they will then be able to assist elderly clients in dealing with. The auto industry will endorse the value of governmentally supported jitney buses in every part of the nation, buses specially equipped to provide safety, convenience, and comfort to elderly passengers. Restaurants, theaters, airlines, and summer camps can argue vigorously for governmentally subsidized travel and recreation opportunities for the elderly. And so forth.

The most formidable lobby of all—the government bureaucracy—critically affects, and in turn is vitally affected by, the prospective success of rent seeking by the elderly. As the working-age population declines in relative size, job opportunities will improve greatly for groups that are currently highly active and visible in the political allocation process. Job opportunities in the private sector should also improve for government bureaucrats. Hence, the brokers of rent-seeking activity will face higher opportunity costs in their brokerage activity, and their current clientele will grow smaller, certainly in relative share of the population, and perhaps in absolute numbers. Thus, there are important forces working to diminish the large size and excess capacity of the rent-seeking brokerage industry.

It does not follow, however, that the brokers will care to see their influence diminished without a fight. Recent years have witnessed a rapid growth of government wages compared with wages paid for equivalent work in the private sector.[7] One explanation of that growth would hold that higher government wages were necessary to bid away the required talent out of private-sector employment. That explanation is hard to reconcile with the rapid surge in the numbers of new accessions to the labor force and the persistent stickiness of unemployment rates. An alternative explanation would hold that the growth in government employment was in part supply driven. Increases in the numbers of new workers created a demand for jobs, which were provided by government. With growth in the numbers of government employees came an increase in their political power, which they used to legislate that higher compensation in government employment while maintaining a strong demand for public employees.[8] That political power mechanism may be used to preserve government employment opportunities at high pay.

The future level of government employment will depend largely on the legislated response to the lobby for high relative wages in government employment and for continuing growth in government employment opportunities. If government employment were a market-determined process, we would expect, from both the currently visible anti-government-growth temperament and forecasts of increasing ease of access to employment in the private sector, that relative government wages will decline in the future. A decline in relative government wages will result in a smaller bureaucracy and a reduction of the rent-transferring and monopoly-franchising services provided by government employees.

But suppose, in contrast, that government employees manage, by the exercise of political power, to preserve their relative wage advantage. It then becomes crucial that groups on behalf of whom bureaucrats have traditionally operated (blacks, hispanics, native Americans, women) will find increased opportunity in the private sector. Idle hands of bureaucrats can be expected to try to fill their time by operating on behalf of the elderly.

But even if the size and vigor of the bureaucracy is preserved in

---

[7] Sharon Smith's work documents this fact, despite all protestations of the civil service bureaucracy that they seek only parity with the private sector. See her "Pay Differences between Federal Government and Private Sector Workers," *Industrial and Labor Relations Review* 29 (January, 1976): 179–197.

[8] For purposes of this discussion, government consultants and government employees are the same thing.

the face of superior private opportunity, it may prove politically difficult to make extensive transfers that benefit the elderly as a group. In
the past, two powerful supporting arguments often were made in cases
where proposals for transfer payment programs succeeded: it was
shown either that certain people could not find work because of general lack of opportunity, labor-market prejudice against particular
groups, or undeveloped skill, or that those who had work were growing increasingly wealthy. It probably will not be possible to mount the
first of those arguments on behalf of the elderly, and the second is
jeopardized by the recent leveling of real wages.

The first argument carries decreasing conviction because non-
labor productive resources, especially energy resources, are growing
considerably more expensive, indicating a demand shift toward labor.
Productivity per capita and real wages now are barely growing and in
some sectors are in decline. These tendencies could induce a reduction in rent seeking in general and among the elderly in particular. A
perception of unchanging real income blunts the type of equity argument that has underlain much of the past defense of transfer programs:
somehow it is easier to justify taking away from a relatively well-off
person whose income is growing than from one whose income is static.
Meantime, those same forces will make productive work more easily
available to persons over sixty-five. Wages probably will not grow
much, but they may well grow rapidly relative to the expected return
on rent seeking.

Following the world wars, market exchange virtually terminated
in the presence of a veteran: all manner of special dispensations and
exceptions were made for this group, in health care, housing, mort-
gage insurance, education, and employment. This group, in the late
1940's and early 1950's, may have numbered 11 million, or about 7.5
percent of the population. Because most of them were easily assimila-
ted into normal economic roles, their claims in most years appeared as
a modest tally against the national wealth, and (with no intent of as-
serting cost-effectiveness) we should note that many of their benefits
enhanced the productivity of the individual recipients. Similarly, the
numerous compensating and equalizing measures proposed and enacted on behalf of social and cultural minorities, although they have
affected a somewhat larger portion of the population (perhaps 15 percent) can be defended on the ground that they should enhance the

productivity of benefited individuals. Legislation on behalf of the aged, however, is a process of transfer pure and simple, which benefits and injures all recipients to about the same degree. By no stretch of imagination can such legislation claim to be recompense for past injuries suffered; neither does it contribute to the fund of productive skill within the society. Such transfer programs are classics from the pork barrel: of benefit to the bureaucrats who administer them and to the industries that supply them when they call for assistance in kind.

The pork-barreling dimension aside, I have here portrayed rent seeking by the elderly as an unambiguously negative-sum game. The interests of the intended beneficiaries are not served, and in a future world of labor scarcity the use of resources in lobbying for and administering such programs is wasteful. Two battles that will be fought over the next couple of decades will decide whether rent seeking by the elderly is to be an important social force. First is the battle to control the population of brokers for rent seeking employed in the bureaucracy. To win this battle, relative wages in government employment (including contract and grant consulting by "private" employees) must be cut. Second is the battle to stifle the activity of interested third parties who might like to become involved in providing benefits in kind for the elderly. This battle can be won only if the economically sound ideology of self-provision, which rejected social security as charity, can be strengthened and maintained as a political force.

APPENDIX TO CHAPTER 13

A word on the methods employed in forecasting population levels should be included. Beginning with the 1970 census, estimates for July, 1976, are prepared and checked by sampling methods. Projections into the future then are made, using the "inflation-deflation" variant of the "standard cohort component" method. This neat bit of jargon is explained by the U.S. Bureau of the Census:

> In the cohort-component method, the components of population change (births, deaths, and net immigration) are projected separately for each birth cohort (persons born in each year). The initial (base year) population is carried forward year by year using projected survival rates and projected net immigration by single year of age, sex, and race. Annual births are projected for each future year and are carried forward in the same manner as the cohorts born before the base year.

The inflation-deflation procedure starts with the latest census population adjusted for estimated net census undercount by age, sex, and race. This inflated population is carried forward to the base date (with data on births, deaths, and net migration) and on to future years using the cohort-component method. For each future year the projected population is deflated to reflect the percent of estimated net census undercount by age, sex, and race at the latest census. Finally, a small pro rata adjustment is made in the deflated figures by age, sex, and race to bring them into exact agreement with an independent estimate of the population in each sex-race group obtained by carrying forward the census population with information on subsequent births, deaths, and net immigration without regard to age. [U.S. Bureau of the Census, Current Population Reports, *Projections of the Population of the United States, 1977–2050*, No. 704, July 1977, p. 11.]

The two sets of projections reported in table 13.1 begin from the same base population, employ the same mortality assumptions, and assume a net immigration level of 400,000 per year. They differ in assumption about fertility rates: the series II projections assume a fertility rate of 2.1 lifetime births per woman, whereas the series I projections use a figure of 1.7. Both sets of projections make the same assumptions about childbearing age frequency, another factor that affects population growth.

14

Mercantilism as a Rent-Seeking Society

by

BARRY BAYSINGER, ROBERT B. EKELUND, JR.,

and ROBERT D. TOLLISON

> The proposal of any new law or regulation of commerce which comes from this order [merchants and manufacturers], ought never to be adopted till after having been long and carefully examined, not only with the most scrupulous, but with the most suspicious attention. It comes from an order of men, whose interest is never exactly the same with that of the public, who have generally an interest to deceive and even to oppress the public, and who accordingly have, upon many occasions, both deceived and oppressed it. —Adam Smith, *Wealth of Nations*

MERCANTILIST economic doctrines are typically summarized in terms of the central tendencies found in the literature of the period, roughly dated from 1500 to 1776. Among the most often-stressed tenets of the mercantilists are the equation of specie with wealth, regulation of the trade sector to produce specie inflow, and emphasis upon population growth and low wages. Absolutist historians of economic thought tend to stress the presence of grave errors in mercantilist logic, which were exposed by David Hume, Adam Smith, and the classical economists generally. The primary example of such faulty reasoning was, of course, the failure of the mercantilists to recognize the self-regulating nature that the "specie-flow mechanism" imposed on the mercantilist objective of a perennial trade surplus.[1] Relativist histo-

[1] Keynes defended the mercantilists on the grounds that a favorable balance of trade was the only feasible means available to a country at that time of lowering domestic

rians of thought tend to view the mercantilists more charitably. Writers in the German Historical School, such as Gustav Schmoller, and their English disciples argued that mercantilist policies were very rational for a period in which the attainment of state power was the overriding goal of the polity.

Methodological preferences aside, the major students of mercantilism seem to organize their interpretations of this period and its writers around a paradigm that stresses that certain regulatory implications follow from a balance-of-trade and specie-accumulation objective.[2] Adam Smith, perhaps the keenest student of the mercantilists, suggests a different view. He argues (in Mark Blaug's words) that "mercantilism is nothing but a tissue of protectionist fallacies foisted upon a venal Parliament by 'our merchants and manufacturers,' grounded upon 'the popular notion that wealth consists in money.'"[3] In this view causation is reversed in the mercantilist paradigm, that is, the balance-of-trade objective is seen as flowing from the effective demand for regulatory rents by domestic economic agents.

We will develop such an interpretation of mercantilism in this paper.[4] In doing so, we will concentrate on the gains to economic agents in using the state for profits, and we will use concepts from modern developments in the theory of the rent-seeking society to explain mer-

---

interest rates and increasing home investment and employment. See J. M. Keynes, *General Theory of Employment, Interest and Money* (New York: Harcourt, Brace and World, Inc., 1936), chapter 15. Heckscher argued in rebuttal that unemployment in mercantilist times was essentially voluntary and not sensitive to changes in aggregate demand. See Eli Heckscher, *Mercantilism*, trans. Mendel Shapiro, 2 vols. (London: George Allen and Unwin Ltd., 1934).

[2] The two great writers on mercantilism were, of course, Heckscher, *Mercantilism*, and Jacob Viner, *Studies in the Theory of International Trade* (New York: Augustus M. Kelley, Publishers, 1967; first published, 1937).

[3] Mark Blaug, *Economic Theory in Retrospect* (Homewood, Ill.: Richard D. Irwin, Inc., 1968), p. 11.

[4] In other work on the general topic of mercantilism, two of the present authors have (1) expanded the theory of the emergence of the modern corporation (R. B. Ekelund and R. D. Tollison, "Mercantilist Origins of the Corporation," *Bell Journal of Economics* (forthcoming); (2) developed a cartel interpretation of mercantile French business organization (Ekelund and Tollison, "A Cartel Theory of French Mercantilism," unpublished manuscript, 1979); and (3) analyzed the role of the justices of the peace and the mercantile judiciary in the domestic regulation of mercantile England (Ekelund and Tollison, "Economic Regulation in Mercantile England: Heckscher Revisited," *Economic Inquiry*, forthcoming).

cantilist doctrine and policy.[5] Methodologically, we will not evaluate mercantilist economics from the standpoint of modern economic theory (à la Keynes); we will simply try to explain the doctrines of the mercantilists in terms of the larger rent-seeking society in which they lived. In other words, we are engaging in an exercise in positive economics, not arguing that the mercantilists were good economists from the standpoint of modern economic theory.

The model developed in this paper explains the rise and fall of mercantilism in the positive terms of costs and benefits accruing to the participants in the often deadly game of mercantile rent seeking. Merchants, monarch, and the public (as represented by democratic institutions, legislative and judicial) are featured as self-interested protagonists in institutional change. Focusing upon specific examples of rent seeking in England and France, as well as upon the comparative institutional frameworks in these countries, we seek to explain with our theory (1) why mercantilism declined in England at the same time it was being strengthened in France, and (2) how an analysis of self-interested forces reacting to shifting costs and benefits to rent seeking presents a more satisfying explanation of mercantilism than the well-known alternatives.

With respect to the latter point, there appear to be two wholly consistent views of mercantilism in the literature. The first view, espoused and promulgated to a large extent by the historians (with modified and improved versions by Jacob Viner and Eli Heckscher), emphasizes mercantilism as a concerted policy of nationalism or state-building, stressing an exogenously determined economic policy divorced from the endogenous interplay of self-interested forces. Thus, a policy of taxing the import and subsidizing the export of "finished" goods is seen as a method of state-building or of accumulating specie or promoting domestic employment, rather than as the simple product of rent maximization by parties to the resulting income distribution. "Mercantile policy," in this view, achieved a life of its own, and

---

[5] In particular, we refer to the work of George J. Stigler, "The Theory of Economic Regulation," *Bell Journal of Economics and Management Science* 2 (Spring, 1971): 3–21; Gordon Tullock, "The Welfare Costs of Tariffs, Monopolies, and Theft," chapter 3 in this volume; Anne O. Krueger, "The Political Economy of the Rent-Seeking Society," chapter 4 in this volume; and Richard A. Posner, "The Social Costs of Monopoly and Regulation," chapter 5 in this volume.

the underlying forces that produced it (which, to us, is the important matter) remain unexplored and, worse, unexplained.

A second tactic of historians of thought in dealing with the mercantile era, which does not compete with the first view, has been to argue, at least implicitly, that the achievement of laissez-faire was the product of the subjective philosophical forces of the times. Here, we encounter "anticipatory" works on individualism and the natural ordering of economic phenomena, ranging from the writings of John Hales, John Locke, William Petty, and Richard Cantillon through those of Bernard Mandeville, David Hume, and the Physiocrats. Indeed, most common references imply that the intellectual case for free trade (Adam Smith, David Ricardo, and earlier writers) made such an impression on legislators that they quickly transformed the policy proposals of these authors into practice.

Although the latter of these positions may possess merit as an auxillary, supporting explanation of the mercantile era, the former in our view obfuscates an understanding of the period, and, especially, of its tortuous evolution to laissez-faire. Although neither position is inconsistent with our own, we reject both these interpretations of mercantilism and of the movement to a free economy in England as a primary explanation for the emergence of liberalism. They are simply incomplete. Rather, we seek explanations in terms of institutional changes (e.g., the growth of the rule of law), which altered the costs and benefits of regulation to rent seekers. The emergence of a modern theory of rent seeking greatly facilitates such a re-evaluation.

We begin in the next section by presenting a model of the use of the state for profit in the mercantilist era. We stress the importance of institutional developments to the relative profitability of rent seeking in these times. In particular, our model stresses the role of an unfettered monarchy as an almost perfect setting for the creation of regulatory rents and state interference in the mercantile economy. Additionally, the rise of representative democracy and the consequent struggle over the power to supply legislation may be viewed as the primary reasons for a fall in relative rates of return to political investments (e.g., lobbying) under mercantilism and for the demise of mercantilism and the rise of a free economy in England.[6] In the subse-

---

[6] On the latter point see the hint of a suggestion by Friedrich A. Hayek, *The Constitution of Liberty* (Chicago: University of Chicago Press, 1960), p. 163.

quent three sections, we apply our model to the mercantile economies of England and France. Our purpose in these sections is to show how well the rent-seeking model elucidates the doctrines and policies of these economies relative to the paradigm of mercantilism as a confused collection of ideas centered around the concept of specie accumulation. We also seek to show how our model is useful in interpreting differences in English and French mercantilism. Some concluding remarks are offered in a final section.

Rent Seeking in the Mercantile Economy

The central purpose of our model will be to explain the record of the mercantile era as individual rent-seeking behavior in a variety of institutional settings. Our positive model seeks to explain the development of the mercantile state and its evolution into modified laissez-faire, as the result of consistent individual behavior under slowly changing institutional constraints. The blend of methodological individualism and slowly changing institutional constraints is central to our main thesis concerning the rise and fall of mercantilism. If we define the mercantilist era as a collection of economic phenomena, then we may explain these phenomena using the standard theory of choice, without recourse to historical or dialectical explanation. Given the standard (timeless) assumptions of individual choice theory, the model of rent seeking simplifies into a specification of the constraints that modify economic behavior. Once the model is developed, we may turn to the historical record and seek the institutional features that served as constraints to explain observed phenomena.

THE RISE OF MERCANTILISM

We assume for purposes of initial exposition that monopolies are created by the rent-seeking activities of individuals, rather than spontaneously appearing or being independently created by governmental authorities. At some point, emergent competition is the rule in the production of goods and services, and there exists a state or government with authority to order society as it chooses within the limits of feasible production possibilities (which include enforcement costs). In this context we imagine individuals who see potential gains accruing from the sole rights to produce particular goods and services. These

FIGURE 14.1

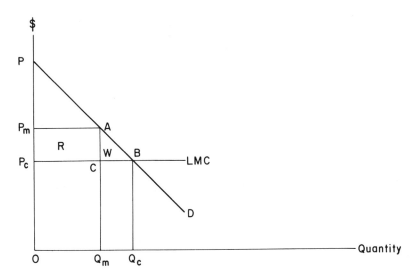

individuals will attempt to subvert the forces of the market and to monopolize the production of goods and services by having the state limit
production to themselves by fiat. The process may be simply illustrated by figure 14.1.

It is clear that the entire triangle, P_cPB, is a measure of surplus in
the case of competitive organization, a surplus to which no one has a
property right. It exists because of technological conditions that preclude producers from perfect price discrimination. The entire area be-
longs to no one, yet consumers and producers can both attempt to
claim it. This situation is further illustrated in figure 14.2.

From the point of view of the contenders for the surplus, the
problem is not one of efficiency. Monopolists seek to achieve a position
on the contract curve close to P_m, and consumer forces to seek a position toward P_c. There is nothing in the theory of choice that assigns
preference to either position; both are on the contract locus.[7] Thus,
the issue of dynamic monopoly creation is (net of the welfare triangle)
a matter of bilateral monopoly.

It stands to reason that in such matters the two parties will retain

    [7] Figure 14.2 adjusts for the monopoly welfare loss involved if the market solution
is P_m.

FIGURE 14.2

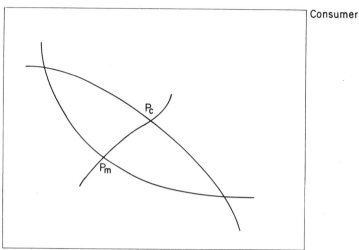

Consumer

Monopolist

brokers (lobbyist-lawyers) to assure a favorable outcome, and each will devote resources equal to an epsilon below the potential gains in their efforts. That producers are better able to effect the P_m solution is well known but is no more undesirable (net of the welfare triangle) than the technological constraints precluding perfect price discrimination. The social waste of monopoly thus involves the traditional welfare triangle, which measures both the portion of consumers' surplus that is lost to society because some individuals refrain from purchasing the monopolized output at higher prices (area W in figure 14.1) and also the use of lobbyist-lawyer resources to effect a pure transfer (area R in figure 14.1).[8]

If an incipient monopolist is successful in his dealings with government, he will be able to impose the classic monopoly solution of P_mQ_m in figure 14.1, receiving a return on his rent-seeking investment of P_mACP_c. With the gain in rents so depicted, we expect several other features of the rent-seeking society to be present. There is no reason to believe that only one individual will discover the gains from seeking

[8] On the static welfare loss from monopoly, see Arnold C. Harberger, "Monopoly and Resource Allocation," *American Economic Review* 44 (May, 1954): 77–87. For the original statement of the rent-seeking welfare loss from monopoly, see Tullock, "The Welfare Costs of Tariffs, Monopolies, and Theft."

monopoly rights sponsored by the state. We thus expect numerous rent seekers to compete for these rights, and that in the long run this competition will dissipate the returns from using the state as a source of profit.[9] Also, as the above discussion intimates, we expect those who stand to lose from the monopolization of an activity to have an interest in preventing such losses. Consumers stand to lose P_mACP_c, the rent gained by the successful monopolist, plus the deadweight welfare loss, ABC. In a costless world consumers would invest resources to retain this surplus, but we will abstract from such behavior here, because of the well-known transaction costs in organizing consumer efforts to resist government action in raising prices.[10]

But what about the remaining party in the rent-seeking society, that is, the state authority holding the power to grant monopoly rights? The interest of the rent seekers is clear, but what are the interests of the supplier of monopoly rights? One may conceive of a range of possibilities. At one extreme we may picture the state as a unified, revenue-seeking leviathan, where fiscal needs (defense, court expenses, and so forth) prompt the sale of protective legislation. For example, to "the mercantilist politician, the state was more or less the leviathan, absolute and all powerful."[11] In the rent-seeking society this case corresponds to an absolute monarchy. Entry into the business of granting monopoly rights is completely limited in this case because—in the extreme case at least—the monarch rules by divine right, the supply of which is very inelastic. This type of institutional arrangement tilts the bargaining power in the market for monopoly strongly in favor of the crown. If enforceable monopoly rights cannot be bought elsewhere in the dominion, the king should be able to price-discriminate effectively in the award of such rights. Most of the consumer surplus in figure 14.1 will end up in the king's coffers under these circumstances.

As we will develop more fully in the next two sections, revenue seeking was an important aspect of European history in the early mercantilist era. For example, one historian of the period characterizes

---

[9] See Posner, "The Social Costs of Monopoly and Regulation," for this argument.

[10] On this point see especially James M. Buchanan and Gordon Tullock, "The 'Dead Hand' of Monopoly," *Antitrust Law and Economics Review* 1 (Summer, 1968): 85–96.

[11] C. H. Heaton, "Heckscher on Mercantilism," *Journal of Political Economy* 45 (June, 1937): 392.

mercantilism "as a negative and restrictive factor, which had its principal source, not in any deliberate plan of promoting economic progress, but in the fiscal exigencies of short-sighted and inpecunious government."[12] C. H. Heaton, reflecting on this appraisal, concurs, adding that "rarely in framing government policy did a government have the deplorable condition of the exchequer far out of mind, and every 'projector' who presented a scheme to his ruler stressed the benefit that would directly or indirectly flow into the royal coffers."[13] Further evidence comes from Heckscher: " . . . one of the most important features of economic policy if not the most important of all [was] what is called in French *fiscalisme*. . . . The state, by its intervention, wanted to create large sources of revenue for itself. . . . The state exploited for its own ends the monopolistic advantages which the guilds had secured for their members or the owners of private producers had received for themselves."[14]

In general, then, we may analyze the situation faced by the monarchical state authority and potential rent seekers in the context of an Edgeworth-box diagram. Given royal prerogative, consumer interests are effectively left out of consideration. Hence, under competitive organization, with the crown at one corner of an Edgeworth box and "projectors" at the other, the solution is off the contract curve, and each party stands to gain from cooperation. The remaining issue is merely the location of the solution on the contract curve. With a unified state authority the ease with which mutual interests were recognized and realized was relatively great.

In sum, we posit that the pursuit of special favor by individuals was the driving force behind the rent-seeking activities that flourished during the mercantile era. "The incentive rarely came from a whole class, for a class was too unwieldy, too class-unconscious, and too much torn by conflicting factors or interests to have one will or voice. Action came from individuals or compact groups who saw an opportunity to profit by protection or promotion."[15] The ascension of mercantilism in the early part of the era is readily explained by the institutional setting

[12] R. H. Tawney (ed.), *Studies in Economic History: The Collected Papers of George Unwin* (London: Royal Economic Society Reprint, 1958), p. lxiv.

[13] Heaton, "Heckscher on Mercantilism," pp. 375–376.

[14] Heckscher, *Mercantilism*, I, 178.

[15] Heaton, "Heckscher on Mercantilism," p. 387.

facing the participants in the process of monopolization. Since the transaction costs required for seeking rents were low with a unified state authority (the monarch), the flowering of mercantilism during this period is explained. That is, since the cost of seeking monopolies was relatively low under absolute monarchy, other things equal, we expect to observe relatively more of this activity in this institutional milieu.

THE DECLINE OF MERCANTILISM

At the other extreme from the rent-seeking leviathan was the rise of representative democracy. This historical development in England was embodied in a struggle over the power to supply legislation in a rent-seeking context. This struggle ultimately led to the demise of English mercantilism because of the profound changes that took place in the institutional environment. Under the assumption that self-interest is independent of time, the source of the fall of mercantilism must be found in the changing cost-benefit structure facing potential rent seekers. We have thus far suggested that mercantilism arose because the relative costs of negotiating favored treatment with a state in which authority was vested in a central figure were low. Prior to the centralization of authority, rent seekers had to deal with a multitude of feudal rulers, which made the costs of negotiating and enforcing exclusive rights relatively higher. The correlated rise of mercantilism and central monarchies was thus the result of changed cost conditions, and the fall of widespread mercantile activity in England may be explained as a manifestation of changes in the bargaining environment, which occurred as the result of political upheaval.

In seeking an explanation for the decline of English mercantilist policies within the rent-seeking paradigm, we follow Friedrich Hayek when he notes that "it was finally in the dispute about the authority to legislate in which the contending parties reproached each other for acting arbitrarily—acting, that is, not in accordance with recognized general laws—that the cause of individual freedom was inadvertently advanced."[16] Throughout his discussion of the emergence of the rule of law in England, Hayek stresses that economic freedom came about as a by-product of a struggle for the power to supply legislation. In this

---

[16] Hayek, *The Constitution of Liberty*, p. 163.

struggle several important institutional changes occurred, which dramatically affected relative rates of return on rent-seeking investments. We seek to explain the deregulation of mercantile society in terms of these changes.

As the power of the monarchy in England declined, the movement toward representative democracy shifted the locus of rent-seeking activity to new forums, primarily the legislature and the judiciary, with predictable implications for the decline of the rent-seeking society of mercantilism. For example, the costs of lobbying a representative body are higher than the costs of lobbying a unified monarchy for monopoly charters because there are many decision makers rather than one. The rational rent seeker will reduce his bid for a monopoly right when lobbying costs rise. Moreover, the uncertainty costs facing the rent seeker will rise under representative government. Logrolling in the legislature will mask current votes to some extent, making current legislative outcomes more uncertain. There will be turnover among politicians and uncertainty about the durability of legislation from session to session of the legislature.[17] For these and other reasons, the costs of lobbying to rent seekers will rise under representative democracy, and we would therefore expect to see a decline of government interference in the economy because of these higher costs.

With respect to the mercantile judiciary in England, there was an important jurisdictional competition between the common law courts and those supporting the king's interests. The common law courts evolved a doctrine that held that royal monopoly and prerogative were illegal, whereas the special interests sanctioned by Parliament were legitimate. The king's courts obviously disagreed with this doctrine. The net result was a legal conflict in which one court system would rule that a monopoly right was valild and the other that it was invalid. There was, in effect, no legal basis for a completely valid monopoly right under these conditions. So, even if a rent seeker could obtain a monopoly grant from the king or Parliament, he had no guarantee that it could be sustained against interlopers. Seeking monopoly through the shelter of the state was clearly going to be a less profitable activity under these circumstances.

[17] For further discussion of the durability of special-interest legislation, see William M. Landes and Richard A. Posner, "The Independent Judiciary in an Interest-Group Perspective," *Journal of Law and Economics* 18 (December, 1975): 875–901.

As we shall outline in the next sections, a great struggle evolved in England between the king and Parliament and between the king's courts and the common law courts allied to parliamentary interests. This struggle, which had important religious and political bases, was also a struggle over who was to run and to profit from the rent-seeking economy of English mercantilism. This conflict over authority to legislate and to adjudicate legal disputes meant that the costs of seeking monopoly protection from the state ultimately exceeded the potential benefits for rent seekers, and state interference in the economy consequently declined.[18]

SUMMARY

Our argument here is that the theory of the rent-seeking society is a more useful paradigm for explaining the rise and fall of mercantilism than the usual specie-accumulation interpretation. The rent-seeking paradigm rationalizes the emergence of the social order of mercantilism and its demise in terms of individual behavior in the face of varying institutional arrangements, rather than in terms of such arguments as that mercantilism was a highly irrational social order.

Mercantilism as a Rent-Seeking Society: Some Historical Evidence

Although historians of economic thought are wont to label the period 1500 to 1776 as (roughly) the "mercantile period," this convenient generalization fails when one considers rent seeking as a primary feature of the mercantile economy. The battle for property rights (i.e., the right to rent seek) arose in an environment where industrial and constitutional interests were emerging in the context of ongoing monarchies. This process, though historically complex, is clearly discernible, under vastly different institutional structures, in England, France, the Netherlands, and Spain between the thirteenth and eighteenth centuries.

It is instructive to contrast some of the central features of the institutional structures of England and France vis-à-vis the fisc in those

---

[18] See Ekelund and Tollison, "Economic Regulation in Mercantile England: Heckscher Revisited," for a more detailed discussion of the role of legislative and judicial conflict in explaining the demise of English mercantilism.

countries before proceeding to some historical evidence that illustrates our theory of the rise and fall of mercantilism. In the first place, French and English monarchs differed greatly in their power to tax over this long period, and the "mercantile" systems of venality, which the power to tax (or lack thereof) created, were accordingly vastly different. The "French system" was absolutist in the sense that, from the time of Charles VII and the Ordinance of 1439 the Estates General gave the king the absolute power to tax without popular consent, a power that molded the form of rent-seeking in French society for over three hundred years.

In contrast, there were early consensual constraints on the English monarch's ability to tax. (England's Parliament was already well established when France's first Estates General met in 1302.)[19] These elements of parliamentary consent were not absolute until the revolutionary period of the mid-seventeenth century, largely engendered by conflict between monarch and the House of Commons over authority to collect rents to support armed struggles. As noted previously, costs and benefits of regulation were changing over this period (late sixteenth and early seventeenth centuries), and these changes led to the fall of a predominantly rent-seeking society in England.

MERCANTILE MONARCHY IN ENGLAND

The process of rent seeking described in the last section of this paper was a prominent feature of English government for centuries before 1649 and the execution of Charles I. The conduct of the wool trade in fourteenth-century England provides a very clear example of this process, which, during the reign of the three Edwards, precipitated constitutional crisis, presaging those of the seventeenth century. The first crisis was over the taxation of wool.

The wool trade of medieval England included a large number of competitively organized wool producers, a smaller number of large-scale producers (mostly monasteries), and an even smaller number of wool exporters. An export monopoly was fostered by the combined

---

[19] Martin Wolfe, *The Fiscal System of Renaissance France* (New Haven: Yale University Press, 1972), pp. 10, 33. For an interesting examination of fiscal policy and alterations in population and property rights as causal factors in the emergence of efficient economic organization, see Douglass C. North and Robert P. Thomas, *The Rise of the Western World* (Cambridge: Cambridge University Press, 1973). Our analysis of mercantilism is broadly in the spirit of their investigation.

rent-seeking interests of large merchants and exporters in bilateral negotiation with the king. The mechanism through which these activities took place was an "assembly of merchants" called by the king as
early as the late thirteenth century for the purpose of advice and consent on the matter of export and other taxation, especially on wool.
This body, which rivaled Parliament in its functions, was willing to
consent to taxation, given that monopoly and other privileges could be
exacted from the crown.[20] In short, merchants would accept the costs
of taxation and regulation so long as the benefits conferred by regulation exceeded these costs.

The ability of merchants to shift the incidence of the wool tax,
both backward to wool growers, large and small, and forward to foreign consumers (depending, of course, upon elasticity of demand),
forced a polarization of parliamentary interests, which came to recognize the deleterious effects of higher wool prices. This interest group
was composed of lay and ecclesiastical magnates (the large wool producers) and the knights of the shire, who represented more than a million small freeholders in Commons. Parliament's fight for the abolition
of the tax was thus premised upon their objection to the income-
reducing effects of the regulation of the wool market by the king (Edward I) and the wool merchants. Significant constitutional crises,
which occurred in the 1290's and 1330's, resulted principally because
of realigned and eventually shared interests between Parliament and
the merchants. The costs of monarchial regulation (taxes) exceeded
the benefits (entry-restricted monopoly) only so long as the king did
not impose *new* taxes on the wool merchants. When this did in fact
occur, owing to war and other pressures on the English fisc, wool merchants clearly recognized that the bilateral form of rent seeking was
one-sided and unprofitable. Merchant voices thus joined those of Parliament calling for *abolition* of the tax.[21]

[20] Eileen Power, *The Wool Trade in English Medieval History* (London: Oxford
University Press, 1941), p. 71.

[21] The alienation of merchants was furthered when the king shifted his favor to a
group of "rogue financiers," less than thirty in number, who advanced money to the
crown on wool granted to him. Power notes that the "king was . . . compelled to impose
an embargo on general export for a time (sometimes a whole year) in order to enable his
financiers to dispose of the wool on his behalf. And every time this happened a virtual
monopoly of a financial group was established" (ibid., p. 83). The result was the dissolution of the larger group of merchant exporters, with those "shut out" becoming disposed
(in their self-interest) to urge Parliament to impose constraints on the king.

Though Parliament was unsuccessful in abolishing the periodically imposed ("extraordinary") wool tax ("maltote"), the increased demand of the sovereign for funds at the outbreak of the Hundred Years War (1336) was met by a tax, but with domestic price controls on wool as quid pro quo.[22] In 1350 Parliament finally gave up on the issue of abolishing the tax, but got control over it and converted it into a parliamentary subsidy for specified time periods. A quasi-monopoly of the wool trade (the English Company of the Staple) remained, and as Power reports, " . . . it is by virtue of this monopoly alone that they were able to shoulder the subsidy," the latter contingent on the will and consent of Parliament.[23]

A MERCANTILE PATTERN OF RENT SEEKING

The pattern and effects of mercantile monarchy, as developed in our theory of rent seeking, may be seen in the early history of the medieval wool trade. Again and again in the mercantile period—most significantly in the sixteenth and seventeenth centuries—Parliament was strengthened to limit and oppose the crown's ability to regulate. In England the rent-seeking proclivities of the crown were strengthened by a legislative constraint on its possible revenues. Extraordinary expenditures, which arose with ever-increasing frequency in order to conduct wars, meant that English monarchs were always in need of funds. (The French crown was often in similar need, but it did not face the same constraints, as we shall see in a later section.) The crown's reaction to this situation was initially to offer special favors, monopoly-entry control, to growing national industries (large exporters were often fewer in number, organized with lower transactions costs, and more easily controlled), who, in return, submitted to taxation.

Reactions to this state of affairs were twofold, and both eventually brought about the decline of monarchial rent seeking and an increase in costs to legislative supply of regulation. First, Parliament, which represented "society's" and, ultimately, merchants' interests, grew restive at the rent-seeking franchises of the king. As the mercantile period wore on, this restiveness became more pronounced. Second, and more important perhaps, the absolutism of the English monarchy

---

[22] At this point the wool merchants were still sanguine about the export monopoly franchise, since the prospect of passing the tax forward still existed (ibid., p. 81).

[23] Ibid., p. 85.

was more and more eroded with the aid and action of the merchant classes themselves. Great uncertainty crept in as merchants grew wary of the net benefits of a regulatory alliance with the king. Specifically, this uncertainty of benefits drove merchants to support parliamentary interests, which reduced the powers of the monarch in economic as well as in legal and religious matters. Thus, the caprice of monarchial power, which led to uncertainty among merchants, landowners, and freeholders, resulted in the emergent constitutional solution of the late sixteenth and seventeenth centuries.

THE DECLINE OF ENGLISH MERCANTILISM

We must now amplify and further illustrate the pattern of rent-seeking discerned in the medieval wool trade and described by our theory. Here, we focus upon a "high period of mercantile monarchy," followed by its fall in 1640 or so. Roughly, our treatment extends from the reign of Elizabeth I (the last Tudor monarch) through those of James I and Charles I (the first two Stuarts).

The constraints on regulatory supply and demand between the death of Henry VIII (1547) and the execution of Charles I (1649) were in kind very much like those of the earlier period. The monarch still required the consent of the taxed in order to obtain revenue. He still depended, in other words, upon the good will and self-interest of the wealthy gentry and landowners in order to function, especially when he had to meet "extraordinary" expenses. Over this period the three major checks upon the crown's power and rent-seeking activities were (1) private local interests composed of increasingly wealthy city merchants and magistrates, (2) the common law courts, and (3) the House of Commons. The latter two institutions were increasingly representative of and peopled by the wealthy merchants from whom the king wished to extract rents.[24]

[24] Here, we must emphasize that we are not trying to explain the decline of rent seeking solely in terms of the rise of constitutional democracy, though we argue that it is a major causal factor in explaining mercantile policies. Technological growth and an emergent factory system, a familiar *deus ex machina*, may have (for example) fostered powerful interests (such as wool buyers or household producers), which arose to compete with the large wool producers and exporters for rents in Parliament, thereby dissipating them. North and Thomas, *The Rise of the Western World*, emphasize still other changes as the grounds for economic development and the emergence of property rights. While their arguments concern somewhat more fundamental causal features of development, they do not emphasize, as we do, the role of rent seeking in the decline of mercantilism.

The actual means of rent seeking and the king's ability to enforce it were likewise in transition, being eroded by self-interested forces and developments in constitutional law. Basically the crown had to depend upon three means of imposing industrial regulation: (1) enactment of regulation by statutes of Parliament, (2) royal proclamations and letters patent, and (3) orders of privy council or decrees instituted by privy council sitting in Star Chamber (the king's court). Developments of the period 1547–1640 led to the utter supremacy of Parliament in imposing regulation. The concept of the "crown in council" as ultimate authority—the great Tudor contribution to administrative government—was also swept away by the events of these years, though the "council" form of executive administration survives and, indeed, is enshrined in the forms of most contemporary representative governments.[25] During this period, self-interested forces successfully opposed every attempt of the crown to impose and enforce industrial regulation. We now turn to a few examples of these forces.

EXAMPLES, 1563–1597

The reign of Elizabeth I (1558–1603) is regarded by many as the high time of successful mercantile policy. Historical facts do not appear to justify this view, however. To echo a modern directive, regulation should be judged not on the basis of its aims or intent, but on grounds of its effects.[26] In fact, Elizabeth opened her reign with a great deal of patent granting and lusty rent seeking from industry, but closed it by meekly admitting that patent monopoly was a dangerous innovation contrary to common law.

In common with successful French systems of regulation, the English monarch would have liked to have controlled industry locally through the guild system and crown representatives like local magistrates, justices of the peace, and their subordinates. Much regulation to this end was imposed during the reign of Elizabeth. In 1563 a Statute of Artificers was passed commanding craftsmen to serve a seven-year apprenticeship and regulating wages in all occupations

[25] Bureaucratic reforms in Tudor administration are treated exhaustively in G. R. Elton, *The Tudor Revolution in Government: Administrative Changes in the Reign of Henry VIII* (Cambridge: Cambridge University Press, 1966).

[26] The growing literature of the "effects and effectiveness" of regulation dates to George Stigler and Claire Friedland, "What Can Regulators Regulate? The Case of Electricity," *Journal of Law and Economics* 5 (October, 1962): 1–23.

then existing.[27] In 1596–1597, by an act of the privy council, Elizabeth attempted to fix the prices of grain, bread, ale, beer, and malt, and, for a time, those of building materials, bricks, and the wholesale price of coal. The crown's response to new and growing industries, such as tobacco pipe makers, gun makers, and spectacle makers, and to the nascent manufacturing towns they supported, was to incorporate these industries (an attempt to bring them under the umbrella of guild regulation) and to enact statutes aimed at keeping industry from moving from old towns to the country, where many regulations did not apply.

THE LOCAL REACTION TO REGULATION

Such regulations yielded Elizabeth very meager results, except to implant in the minds of most of those she attempted to regulate the notion that self-interest and progress demanded nonregulation. Reasons for the failure to impose price and wage controls could not be more clear. It was a question of unpaid enforcers (local justices of the peace), or highly self-interested magistrates (industrial merchants harmed by regulations) attempting to enforce a system of regulation that injured the influential majority of those it affected. The opportunity cost structure for regulatory enforcement was changing drastically. As John U. Nef has noted, "During the eighty-five years which followed the accession of Elizabeth and culminated in the civil war, the privy council was not able to strengthen the royal authority for enforcing industrial legislation by introducing new, disinterested officials into the local administration to help the justices of the peace in performing the increasingly heavy duties imposed on them by the new enactments."[28] Heckscher goes even further on the matter, noting that "neither before nor after 1688 was there in England a paid *ad hoc* bureaucracy to supervise the enforcement of industrial legislation which Colbert had been at pains to create in France."[29]

As mentioned above, the statutes regulating wages applied only

---

[27] See the discussion of the statute in Heckscher, *Mercantilism*, I, 227 ff.

[28] John U. Nef, *Industry and Government in France and England, 1540–1640* (Ithaca: Cornell University Press, 1957; first published, 1940), p. 36. We question the extent to which local officials were disinterested (see Ekelund and Tollison, "Economic Regulation in Mercantile England: Heckscher Revisited").

[29] Heckscher, *Mercantilism*, I, 263. Professor Hartwell has recently amplified Heckscher's point, contrasting his view to the character of nineteenth-century administration. See R. Max Hartwell, "Capitalism and the Historians," in *Essays on Hayek*,

to existing industries. It takes little imagination to predict what happened, given this loophole in the law. Large numbers of new industries forming between 1575 and 1620 were simply exempt from the laws. Other industries such as textiles, which were undergoing a transition to large-scale manufacturing, simply evaded the laws altogether by moving to the countryside (where the laws did not apply), by importing cheap unskilled labor from the country, or by "letting" or "putting out" the finishing of textiles to large numbers of workmen in their homes. Outright disobedience of the law was facilitated by self-interested local magistrates and justices of the peace and by decisions of the common law courts limiting the applicability of local regulations over industry.[30]

MONOPOLY REGULATION

Apart from the attempt to impose local industrial regulation, which was virtually swept away by parliamentary acts of 1575–1576 and 1623–1624, there was no dearth of attempts by industrial rent seekers and crown to institute monopolies over specific branches of trade. But in these cases, the self-interest of those left out (potential competitors) and eventually of those protected—together with the common law judges and a House of Commons pliant to the wishes of merchant-capitalists—combined to overthrow and render ineffective monopolies created by patents, royal decree, or proclamation of the crown's privy council. Examples are numerous, and here we might note the attempted monopolization of the saltpeter, gunpowder, salt, and paper industries and the attempt of the queen to tax mines and mineral extraction, most of which failed to provide any rents to the crown.[31]

On familiar grounds of national defense, Elizabeth claimed exclu-

---

ed. Fritz Machlup (New York: New York University Press, 1976), p. 84. Hartwell's interpretation of Heckscher is certainly correct with respect to England and perhaps the Netherlands, but this was not the case in France and Spain, as we shall see. Moreover, Hartwell does not provide a cogent explanation for the *origins* of bureaucratic control in nineteenth-century administration.

[30] The classic judicial decisions of Sir Edward Coke in the Tolley case and others were of singular importance in bringing about legal limits on crown regulation. See D. O. Wagner, "Coke and the Rise of Economic Liberalism," *Economic History Review* 6 (March, 1935): 30–44.

[31] See Nef, *Industry and Government in France and England*, pp. 88–112.

sive rights to the manufacture of saltpeter and gunpowder. A monopoly was granted to George and John Evlyn. The Evlyn family enjoyed the rent splitting for almost fifty years (until 1635).[32] But steady opposition from both merchants and the common law courts (dating from the initial award) finally brought the monopoly restrictions down. Subsequently, the manufacture of both saltpeter and gunpowder became the object of open competition. Principal opposition came from the merchants and "from the increasing number of town traders and landed gentlemen with money to invest in the new industries, the same persons who were becoming lax about complying with royal industrial legislation. They objected to all industrial monopolies as trenching upon the liberty and the property of the subject, whose rights, they claimed, were guaranteed by the fundamental law of the country."[33]

Other examples may be cited. The rights to the royalties from ores other than gold and silver were removed from the crown in a court decision of 1566, which limited regalian rights to gold and silver only (none in England). Officials charged with dealing with mining leases *on royal lands* were not above the lure of self-interest, moreover. Thus Professor Nef notes, "Even in royal manors and forests, where the king or queen like any other landlord owned the minerals and appointed special officials to deal with their mining lessees, these officials, like the justices of the peace and the sheriffs, were always local men who were frequently more mindful of the wishes of their rich neighbors with investments in the mines than of the interests of their royal masters."[34]

Elizabeth tried to imitate the French king's successful and lucrative salt tax (the *gabelle*), but these efforts were also doomed. In 1564 Elizabeth attempted to establish a patent monopoly in salt, but the patentees gave up after five years, leaving huge salt pans rusting on the

---

[32] Though Elizabeth claimed regalian rights on grounds of national defense, she stood to gain monetarily by the conditions of the rent-split. All unused gunpowder could be sold by her at a profit to both domestic and foreign consumers. Since by law she claimed *all* Evlyn's output, a time of peace meant pure profit to Elizabeth.

[33] Nef, *Industry and Government in France and England*, p. 92. An issue of "illegal search and seizure" was also involved here, since the collection of saltpeter required entry to henhouses and barnyards across England.

[34] Ibid., p. 101.

English coast. At this point private capitalists, without franchise, entered the industry and profitably produced and marketed salt over the next three decades in spite of repeated attempts by the crown to reestablish monopoly rights.

Yet another example of the futile attempt of Elizabeth's councillors to grant monopolies to court favorites was the paper monopoly, originally granted to one John Spilman in 1588. Spilman claimed to have a new process for producing white paper. Although patents issued to protect a new process or invention were ordinarily unopposed by Commons and the common law courts, they were often extended, enabling patentees to "engulf" closely related products. Such was the case with Spilman, who in 1597 was granted a monopoly over *all kinds* of paper. The monopoly privileges were not enforceable, however, and within six years Spilman had to rest content with "such a share of the expanding market for paper as the efficiency of his machinery, the skill of his workmen, and the situation of his mills enabled him to command."[35] Elizabeth's luckless adventures into the creation of monopolies ended in 1603 (the year of her death), when she personally declared, with respect to proposed monopoly on playing cards, that such patents were contrary to common law, and that such issues were to be decided by Commons and the courts.

POST-ELIZABETHAN RENT SEEKING

Opposition to crown attempts to monopolize industries during Elizabeth's reign grew, culminating in civil war, during the next forty years. Generally, it may be said that after 1603—despite even more vigorous attempts to establish monopolies on the part of Elizabeth's successors—no acts establishing national monopolies were enforceable that reduced the profits of merchants and the interests of those represented by Commons and the courts. At this point we find the de facto end of monarchial mercantilism when, in the context of expanding industries, the net benefit from open competition outweighed the net benefit from crown protection. The *demand* for regulation was reduced owing to rising franchise costs in the form of taxes, together with the uncertainties of regulation by the crown. Potential competition for investment outlets and political pressures upon Commons by

[35] Ibid., p. 106.

affected merchants must have greatly increased the uncertainty of gains from crown-created monopoly.

James I and Charles I revived Elizabeth's early policy of patent grants as sources of revenue, but both met with very limited success (principally in the cases of alum and soap manufacture). Meanwhile, Commons gathered all its strength to fight the king's prerogative to seek rents via monopolization. After a protracted struggle with James over the issue, Commons revived impeachment as a means of punishing monopolists within their ranks and of reminding the king of their total intolerance for his claimed prerogative to seek rents in this manner. Thus, in 1621, for the first time in almost two hundred years, Commons impeached Sir Giles Mompesson and Sir Francis Mitchell for "fraud and oppression committed as patentees for the exclusive manufacture of gold and silver thread, for the inspection of inns and hostelries, and for the licensing of ale houses."[36] The House of Lords rendered the judgment and imposed fines and imprisonment on both men. Commons's objection to the crown's supposed right to supply regulation reached its zenith in 1624, when the famous act concerning monopolies legally stripped the king of all prerogative in patents and other means to monopolize industry.[37]

In 1625 Charles I came to the throne and promptly set about attempting to restore the "divine right of kings," which, of course, included a reassertion of rights to grant monopoly via letters patent or by order of privy council. In doing so, Charles was led to a direct confrontation with constitutionalists, a battle he ultimately lost, along with his head, in 1649. Together with his persuasive and powerful minister Francis Bacon, who supported the royal prerogative to supply regulation, Charles found a loophole in the 1624 statute: the statute did not apply to corporations for benefit of trade or to companies of merchants. Thus, after the repeated refusal of Parliament to fund the king's military adventures and the king's dissolution of Parliament in 1629, Charles tried to make deals with large producers in many indus-

---

[36] Hannis Taylor, *The Origin and Growth of the English Constitution*, Part II (Boston: Houghton, Mifflin and Company, 1898), p. 246.

[37] Exceptions granted were for "patents of Invention" and the alum and soap monopolies. The latter were excepted because the patents were soon to expire and, further, because the privy council agreed not to renew them.

tries.[38] Alum and soap monopolies had been exempted from the 1624 act, but the king encouraged the formation of huge corporations in coal, salt, brickmaking, and others, to which monopoly protection was given (for fourteen years) in return for rents to the crown. Between 1629 and 1640 the alum patent brought in £126,000, with an additional revenue from soap (between 1630 and 1640) of £122,000, but the *new* rent seeking of Charles was doomed to failure.[39] The circumstances of this failure should be, by now, very familiar. The king's monopoly protection and taxing arrangements were *too costly* for *all* the merchants to continue to acquiesce to them. A competitive system in this period of rapid industrial expansion yielded them higher rents than could be obtained through legalized entry control, price fixing, *and* taxation. Thus, cartel arrangements broke down as participants blithely evaded price-fixing agreements or laws when profitable. Moreover, these attempted new monopolies aroused the hostile and vociferous opposition of those merchants left out. The nonmerchant voices correctly perceived monopoly (recall the wool trade example) as inimical to their interests.

Thus the cartel breakdown and the more fundamental problems of enforcement brought on by strong consumer and excluded merchant objections combined to yield the patents of Charles I ineffective three years after they were issued. Antimonopoly interests opposed to the king—reflected in self-interested inaction or adverse decisions by justices of the peace and by Commons—joined forces with legal and religious objections to the king's blatant and audacious assertion of supreme rights and signaled an end to his authority. In a landmark reassertion of rights, Parliament ended the despotism of monarchy and established fundamental constitutional rights. Included in this legislation was the passage in 1640 of a statute putting an end to all but one of the exceptions in the statute of 1624.[40] Monarchial mercantilism

---

[38] Parliament was demanding a restoration of sovereignty and other constitutional rights in return for the subsidy.

[39] Nef, *Industry and Government in France and England*, p. 115.

[40] Although some of the more scientifically minded merchants and gentlemen supported the exemption of limited "patents for invention" in the Statute of 1650 in order to encourage inventors (i.e., in permitting internalization of benefits), the self-interest of members of Parliament, judges, and magistrates may have been a larger factor in this decision. Nef notes, in this connection, that "the increasing industrial investments of the

was repulsed by sharply limiting the ability of the king to *supply* regulation. More important for understanding the course of constitutional
history and regulation, the monarch lost this ability largely because
actual and potential demanders found the effects of these regulations
very uncertain, and most often of negative benefit, given the sa-
lubrious state of the competitive system in the English economy of the
time.

As argued in the theoretical section of this paper, future attempts
to demand and supply monopoly privileges through regulation were
far more costly to participants because of the higher transactions costs
associated with collective decision-making in a representative body
such as Parliament. Thus, the attempt by merchants in the short run to
wrest power to confer monopoly from the monarch (culminating in the
mid-seventeenth century) led to a long-run situation, lasting until the
latter part of the nineteenth century, which severely inhibited the possible formation of rent-seeking regulation.

Customs, Monopoly, and Dualism

Of special interest in a mercantile context is the issue of tariffs and
quotas, that is, the issue of tariffs and quotas in protection or encouragement in international competition. Clearly, the nexus of power
to levy customs duties ("tonnage and poundage") shifted often from
the medieval period through the seventeenth century. Indeed, one of
the major factors leading to the constitutional revolt in the reign of
Charles I was exactly the matter of prerogative in customs duties.
Charles claimed an "ancient right" to customs, but Parliament finally
seized the exclusive power to set these duties in 1641.[41] While Parliament was dissolved, however, an event took place that reveals that
vested interests were operative in the matter of trade policy. In the

---

wealthy merchants and the improving landlords, represented in parliament, in the
courts, and in the town governments, led them to welcome any invention designed to
reduce costs of production and to increase profits. . . . Such industrial adventurers and
their political representatives saw in the granting of patents a means of encouraging the
search for the new inventions with which their prosperity was increasingly bound up"
(ibid., p. 119).

[41] Parliament later gave William and Mary customs and port duty for *limited* terms
of four years, partially a ploy to guarantee frequent parliaments (Taylor, *The Origin and
Growth of the English Constitution*, pt. II, p. 419).

interim in which Charles claimed absolute authority to levy taxes, merchant importers refused (in their own interests) to pay customs to the king, obeying a remonstrance of Parliament to refuse to pay any duties not authorized by Parliament. The king ordered the seizure of goods, whereupon several merchants resisted and were brought before the privy council. One of them, Richard Chambers, declared that "merchants are in no part of the world so screwed as in England. In Turkey they have more encouragement."[42]

This incident, small in itself, reveals that, although motives of unification and state power building may be pressed to explain protectionist trade policies, self-interest was never far from the surface in shaping those policies which we regard as typically mercantile in nature. That is to say, there is a commonality about rent seeking, whether its subject is international trade controls or domestic industrial regulation.[43] Although a number of writers have noted a "dualism" in *mercantile writers'* approach to domestic controls on the one hand and to protectionist "mercantile" policies in trade on the other, the apparent contradiction may be resolved when mercantilism is viewed in terms of rent-seeking activity.[44]

An example drawn from Heckscher will illustrate this point:

[42] Quoted in ibid., p. 274. Prison was the cost to Chambers for his flippancy.

[43] Adam Smith made this point very emphatically: ". . . in the mercantile system, the interest of the consumer is almost constantly sacrificed to that of the producer; and it seems to consider production, and not consumption, as the ultimate end and object of all industry and commerce. . . . In the restraints upon the importance of all foreign commodities which can come into competition with those of our own growth, or manufacture, the interest of the home-consumer is evidently sacrificed to that of the producer. It is altogether for the benefit of the latter, that the former is obliged to pay that enhancement of price which this monopoly almost always occasions" (*Wealth of Nations*, ed. Edwin Cannan [New York: Random House, 1937], p. 625). All restrictions, domestic and international, were for the benefit of merchants and manufacturers. Smith even extends the self-interest axiom to an explanation for the Navigation Acts and to colonial policy: "To found a great empire for the sole purpose of raising up a people of customers, may at first sight appear a project fit only for a nation of shopkeepers. It is, however, a project altogether unfit for a nation of shopkeepers; but extremely fit for a nation whose government is influenced by shopkeepers" (p. 579).

[44] That there was a contradiction in English mercantile *statements* concerning the desirability and efficacy of applications of natural law and free trade is beyond doubt. See A. F. Chalk, "Natural Law and the Rise of Economic Individualism in England," *Journal of Political Economy* 59 (August, 1951): 330–347; or W. D. Grampp, "The Liberal Element in English Mercantilism," *Quarterly Journal of Economics* 66 (November, 1952): 465–501. Their observation that the emergence of a philosophical defense of the domes-

. . . from the end of the Middle Ages onwards, the import of wool cards into England was prohibited. They constituted an important means of production in the textile industry, which normally enjoyed greater favour than any other. A decree of 1630 went so far as to proscribe the sale of cards produced within the country from worn-out patterns. The maintenance of employment was given as the official motive for the measures, but in fact, as least as regards the latter prohibition, the object was to assist one of the oldest industrial joint-stock companies, the Mineral and Battery Works.[45]

The point that this quotation illustrates is that the "official" motive for protectionist measures was, in all likelihood, seldom if ever the real motive. Most writers on mercantilism identify some sort of "homogeneous" mercantile trade policy, employment policy, population policy, domestic policy, and so on, as if interests independent of those which drive economic man in all ages were responsible for the economic policy called "mercantilism." We, however, agree with Smith's assessment that mercantilism was but a tissue of protectionist fallacies supported by merchants, and we go further and argue that thinly varnished rent seeking by merchants, monarch, and ultimately by the masses represented by Parliament explains the sum total of the economic intervention, as well as a good deal of the political and legal change, over the period. A "philosophical dualism" may have existed, as philosophers were converted to individualism (Locke) and natural law as a guide to economic conduct (Mandeville, Petty, Cantillon, Hume, and Smith). But, as we have seen, the philosophical revolution was fostered by the conduct of rent seekers, constrained by a particular form of polity. The form of that polity, moreover, changed fundamentally through the interplay of these self-interested economic forces. Mercantilist writers, Jacob Viner suggests, created "an elaborate system of confused and self-contradictory argument."[46] Our ap-

---

tic market economy came in the late sixteenth century is indisputable. But to defend free trade internally and simultaneously support import and export controls is not "dualistic," if both are of net benefit to the individual involved. When mercantilism is viewed as a rent-seeking process, moreover, the explanation for why mercantilism as a *system* has eluded all attempts at characterization by historians of economic thought becomes readily understandable. Thus, our conclusion extends Viner's belief that "pleas for special interests, whether open or disguised, constituted the bulk of the mercantilist literature. The disinterested patriot or philosopher played a minor part in the development of mercantilist doctrine" (*Studies in the Theory of International Trade*, p. 115).

[45] Heckscher, *Mercantilism*, I, 148.

[46] Viner, *Studies in the Theory of International Trade*, p. 109.

plication to mercantilism of the theory of the rent-seeking society suggests that the practitioners of mercantilism were anything but confused and self-contradictory. Through their actions, self-interested individuals ultimately altered the constraints within which rent-seeking activity took place.

France: The Venal Society

The French experience at rent seeking and the environment under which it took place contrast at almost every point with the case in England. If mercantilism means "a system of extensive economic controls," one could hardly find a better example than France from the thirteenth to eighteenth centuries. The source of this difference lies in large measure with the absolutist property rights in taxation vested in the crown from 1439 through the French Revolution of the late eighteenth century. With minor alterations the tax system of the Old Regime followed that of the Renaissance. Characterized by institutionalized venality, French monarchs shared the power to tax with the French aristocracy over the entire mercantile period. Rent seeking by the monarch in the form of contracting to enterprises or to "tax farmers" was common as early as the thirteenth and fourteenth centuries. A scholar of fiscal systems of the period aptly describes the situation: " . . . the most important local revenues were 'farmed out' to enterprisers, who received the right to collect the domaines in return for lump sum payments. Amounts in excess of this sum became the revenue farmers' profits; and, if they collected less than the amounts paid, it was their loss—not the king's."[47] Corruption permeated a gigantic fiscal bureaucracy, and, as in certain modern political systems, it became a way of life. Property rights shifted as the centuries passed, with tax farming and other "leases" becoming hereditary. Legal and judicial offices were sold by the crown, for example, and provide an interesting example of venality. Revealing the utter hypocrisy of the system, the oath of office in the case of justices and crown lawyers required a state-

[47] Wolfe, *The Fiscal System of Renaissance France*, p. 12. Also see B. F. Hoselitz, "The Early History of Entrepreneurial Theory," in *Essays in Economic Thought: Aristotle to Marshall*, ed. J. J. Spengler and W. R. Allen (Chicago: Rand McNally & Co., 1960), pp. 234–257; and R. B. Ekelund and R. F. Hebert, "A Tale of Two Theories: Concepts of Competition in Economic Literature," unpublished manuscript, Auburn University, 1978.

ment that they had not paid any money for their position. It has been observed that "for the whole sixteenth century the justices and royal lawyers began their careers with an act of perjury."[48]

Royal venality was of such magnitude at the end of Louis XIII's reign (between 1636 and 1642) that the French monarch was collecting between three and four times the per capita taxes from his subjects as Charles I, who was locked in a death battle with Parliament at the time. The mercantile writer Gregory King estimated the "general income" of France in 1688 at £80,500,000 sterling and that of England at £41,700,000, estimates rough in themselves but sufficient to indicate a much larger success of royal rent seeking in France over the "mercantile" period.[49]

THE INSTITUTIONAL FRAMEWORK OF RENT SEEKING IN FRANCE

The rent-seeking coalition of crown and aristocracy was facilitated in France by a number of institutional features stemming from and related to the absolute power to tax by the crown. There are the interrelated matters of (1) the enforcement of industrial regulation, (2) the degree of *effective* crown rent-seeking interference with old and new industries, and (3) the incidence of the tax structure and the incentives established thereby.

The guild system in France grew stronger from the time of the Middle Ages onward, in contrast with the English experience. At the opening of the sixteenth century, most local industry was done by free craftsmen, but by the reign of Henry IV (1589–1610), the guild regime was dramatically strengthened. Two crown edicts (1581 and 1597) laid down uniform rules for the organization of handicrafts all over France and permitted master craftsmen who were not members of guilds to organize and obtain from rent-seeking royal officials all the advantages of formal guild membership—regulated apprenticeships and entry, hours of work permitted, and so forth. Guild regulations, moreover, were confirmed by royal letters patent. The result of these activities was a massive extension of royal prerogative, superseding guild and local prerogative in the matter of decentralized royal control over

[48] Wolfe, *The Fiscal System of Renaissance France*, p. 297.

[49] Gregory King, quoted in Nef, *Industry and Government in France and England*, p. 128.

industrial activity. Entry control, the imposition of maximum wage rates upon journeymen, price controls, and the establishment of rent-seeking offices, which all this engendered, became centralized crown prerogatives.

Although these developments set the stage for a venal society with centralized property rights, further developments significantly strengthened the control of the king's officers over municipal authority. *Intendants des provinces*, tried servants of the crown, were sent as commissioners to the provinces to establish administrative reforms. Gradually, under the aegis of Richelieu and Louis XIII, these well-paid *intendants* took over and consolidated most of the functions of earlier royal provincial administrators, thereby permitting crown ministers far greater assurance that the crown's policies would be undertaken. Adjudication of regulatory disputes at the local level was also more and more becoming the business of the crown courts by invocation of the principle of *cas royaux*, whereby disputes over guild regulations and other industrial encumbrances could be tried in royal courts due to "crown interests." Certainly Colbert, minister of France between 1661 and 1683, must have found these inherited institutions a great advantage in implementing the intensified rent seeking of Louis XIV.

Over this important period, then, the institutions of legislative and judicial enforcement over industry and trade were developing along sharply opposed lines in England and France. During the crucial century from 1540 to 1640, institutions that facilitated rent seeking by crown and aristocracy were greatly strengthened in France, while such "enforcement" institutions, legal and administrative, were becoming atrophied in England. The French crown did not have to brook the *combined* opposition of enforcers, those disgruntled by regulation, and the public in its quest for economic rents.

The administrative machinery that served rent seekers vis-à-vis local handicraft regulation was duplicated over specific industries in a manner that could only be pitifully imitated by the English. Tight royal control over mines, saltpeter and gunpowder, and salt was greatly facilitated by decentralized local production, with centralized control over rent-producing "franchises."

In the matter of saltpeter and gunpowder manufacture, the "grand master of the artillery" (the Minister Sully served for a long while) was given exclusive management. In imitation of the tax-collection system, these rights were "farmed out" to commissioners, who represented the grand master in granting or revoking rights to produce. Commissioners, in turn, exacted a split in the rents created for themselves. Concession rights to the produce of mines were likewise farmed out to court favorites through an elaborate administrative machinery. Revenues in the form of lump-sum payments went to the crown, as did a regalian tax on ores (*droit du dixième*). Entry, exit, and abandonment were all regulated to the mutual advantage of aristocratic franchise holders (*concessionaires*) and the king.

The French crown, in common with its English counterpart, granted patents for new inventions and, along with them, money subsidies and official salaried help for inventors. But the French went much further, determining the entire direction of technology. By granting a large number of limited tax-exempt concessions, kings from Henry IV and Louis XIII directed technological change by shifting emphasis toward new branches of *artistic* craftsmanship (cloth, glass, tapestries) and away from cost-reducing devices necessary for the introduction of quantity-oriented, large-scale production. Though patents for the latter were not refused, crown advisors were establishing conditions that greatly favored the establishment of high-quality artistic productions. Such emphasis expanded into the well-known government studios and art factories of Louis XIV and his royal successors.

Perhaps the single most successful application of venality by the French crown related to the salt monopoly. Claiming regalian rights (which roughly corresponded to the salt tribute of the imperial Roman state) in most of the provinces of France, the crown imposed intricate regulations on salt producers, requiring them to sell all salt produced to royal storehouses at prices fixed by the king's officers. Consumers were then forced to purchase salt, with required quantities per parish, at rates four times as high as free market rates.[50] Although there were infractions, monopoly conditions were rigorously enforced, in large measure because of the fidelity of royal representatives at the local levels.

The *gabelle* and other taxes on salt became the single most important revenue source next to the infamous *taille*. The *taille* was a tax

---

[50] These are Nef's estimates.

levied on the income and real property of peasants, shopkeepers, and craftsmen, who were not exempted by virtue of participation in royal manufactures. In real terms receipts from the *gabelle* rose eight or ten times between 1523 and 1641.[51] The imposition of both the *gabelle* and the *taille* had stark implications for the distribution of income and economic growth. Both these taxes and the indirect taxes on commodities fell heavily upon the poor, discouraging capital formation. Unbridled taxing powers facilitated redistributions to the nobility and to the clergy, who utilized wealth redistributions for "artistic consumptions."

A POSTSCRIPT ON THE VENAL SOCIETY

Institutionalized rent seeking had a number of implications for the ultimate form of the French mercantile state. Growth in real output lagged far behind that of England due to a dearth of investment opportunities and, more importantly, to a lack of incentive for capital formation. Absolutism created so much uncertainty in property rights that, as has been remarked of the Spanish mercantile system of the time, one became a student, monk, beggar, or bureaucrat, since there was nothing else to be.[52] The best minds, as in all controlled societies, were attracted to the areas of highest return. In France this meant that they sought a bureaucratic sinecure that could be passed on through hereditary rights.

The certainty of absolute power and of an imposed system of rent seeking contrasted sharply with the uncertainty of private entrepreneurial returns in France. The high *private* returns of a relatively unfettered competitive system, which proved sufficient to bring down mercantile monarchy in the English case, were not possible in France. The tradition of the venal system created there was so strong that the emergence of a liberal order was postponed until the late eighteenth century.

Conclusions

Historical episodes from France and England appear to fit the theory of mercantilism as rent-seeking activity, as well as to provide a solid

[51] Nef, *Industry and Government in France and England*, p. 83.
[52] North and Thomas, *The Rise of the Western World*, p. 131.

base for explaining its decline in England. In the latter case, higher cost due to uncertainty and growing private returns reduced industry demands for regulation and controls. All this strengthened the emergent constitutional democracy, which created conditions making rent-seeking activity on the part of both monarch and merchants more costly. When the locus of power to seek rents shifted from the monarch to Parliament via more stringent controls on the king, the costs of supplying regulation through legislative enactment rose because transaction costs to rent seekers went up. Moreover, a competitive judiciary created massive uncertainty about the durability of *any* monopoly right. In addition, the inability of the monarch to enforce even simple local regulations was premised upon the political structure of England and, as we have seen, upon the changing cost-benefit structure to royal representatives charged with such enforcement.

The pattern of mercantile rent-seeking in France until the late eighteenth century was manifestly different. Absolute tax powers and ever more efficient royal enforcement at local levels permitted and supported a system of outright venality administered by an institutionalized aristocratic bureaucracy. Monarchial controls over technology further altered the cost-benefit structure of the demand for monopoly franchises by reducing the returns to production and participation in the private economy. Along with monopoly in the supply of franchises, it is easy to understand the persistence and growth of venality in France. The absence of meaningful representative institutions or conditions that would facilitate their emergence is sufficient to explain the historical pattern.

We have argued that the application of the theory of the rent-seeking society to the mercantile period yields new insights into the rise and decline of mercantile restrictions in England and France. Surely our argument would not have surprised Adam Smith, and we view it as an extension of Smith's (admittedly) fragmentary analysis of the rent-seeking modes of the period.[53] As noted throughout the pres-

---

[53] One of Smith's principal themes in the *Wealth of Nations* was that mercantilism was equivalent to the demand for regulation and rents by merchants and manufactures (see pp. 250, 403, 420, 425, 460–461, 695). Smith attributes mercantile restrictions of all kinds—colonization, restrictions designed for specie accumulation, and so forth—to the self-seeking interests of merchants. Typical of Smith's "capture" theory is the following "It cannot be very difficult to determine who have been the contrivers of this whole mercantile system; not the consumers, we may believe, whose interest has been entirel

ent paper, however, there is no dearth of arguments concerning the decline of overt mercantile policies in England, although the reasons for this significant episode of deregulation are largely unexplored in the literature. Credit is given implicitly to Adam Smith and his "liberal" predecessors, who advocated the advantages of the free and spontaneous coordination of economic activity, for making such a forceful intellectual case for their point of view that it was translated into public policy. Our interpretation of mercantilism as a rent-seeking society does not suggest that intellectual developments will have much impact on public policy. We thus tend to disagree with Keynes, who was certain "that the power of vested interests is vastly exaggerated compared with the gradual encroachment of ideas."[54] As fine an academic scribbler as Adam Smith was, we suspect that the roles of special interests and ideas were either reversed or subsidiary to other forces in the ascension of free enterprise over mercantilism. Certainly Smith himself characterized mercantilism correctly as a system built entirely upon self-interest.[55]

We believe, in short, that commentators on mercantilism, such as Heckscher, have "overscholarized" the period. It is not that these renowned writers have not greatly added to our knowledge of the pe-

---

neglected; but the producers, whose interest has been so carefully attended to; and among this latter class our merchants and manufactures have been by far the principal architects" (p. 626). Although Smith featured the monarch as a rent seeker, he did not elaborate much on the self-interested aspects of politicians, but probably more so than Professor Stigler believes (see G. J. Stigler, "Smith's Travels on the Ship of State," *History of Political Economy* 3 [Fall, 1971]: 265–277).

[54] Keynes, *The General Theory*, p. 383.

[55] Other types of explanations are equally unlikely. For example, within the context of our rent-seeking model, the movement to free enterprise might be explained as a general process of Pareto-optimization. The inefficiencies concommitant to monopoly organization offer a range of mutually beneficial gains from exchange. Presumably, consumers could offer to buy monopolists out to the net benefit of both parties. The difficulty with such a solution is the existence of prohibitively high transaction costs to consumers, which implies that monopoly and regulation will persist despite the potential social gains (Buchanan and Tullock, "The 'Dead Hand' of Monopoly"). Moreover, perhaps there were fewer consumers in mercantilist times and more such Pareto-superior bargains could be struck. If this were operationally so, the movement to free enterprise from the monopolistic policies of mercantilism would be susceptible to rational explanation. This is, however, an extremely unlikely explanation of the decline of mercantilism, since the mathematics of transaction costs imply that the number of transactors must be very small before meaningful reductions in transaction costs obtain. It is therefore quite likely that in mercantilist times the organizing costs to consumers would have dominated the returns from abolishing monopoly via Pareto-superior moves.

riod, but rather that they have implicitly emphasized ideas as primary causal forces of change rather than as (sometimes interesting) rationalizations based upon one's position in the rent-seeking game of income redistribution. The motives of mercantile writers, as Smith cunningly indicated, should always be suspect. Heckscher, for example, has pointed out, with reference to "intellectual arguments," that "there was little mysticism in the arguments of the mercantilists. . . . they did not appeal to sentiment, but were obviously anxious to find reasonable grounds for every position they adopted."[56] We certainly do not disagree that writers of *all* persuasions sought reasonable grounds for their arguments, but we argue that these grounds in the main were laid over the underlying self-interested forces of the times. It is our thesis, in short, that rent seeking engendered forces that drastically altered institutions in England, while producing, in a milieu of French constraints, a mercantile rigidity lasting until the nineteenth century. As such, our view is a reassertion of Smith's primitive analysis of mercantilism. It is, moreover, an elaboration of that view, in that it finds a crucial link between rent-seeking activities and fundamental institutional change.

[56] Heckscher, *Mercantilism*, I, 308.

15

The Cost of Transfers

by

GORDON TULLOCK

MOST discussions of transfers have assumed that they are costless. They are movements from one point to another on the same Pareto-optimal production frontier. In utility terms they may actually move the Pareto-optimal frontier out because, with interdependence of utility functions, everyone may feel better off after they are completed. The point of this essay is to demonstrate that transfers may well involve significant costs. Further, we shall demonstrate that the mere possibility of transfers imposes certain costs on society. We are thrown into a game that we cannot avoid playing and that is, unfortunately, negative-sum. This game, moreover, applies to a number of situations in addition to those we have traditionally denominated transfers. Specifically, bargaining, voluntary charity, government-sponsored income redistribution, theft, and war all produce somewhat the same structural problems. As we shall see, our analysis will fit all of them. It should not be taken, however, as a proof that government income redistribution is theft. It is perfectly possible to be in favor of one and not the other. It will remain possible for those readers who favor income redistribution but who are firm pacifists to keep that pair of beliefs, and those readers who believe we should really hit the Communists hard but that government income redistribution is undesirable will be able to retain those beliefs also.

Let us begin with a simple bargaining example. Suppose that we have a two-person society with K and T the citizens. Currently, they are at point O on figure 15.1. Most economists would agree that movement into the area above and to the right of O (to such a point as A) is unambiguously desirable because it benefits at least one person and in most cases both. Movement to point B, however, is normally regarded

FIGURE 15.1

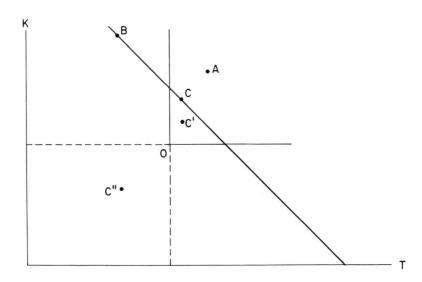

as ambiguous. It clearly benefits Mr. *K*, but it also injures Mr. *T*. The Paretian solution is compensation. Since compensation involves simply a transfer of resources from one party to the other without any change in their quantity, it can be represented by a forty-five-degree angle drawn through *B*. This line passes to the right and above *O*, and hence there is some point such as *C* that could be reached by Mr. *K* and Mr. *T* through agreement and would have the same resource input as point *B*.

This argument as conventionally presented, however, does not fit the real world. If some technological possibility exists that would permit the "society" to move to point *B* and *T* has a veto over the movement, then movement to point *C* will probably require a good deal of negotiation between *K* and *T*. Since this negotiation absorbs resources, the actual point achieved would not be *C* but some point within the line upon which *B* lies, such as *C'*. We can indeed imagine a situation in which the investment of resources in bargaining would be so great that the end product would be at *C''*, which is below and to the left of the original position. As movement up and to the right is unambiguously desirable, movement down and to the left is unambiguously undesirable. Movement into the dotted rectangle is movement to an area where at least one person is injured and no one is benefited. It is only a movement into the areas above and to the left or below and to the right of the starting point that raise doubts about desirability or undesirability of a change.

Granted that some technological change occurred that made it possible to move to B, we would expect the bargaining between the two parties to lead to some point such as C', rather than a point such as C'', simply because both parties must enter into the bargaining voluntarily, and it is unlikely (although surely not impossible) that they will miscalculate to the point where they actually suffer a loss. If they both make estimates of the likely outcome before beginning bargaining, then each must foresee a positive gain. On the whole, one would anticipate that over time these prebargaining estimates would turn out to be correct and hence that voluntary bargaining would not lead to such points as C''.

As we shall see, voluntary charity shares this feature with voluntary bargaining, whereas government income transfers, theft, and war are in this respect different. Before going on to these issues, however, let us briefly pause and consider some special aspects of the Paretian criteria, using figure 15.2. Suppose once again that we are at point O.

FIGURE 15.2

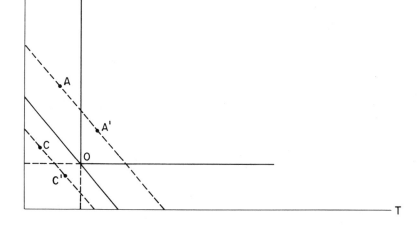

Some technological change occurs that makes it possible for society to move to point A, which lies on the diagonal line running through A'. We know from the location of point A that it is possible for society, by compensation, to reach some such point as A'. Further, if T is given a veto on movement from O to A unless he is compensated, both T and K will have incentives to reach a bargain that will fall somewhere in the Paretian area. Unfortunately, they each also have an incentive to try to gain the bulk of the profit for themselves, and this means that they will most assuredly use resources in bargaining against each other.

If, however, a proposal is made to move to point C, we know, first, that compensation could not lead to some point above and to the right of O; there is, in fact, a genuine reduction in the total resources available to society at point C. Further, there is no incentive for either K or T to engage in bargaining, since from the standpoint of at least one of them any location in the resource area available from point C will be a reduction in welfare. We can, mentally perhaps, say that A is in a location equivalent to something like A', and C equivalent to something like C'; hence, in the first case everyone can conceivably be benefited, and, in the second, of necessity, there will be injury.

It would be possible to argue that social changes that lie above the diagonal line running through O should be adopted, on the grounds that society in some sense will have its resources enlarged by such a move. The counterargument, of course, would be that changes such as C should never be adopted for the same reason. This, as stated, violates the Paretian taboo on the comparison of utilities. It is possible, however, to argue for something like it, on strictly individualistic and Paretian terms. Suppose we anticipate that in the future there will be a large number of opportunities open, some of which will be like A in that they would lead society to a new point above the diagonal line running through O and some like C in the sense that they would lead to a point below. Assume further that we do not anticipate that these changes, as a whole, will favor one person or one group in society. Under these circumstances, both K and T might agree on a general rule that all changes that lead to movement of the frontier out and to the right will be accepted, regardless of their distributional characteristics, simply because the present discounted value of such a rule would for each one of them be an improvement in welfare. Note that the pro-

duction frontier would presumably not have the straight line characteristic of the line passing through A on our figure. The line represents
the transfer possibilities, not the production frontier.

This, of course, involves the assumption that the progress will be
at least evenly enough divided so that each party would anticipate that
his particular position would be improved by a large number of such
technological improvements and that no party has too much risk aversion. By parity of reasoning, and much less controversial, movement
to points that move the frontier back (such as point C) would be undesirable. It seems likely that most people would agree that changes
that lie above the diagonal line lying through O have at least something to be said for them, and changes that lie below it are undesirable, although this rule will offend the Paretian orthodoxy.

The investment of resources in bargaining is always a negative-
sum game. As a handy example, suppose that T wishes to purchase a
house from K and would be benefited by obtaining the house for any
price under $18,000. K, on the other hand, is willing to sell it at any
price over $12,000. If both truthfully stated their reservation price,
they could split the difference. Each, however, is motivated to attempt
to get the entire bargaining cost himself and, therefore, to lie about his
own reservation price. Figure 15.3 shows the game matrix. T stands
for truthful statement and L for lie. If both speak the truth, the expected outcome is shown in the upper lefthand corner; if T speaks the
truth and K lies, then K should be able to get almost the entire bargaining range and T only a tiny part of it; if both lie, the investment in
resources involved in sorting out the false statements, together with
the cost of the possibility of the bargain being missed, leads to the result in the lower right corner. It can be seen, of course, that this is a
prisoner's dilemma game and that the parties will (as in fact they do in
real life) attempt to mislead each other, with the result that there is a
social loss. If either of the two parties chose to behave in the socially
optimal manner, he would suffer considerable loss himself and the
other party would make very large gains. Prisoner's dilemma matrices
of this general sort will be characteristic of all the situations with
which we will deal in this essay.

So much for bargaining. Now let us turn to voluntary charity. In
order to do this, we must redesign the standard diagram we have used
so far and put, not physical values or dollar values, but utility on the

FIGURE 15.3

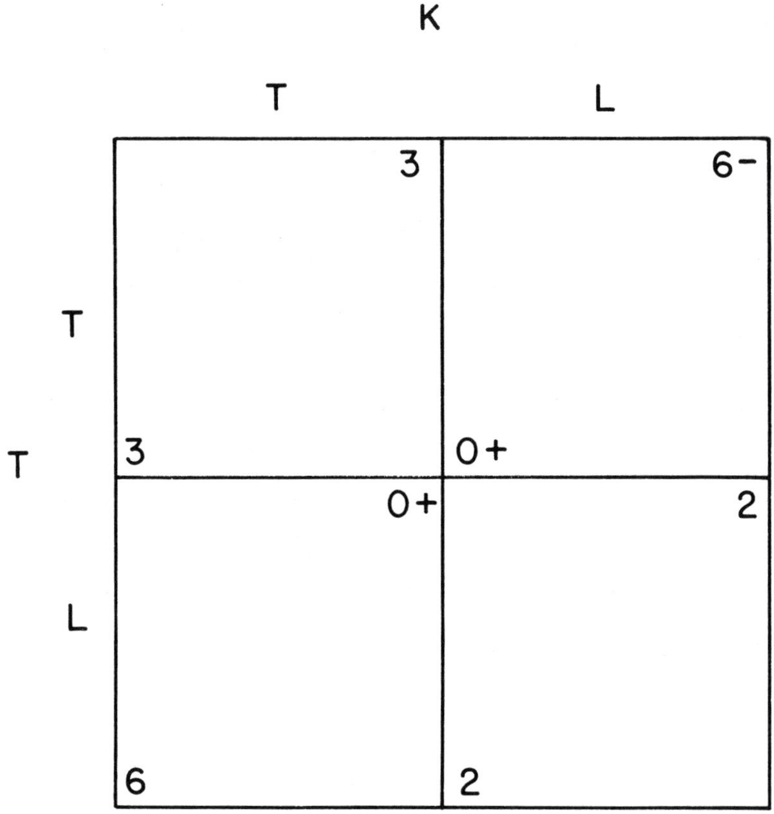

two axes.[1] Thus, suppose that once again K and T are a two-man society and society is at O on figure 15.4. If K is oppressed by T's poverty, he may wish voluntarily to make a gift to T, and such a gift would increase his utility. If nothing more happened, then the gift from K to T might move the society to point A, which is equivalent to a movement outward into the Pareto-optimal region. Thus, a movement that would appear to be simply a movement along the diagonal line, if we

[1] More elegant but complex methods would retain the physical value measure on the chart but design the indifference curves of the two parties appropriately. For an introduction to complexities involved in such voluntary charity, see Thomas R. Ireland and David B. Johnson, *The Economics of Charity*, ed. Gordon Tullock (Blacksburg, Va.: Center for Study of Public Choice, 1970).

drew figure 15.4 in terms of physical product, is a Pareto-optimal move in utility terms. The fact that such moves are possible presumably accounts for voluntary charity.

Unfortunately, the situation is not that simple. Suppose that T perceives that K may make a charitable gift. Under these circumstances, he would be well advised to invest resources in becoming a more suitable object of K's charity. This moves the system to O'. Indeed, in the particular cases with which I am most familiar—Chinese beggars—it may move it to a lower level of utility for both T and K. When I was in China, I occasionally used to see beggars who had deliberately and usually quite horribly mutilated themselves in order to increase their charitable take, and I always found the mutilations inflicted a considerable negative utility in me.

In the Western world, of course, these drastic measures are not normal, but anyone who is at all familiar with people who are objects of charity must realize that they do engage in a certain amount of resource expenditure to improve their receipts. Granted, however, that the potential object of charity may behave in this way, the potential giver is apt to invest resources in attempting to control such activity. This moves the system to O''. Let us once again turn to a traditional area: the hiring of an almsmonger by medieval princes was an effort to

FIGURE 15.4

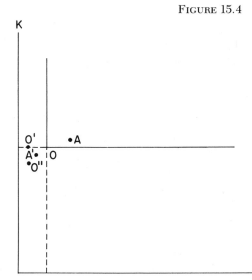

reduce the use of resources in becoming objects of charity by potential beneficiaries of the royal largesse. In modern times, such protection is one of the major objectives of professional administration of charitable programs.

So far, we have moved into the Pareto-dominated area. It should be noted, however, that there is no need for us to remain there. The gift from K to T might still move us to A. It is, of course, possible that it might lead only to A' and hence that the society would be worse off, even in utility terms, after the charitable transaction than it would have been had no one thought of the possibility of such charity. Once again, however, the operation is voluntary on both sides, and it thus seems likely that the end product will be a Pareto improvement rather than Pareto dominated.

The problem, as was the case in bargaining and as will be the case in the other matters to which we will shortly turn, is that, although the actual operation of charitable giving is profitable to both parties, its mere possibility sets off behavior on the part of each party that is aimed at improving his own utility and that uses resources. This behavior is mutually offsetting and, taken in and of itself and ignoring the eventual gift, moves the society into the Pareto-dominated area. The movement from O to O'' is Pareto dominated. If it were possible to see to it that the Pareto-dominated moves never occurred, clearly society would make net gains out of all charitable transactions. There is no way, however, of providing such assurance. Thus, it is almost certain that at least occasionally charitable actions, like bargains, will go wrong, and the net effect will be that society is injured. We may find this unfortunate, but there is no evidence that the world was designed for our convenience.

So far, however, we have been discussing transactions that are voluntary on both sides. There is a sense in which any transaction is voluntary. For example, when the gunman says, "Your money or your life," you make a deal with him that benefits both of you. The involuntary part of this transaction, from your standpoint, is the arrival of the gunman, not the trade you make with him once he has put in an appearance and threatens your life. Indeed, the minor paradox that is sometimes used in teaching—the question of whether this is or is not a voluntary transaction—is very easily answered. There is a trade of the victim's life provided by the gunman against the victim's money, which makes both parties better off; the only thing the victim can complain about is that the gunman, without his consent, placed him in a situation where he faced a decision on such a trade. The appearance of the gunman very sharply reduced the victim's utility. The trade that he later made with the gunman improved both his and the gunman's utility. Thus the transaction can be divided into two acts, the first of which was not Pareto-optimal and the second of which was.

Let us return, however, to our main theme. Theft, war, and governmental income redistribution all involve transfers that are not voluntarily entered into by both parties, in the sense that both parties are satisfied with the entire transaction. Note that government income redistribution is only in part involuntary. Presumably, the taxpayer-citizens are interested in making charitable gifts to other persons and may choose to use the state as a cooperative instrument for that end. Insofar as this is true, the redistribution of income is voluntary and should be analyzed as such. It seems likely, however, that government income redistribution is carried well beyond the point where those who are paying for the redistribution benefit in utility. The argument that appears below, then, applies only to that component of government income redistribution which is not simply a special way of organizing a voluntary gift. As a subjective judgment, I would think that something on the order of 90 percent of the income transfers by governmental process are of this nature, but I could be very far wrong in this guess. We can, I think, all agree that such major redistributions as the farm subsidy program, the very extensive facilities provided at the expense of the general taxpayer to make private airplane flying cheap and easy, or the transfers to owners of steel mills through restrictions on the import of steel are not the result of deliberate desires on the part of the "donors" to make these gifts. They are the result of activities on the part of the recipients combined, perhaps, with indifference, or, more likely, with ignorance and political weakness on the part of the people who actually pay for them.

Let us then consider such redistribution. Note that there is no increase in the total product measured in physical terms or in general utility. Thus, the physical transfer falls on a straightforward diagonal line. No improvement in efficiency in society is expected from such a

FIGURE 15.5

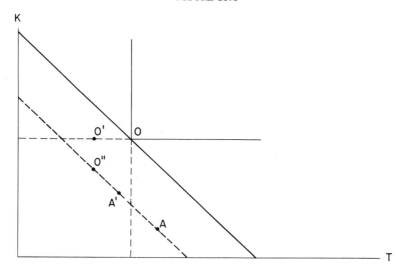

FIGURE 15.5

transfer. The victim will be injured as much as the beneficiary gains.[2]
Assume then that we are now at point *O* on figure 15.5. Some pressure
group—let us say the citizens of Tulsa, who would like their city to be
a deepwater harbor—invest a certain amount of resources in lobbying
in Congress. This moves society to point *O'*. The amount of resources
they would invest would in part be a function of the counterinvest-
ment of resources they expect, but let us defer that discussion for the
moment.

People who would rather not have their tax dollars spent dredging
the river to make Tulsa a deepwater port—*K* in our diagram—now invest resources in lobbying against the measure, with the result that
society moves to *O''*. Congress then acts. If the measure to dredge the
river to Tulsa is defeated, we would remain at *O''*. Unfortunately, in
the real world, the measure carried. There was thus a transfer of resources from *K* to *T*. Since the lobbying activity had lowered the total
number of resources, this was a forty-five-degree movement from *O''*.[3]

[2] This, strictly speaking, is not a necessary condition for the analysis that follows. It
could be that, although the "donor" would rather not give this particular amount, he
nevertheless acquires some utility from the gift, albeit less than its cost to him. This
would lead to more elaborate analysis but no fundamental change in our conclusion.

[3] This particular transfer might be a movement that, in and of itself, impoverished
society. That is, the dredging might have been worth much less to the citizens of Tulsa

If the citizens of Tulsa—represented by T in our diagram—had calculated appropriately, the transfer of resources would be such that they would be benefited as a result of the entire transaction, that is, they would reach some such point as A. If they had calculated inappropriately, the transfer might be less than the loss of resources invested in the effort to obtain the dredging operation; hence, they might end up at A'.

We could, I think, assume—looking at the matter solely from the standpoint of those persons engaged in lobbying to cause such transfers—that when the transfer was successful, it would turn out that they had made a net profit on the operation. When the transfer was unsuccessful, of course, they would lose. What the present discounted value of the stream of several such operations would be, we cannot say. It might well be some such point as A'. If we assume, however, that everyone is engaged in attempting to get such transfers and that there is a tendency for them to cancel out among different members of society, then clearly we end up in the Pareto-dominated area. In any event, it is clear that the action as a whole has not benefited "society," and that if asked whether we would like such transactions to occur in the future, not knowing whether we would be the beneficiaries or victims of them, we would be opposed. The ex ante value of a stream of such redistributions is negative for the average person.

Let us consider briefly the calculation undertaken by some party who finds himself either interested in obtaining a transfer from someone else by lobbying or interested in avoiding a transfer from himself. Under these circumstances, he invests resources in lobbying as shown in figure 15.6. For the lobbying costs and potential gains from lobbying (assuming that his opponent is undertaking some fixed amount of counterlobbying) as shown in figure 15.6, he would choose to invest amount A in lobbying activity and would purchase some particular probability of success. Looked at from his standpoint, this is ex ante a sensible investment of his resources. Ex post, he may win or he may lose, but over time a policy of always making this kind of calculation

---

than its cost to other people. Under these circumstances, the movement would be along a line at a steeper angle than forty-five degrees. It would be an inefficient transfer. Although in the real world individual transfers may have this type of inefficiency attached to them, it seems sensible to confine our discussion to the simple case where the transfer does not in and of itself involve inefficiency.

FIGURE 15.6

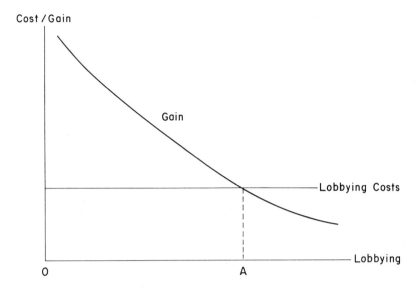

and investing an appropriate amount in lobbying would maximize his income stream.

Note, however, that we have assumed that the other party's lobbying activities are fixed. In the real world, each of the two parties would adjust lobbying activities to that of his opponent, and the end result would be a standard reaction diagram with (assuming everything is normal) the two curves intersecting at an equilibrium point. Since the resources used in lobbying are self-cancelling—T's resources in part simply offset K's—they represent net social loss. If we could predict the outcome in advance, both parties could benefit by accepting that outcome without the investment of resources. Nevertheless, in the real world the individuals would be irrational *not* to make the investment in lobbying, and we can anticipate that this type of prisoner's dilemma will lead to large-scale investment in lobbying in those situations in which transfers are possible.

This article has been entitled "The Cost of Transfers." As can be seen from the diagram, it could also have been called "The Cost of Resistance to Transfers." The problem is that the possibility of a transfer leads people to invest resources in either obtaining the transfer or preventing it. People who hope to receive the transfer will invest resources until the return in probability of receiving the transfer on the last dollar is worth one dollar. Those against whom the transfer would work will invest similarly. One side or the other will win, but from the social standpoint the resources invested in the conflict between the two groups are entirely wasted.

There is, of course, no a priori argument for one side or the other being favored in elimination of this conflict. If we return to the customs of Gladstone's England, in which the government engaged in substantially no transfers and it was known to all parties that the lobbying cost of introducing a change in this custom for their own benefit would almost certainly be much in excess of the benefit received, we would find very little such resource investment. If, on the other hand, the converse situation existed—it was widely believed that any proposal for a transfer would automatically go through, and hence it was a waste of resources to resist the transfer—once again, few resources would be wasted in conflict. The reason being, of course, that with little resistance to transfers, there would also be very little resources invested in obtaining the transfers.[4] One might choose between these two social situations in terms of a general attitude toward transfers, but this would be outside the scope of this essay.

So much for government-imposed redistribution of income or wealth. As can readily be seen, war and theft can be analyzed by the same apparatus and, indeed, shown on the same diagrams if we change the labeling a little bit.[5] In each case, resources can be invested to obtain transfers, and in each case, if the other side invests very little resources, this will be a profitable operation. The Mexicans, for example, are a very poor people living next to the wealthiest nation in the world. Further, as far as I can see, they rather dislike the citizens of the United States. Under the circumstances, conquest of the United States would clearly be highly desirable for Mexico. The reason they do not do it, of course, is that with our present armament it would be a militarily impossible operation. If, however, we unilaterally disarmed and hence made conquest of the United States cheap, they would be fools not to undertake the action. Needless to say, our military forces right now are not aimed against the Mexicans. They are aimed at other

[4] There might be large investments in attempts to determine which particular transfers were to take place.

[5] This also applies to revolutions.

enemies who are so powerful that it is necessary to maintain forces vastly superior to those maintained by Mexico. Under the circumstances, we are probably suffering nothing from the enmity of Mexico, and the Mexicans have nothing to fear from us militarily.

If, however, we have two major powers, both of which are heavily armed, it is likely that the conflict between them will cost more than the benefit; hence, one would anticipate that on the whole they would choose not to engage in the conflict, although the competitive armament itself is a form of conflict. It should be noted, however, that this is simply because the armament level is high enough so that the costs of conflict are very great. If the armament level by either or both were permitted to slip back to the point where the costs of conflicts would be low, the probable profits of the war would reappear. Consider, for example, the North Vietnamese government's first attempt to overthrow the government of Cambodia. Granted the military preparations that Cambodia had, it seems to me that the decision to make this attempt was a rational one ex ante, regardless of its results ex post.

To summarize, it is customary to say that transfers are costless economically and raise essentially noneconomic problems. I do not wish to quarrel with the statement that transfers normally raise noneconomic problems; the point of this essay has been simply to point out that they also do involve purely economic costs. The transfer itself may be costless, but the prospect of the transfer leads individuals and groups to invest resources in attempting either to obtain a transfer or to resist a transfer away from themselves. These resources represent net social waste. Transfers lead to conflict, and conflict is always an example of social waste from the standpoint of society as a whole. Unfortunately, it is very commonly rational for the individuals engaged in it.

16

On The Welfare Cost
of Transfers

by

Edgar K. Browning

IN a recent article, Professor Gordon Tullock elaborates on the idea
that government transfers involve a real resource cost to society even
if traditional excess burdens are ignored.[1] The cost reflects the investment of resources in lobbying designed to obtain or prevent the transfers of income: "The transfer itself may be costless, but the prospect of
the transfer leads individuals and groups to invest resources in attempting either to obtain a transfer or to resist a transfer away from
themselves. These resources represent net social waste."[2] Furthermore, Tullock suggests that this waste, or welfare loss, can be quite
large. It is possible, for instance, that the recipients of government redistribution of income will invest more resources in lobbying for the
transfer than they ultimately receive, so the supposed beneficiaries of
the redistribution are actually worse off on balance. This would truly
be a welfare loss with a vengeance.

Although correct in arguing that resource investment in lobbying
represents a welfare loss, Tullock greatly overstates the likely size of
this loss. Indeed, for a great many government transfer policies it can
be shown that the "Tullock welfare loss" will be virtually nonexistent.

NOTE: I would like to thank William Breit and Roland N. McKean for their comments on
an earlier version.

[1] Gordon Tullock, "The Cost of Transfers," chapter 15 in this volume. Tullock
makes the same argument in *Private Wants, Public Means* (New York: Basic Books,
1970), pp. 250–251, and in "The Welfare Costs of Tariffs, Monopolies, and Theft," chapter 3 in this volume. Some closely related matters are discussed in Gordon Tullock, "The
Charity of the Uncharitable," *Western Economic Journal* 9 (December, 1971): 379–392.

[2] Gordon Tullock, "The Cost of Transfers," p. 282.

Suppose the transfer policy in question is the degree of progressivity of the income tax structure. Our problem is to determine the quantity of resources devoted to lobbying to affect the policy outcome. Since tax reforms are frequently on the political agenda, let the reader ask himself what resource investment in lobbying he made to influence this policy when it last arose. If my case is at all typical, and I shall argue that it is, the answer is that no voluntary contribution to lobbying was made. As a first approximation, then, it appears that individuals do not commit resources to lobbying in this type of case.

Such behavior is perfectly rational, despite the fact that lobbying might favorably affect the policy choice. The salient feature of this tax reform, as well as most other government programs that redistribute income, is that it transfers income from one group of millions of people to another group of similarly large size. Lobbying activity that affects the policy decision then has the attributes of a public good: an increase in the probability of a more progressive tax has indivisible benefits for millions of taxpayers (and indivisible costs for millions more), with it being very difficult to exclude the effects from those who do not contribute to the lobby. Since lobbying is a public good, the free-rider problem becomes the central element in the analysis of an individual's decision to invest in lobbying. It is no surprise, then, that individuals would not invest in lobbying, since their *individual* contributions would not significantly affect the policy outcome and they will enjoy the same benefits (or bear the same costs) regardless of whether they contribute.

Consider Tullock's explanation of why individuals would lobby: "In any situation in which transfers are likely, it must be assumed that profit-seeking individuals will invest resources in attempting to get them or prevent them, if the transfer is away from the individual."[3] But the fact that high-income taxpayers might *collectively* profit from investing in lobbying to reduce progression is no reason to suppose that it is in the *individual* interest of even a single one of them to lobby. Tullock has forgotten the free-rider phenomenon. (It is worth mentioning that this is an instance where free-rider behavior is a positive advantage in a social system. There are other examples: for instance, the free-rider problem is a factor that inhibits collusive agreements

[3] Ibid. The quoted passage is in the "Summary" attached to the original article but not reprinted in this volume.

among firms trying to establish a cartel.) Therefore, the "Tullock welfare loss" would be nonexistent, or at most negligible, in this situation.

Tullock's argument is thus an incomplete explanation of the existence of lobbies. But lobbying activity is a prevalent feature of the political landscape, and we must now attempt to explain why it does occur. To put the matter most simply: under what conditions can a group overcome the free-rider problem and provide a public good? Mancur Olson, Jr., has examined this problem in detail, and the following remarks rely on his trenchant analysis.[4]

Olson identifies three circumstances in which a public good such as lobbying can be provided. First, the group may be of sufficiently small size that the free-rider problem can be at least partially overcome. Thus, if the government redistributes income in favor of a small group, some lobbying may occur. For example, a tariff to protect the firms in a concentrated industry often calls forth lobbying effort. In the small-group case, however, the amount of lobbying will tend to be less than the amount that maximizes profits for the entire group. In any event, the bulk of government redistribution is probably not of the small-group variety.

Second, an organization may be able to coerce individuals into supporting a lobby. Coercion presumably accounts for Tullock's example of the citizens of Tulsa's lobbying to have the federal government dredge the river to make Tulsa a deepwater port. The citizens of Tulsa, being a large group, would not voluntarily contribute to this effort, but the government of Tulsa may use its power to levy taxes to finance a lobby. Even so, the lobbying effort would be constrained by the existence of a large number of local governments (i.e., if the federal government is deciding whether to dredge a hundred rivers, there would be a free-rider problem affecting local governments themselves), by differences of opinion within the locality, and by the mobility of people among local governments. Nevertheless, some lobbying activity surely does take place by local governments, as well as by other organizations that have coercive power.

A third way lobbies can be supported arises when an organization is financed by selling an essentially private good to people and using some of the proceeds to finance the lobby. This is Olson's by-product

---

[4] Mancur Olson, Jr., *The Logic of Collective Action* (New York: Schocken Books, 1968).

theory of pressure groups, with the lobbying activity a by-product of an organization that provides some other nonlobbying service. Labor unions and the American Medical Association are good examples of lobbies organized in this way.

The "Tullock welfare loss" is not a necessary consequence of government redistribution but results from the possibility of redistribution in conjunction with one or more of the factors enumerated above. Granted that some lobbying does occur on redistributive issues, however, can we follow Tullock and conclude that the welfare loss is likely "vastly larger" than the conventional excess burden of the price-distorting effects of the transfers?[5] There are several reasons for doubting that this is so. First, not all redistribution will call forth lobbying effort, as we have seen. Second, even when the conditions enumerated above do result in lobbying, there is no reason to suppose that it will be the amount of lobbying that maximizes profit for the relevant group. In all likelihood it will be a much smaller amount.[6] Third, it may be that the cost of lobbying is greater than the expected increase in transfers to the group, in which case it would be irrational, even collectively, for the group to lobby. The fact that some lobbies do exist does not prove that possible benefits are *generally* greater than costs. Fourth, some lobbying may be desirable to convey information to legislators, just as some advertising may be a good thing. Fifth, we should not be misled into thinking that all special-interest legislation that redistributes in favor of some group results from a lobbying effort.[7] As Richard Wagner emphasizes in his review of Olson's book, politicians may enact special-interest legislation to gain votes without any lobbying being involved.[8] Sixth, and finally, the traditional excess burdens are quite large themselves. A conservative estimate of redistribution by the federal government in the United States (including budgetary items and rough guesses of the distributive impact of its promotion of business and labor monopoly) is $150 billion annually. The excess burden of this redistribution is probably at least 10 percent of the amount

---

[5] Tullock makes this claim explicitly in *Private Wants, Public Means*, pp. 250–251.

[6] The difficulties faced by a lobby attempting to maximize the "profit" of its members are closely analogous to those facing a cartel. See George Stigler, *The Theory of Price*, 3rd ed. (London: The Macmillan Company, 1966), chapter 13.

[7] Tullock, to be sure, does not claim this explicitly.

[8] Richard E. Wagner, "Pressure Groups and the Political Entrepreneurs: A Review Article," *Papers on Non-Market Decision Making* 1 (1966): 161–170.

transferred, or $15 billion, and may be considerably more.[9] For these reasons it is far from obvious that the "Tullock welfare loss" from lobbying for and against government redistribution will dwarf conventional excess burdens, but this issue must ultimately be resolved by empirical research.

These critical remarks should not obscure the genuine contribution Tullock makes. Tullock suggests that more is at stake with government redistribution than simply the price-distorting effects of the taxes and subsidies. In this he is clearly correct, although we may differ as to how important we think "Tullock welfare losses" are quantitatively. Tullock's analysis also suggests the importance of analyzing redistributive schemes within an explicit public-choice framework. Further analysis of this sort may well disclose other "hidden" welfare losses (and perhaps welfare gains as well) that are not apparent in the conventional emphasis on price distortions. For example, I conjecture that a major impact of legislators' spending so much time designing a multitude of redistributive programs is that they are less well informed about other government programs. If this is so, perhaps the place to look for the hidden welfare losses of government redistribution as presently carried out is in the inefficient performance of other government policies.

[9] It should be recalled that transfers have a double excess burden, since there is a distortion introduced by the tax as well as the benefit payment. If the excess burden per dollar of revenue (ideally including administrative and compliance costs) is 5 percent and the excess burden per dollar of expenditure is also 5 percent, we would then have the 10 percent figure given in the text. I have made a very rough estimate of the excess burden for a specific negative income tax, considering only labor supply distortions and ignoring administrative and compliance costs, and the result was an excess burden equal to 15 percent of the amount transferred (see Edgar K. Browning, "Income Redistribution and the Negative Income Tax: A Theoretical Analysis" [Ph.D. dissertation, Princeton University, 1971], chapter 4, appendix B).

17

More on the Welfare Cost
of Transfers

by
Gordon Tullock

THAT lobbying for income transfers in many cases generates public goods or bads cannot, I think, be denied. If this is so, then the investment in obtaining such a transfer would be less than the total present discounted value of the transfer. As I shall argue below, this offers an explanation for the fact that in democracies we see a very large amount of self-cancelling transfers of income back and forth within the middle-income groups.

Before turning to this matter, however, I should like to discuss the political costs of transfer mechanism. Edgar Browning is, of course, quite correct in his final remark about cost of "legislators' spending so much time designing a multitude of redistributive programs . . . that they are less well informed about other government programs."[1] What we actually have for many of these programs is what we might call Wagner-type lobbying.[2] The congressmen consider that the voters in their district are more interested in getting projects in the district than in almost anything else, and hence spend much of their time in attempting to get transfers to their districts. Some congressmen also specialize in obtaining transfers to special groups in society who are represented in their district but are also of wider scope: the elderly, farmers, and so forth.[3] Surely this cost in terms of that

[1] Edgar K. Browning, "On the Welfare Cost of Transfers," chapter 16 in this volume, p. 287.

[2] Richard E. Wagner, "Pressure Groups and Political Entrepreneurs: A Review Article," *Papers on Non-Market Decision Making* 1 (1966): 161–170.

[3] Although this article and Browning's article are based primarily on American data, as far as I can see these phenomena are universal in democracies.

very scarce resource, legislators' time, must be immense. Further, it must have exactly the offsetting characteristics that I discussed in the original article.

We can go further, however. Another group of people who engage in active lobbying are bureaucrats in each government bureau. These bureaucrats are essentially interested in transfers to themselves by way of expanding their particular bureau, but the social costs must be immense.[4] Once again, competition between the bureaus would set off the kind of phenomena that I described in my original article.

Note that in both these cases, however, the actual effect of this kind of lobbying is much greater than the direct resource cost because a great many people who are not involved in lobbying find themselves affected by the outcome. A dispute between the Department of Interior and the Army Corps of Engineers for appropriations would lead to an investment of resources by those two bureaus that probably fairly well discounted the value to the two bureaus of the switch in appropriations between them that they are fighting for. The effect of that appropriation on the economy as a whole may be vastly greater. But since these are the only people involved in the actual conflict for or against the appropriation, we would anticipate that the effect on the economy as a whole would tend to be relatively random. If so, we would expect that the transfer effect of the outcome of this dispute on the economy as a whole would only by coincidence fit some idea of social policy. Basically, it would simply be a random transfer.

In my original article, I talked mainly about transfers of this sort, that is, decisions on appropriations or programs that had a fairly concrete and narrow direct effect for some limited group of people. Browning refers to "tax reform" as a typical example and says, "The salient feature . . . , as [of] most other government programs that redistribute income, is that it transfers income from one group of millions of people to another group of similarly large size." His example is "the degree of progressivity of the income tax structure." He argues that "no voluntary contribution to lobbying" was made on this issue.[5]

Clearly we are talking about different types of programs, and I am willing to argue that the type Browning describes is relatively rare.

---

[4] See David L. Shapiro, "Can Public Investment Have a Positive Rate of Return?" *Journal of Political Economy* 81 (March–April, 1973): 401–413.

[5] Browning, "On the Welfare Cost of Transfers," p. 284.

First, when we turn to facts, the new Musgrave and Musgrave text summarizes the situation fairly well.[6] The total tax burden on Americans is approximately proportional to their income for a long range from about $5,700 a year to about $35,000 a year.[7] Taxes below $5,700 are lower and they rise above $35,000, although not very steeply. If one turns to the net result of government action,[8] somewhat the same picture emerges. In other words, the net effect of our tax and government activity is not particularly progressive.[9]

In practice it seems to be necessary for most governments to have a nominally progressive tax system, and the fact that it must be nominally progressive no doubt does indeed have some real effects. In the United States, for example, all basic changes in the tax structure apparently require some increase in the nominal degree of progressivity. However, in practice this progressivity is more illusion than reality. Thus, on this matter for which Browning says there is very little lobbying, it is also true that it is not obvious that the government has any particular policy. The actual "degree of progressivity of the income tax structure" is, however, the result of very intense lobbying on a myriad of detailed provisions.

If one looks at the U.S. income tax in detail, one finds an immense body of law and regulation. Buried in this mass of literature is a gigantic number of special provisions that benefit various small special groups. I believe, and I do not expect that Browning will contest it, that these provisions have all been put in by active lobbying by those particular groups. In many cases the lobbyist is, of course, a congressman rather than a professional, but private lobbyists make major contributions, also.

Since such provisions are normally public goods (or bads), albeit for normally quite a small group of people (perhaps 10,000), the theoretical objection raised by Browning would appear to apply here,

---

[6] Richard A. Musgrave and Peggy B. Musgrave, *Public Finance in Theory and Practice* (New York: McGraw-Hill, 1973).

[7] Ibid., p. 369.

[8] Ibid., p. 376.

[9] Indeed, in my opinion it may be sharply regressive. The services given by the government are normally evaluated on their resource cost. It seems likely that many of these services, such as elementary education, in fact are of considerably less value to the poor than to the well-off. If this is so and the value of benefits given by the various governments is adjusted accordingly, we might find that in the middle ranges (which, after

also. Indeed, I think it does. However, we do observe these lobbies; let us consider how that happens.

If we consider some action of the government that will affect a number of people, it is normally true that it will affect different people differently. There may be some for whom the effect is quite large and a number for whom the effect is small. If there are some for whom the effect is quite large, it may be wise for them to invest resources in attempting to get a change in government policy.

In general, the desirability of such an investment from their standpoint will depend on how much the return to them would be from the change in government policy, and, secondarily, on what likelihood there is of opposition. If there is going to be no opposition— that is, there are no people on the other side for whom there would be a concentrated harm imposed—then the cost of generating the change will be much lower; indeed, it will simply be the cost of overcoming the inertia of the government system. On the other hand, there may be similar concentrated interests on the other side, and hence we may have a conflict. In any event, there surely are very many cases in which it is sensible for at least some people to invest at least some resources in lobbying for or against the change.

Insofar as these people do invest resources in attempting to make such a change, then the argument that I offered in my original article would tend to be true, although of course its strength is diluted. For those people who are affected by the redistributional change but for whom the effect is small enough so that it is not worth their time to invest any resources in it, the outcome is apt to be random. For some of these changes they will benefit, for some they will lose. We would anticipate that, over the population as a whole, individuals who are not involved in active lobbying would tend to gain about as much as they lose. Browning gives $150 billion as the total of transfers in the United States. I see no reason to doubt this, but it should be pointed out that

---

all, include almost the entire population) the net effect of the government is to make the income distribution markedly less equal than it would be without government activity. Once again, although I am using American data, I regard this as characteristic of most democracies. See Adrian L. Webb and Jack E. B. Sieve, *Income Redistribution and the Welfare State* (London: Social Administration Research Trust, 1971), for data on the situation in England.

the transfer from the wealthy and to the poor is only a very small part of that amount. [10]

The bulk of transfers, however, are back and forth within that massive group of people who make up the bulk of society and pay the bulk of the taxes. Although individual members of this group may suffer very pronounced negative transfers or receive very pronounced positive benefits as a result of what amounts to participating in a lottery, surely most of them end up with about the same income they would have had to begin with, except, of course, insofar as the excess burden reduced their total income. The people who are interested in obtaining or preventing transfers, on the other hand, do invest resources and have a cost that is related to whatever transfer they receive or prevent. Thus, the population either invests resources in lobbying or participates in a lottery. For the first group, which is probably small, my original description is more or less correct. For the second, and much larger group, there is an excess burden but, on the average, no net transfer.

---

[10] There are allegations occasionally found in the literature that the wealthy do not in fact suffer any negative transfers from the tax system. With careful reading, it will usually be found that the author's actual feeling is that the wealthy should have larger transfers of income away from them than they now have, not that they now have no loss through the transfer system.

18

Wealth Transfers in a Representative Democracy

by

ROBERT E. MCCORMICK *and* ROBERT D. TOLLISON

IN the theory of economic regulation, interest groups seek transfers of wealth from consumer-voters. The basis for wealth transfers to successful interest groups is shirking by voters. In a world of costless voting and Wicksellian unanimity, there would clearly be no Pareto-inferior moves; all transfers would enhance individually perceived welfare. Costly voting encourages transfer-seeking activity because it makes shirking efficient for some voters. Indeed, some voters may even shirk under a unanimity rule if the costs of voting and becoming informed exceed the benefits of voting.

Building on these widely recognized points, we can develop the concept of a supply of wealth transfers. Individuals will let their wealth be taken away from them so long as the costs of changing such political outcomes are less than the amount of wealth taken away. If collective decisions are easily influenced, there will be a small amount of wealth transfers supplied. As the costs of monitoring and sanctioning collective decisions rise, a larger quantity of wealth transfers will be supplied.

Where there are costs associated with obtaining wealth transfers, not all individuals or groups will find it worthwhile to seek them. As George Stigler observes, "many stakes are so small that trifling costs of

NOTE: We are grateful to participants in the Economics Workshop at the Graduate School of Management, University of Rochester, especially John Long, Cliff Smith, and Jerry Zimmerman, and to Arleen Leibowitz and George Stigler for helpful comments on earlier drafts of this paper. The usual disclaimer applies.

representation are sufficient to silence them."[1] Those individuals or groups who do find such activity profitable are customarily called lobbyists or interest groups. The purpose of this paper is to develop a testable economic theory of the lobbying behavior of interest groups in the pursuit of wealth transfers. This theory will be expressed in terms of a maximization process, in which the lobbyist seeks to maximize the returns to his interest group (net of total lobbying expenses) from legislation.[2] Such a theory is presented in the following section, where we derive the conditions that indicate how the lobbyist will allocate his lobbying budget in a bicameral vote market so as to maximize his interest group's returns from legislation. Moreover, the properties of this theory, when the size of the legislature and the relative sizes of the two houses of the legislature change, are developed in this section. A number of testable implications come from this analysis. Perhaps the primary ones are that the lobbyist will fare better in procuring returns from legislation for his interest group (1) where the size of the legislature is small, and (2) where the sizes of the senate and house are close to equal. These implications of the analysis, along with several others, are subjected to two empirical tests in the second section below. Some brief remarks are offered in a concluding section. Finally, the first chapter appendix briefly outlines how considerations of the size of the interest group can be incorporated in the analysis.

Maximizing the Returns from Legislation in a Bicameral Vote Market

We will basically follow Stigler's lead in this section, stressing that legislative influence is analogous to market influence and that it is not appropriate to think in strict majoritarian terms when analyzing the concept of political influence.[3] Here the activity of the lobbyist is analyzed in terms of how he derives and allocates his budget in the buying of legislative influence so as to maximize the returns to his interest group from legislation. We do not presume that the lobbyist has to buy

[1] George J. Stigler, "The Sizes of Legislatures," *Journal of Legal Studies* 5 (January, 1976): 18.

[2] We are speaking here, and subsequently in the paper, in terms of a rate of return to the interest group, and not to society.

[3] George J. Stigler, "Economic Competition and Political Competition," *Public Choice* 13 (Fall, 1972): 91–106.

a majority of legislators in order to reap returns from legislation. Later in the section, the analysis is recast into terms of purchasing a simple majority of legislators in both houses. In either case the presumption of an economic approach to the market for special-interest legislation is that increasing levels of expenditures by an interest group will increase the influence or votes the group receives on an issue. The naive view that influence in one chamber is useless without influence in the other is rejected.

Second, although it could be argued that demand and supply factors generate a single market-clearing price of legislation, it should be clear from our earlier discussion that no two pieces of legislation will evoke uniform support or opposition. Small groups or groups that face low costs of controlling free-riding behavior among their members can offer politicians greater support (e.g., campaign contributions and votes) in return for the politicians' support on legislation. The amount of influence purchased per dollar will vary among interest groups as their ability to support politicians varies. In other words, every piece of legislation will have a different demand and supply function, so that, practically speaking, each legislative transaction will carry a separate price.[4]

THEORY

The interest group must decide how much to spend on buying legislative influence, and its functionary must decide how to allocate this budget across the two houses of the legislature so as to maximize the organization's returns from legislative influence. Whether the group can "afford" the price necessary to win returns through legislation will again be a function of its comparative advantage in collecting votes and contributions for politicians. The organization knows that the votes (V) it will receive in each house are a function of its expenditures in each house $(E^h$ and $E^s)$ and the size of each house $(h$ and $s)$. That is, $V^h = V^h(E^h, h)$, and $V^s = V^s(E^s, s)$. The economic problem faced by the interest group is therefore to maximize the net returns (Y_n) from legislative influence, that is, $Y_n = Y - E$, where E is the size of the group's lobbying budget.

$$Y_n = Y - E, \qquad (1)$$

[4] The formal analysis underlying the discussion in this paragraph appears in the first appendix at the end of the paper.

$$E = E^h + E^s, \tag{2}$$

$$Y = Y(V^h, V^s, L, W, P), \tag{3}$$
$$Y_1, Y_2, Y_4, Y_5 > 0, \text{ and } Y_3 < 0.$$

$$V^h = V^h(E^h, h), \text{ and} \tag{4}$$
$$V^s = V^s(E^s, s). \tag{5}$$

$$V^h_1, V^h_2, V^s_1, V^s_2 > 0$$
$$V^h_{11}, V^h_{22}, V^s_{11}, V^s_{22} < 0$$
$$V^h_{12}, V^s_{12} > 0.$$

Equation (3) maps the level of house and senate influence, V^h and V^s, into income. Increasing levels of influence enhance the returns from lobbying ($Y_1, Y_2 > 0$). Rather than votes, influence is employed as a more general measure of what interest groups seek. The degree of correspondence between influence and votes will be a function of the homogeneity of legislators. If legislators are identical and come from identical districts, influence and votes will be equivalent. However, if legislators are different (e.g., they have different term lengths), their ability to manipulate political processes will vary, and the correspondence between influence and votes will diverge. In this case, which is the one most frequently observed, the purchase of influence by an interest group is the more general case and will be formalized first. The purchase of votes is a special case of the purchase of influence, a case to be analyzed later in this section.

The wealth (W) of a community influences lobbying in two ways. As wealth increases, the costs to individual voters of monitoring the political process increase (a substitution effect), and the income obtained by a lobbying group should thus rise in wealthier jurisdictions. However, if monitoring the political process is an income-elastic consumption good, an argument that is often made, there is an income effect of increasing community wealth on monitoring, which cuts in the opposite direction from the substitution effect. In our analysis we will claim that the substitution effect dominates ($Y_4 > 0$).

As population (P) increases, the probability of any one voter's influencing collective decisions decreases. Moreover, for a given transfer (W^o), the per capita share of the costs falls as P increases. For both these reasons more transfers will be forthcoming from larger populations ($Y_5 > 0$).

Legislative size (L), which is $h + s$, has an important effect on the interest group's returns from legislation, which is examined in detail below.

Equations (4) and (5) are the vote-production functions in the two houses. These vary as the institutional character (e.g., term lengths) of the two houses varies. We assume that there are diminishing returns of influence, wealth, and population on income in each house and across both houses taken together. The presumption of diminishing returns in equations (3), (4), and (5) is based upon two arguments.

The first argument derives from our earlier statment that each piece of legislation carries a separate price. As various legislators arrive from different constituencies, their relative prices to interest groups, based on potential campaign support by the various groups, will result in an ordering of supply prices among legislators.[5] In other words, the politician must pay careful attention to the opposition (or "losers"), so that at the margin the political gain to him from the last dollar transferred just equals the loss. Since an interest group will first purchase that legislative influence which carries the lowest supply price, there are diminishing returns of expenditures to votes, as given in equations (4) and (5).[6] Second, and similarly, an interest group will first convert its influence into those projects which have the greatest impact on its income. We assume that the various legislation an interest group seeks will have descending impacts on its income, and that there are therefore diminishing returns of influence to income. It will turn out that diminishing returns in either case is a necessary condition for a determinate solution to the optimal level of spending (E) by an interest group.

For several reasons legislative size plays an important role in the lobbying process. First, increasing legislative size increases the number of vote suppliers and reduces the costs of influence or votes. Since in this theory politicians are brokers between winners and losers in

[5] This theory does not depend upon a monolithic idea of legislators as vote sellers. Lobbying frequently conveys information to legislators, for example, about the proportion of voters who favor or oppose a particular proposal. Thus, based upon personal convictions, attitudes toward risk, reelection prospects, and so forth, various legislators will have different Marshallian "convincing prices." What this means is that there is an ordered array of prices of influence facing the interest group, and for analytical simplicity we simply assume that all influence is purchased.

[6] Again, see the first appendix for a more detailed analysis of this aspect of the analysis.

the wealth-transfer process, the degree of competition in the legislative process will affect their brokerage fee. As some analysts have argued, the presence of a few firms does not necessarily imply a noncompetitive outcome.[7] What it does suggest, however, is a relatively low cost of colluding. The latter point is especially important in the case of a legislature, where entry is not costless and the size of the legislature is fixed. For such reasons increases in house size will reduce the price of influence because of reduced monopoly power among suppliers, but this effect should diminish quite rapidly (V_2^h, $V_2^s > 0$). In other words, for a fixed level of lobbying expenditures in either chamber, a larger house size will increase the level of influence obtained, but at a diminishing rate. Second, there is a perhaps more important effect of legislative size because larger legislatures mean smaller relative influence for any individual legislator. This might be termed the "small fish in the big pond" effect. Larger legislatures are thus characterized by relatively weak individual legislators, weak in the sense that the influence of any one of them is likely to have a small impact on the income of a lobbying group. Third, another effect, perhaps an insignificant one, is that a larger legislature reduces the number of voters per legislator, and this might lead to improved policing by voters. In other words, larger legislatures will more closely represent the entire citizenry, and hence there will be a smaller level of wealth transfers. (Consider the limiting case where all voters are in the legislature.) It is less expensive for losers in the wealth-transfer process to affect political outcomes when legislative size is large, and thus, when legislative size increases, an interest group will find that its fixed stock of votes or influence yields fewer transfers.

We capture these effects in equation (3) by signing $Y_3 < 0$. That is, as legislative size increases, any particular absolute amount of influence obtained, V^h and V^s, will be less valuable, because in a relative sense the influence obtained has actually declined.[8]

---

[7] See Eugene F. Fama and Arthur B. Laffer, "The Number of Firms and Competition," *American Economic Review* 62 (September, 1972): 670–674.

[8] Consider the following example. A firm wins the influence of one legislator out of fifty. Facing a six-month delay in obtaining permission from the environmental board to discharge a certain amount of waste, the firm requests the legislator to phone the board. The delay is reduced to two months at the legislator's insistence. Now consider the same example where there are seventy-five legislators. The environmental board will be less

If we insert equations (2) through (5) into equation (1), we find that the first-order conditions necessary to maximize the group's net income with choice variables E^h and E^s are:

$$Y_1[V^h(E^h, h), V^s(E^s, s), L, W, P] \, V_1^h(E^h, h) = 1, \text{ and} \tag{6}$$

$$Y_2[V^h(E^h, h), V^s(E^s, s), L, W, P] \, V_1^s(E^s, s) = 1. \tag{7}$$

These two conditions taken together imply that

$$\frac{V_1^h(\cdot)}{V_1^s(\cdot)} = \frac{Y_2(\cdot)}{Y_1(\cdot)}, \tag{8}$$

or that the lobbying group will spend to influence votes until the ratio of the marginal impact of its expenditures on votes in the two houses equals the ratio of the marginal impact of relative votes in the two houses on its income.[9]

As we noted in the presentation of the model, legislative size plays an important and complex role in the lobbying process. To understand this aspect of our analysis more fully, we now explore the response of an interest group to changes in the size of the legislature and to changes in the ratio of house sizes (holding total legislative size constant). More specifically, we want to know what happens to lobbying expenditures, the amount of influence obtained from these expenditures, and the change in an interest group's net income from lobbying in the presence of these two types of changes in the size of the legislature.

---

concerned about the request of any one legislator because there are more of them, each with proportionately less control over the activities of the agency, and the legislator's phone call will be worth less under these circumstances. The moral of the story is that only by increasing relative influence can income from lobbying be increased.

  [9] The second-order conditions sufficient to guarantee a maximum of equation (1) are

$$(V_1^h)^2 Y_{11} + Y_1 V_{11}^h < 0, \tag{1'}$$

which is satisfied by an assumption of diminishing returns of votes to income and of expenditures to votes, and

$$(V_1^h)^2 (V_1^s)^2 (Y_{11}Y_{22} - (Y_{12})^2) + Y_{11}Y_2 V_{11}^s (V_1^h)^2$$
$$+ Y_1 V_{11}^h Y_{22}(V_1^s)^2 + Y_1 Y_2 V_{11}^h V_{11}^s > 0. \tag{2'}$$

A sufficient, but not necessary, condition for (2') to hold is that $Y_{11}Y_{22} \geq (Y_{12})^2$. This condition will hold if diminishing returns of votes on income within each house are at least as large as the diminishing returns of votes on income across both houses taken together. We maintain such an assumption in the subsequent analysis.

CHANGES IN LEGISLATIVE SIZE

To examine the effects on E^h, E^s, V, and Y_n when the total size of the legislature changes, we displace equilibrium in our model by taking the total differential of equations (6) and (7). For simplicity we will change only the size of the lower house, that is, we set $ds = 0$.

Via Cramer's rule, the effect on expenditures in the house, as the size of the house increases, is

$$\frac{\partial E^h}{\partial h} = \frac{1}{|H|} \cdot \{V_1^h V_2^h (V_1^s)^2 [(Y_{12})^2 - Y_{11}Y_{22}]$$
$$+ V_1^h (V_1^s)^2 [Y_{12}Y_{23} - Y_{22}Y_{13}] - (V_1^s)^2 V_{12}^h Y_1 Y_{22}$$
$$- V_1^h V_2^h V_{11}^s Y_2 Y_{11} - V_1^h V_{11}^s Y_2 Y_{13}$$
$$- V_{11}^s V_{12}^h Y_1 Y_2\},\tag{9}$$

where $|H| = (V_1^h)^2 (V_1^s)^2 [Y_{11}Y_{22} - (Y_{12})^2] + (V_1^h)^2 V_{11}^s Y_2 Y_{11}$
$$+ (V_1^s)^2 V_{11}^h Y_1 Y_{22} + V_{11}^h V_{11}^s Y_1 Y_2 > 0$$

by the second-order conditions. Since $(Y_{12})^2 - Y_{11}Y_{22}$ is assumed to be nonpositive to ensure that the second-order conditions are met, we know that a larger house size reduces the interest group's house expenditures if $Y_{12} Y_{23} < Y_{22}Y_{13}$. If the effect of increasing legislative size reduces the marginal impact of influence on income equally in the two houses, and if the marginal effect of influence on income diminishes more rapidly in each house than across both houses, then $Y_{22}Y_{13} > Y_{12}Y_{23}$, and larger houses will result in smaller expenditures by interest groups in the house, that is, $\partial E^h/\partial h < 0$.

Similarly, we know that,

$$\frac{\partial E^s}{\partial h} = \frac{V_1^s}{|H|} \{(V_1^h)^2 (Y_{12}Y_{13} - Y_{11}Y_{23})$$
$$+ Y_1 Y_{12} (V_1^h V_{12}^h - V_2^h V_{11}^h) - V_{11}^h Y_1 Y_{23}\}.\tag{10}$$

Recalling that $Y_{11}Y_{23} > Y_{12}Y_{13}$, we know from direct observation that the first and third terms in brackets in equation (10), including their signs, are negative. We can also show that $V_1^h V_{12}^h - V_2^h V_{11}^h > 0$, and that the second term in brackets in equation (10) is also negative.[10] Con-

---

[10] Visualize a production mountain of votes, depending upon house size and lobbying expenditures. The iso-vote curves in this map will be convex, because V_1^h and V_2^h are both positive and because V_{11}^h and V_{22}^h are negative. The slope of these iso-vote curves is $-V_1^h/V_2^h$. The rate of change of the slope, as we increase E^h holding h constant, is $\partial(-V_1^h/V_2^h) / \partial E^h = -(V_{11}^h V_2^h - V_{12}^h V_1^h)/(V_2^h)^2$. If V^h is linearly homogeneous in E^h and h or is homothetic, the

sequently, the interest group will also reduce its expenditures in the senate when the house size increases. Moreover, the interest group will decrease its expenditures on influence buying in the face of an increase in legislative size, since its expenditures in both chambers decrease under these conditions.

Finally, we can deduce the effect on the net income of the interest group of an increase in the size of the house. Since $Y_n = Y - E$,

$$\partial Y_n / \partial h = \partial E^h / \partial h \ (Y_1 V_1^h - 1)$$
$$+ \ \partial E^s / \partial h \ (Y_2 V_1^s - 1) + Y_1 V_2^h + Y_3.$$

By the first-order conditions, both $Y_1 V_1^h$ and $Y_2 V_1^s$ are equal to one at the optimizing level of expenditure. Hence, $\partial Y_n / \partial h = Y_1 V_2^h + Y_3$, and the interest group's net income will fall if the income effect of the decline in relative influence exceeds the gain in value due to cheaper influence. Our conjecture is that the former effect dominates, and that the interest group's net income falls under these conditions.

Moreover, the change in influence for an increase in house size is

$$\partial V / \partial h = V_1^h \ \partial E^h / \partial h + V_2^h + V_1^s \ \partial E^s / \partial h.$$

The effect of house size on influence thus depends upon the magnitudes of the relevant variables, even though the lobby group has spent less money. For example, where the impact of size on the price of influence is small (i.e., V_2^h is near zero), $\partial V / \partial h < 0$, and increasing house size will reduce the total influence obtained by an interest group. On the other hand, if the marginal impact of lobbying expenditures on votes in the two chambers is sufficiently small compared with the effect of size on the price of influence in the house, then the total votes obtained will increase as house size grows.

Again, the reader might consider the limiting case where all voters belong to the house (i.e., referenda for state legislation). There would seem to be no doubt in this case that milk lobbyists, for example, would have a tougher time collecting rents from price supports under referenda voting. In this case it is clear that V_2^h is near zero, and hence the amount of influence obtained will also go down as house size increases.

In sum, then, there are good reasons to believe that as house size

---

slopes of the iso-vote functions are less negatively sloped, as we increase E^h holding h constant. It then follows clearly that $V_1^h V_{12}^h - V_2^h V_{11}^h > 0$.

increases, expenditures by the lobbying group go down, and the amount of influence obtained from these expenditures also falls (i.e., V_2^h is close to zero and $\partial V/\partial h < 0$).

CHANGES IN THE RATIO OF HOUSE SIZES

A second set of relevant exercises in comparative statics deals with the effects of a change in the ratio of house sizes on the interest group's expenditures in the two houses, the influence obtained from these expenditures, and the net income of the interest group from legislation. In deriving these results, we will set $\partial s/\partial h = -1$ to avoid the confounding effect of a simultaneous increase in the total number of legislators and an overall lower price of votes.

We again employ Cramer's rule to obtain the effect on expenditures in the house as house size increases at the expense of senate size.

$$\left.\frac{\partial E^h}{\partial h}\right|_{\frac{\partial s}{\partial h} = -1} = \frac{1}{|H|} \cdot \{V_1^h(V_1^s)^2V_2^h[(Y_{12})^2 - Y_{11}Y_{22}]$$

$$+ V_1^hV_{11}^sY_2(V_2^sY_{12} - V_2^hY_{11}) - V_1^sV_{12}^hY_1Y_2$$

$$- V_1^hV_1^sV_{12}^sY_2Y_{12} - V_{12}^h(V_1^s)^2Y_1Y_{22}\}.$$

If we assume that the diminishing returns of votes to income within each house are the same as the diminishing returns of votes to income across both houses (i.e., that $Y_{11} = Y_{12} = Y_{22}$), then expenditures in the house will decrease when the house-to-senate ratio increases. That is,

$$\left.\frac{\partial E^h}{\partial h}\right|_{\frac{\partial s}{\partial h} = -1} = - V_{11}^sV_{12}^hY_1Y_2 - V_1^hV_1^sV_{12}^sY_2Y_{12}$$

$$- V_{12}^h(V_1^s)^2Y_1Y_{22} < 0.$$

Analogously, the effect on expenditures in the senate as house size is increased at the expense of senate size is

$$\left.\frac{\partial E^s}{\partial h}\right|_{\frac{\partial s}{\partial h} = -1} = \frac{1}{|H|} \cdot \{(V_1^h)^2V_1^sV_2^s[Y_{11}Y_{22} - (Y_{12})^2]$$

$$+ V_1^sV_{11}^hY_1[V_2^sY_{22} - V_2^hY_{12}] + (V_1^h)^2V_{12}^sY_2Y_{11}$$

$$+ V_{11}^hV_{12}^sY_1Y_2 + V_1^hV_1^sV_{12}^hY_1Y_{12}\}.$$

Again, if $Y_{12} = Y_{11} = Y_{22}$, increasing the house-to-senate ratio will increase the interest group's expenditures in the senate because

$$\frac{\partial E^s}{\partial h}\bigg|_{\frac{\partial s}{\partial h} = -1} = (V_1^h)^2 V_{12}^s Y_2 Y_{11} + V_{11}^h V_{12}^s Y_1 Y_2$$
$$+ V_1^h V_1^s V_{12}^h Y_1 Y_{12} > 0.$$

The assumption of the equality of diminishing returns of votes to income within and across houses is a sufficient, but not necessary, condition for house expenditures to fall and senate expenditures to rise when the ratio of house-to-senate size increases. If the diminishing returns of votes to income are not equal, the results are ambiguous and depend upon the relative magnitudes of the variables.

Consider next what happens to the total number of votes that the interest group's expenditures convince with an increase in h at the expense of s. The change in V for the parametric change in house to senate size is given by

$$\frac{\partial V}{\partial h}\bigg|_{\frac{\partial s}{\partial h} = -1} = V_1^h \frac{\partial E^h}{\partial h}\bigg|_{\frac{\partial s}{\partial h} = -1} + V_2^h + V_1^s \frac{\partial E^s}{\partial h}\bigg|_{\frac{\partial s}{\partial h} = -1} - V_2^s.$$

If $Y_{11} = Y_{12} = Y_{22}$, then

$$\frac{\partial V}{\partial h}\bigg|_{\frac{\partial s}{\partial h} = -1} = \frac{Y_1 Y_2 (V_{11}^h V_1^s V_{12}^s - V_1^h V_{12}^h V_{11}^s)}{|H|} + V_2^h - V_2^s. \quad (11)$$

Since $s < h$, increases in s should have a greater impact on the price of influence than equal increases in h, and a greater impact on votes, or $V_2^h - V_2^s < 0$. Then, if the ratio of the marginal products of expenditures (to votes) is greater than the ratio at which they diminish, weighted by the ratio of the marginal impact of chamber size to marginal product of expenditures (i.e., $V_{11}^h V_1^s V_{12}^s < V_1^h V_{12}^h V_{11}^s$), we know that the total influence obtained will decrease if the house-to-senate ratio increases. Otherwise, it again becomes a question of the relative magnitudes of the variables.

Finally, the change in the lobby's return from seeking legislation is

$$\frac{\partial Y_n}{\partial h}\bigg|_{\frac{\partial s}{\partial h} = -1} = \frac{\partial E^h}{\partial h}\bigg|_{\frac{\partial s}{\partial h} = -1} (Y_1 V_1^h - 1)$$

$$+ \left. \frac{\partial E^s}{\partial h} \right|_{\frac{\partial s}{\partial h} = -1} \quad (Y_2 V_1^s - 1) + Y_1 V_2^h - Y_2 V_2^s.$$

We know that $Y_1 V_1^h = Y_2 V_1^s = 1$, and hence

$$\left. \frac{\partial Y_n}{\partial h} \right|_{\frac{\partial s}{\partial h} = -1} = Y_1 V_2^h - Y_2 V_2^s \gtreqless 0, \text{ as } \frac{Y_1}{Y_2} \gtreqless \frac{V_2^s}{V_2^h}. \tag{12}$$

Equation (12) is not strictly determinate. Since we have assumed that $V_2^s > V_2^h$ and $h > s$, and since it is quite plausible that at the optimizing level of expenditures the marginal impact on income of senate influence is at least as large as the marginal impact of house influence on income (i.e., $Y_2 \geq Y_1$), we believe that

$$\left. \frac{\partial Y_n}{\partial h} \right|_{\frac{\partial s}{\partial h} = -1} < 0.$$

A MAJORITARIAN INTERPRETATION OF THE MODEL

As we noted at the outset of our analysis, we have heretofore been using votes in the broad sense of influence, rather than in the strict sense of one man–one vote. What happens if we suppose that the success of an interest group is based upon whether it achieves a simple majority of the legislators in each house? In this case we can easily show that if $V^h(\tilde{E}, h^0)$ is equal to $V^s(\tilde{E}, s^0)$ where $h^0 = s^0$, the total vote obtained by a lobbyist will be maximized for any given level of expenditures, $\tilde{E}$, if the two chambers are of equal size.[11]

Consider a legislature of 100 members equally divided between house and senate. A simple majority voting rule dictates that 26 votes in each house are required for legislative success. Suppose that convincing those 52 votes costs E^* dollars. Compare E^* with the cost of convincing a simple majority where the 100 legislators are divided into

---

[11] Simply maximize V subject to $h + s = a$ constant, and observe that $V_2^h(\cdot) = V_2^s(\cdot)$ is a necessary condition that will hold only if $s = h$. Other institutional characteristics of the two houses, such as term lengths, will obviously affect the application of this result. Our assertion here holds to the extent that these other characteristics are approximately the same in both houses. The second-order conditions are guaranteed by the assumption of diminishing returns of chamber size to votes, that is, that both V_{22}^s and V_{22}^h are negative.

66 representatives and 34 senators. If the costs of making collective decisions increase at an increasing rate, the extra cost of convincing 8 more votes in the house will exceed the saving from buying 8 less votes in the senate, and the total expense, $\hat{E}$, of obtaining 52 votes in this fashion will exceed E^*, the cost when the legislators were equally divided between house and senate. An important principle thus emerges—interest groups will be most successful where the two houses of a bicameral legislature are of equal size, *ceteris paribus*.

TESTABLE IMPLICATIONS

There are essentially four testable implications of this theory of lobbying. First, interest groups will fare better in the market for legislation where the two houses of the legislature are more equal in size. Second, larger legislatures will frustrate the rent-seeking activities of interest groups. Third, wealthier jurisdictions will exhibit more rent seeking. Fourth, a larger population will induce more rent seeking. We now turn to the presentation of some empirical tests that support these implications of the theory.

Empirical Evidence from U.S. State Legislatures

The major empirical implications of our analysis concern the effects of a bicameral vote market on the returns from lobbying. We expect that where the ratio of house-to-senate size is lower and where the overall size of the legislature is smaller, the rate of return to interest groups from lobbying will be higher. In this section we present two sets of evidence consistent with these implications of the theory.

THE DEGREE OF ECONOMIC REGULATION ACROSS STATES

If one subscribes to the major findings of theory of economic regulation, then a reasonable proxy for the success of interest groups would be the degree of economic regulation qua monopoly across states. In other words, the level of economic regulation as measured, for example, by the amount of enforcement activity, is one possible measure of the level of monopoly privileges granted by a legislature, ostensibly in response to lobbying activity. If our theory holds, the level of enforcement activity will be predictably related to the ratio of house sizes, legislative size, wealth, and population across states (see second appendix to this chapter for correlation matrix of the independent variables).

To test these implications of our theory, we estimated four versions of the following model.

$$REG = a_0 + a_1(RATIO) + a_2(ASSOC) + a_3(YPC) + a_4(RPC)$$
$$+ a_5(SPC) + a_6(POP) + a_7(POP^2) + a_8(SIZE) + \mu,$$

where

REG = protective inspection and regulation expenses,
$RATIO$ = ratio of house-to-senate size,
$ASSOC$ = number of trade associations,
YPC = per capita state personal income,
RPC = number of representatives per capita,
SPC = number of senators per capita,
POP = state population,
$SIZE$ = size of legislature, and
μ = a random error term.

The results of estimating four specifications of this model by ordinary least squares are reported in table 18.1.[12]

Our estimates strongly suggest that the level of economic regulation across states is related negatively to the disparity in house sizes. In all specifications the coefficient on *RATIO* is negative, and it is significant in each case except the specification where *SIZE* appears without population-squared. The latter result is most likely the result of the rather high correlation between *SIZE* and *RATIO* (0.80), which acts to reduce the *t*-statistics on both variables. The coefficient on *SIZE* is also negative, being significant in one specialization but not in the other. Moreover, the pattern of results on the other independent variables is generally consistent with our analysis. As we hypothesized, population plays an important role in the determination of the level of economic regulation in all the specifications. The wealth of a

[12] The coefficients in table 18.1 are estimated from 1975 data on U.S. states. Estimating this model by weighted least squares, where the weighting device is the square root of population, does not appreciably change the results in table 18.1. Nebraska's unicameral legislature presents an interesting problem for our theory—that is, special interests should be very successful in Nebraska because there is no second house in the legislature. Econometrically, we handle this problem by aligning the Nebraska legislature with state senates, thus setting $h = 0$. Nonetheless, our empirical results are basically unchanged if we simply drop Nebraska.

TABLE 18.1
Regression Results for Protective Inspection and
Regulation Expenses (1975)

Explanatory Variable	Coefficient/t-statistic			
Constant	−643.98	11285.5	8059.7	11809.5
	(−0.07)	(2.03)[b]	(0.88)	(1.91)[b]
ASSOC	18.27	15.92	20.60	16.1
	(5.03)[c]	(6.92)[c]	(5.73)[c]	(6.41)[c]
RATIO	−4617.7	−2238.4	−2057.7	−2086.3
	(−2.92)[c]	(−2.24)[b]	(−1.11)	(−1.66)[a]
YPC	10116.8	9041.2	1687.9	8576.0
	(0.66)	(0.93)	(0.11)	(0.85)
RPC	151136	65148	123392	63440
	(2.82)[c]	(1.93)[b]	(2.36)[b]	(1.81)[b]
SPC	−232075	−27794	−178364	−27522
	(−1.50)[a]	(−2.83)[c]	(−1.20)	(−2.75)[c]
POP	5.0		5.09	
	(11.1)[c]		(11.78)[c]	
(POP²)		0.26x10⁻⁶		0.26x10⁻⁶
		(19.1)[c]		(18.8)[c]
SIZE			−80.4	−4.71
			(−2.36)[b]	(−0.20)
R^2	0.93	0.97	0.94	0.97
F-statistic	96.6[c]	249.1[c]	92.3[c]	208.7[c]

SOURCES: Calculated from Council of State Governments, *Book of the States, 1976–1977* (Lexington, Ky.: Iron Works Pike, 1976); Gale Research Company, *Encyclopedia of Associations* (Detroit: Ruffner, 1973); *Statistical Abstract of the United States, 1977* (Washington, D.C.: U.S. Government Printing Office, 1977); U.S. Department of Commerce, Bureau of the Census, *State Government Finances* (Washington, D.C.: U.S. Government Printing Office, 1976).
[a] t-value significant at the 10 percent level.
[b] t-value significant at the 5 percent level.
[c] t-value significant at the 1 percent level.

state is proxied by income per capita, and in all specifications we obtain positive but insignificant signs. Moreover, as one might reasonably expect, the number of trade associations is positively and significantly related to the measure of economic regulation.[13]

Two additional remarks about these results are relevant. First, if the reader is concerned that the total amount of regulation is the

[13] Similar results are obtained if *ASSOC/POP* is used rather than *ASSOC*.

wrong way to measure monopoly power across states, our results are consistent if we define the dependent variable in per capita terms (*REG/POP*). The coefficients show the predicted signs at comparable levels of significance in such a specification, though we obtain a smaller R^2, as one might reasonably expect. Second, there may be some concern that the number of trade associations is a product of a fertile breeding ground (e.g., a low *RATIO* and a low *SIZE*), and *ASSOC* is therefore endogenous to the model. A two-equation estimation yields the same results cited here.

Degree of Occupational Regulation across States

Occupational licensing is a specific and important manifestation of the theory of economic regulation. Few careful observers would disagree that the benefits of licensing accrue to members of the licensed profession in the form of increased rents due to entry limitations and restrictions on price competition within the profession. Moreover, such legislation typically results from lobbying pressure by practitioners in the occupation. For example, "the sponsoring group usually drafts the legislation and then has it introduced by a friendly legislator. Members and friends participate in an organized letter-writing campaign to support the legislation; practitioners and paid lobbyists call on legislators in person to obtain commitments for the law."[14] If the size of the legislature and the ratio of house sizes are important to the success of lobbying, then the number of licensed occupations in a state ought to be sensitive to such variables.

As an important additional test of the theory of lobbying, we therefore propose to examine whether states with larger legislatures and higher ratios of house-to-senate size are characterized by less successful lobbying for occupational licensing. Moreover, the data for this additional empirical work is based upon a 1952 cross-section of forty-eight state legislatures and the occupations licensed by each state. Applying the theory to explain the extent of occupational licensing in this earlier period presents a challenge in two senses. First, there is not a large variation in the 1952 data on the number of occupations licensed

[14] B. Shimberg, B. F. Esser, and D. H. Krueger, *Occupational Licensing* (Lansing: Educational Testing Service and Michigan State University Press, 1972), p. 14.

across states to be explained. Arizona and Utah licensed twenty-eight occupations (the most), and Mississippi licensed eighteen (the least). Indeed, it must be kept in mind throughout our empirical work that competition among these highly open state jurisdictions will lead to substantial uniformity in monopoly power across states, and that we have, in general, selected a difficult cross-sectional basis for testing our theory. Second, checking the explanatory power of the theory on data from an earlier period should give some idea of the robustness of the model (see second appendix to this chapter for correlation matrix of the independent variables).

Since there is a high statistical correlation between size of the legislature and the ratio of house sizes in the 1952 data (0.81), we report the results of estimating three specifications of the following model.

$$LIC = b_o + b_1(Y) + b_2(DEN) + b_3(PROFARM) + b_4(SIZE) + b_5(RATIO) + \mu,$$

where

LIC = natural log of the number of licensed occupations per state,

Y = state personal income,

DEN = state population density,

$PROFARM$ = proportion of the state population employed in agriculture,

$SIZE$ = size of state legislature,

$RATIO$ = ratio of house to senate size, and

μ = a random error term.

The results of estimating this model by ordinary least squares are given in table 18.2.[15]

When entered alone, both $RATIO$ and $SIZE$ are negative and sig-

[15] As in the case of the first empirical model above, least-squares estimates of this model weighted by the square root of population differ hardly at all from the results given in table 18.2. Three further points are relevant to the estimation of the occupational licensing model. First, following Stigler, "The Sizes of Legislatures," one might be concerned that legislative size is endogenous. However, estimation of our model with Stigler's equation for legislative size yields essentially the same results as those obtained by ordinary least squares. We thus report only the latter results here. Second, logarithmic and linear specifications product similar results. Third, while we still obtain negative signs on $SIZE$ and $RATIO$, regressions of this model that incorporate RPC and SPC are not significant.

TABLE 18.2
Regression Results for Occupations
Licensed by the States, 1952

Explanatory Variable	Coefficient/*t*-statistic		
Constant	3.25	3.25	3.25
	(66.4)[c]	(66.0)[c]	(64.81)[c]
Y	0.29×10^{-13}	0.41×10^{-13}	0.32×10^{-13}
	(1.21)	(1.75)[b]	(1.17)
DEN	−0.12	−0.09	−0.11
	(−1.12)	(−0.86)	(−1.01)
PROFARM	−1.33	−0.92	−1.24
	(−1.89)[b]	(−1.37)[a]	(−1.57)[a]
SIZE		-0.38×10^{-3}	-0.98×10^{-4}
		(−1.78)[b]	(−0.23)
RATIO	−0.012		-0.96×10^{-2}
	(−1.95)[b]		(−0.78)
R^2	0.19	0.18	0.20
F-statistic	2.48[a]	2.31[a]	1.95

SOURCES: Calculated from Council of State Governments, *Occupational Licensing in the States* (Chicago: Council of State Governments, 1952), and *Statistical Abstract of the United States, 1953* (Washington, D.C.: Government Printing Office, 1953).
[a] *t*-value significant at the 10 percent level.
[b] *t*-value significant at the 5 percent level.
[c] *t*-value significant at the 1 percent level.

nificantly different from zero at the 5 percent level. These highly related characteristics of legislatures thus continue to be important predicators of lobbying success. When entered together, both are negative, but not statistically significant, a result possibly due to their high simple correlation.[16] State personal income, population density, and the proportion of farm workers account for cross-sectional differences in state wealth, the potential supply of wealth transfers, and economic homogeneity. In each case we find the expected sign. Higher state income or wealth is associated with greater lobbying success—that is, more licensed occupations.[17] Higher population densities frustrate lobbying, because the suppliers of wealth transfers find it less costly to

[16] The sequential *F*-statistic on *SIZE* and *RATIO* is 1.88 and is significant at the 20 percent level.

[17] We employ *Y* rather than *Y/POP* in this specification because it provides a better fit to the data. The results are basically unaltered by the use of *Y/POP*.

defeat special-interest legislation where they can more easily associate physically with one another.[18] In those states where the proportion of the population employed in agriculture is large, occupations are less successful in obtaining licensing legislation, a not so surprising result, since the extent of agriculture is a proxy for the degree of homogeneous interest in a population.[19]

SUMMARY

The two sets of evidence presented in this section offer strong support for our theory of interest-group lobbying. Two measures of the degree of monoply power obtained through legislation were found to be negatively and significantly related (as postulated) to legislative size and the ratio of house sizes across states. Moreover, the other explanatory variables in our theory, such as commodity wealth and population, exhibited the postulated relationships to the measures of legislatively inspired monopoly power.

Concluding Remarks

In this paper we propose a testable economic theory of the behavior of an interest group in lobbying a legislature for wealth transfers. Our basic argument is that certain constitutional aspects of the legislature, primarily its size and the ratio of chamber sizes, will predictably affect the rate of return that interest groups earn from legislation. Our major conclusions, supported strongly in two empirical tests, are that more equal chamber sizes and smaller legislatures favor the activities of interest groups in capturing and sustaining rents via the political process.

APPENDIX 1 TO CHAPTER 18

A more complicated version of our model formally incorporates the role of group size into the rent-seeking calculus of the special-interest group. Suppose that the interest group has the prerogative to control the number of its

[18] Higher density, of course, lowers the costs of organizing and controlling free riding for both winners and losers in the wealth-transfer process, but it lowers these costs *relatively* more for the losers because they face a more acute free-rider problem by definition.

[19] *PROFARM* is a proxy for the extent of special-interest activity in this model. We

members. The group is thereby faced in our analytics with the problem of selecting not only its level of lobbying expenditure, but also the income-maximizing group size. In this context group size is a two-edged sword. Increasing group size offers the opportunity for the group to provide increased support for politicians, as the costs of preventing free riding are low, which reduces the costs of influence or votes to the group. But the returns from increasing group size diminish rapidly as free riding by group members (e.g., not voting) becomes increasingly expensive to prevent.

In our basic model of income maximization by an interest group, as given in equations (1) through (5) in the text, a modification to include considerations of group size occurs in the original equations (4) and (5). The new specifications are

$$V^h = V^h(E^h, h, N) \text{ and} \tag{4'}$$

$$V^s = V^s(E^s, s, N), \tag{5'}$$

where N is the number of members in the interest group. Once again, we maximize the group's net income, as given in equation (1), by inserting equations (2) through (5) into equation (1), but now the group's choice variables are E^h, E^s, and N. The necessary conditions for a maximum are

$$Y_1 V_1^h = 1,$$
$$Y_2 V_1^s = 1, \text{ and}$$
$$\frac{V_3^h}{V_3^s} = \frac{Y_2}{Y_1} .$$

By assuming that both V_{33}^h and V_{33}^s are nonpositive, we know that income is concave in lobby size, as

$$\left. \frac{\partial^2 Y}{\partial L^2} \right|_{V^s = 0} = Y_1 V_{33}^h + (V_3^h)^2 Y_{11} < 0, \text{ and}$$

$$\left. \frac{\partial^2 Y}{\partial L^2} \right|_{V^h = 0} = Y_2 V_{33}^s + (V_3^s)^2 Y_{22} < 0.$$

V_{33}^s and V_{33}^h are zero in the range of group sizes where free riding no longer influences the political support or participation of the group's membership. In this range, for example, some absolute minimum number of group members, who vote for reasons other than their interest group's concern (e.g., consumption), will support particular politicians, albeit at a low level, and thereby reduce the cost of special-interest legislation to their group. Thus, ever increasing group size beyond some point maps into asymptotic voter support for politicians at election time and therefore into a constant level of influence from politicians in support of the group.

---

would have preferred to use *ASSOC*, as in the regulation expenses model, but there are no data on this variable for 1952.

It should be stressed that the optimal group size will vary considerably among interest groups. Numerous factors will work to influence the level of free riding, i.e., $V^h(O, h^0, N)$ and $V^s(O, s^0, N)$. As the group improves its ability to control free riding, the functions $V^h(\cdot)$, $V^s(\cdot)$, $V_3^h(\cdot)$, and $V_3^s(\cdot)$ will all shift upward, improving the marginal productivity of vote buying.

The purpose of this analysis, outside an intrinsic interest in its own right, is twofold. First, an equilibrium in this market will generate zero returns at the intensive and extensive margins. Small groups and groups with uncommon abilities to control free riding should enjoy inframarginal gains relative to the market, but zero returns at their own margin. Larger groups will likely find that even inframarginal returns are low or zero because their vote production functions are low and flat as they offer little in the way of support for politicians. Second, our analysis here demonstrates that the theory of economic regulation does not necessarily imply that successful interest grouups are small. Consider that interest groups can offer politicians both dollars and votes in return for political favors. Politicians can convert votes into dollars through reduced campaign expenditures and higher present values of their seats. This implies that an interest group need not be small to be successful in receiving transfers from the state.

APPENDIX 2 TO CHAPTER 18

For the reader's inspection the correlation matrices of the independent variables in our two empirical tests are given here. Variable definitions and data sources appear in the text.

	ASSOC	YPC	SIZE	Y	RPC	SPC	POP	RATIO
ASSOC	1.0							
YPC	0.30	1.0						
SIZE	0.24	−0.16	1.0					
Y	0.75	0.32	0.23	1.0				
RPC	−0.21	−0.18	0.42	−0.40	1.0			
SPC	−0.31	−0.02	−0.25	−0.57	0.60	1.0		
POP	0.71	0.24	0.25	0.99	−0.42	−0.60	1.0	
RATIO	−0.02	−0.16	0.80	−0.01	0.71	−0.07	−0.001	1.0

	Y	DEN	PROFARM	RATIO	SIZE	Y/POP
Y	1.0					
DEN	0.32	1.0				
PROFARM	−0.40	−0.52	1.0			
RATIO	−0.04	0.12	−0.28	1.0		
SIZE	0.17	0.20	−0.13	0.80	1.0	
Y/POP	0.42	0.42	−0.65	0.03	−0.07	1.0

19

Tax Avoidance, Horizontal Equity, and Tax Reform: A Proposed Synthesis

by

Michael L. Goetz

FEW concepts in the area of taxation can generate more discussion and controversy than tax avoidance and tax reform. Debate over these issues is customarily framed in terms of the desire for or the departure from the criteria of horizontal and vertical equity.[1] Irrespective of the usefulness of horizontal and vertical equity as guides for policy, the concepts command a wide degree of popular acceptance and support. Recent papers by Martin Feldstein and Richard Musgrave have argued that horizontal equity be reformulated in terms of utility rather than of ability to pay.[2] Some of the implications of this reformulation are examined in this paper. In particular, by employing the expenditure function it can be demonstrated that questions of tax avoidance and tax reform are inseparable from the definition of horizontal equity.[3]

NOTE: The author wishes to acknowledge the comments of Martin J. Bailey, Jessi Raine, and Allen Soltow on previous drafts and discussions of issues with Cadwell Ray, Steve Steib, and Larry Wofford. Any remaining errors are, of course, the responsibility of the author.

[1] See Carl S. Shoup, *Public Finance* (Chicago: Aldine Publishing Company, 1969), chapter 2, for a general discussion of consensus and conflict criteria of equity.

[2] Martin Feldstein, "Compensation in Tax Reform," *National Tax Journal* 29 (June, 1976): 123–130, and idem, "On the Theory of Tax Reform," *Journal of Public Economics* 6 (July–August, 1976): 77–104. Also see Richard A. Musgrave, "ET,OT, and SBT," *Journal of Public Economics* 6 (July–August 1976): 3–16.

[3] Peter A. Diamond and Daniel L. McFadden, "Some Uses of the Expenditure Function in Public Finance," *Journal of Public Economics* 3 (February, 1974): 3–21; John

The first section analyzes preferential provisions of the tax laws as rent-generating restrictions, the general consequences of which have been examined by Anne Krueger, Richard Posner, and Gordon Tullock.[4] It is argued that if preferential tax provisions are capitalized, they will only temporarily serve the goal of expanding the consumption of the commodity. This view of tax avoidance requires a reinterpretation of horizontal equity and provides an alternative explanation of some recent results presented by Martin Bailey.[5] In the next section, the new, utility-based definitions of horizontal equity are defined in terms of the expenditure function. Some recent empirical results are examined in light of these alternative definitions. The third section examines the distinction between tax design and tax reform, concluding that any such distinction is arbitrary. Moreover, the search for the properties of a "good" tax system is made even more difficult if the results of this paper are accepted. Conclusions are contained in the final section.

Tax Preferences as Rent-Generating Restrictions

Tax avoidance can be defined as the legal reduction of tax through the use of preferential provisions of the tax laws. These preferential provisions of the tax system have been referred to as either tax loopholes, tax incentives, or tax expenditures.[6] The term *tax preferences* is more neutral than the above alternatives and reflects the presumption that a preferential rate of tax is granted to an activity, which is deemed to confer some benefits over and above any tax savings that accrue to taxpayers, in order to expand the level of the activity. The process of tax

---

C. Hause, "The Theory of Welfare Cost Measurement," *Journal of Political Economy* 93 (December, 1975): 1145–82.

[4] Anne O. Krueger, "The Political Economy of the Rent-Seeking Society," chapter 4 in this volume; Richard A. Posner, "The Social Costs of Monopoly and Regulation," chapter 5 in this volume; and Gordon Tullock, "The Transitional Gains Trap," chapter 12 in this volume.

[5] Martin J. Bailey, "Progressivity and Investment Yields under U.S. Income Taxation," *Journal of Political Economy* 82 (November–December, 1974): 1157–76.

[6] The latter term was coined in 1968 by then Assistant Secretary of the Treasury Stanley S. Surry. For more detailed discussions, see Stanley S. Surry, *Pathways to Tax Reform* (Cambridge, Mass.: Harvard University Press, 1973), and Shoup, *Public Finance.*

avoidance results in a misallocation of resources, the measure of which is the excess burden or welfare cost of the tax.[7] These preferential provisions of the tax system are conceptually equivalent to the granting of a privilege to obtain a tax saving. We will argue that this tax saving will be capitalized and, accordingly, tax preferences are an example of rent-generating restrictions.

The premise that rents are capitalized as costs is by no means novel. The process by which rents are capitalized as costs is enshrined in the taxicab problem and can be employed to test the validity of the Tiebout hypothesis.[8] Three recent papers have employed the capitalization process to analyze divergent sets of phenomena. Krueger analyzes the competitive nature of rent-seeking for quantitative restrictions on trade and the relative welfare losses associated with quantitative restrictions and their tariff equivalents.[9] Tullock seeks to explain the apparent long-run inefficiency of government programs.[10] Tullock argues that any government program that confers a privilege—that is, a monopoly position—on any group will ultimately be unsuccessful in that the privilege will only generate transitional gains that will subsequently be capitalized. Therefore, successors to the original recipients of the privilege will be no better off than if the privilege did not exist; however, they would be harmed by the elimination of the privilege.

Posner argues that if obtaining a monopoly is a competitive activity, resources will be drawn into that activity such that the monopoly gains are eliminated and only a normal rate of return is earned.[11] The method by which the monopoly gain is eliminated may take sev-

---

[7] Edgar K. Browning, "The Marginal Cost of Public Funds," *Journal of Political Economy* 84 (April, 1976): 283–298; Arnold C. Harberger, "Three Basic Postulates for Applied Welfare Economics: An Interpretive Essay," *Journal of Economic Literature* 9 (September, 1971): 785–797.

[8] Matthew Edel and Elliott Sclar, "Taxes, Spending, and Property Values: Supply Adjustment in a Tiebout-Oates Model," *Journal of Political Economy* 82 (September–October, 1974): 941–954; Wallace E. Oates, "The Effects of Property Taxes and Local Spending on Property Values: An Empirical Study of Tax Capitalization and the Tiebout Hypothesis," *Journal of Political Economy* 77 (November–December, 1969): 957–971; and Mark V. Pauly, "A Model of Local Government Expenditure and Tax Capitalization," *Journal of Public Economics* 6 (October, 1976): 231–242.

[9] Krueger, "The Political Economy of the Rent-Seeking Society."

[10] Tullock, "The Transitional Gains Trap."

[11] Posner, "The Social Costs of Monopoly and Regulation."

eral forms. For example, if price competition is excluded by law, non-price competition would eliminate the potential gain. Even if nonprice competition were forbidden, resources would be expended in the process of aquiring the right to earn above-normal returns.[12] Whether the gains from monopoly or regulation are eliminated by the capitalization of the value of the privilege or by the expenditure of resources to obtain the privilege, the consequences are the same.[13] Conferring a monopoly privilege will generate only transitional gains; subsequent recipients of the privilege will receive only a normal rate of return and would incur a loss were the privilege to be canceled; any resources devoted to obtaining a privilege constitute social costs of that privilege.

The consequences of the application of the capitalization hypothesis to tax preferences is that the process of adjustment by taxpayers will result in the equalization of rates of return between favored and nonfavored activities. For example, wages will adjust downward in tax-favored occupations, while the tax advantages of home ownership will be reflected in the price of homes.[14] That is, "horizontal equity and capitalization are essentially two ways of saying the same thing."[15] Given the assumptions of a single type of ability and common tastes, horizontal equity will not arise from an existing tax structure, but can arise only from changes in that structure.[16] We have the paradoxical situation in which the elimination of tax preferences commonly thought of as constituting horizontal inequities would itself constitute a horizontal inequity.[17]

Consider a utility-maximizing consumer with well-behaved utility

[12] Ibid., p. 75.

[13] This result assumes either that there are no transactions costs or that, if they exist, they are equal. The result is therefore only a first approximation to the problem. See Eirik G. Furubotn and Svetozar Pejovich, *The Economics of Property Rights* (Cambridge, Mass.: Ballinger, 1974), and Oliver E. Williamson, "Franchise Bidding for Natural Monopolies in General and with Respect to CATV," *Bell Journal of Economics* 7 (Spring, 1976): 73–104.

[14] Feldstein gives a number of examples of this phenomenon in his "Compensation in Tax Reform" and "On the Theory of Tax Reform."

[15] Bruce W. Hamilton, "Capitalization of Interjurisdictional Differences in Local Tax Prices," *American Economic Review* 66 (December, 1976): 744.

[16] Feldstein, "Compensation in Tax Reform," pp. 123–124; idem, "On the Theory of Tax Reform," pp. 94–95.

[17] A possible solution to this problem is actual, as opposed to hypothetical, compensation. Whether tax reform is a "taking" that requires compensation will be considered below.

FIGURE 19.1

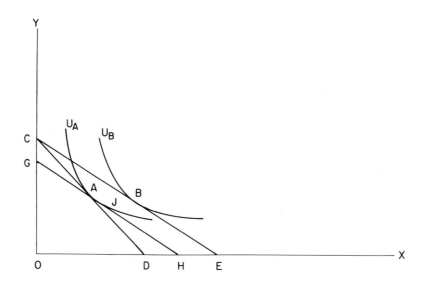

function $U = U(X, Y)$, where X is any commodity and Y is the numeraire commodity. In the absence of any preferential rate of tax on X, the consumer maximizes utility at A in figure 19.1. The costless enactment of a preferential rate of tax on X pivots the budget line from CD to CE with the new equilibrium at B.[18] The preferential rate of tax results in an increase in the taxpayer's real income. The gain in real income caused by the preferential rate of tax represents the maximum sum the taxpayer would pay for the right to pay tax at the lower rate. In terms of the numeraire, this sum is represented by CG, the change in Y such that the original level of utility U_A is attained.

Given the form of the tax preference, the sum CG can be interpreted as the compensating variation (hereafter CV) of the tax preference. The CV of the tax preference may be defined as the increment of income that could be subtracted from the income required at B so that the consumer would be indifferent between B and the income-modified point J, given the relative prices prevailing at B. Alternatively, the compensating variation is the difference between the in-

[18] The slope of CE is $-P_X(1-t)$, where t is the preferential rate of tax. The preferential tax rate is constant and formally equivalent to an open-ended conditional matching grant, that is, a tax deduction.

come available at B and the income necessary to reach the initial level of utility at the new relative prices.[19] In effect, the income effect of the tax preference is converted into the price of the right to obtain the tax saving. In figure 19.1, if the demand functions are integrable, the vertical distance from B to U_A, the compensating surplus, would be equal to CG, the compensating variation. That is, the tax preference has increased the purchases of X and if the maximum price is paid for the tax preference, utility is at the initial level U_A.

The previous result has several consequences. Although we have emphasized that the cancellation of a tax preference will violate horizontal equity, an additional consequence of some importance is also implied. Even if it is true that all factors adjust to the tax so that the tax preference is capitalized, the goal of the legislature, the expansion of the activity, will have been achieved.[20] However, if capitalization is complete, the inducement to expand the activity will be transitory. To see this, let the pre–tax preference equilibrium be X_1 with income in terms of the numeraire Y_1 and prices P_1; the equilibrium level of utility is U_1. After introduction of the tax preference, we have a commodity bundle X_2, income Y_2, prices P_2, and utility level U_2. The CV of a tax preference has a particularly convenient interpretation in terms of the expenditure function.[21]

The expenditure function represents the level of income required by the solution to the dual of the consumer-choice problem.[22] The expenditure function is given by $Y^*(U_1; P_2)$, that is, the minimum level of income required to reach U_1 at prices P_2. The CV of the tax preference is, therefore, $Y_2 - Y^*(U_1; P_2)$. The effect of the tax preference is an increase in X from X_1 to X_2. However, when the CV of the tax preference is capitalized, the consumer is confronted with income $Y(U_1; P_2) = Y_2 - [Y_2 - Y^*(U_1; P_2)]$ and prices P_2. Since $Y(U_1; P_2)$ and Y_1

[19] For a complete discussion of various measures of changes in welfare, see John C. Hause, "The Theory of Welfare Cost Measurement," *Journal of Political Economy* 83 (December, 1975): 1145–82.

[20] I wish to thank the referee of the *Southern Economic Journal* for bringing this point to my attention.

[21] William J. Baumol, *Economic Theory and Operations Analysis*, 4th ed. (Englewood Cliffs, N.J.: Prentice-Hall, 1977); Diamond and McFadden, "Some Uses of the Expenditure Function in Public Finance"; and Hause, "The Theory of Welfare Cost Measurement."

[22] Diamond and McFadden, "Some Uses of the Expenditure Function in Public Finance," pp. 3–4.

both are associated with utility level U_1, real income is constant by Hicks's definition. Therefore, after capitalization, the tax preference has only a substitution effect, and the increment in income designed to encourage expansion of the activity no longer exists. Accordingly, the expansionary impact of a tax preference exists only as long as capitalization is not complete.

If the expenditure function were only to provide an alternative specification of the change in welfare attributable to a tax preference, it would be merely interesting. However, when horizontal equity is defined in terms of utility, the alternative definition is more than a curiosity. "If two individuals would be equally well off (have the same utility level) in the absence of taxation, they should be equally well off if there is a tax."[23] Since the expenditure function gives the income required to attain a variable level of utility, given relative prices, the relationship between the expenditure function and the new definition of horizontal equity is clear. The use of the expenditure function allows utility differences to be converted to income differences. This formulation illustrates the premise that if capitalization is complete, an existing tax preference is not a source of horizontal inequity. In fact, the tax system is horizontally equitable, since the pretax and posttax utility levels are identical and any change in the tax preference would alter the utility ordering and therefore cause horizontal inequity.[24]

By creating the right to reduced taxes, the preferential provisions of the tax laws create an asset that, if correctly priced, eliminates the tax saving conferred by the privilege. An alternative method of illustrating this premise is given below. Commodity X was initially taxed at rate T_1; a preferential rate of tax T_2, $T_2 < T_1$, is enacted for commodity X. In figure 19.2, X_1 units were purchased before enactment of the preferential provision at a price of P_1. At the preferential rate of tax, X_2 units of X are purchased. The excess burden or loss due to tax avoidance is given by BCH. When it is recognized, however, that there exists a potential tax saving of P_1ABP_2 conditioned upon the purchase of X, resources just equal to the tax saving will be expended in order to secure the privilege.[25] The net result is that tax at rate T_1 is paid on X_2

[23] Feldstein, "Compensation in Tax Reform," p. 83.

[24] These results assume identical tastes and a single type of ability. These assumptions will be relaxed in the third section.

[25] If one assumes zero elasticities, the potential tax saving is P_1GBP_2. See Joseph E.

FIGURE 19.2

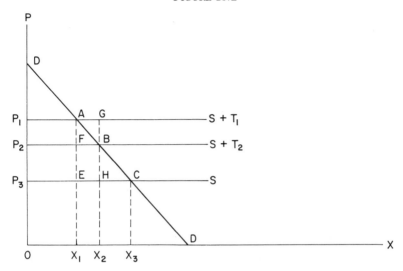

units; P_2BHP_3 is paid in tax while P_1ABP_2 is paid for the privilege to pay tax at a preferential rate. However, the latter payment does not go to the government, but instead to those groups which package tax savings. Any resources so expended are a cost of the tax system. Moreover, the lost revenue must be collected in some other manner, and the welfare costs of these alternative sources of revenue also constitute a cost of the tax system.[26]

The above framework can be employed to amplify some of Bailey's results. With respect to the personal income tax, Bailey argues that "apparent horizontal inequities as a rule shake out in competitive resource allocation and translate into misuse of resources."[27] The horizontal inequities referred to are tax preferences, and the process of competitive resource allocation is either the capitalization or the erosion of tax preferences. Bailey further argues that the true burden of

Stiglitz and Michael J. Boskin, "Some Lessons from the New Public Finance," *American Economic Review* 67 (February, 1977): 296–297.

[26] Tullock, "The Transitional Gains Trap"; Posner, "The Social Costs of Monopoly and Regulation"; and Hause, "The Theory of Welfare Cost Measurement," p. 1167.

[27] Bailey, "Progressivity and Investment Yields under U.S. Income Taxation," p. 1174.

the personal income tax is mildly progressive at the top marginal rates; the tax is less progressive than the progression implied by the statutory rate structure but more progressive than the effective rate structure. The preferential provisions that moderate progressivity are conceptually equivalent to the granting of a privilege to obtain a tax saving.

If the capitalization process were complete, the true burden of the tax would be identical with that defined by the statutory tax rates. Bailey indicates the factors that prevent the above result from occurring. First of all, neither side of the market for tax preferences is perfectly competitive. The interrelation among marginal tax rates, the taxpayer's income, and the before-and-after tax rates of return defines the limit on the buyer's side. Moreover, if the supply side of the tax preference market is likewise imperfectly competitive, suppliers and buyers of tax preferences may be viewed as sharing a portion of the potential tax savings. This process will result in excess profits for suppliers and a moderation of progressivity below statutory levels for taxpayers. In addition, risk aversion on the part of some taxpayers may cause these taxpayers to forgo tax preferences that would otherwise be part of portfolio optimization.

Although Bailey is principally dealing with the problem of taxpayer portfolio optimization, the related issue of the welfare cost of raising tax revenue in a system replete with exemptions, deductions, and credits is also considered. The existence of tax preferences channels resources into those areas in which tax savings may be obtained. The resources expended in the search for these tax preferences are properly included as welfare costs of raising tax revenue. In addition, Bailey correctly cites the reduced before-tax rates of return on investments as a cost of such a system. To the extent that capitalization is complete, the tax preferences are only temporarily effective. The question of whether a less costly method of generating revenue exists immediately arises.

It is of some interest to examine the identity of the gainers and losers from tax preferences. If capitalization is complete, the posttax utility ordering is identical to the pretax utility ordering; this is no more than restatement of Feldstein's definition of horizontal equity. It is possible, however, for taxpayers to achieve a level of utility greater than the pre-preference level but less than the level of utility corresponding to the undiluted preference. Such a situation would occur when taxpayers and those who package tax preferences share the potential gain. In such a situation, relative bargaining power will determine the disposition of the gain. These results are crucially dependent on the assumptions of identical tastes and a single type of ability. The next section attempts to relax these assumptions and examines how horizontal and vertical equity may be restated by using the expenditure function. In addition we examine the implications of capitalization for some recent econometric estimates of tax preferences.

Measuring Horizontal Equity

Horizontal equity refers to the equal treatment of equally circumstanced individuals. While Feldstein and Musgrave have argued for a reformulation of horizontal equity in terms of utility instead of income, some operational content must be given to the notion of equal position or circumstance.[28] The use of utility as an index of horizontal equity complicates this problem. Feldstein has demonstrated that in the absence of identical tastes and a single type of ability (income), no income tax is consistent with horizontal equity; this is more a statement of the problem than a solution.[29] It is possible to gain some additional insight into the proposed definitions of horizontal equity by employing the expenditure function. We will adopt Musgrave's dichotomy and examine possible definitions of equal position, and thus horizontal equity, for the equality and inequality of both options and preferences.[30]

Equality of preferences requires identical tastes; equality of options refers to identical opportunity sets.[31] In tax design, horizontal equity requires that if, in the absence of taxation, two individuals have the same utility level, they should have the same utility in the presence of a tax. Consider initially the case of equal options and preferences. In this case, all individuals will select the same commodity bundle. However, since there is no requirement that individuals receive the same level of satisfaction from the same commodity bundle, such a

---

[28] Feldstein, "On the Theory of Tax Reform"; idem, "Compensation in Tax Reform"; and Musgrave, "ET, OT, and SBT."

[29] Feldstein, "Compensation in Tax Reform."

[30] Musgrave, "ET, OT, and SBT."

[31] Assume a single type of ability of income.

situation need not be one of equal position. As Musgrave recognizes, we must also assume that equal welfare is derived from identical commodity bundles.[32] With this assumption, expenditure functions would be the same for all taxpayers. Alternatively, if we specify an initial level of utility for all taxpayers, the value of the expenditure function may differ for different taxpayers unless Musgrave's further restriction is imposed.[33] If taxes are levied on expenditures, there is no requirement that equally circumstanced individuals, in terms of utility, should pay equal taxes.

When we move to the case of equal preferences with unequal options, and assuming identical baskets yield identical welfare, taxpayers in each subgroup as defined by options are in equal positions and should pay equal tax. If a higher opportunity set implies a higher level of welfare, the level of expenditure will be greater for the higher opportunity set. It is then possible to define vertical equity in terms of the level of expenditure. However, this result is dependent on the assumption of equal welfare for identical commodity bundles.

When we consider the case of unequal preferences with equal options, the definition of equal position becomes even more vague. There exists no necessary relationship among the level of expenditure, the level of welfare, and commodity bundles. Similar remarks hold for the case of unequal options and preferences.[34] The general conclusion is that definitions of horizontal equity in terms of either income or utility encounter equally debilitating problems of definition. This is, unfortunately, an uncomfortable conclusion, and we must agree with Musgrave that more scrutiny must be given to the definition of horizontal equity. If horizontal equity is interpreted to mean that tastes are not to count, then taxes are based on ability to pay, that is, income and prices. In contrast, in a utilitarian framework, tastes are to count and taxes may, accordingly, discriminate on that basis.[35]

---

[32] Musgrave, "ET, OT, and SBT," p. 6.

[33] If the ability to derive welfare from commodity bundles depended directly on income or education, a given level of utility would be associated with a lower expenditure level for richer or more educated families, since the expenditure function is strictly monotonically increasing with utility.

[34] Musgrave reaches virtually the same conclusions in "ET, OT, and SBT."

[35] For an extended discussion of this conflict, see A. B. Atkinson and J. E. Stiglitz, "The Design of Tax Structure: Direct versus Indirect Taxation," *Journal of Public Economics* 6 (July–August, 1976): 55–75. For a summary of empirical results based on this premise, see Stiglitz and Boskin, "Some Lessons from the New Public Finance."

Horizontal equity in tax reform requires that tax changes preserve the utility order.[36] We earlier demonstrated that for identical tastes and a single type of ability, the change in real income attributable to a tax preference will be capitalized in such a way that the pretax and posttax utility levels are the same. The tax preference is not a source of horizontal inequity, but any modification of the tax preference will be a source of horizontal inequity. This result has implications for the distinction between tax design and tax reform. Before proceeding to this issue, we will examine the impact of the capitalization hypothesis on econometric estimates of tax preferences.

A useful point of departure is the work on property tax capitalization of Wallace Oates and the recent response of Thomas King.[37] King's principal argument is that in his regressions, Oates employed the effective tax rate rather than the property tax payment as the measure of tax capitalization. When this substitution is made, the tax payment variable is endogenous and, accordingly, King employs TSLS in his estimation. If tax preferences are capitalized, some measure of this effect should be included in any econometric estimates. For example, Martin Feldstein and Charles Clotfelter exercise particular care to employ an income measure that is not endogenous.[38] However, if there is capitalization, the taxpayer is confronted with a lower price ratio and a lower level of real income, both reflecting the capitalized value of the tax preference. Not to account for this effect would seem to introduce a possible bias into the results, since the dependent variable will reflect the existence of the favorable tax treatment.[39]

There are at least two ways to surmount this difficulty. The first method would be to adjust either the income or the wealth variables to reflect the existence of the capitalization of tax preferences. In this case, wealth would depend on the extent of capitalization, and the possibility of a simultaneous-equation bias would exist, necessitating, for

[36] Feldstein, "On the Theory of Tax Reform," p. 95.

[37] Oates, "The Effects of Property Taxes and Local Spending on Property Values"; Thomas A. King, "Estimating Property Tax Capitalization: A Critical Comment," *Journal of Political Economy* 85 (April, 1977): 425–431.

[38] Martin Feldstein and Charles Clotfelter, "Tax Incentives and Charitable Contributions in the United States," *Journal of Public Economics* 6 (January–February, 1976): 4. Feldstein and Clotfelter, in relating charitable giving to income and other variables, define income to equal total income minus the taxes paid were charitable giving zero.

[39] Ibid. I do not mean to single out Feldstein and Clotfelter as the only example of this error.

example, the use of TSLS. Alternatively, the dependent variable could be adjusted to reflect the existence of capitalization as in King.[40] The difficulty with this method is to obtain an independent estimate of the degree of capitalization. If one views this problem generally as one of errors in variables, the resulting estimates will be inconsistent. Although no attempt to infer a general pattern can or will be made, King's reformulation of Oates's results suggests that accounting for capitalization may be important.[41]

Tax Reform and Tax Design

Pleas for additional preferential treatment or complaints against the perceived inequities of existing preferential treatment mark public discussion of both taxation and regulation. As demonstrated above, there is a relationship between tax avoidance and horizontal equity, although not the relationship that might have been anticipated. It is interesting to note that tax reform is usually synonymous with tax simplification, that is, the elimination of preferential tax provisions. If such an effort is a true reform, the fact that so little of it is undertaken seems surprising.[42] Given the above results, both the desirability and the possibility of tax reform are called into question. The problem is, however, more basic. The process of designing a tax system contains the seeds of its own modification whether by piecemeal reform or by the capitalization of existing privilege. The question is not one of tax design versus tax reform, but rather, if, when, and how tax reform will occur. That is, the distinction between tax design and tax reform is, to a substantial degree, arbitrary.

Adopting the preceding perspective on tax design and/or reform reflects an alternative conception of the contractual content of eco-

[40] King, "Estimating Property Tax Capitalization: A Critical Comment," p. 429.

[41] Ibid.; also see Oates, "The Effects of Property Taxes and Local Spending on Property Values."

[42] For an unequivocal stand in favor of reform, see George F. Break and Joseph A. Pechman, *Federal Tax Reform* (Washington, D.C.: Brookings Institution, 1975). "That tax reform will produce larger gains than losses and is therefore a positive-sum game well worth playing is the firm belief of most fiscal economists. Past failures in the tax reform movement may well be due mainly to the experts' lack of success in conveying this message to the general public" (p. 16). For other views on tax reform, see Feldstein, "Compensation in Tax Reform"; idem, "On the Theory of Tax Reform"; Shoup, *Public Finance*; and Surrey, *Pathways to Tax Reform*.

nomic theory.[43] Succinctly stated, the contract of traditional economic theory is a discrete transaction. An alternative conception of contract is one of an ongoing relationship for which future obligations and duties are vaguely defined and which involves a substantial degree of uncertainty. The adoption of the alternative paradigm for economic contract requires that attention be diverted from the comparative static properties of a solution to the mechanism for adjustment to future unanticipated contingencies. That is, how are the "rules of the game" to be changed once the game is in progress?

In terms of the discrete transaction paradigm, the distinction between tax design and tax reform is sharp and, accordingly, the difficulties that Feldstein outlines, discussed in the second and third sections, are important.[44] If the capitalization process is complete, the taxpayers who appear to be benefiting from the tax preferences are in fact no better off than if the preferences did not exist. Since the gains have been capitalized, however, the taxpayers would incur a loss were the privilege to be canceled. The process of tax reform has the effect of reimposing inequities previously reconciled by the market. It would seem that proponents of tax reform possess two options. The first option involves the payment of actual compensation to those who would lose from a given tax reform.[45] The political feasibility of a reform-with-compensation package remains to be determined. As Tullock argues, such a situation is, in fact, a trap.[46] Once established, the tax preference ceases to be effective. However, once established, elimination without compensation is arbitrary. Elimination with compensation poses the question of raising sums required for compensation. The second option has been put forth by Henry Aaron.[47] The case for reform rests on eliminating future inequities not yet capitalized and the

[43] For an examination of the alternative, the administered contract perspective, see Victor P. Goldberg, "Toward an Expanded Economic Theory of Contract," *Journal of Economic Issues* 10 (March, 1976): 45–61; idem, "Regulation and Administered Contracts," *Bell Journal of Economics* 7 (Autumn, 1976): 426–448; idem, "Commons, Clark, and the Emerging Post-Coasian Law and Economics," *Journal of Economic Issues* 10 (December, 1976): 877–892; and Williamson, "Franchise Bidding for Natural Monopolies in General and with Respect to CATV."

[44] Feldstein, "Compensation in Tax Reform" and "On the Theory of Tax Reform."

[45] Feldstein, "Compensation in Tax Reform," pp. 124–128.

[46] Tullock, "The Transitional Gains Trap."

[47] Henry J. Aaron, *Who Pays the Property Tax?* (Washington, D.C.: Brookings Institution, 1975), pp. 66–67.

consequent reduction in resources devoted to tax avoidance. These gains are to be offset against the loss due to the reintroduced inequities.

The capitalization process provides some insight into another characteristic of tax preferences. The recipients of existing tax preferences often claim that a marginal increase in the tax preference is necessary in order to fulfill the original objective of the tax preference. If the gains are in fact transitional, these claims are correct. However, these gains will only be temporary, and sometime in the future the call for the reassessment of the effectiveness of the tax preference can be anticipated. Another difficulty can be noted. Once capitalization has occurred, the question of compensation is pervasive. In considering the question of adjustment to change, not only must the identities of the gainers and losers be considered, but also the numbers of the gainers and losers and the magnitude of the gains and losses.[48] Further, as Tullock has argued, adherence to the criteria of gains-from-trade in the presence of capitalization makes adjustment to changing circumstances particularly difficult.[49]

With the above results in mind, the results of two recent papers may be fruitfully examined. Posner poses the question of the relative desirability of income and excise taxation and concludes that the income tax is not clearly superior when the costs of avoidance, the costs incurred in the process of rearranging economic activities in response to the tax structure, are considered.[50] With the above discussion in mind, this question can be alternatively posed in the following manner. Is there any presupposition that, after the capitalization of any transitional gains, an income tax is superior to a system of excise taxes? The answer to this question is negative. To the extent that the potential tax savings are transformed into social costs in the process of attempting to realize these tax savings, it is quite possible that a system of excise taxes may be a less costly alternative. This result presupposes that the system of excise taxes contains no transitional gains of its own.

Browning has recently considered the relationship between the

[48] As argued by Sam Peltzman, "Toward a More General Theory of Regulation," *Journal of Law and Economics* 19 (October, 1976): 211–240, the amount of support for a proposed change depends on the number of gainers, directly by providing a larger base of support and indirectly by lowering the gain per member.

[49] Tullock, "The Transitional Gains Trap."

[50] Posner, "The Social Costs of Monopoly and Regulation."

marginal cost of public funds and the proper level of government expenditures.[51] Basically, Browning's argument is that the marginal welfare cost of generating tax revenue provides a measure of the increased productivity of public relative to private expenditure necessary to produce a net gain in welfare. The previous analysis indicates two possible qualifications to Browning's analysis. Browning recognizes the importance of both administrative and compliance costs and incorporates them accordingly. An additional element should also be included in these calculations: the transitional gains generated by the difference in statutory and effective tax rates. Such a modification would increase the marginal cost of public funds and thereby increase the social opportunity cost of government spending.

The second qualification to Browning's analysis implied above is somewhat more serious. This qualification also applies to Posner.[52] Specifically, although it is legitimate to assume that resources are withdrawn from a perfectly competitive private sector in order to establish a theoretical relationship, it is not permissible to infer policy recommendations from such a model, as Browning appears to suggest. One of Posner's principal conclusions is the existence of distortions in the private sector, such as monopoly and regulation, which are transformed into social costs. Given this result, Browning's policy recommendation is not wrong, but rather incomplete. A more correct restatement might read: a government expenditure program will be efficient only if its benefits exceed the direct tax cost by an amount at least as large as the difference in the public and private welfare cost of the funds. The transfer of funds from the private to the public sector results in a reduction of welfare costs in the private sector and an increase in the corresponding cost in the public sector. It is not possible to specify a priori the relative magnitudes of these two components of cost. Therefore, there exists no presupposition as to the "correct" level of government expenditures.

The preceding analysis raises many objections to the treatment of tax design and tax reform. Many of these difficulties stem directly from use of the discrete transaction paradigm of contract. Although the adoption of an administered contracts perspective eliminates some of

[51] Browning, "The Marginal Cost of Public Funds."
[52] Posner, "The Social Costs of Monopoly and Regulation."

these problems, it creates an even larger number of difficulties. Principally, we must be concerned not only with the initial attributes of a tax system, but also with the mechanisms by which the tax system adapts to changing circumstances.[53] The function of tax preferences in an administered contracts perspective remains to be established. However, it would seem useful to consider the length of time over which capitalization occurs and the magnitude of the gains as well as their incidence. Recognizing the existence of frictions in moving toward complete capitalization complicates any discussion of tax reform. Incomplete or protracted capitalization makes the case against tax reform less persuasive.

Generally, tax preferences may or may not possess certain desirable properties in terms of efficiency and equity. Equally important are the adaptive properties of the tax system to future events. Although tax preferences may possess some desirable properties in this respect, the process of capitalization causes the adaptive properties to become ineffective. We are then required to examine the factors that determine the degree and duration of capitalization and, therefore, the usefulness of tax preferences as a mechanism for dealing with change. These difficult questions must be confronted before disputes over tax reform can be resolved.

Conclusion

The application of the capitalization or transitional gains principle to an examination of the structure and reform of preferential tax provisions has been shown to yield several interesting and perhaps novel results. The granting of a preferential rate of tax was shown to be conceptually equivalent to the creation of an asset that, if correctly priced, eliminates the tax saving. The expenditure function was used to provide a measure of this change in welfare. It was demonstrated that complete capitalization resulted in the equality of the pretax and posttax utility levels.

Use of the expenditure function allowed consideration of the new definitions of horizontal equity. It was demonstrated that although defining horizontal equity in terms of utility eliminates some of the diffi-

[53] Feldstein, "On the Theory of Tax Reform," pp. 91–94, recognizes the need to consider the adaptability properties of a tax system.

culties associated with the definitions of ability to pay, it creates a new set of problems regarding equal position when preferences and options differ. It was demonstrated that capitalization poses some significant difficulties for econometric estimates of the effects of tax preferences.

The distinction between tax reform and tax design was then examined under two paradigms of contract. For the discrete transaction mode, if the capitalization principle is operative, the granting of preferential tax provisions should be undertaken with candid recognition of the inherent difficulties. In addition, the burden of a tax was shown to consist of more than efficiency distortions.

Finally, when an administered contracts perspective is adopted, the distinction between tax design and tax reform is blurred. Accordingly, horizontal equity, tax avoidance, and tax reform no longer fall into neat categories. Attention must be concentrated on how the tax system adapts to unanticipated events. More questions than answers have been suggested. The search for the properties of a "good" tax will require, in addition to the customary questions, an examination of the process of adaptation to change.

20

Rent-Seeking Aspects of
Bureaucratic Competition

by

ROGER L. FAITH

A good deal of the literature on the economics of bureaucracy has dealt
with models of budget determination that emphasize the rational behavior of bureaucrats.[1] Among the questions addressed in the literature have been: Is the allocation of resources between the public and
private sector efficient? Is the allocation of resources within the public
sector efficient? What can be done to improve the efficiency of governmental production? The answers to these questions (and any subsequent policy recommendations) depend, of course, on the institutional
structure underlying the model. The aim of this paper is to investigate
the effect that current institutions have on the relationships among individual bureaus.

Conventional models of bureaucracy have been concerned primarily with the interaction between the demanders of governmental
output (the legislature) and the suppliers of governmental output (the
bureaucracy). But "the bureaucracy" is neither a monolith nor a well-
organized cartel. Rather, it is a collection of many individual bureaus,
each seeking its own political and economic reward where the reward
accruing to any one bureau is inextricably related to the activities of all

[1] For a broad survey of the literature in this area see Ryan Amacher, Robert Tollison, and Thomas Willett, "Budget Size in a Democracy: A Review of the Arguments,"
Public Finance Quarterly 3 (April, 1976): 99–121; Thomas Borcherding, ed., *Budgets
and Bureaucrats* (Durham, N.C.: Duke University Press, 1977); Albert Breton and
Ronald Wintrobe, "The Equilibrium Size of a Budget-Maximizing Bureau: A Note on
Niskanen's Theory of Bureaucracy," *Journal of Political Economy* 83 (February, 1975):
195–207; and Jean-Luc Migué and Gérard Bélanger, "Toward a General Theory of Managerial Discretion," *Public Choice* 17 (Spring, 1974): 27–43.

other bureaus. And just as the determination of private sector output depends upon the relationships among individual firms and industries, so the determination of bureaucratic output surely depends upon the relationships among individual bureaus. Any policy recommendation regarding the organization of the government production sector that fails to consider these relationships will be, at best, of uncertain value.

The primary hypothesis presented in this paper is that due to the institutional environment under which bureaus behave, particularly that in which bureaucratic production rights are allocated, a significant portion of a bureau's resources are devoted to rent-seeking activities. Moreover, when the social costs of these rent-seeking activities are recognized, the sometimes-proposed policy of increasing bureau competition is seen not to be *necessarily* desirable.

A Description of Bureaus and Their Environment

Bureaus are governmental organizations. As such they differ from private organizations in that governmental organizations are not economically responsible for some specified set of real losses that they impose on others and cannot sue to capture some specified set of gains that they confer on others.[2] An additional characteristic of most governmental production organizations is that their customers substantially care about what is done with their payments to the organization but cannot easily determine what in fact is done with them. That is, the production and distribution of governmentally produced benefits is important to the legislators who provide the bureau with its revenue, but it is difficult for the legislature, particularly in the absence of a formal marketplace, to tell exactly what and how much is produced with the resources they allocate to each bureau. This aspect of bureaucratic production will play an important role in my subsequent discussions.

The economic advantage of governmental organization is the reduction of certain transaction costs, typically incurred in private markets, which are associated with trying to reach a price agreement prior

[2] This distinction is due to Earl Thompson, "Review of *Bureaucracy and Representative Government* by W. A. Niskanen," *Journal of Economic Literature* 11 (September, 1973): 950–953; and idem, "The Optimal Role of Government in a Competitive Equilibrium with Transaction Costs," *American Re-Evolution, Papers and Proceedings*, ed. Richard Auster and Barbara Sears (Dallas: Criterion Studies, 1977), pp. 9–23.

to providing output. These transaction costs are the sum of the unavoidable joint losses to transacting parties that occur in a world of imperfect information regarding (1) the conditions of an exchange agreement (contract costs), (2) the distribution and location of available exchange offers (search costs), and (3) the final terms of the exchange agreement (bargaining costs). An example, where these costs are reduced by governmental production, is the provision of national defense, which is supplied without first negotiating a price with each of the several consumers of defense services or erecting barriers to exclude nonpayers. Emergency medical care is an example of a noncollective good that is often governmentally produced and supplied without a prior price agreement. The economic disadvantages of governmental organizations are the well-known social losses resulting from inefficient input and output decisions made by managers with attenuated profit motives.[3] If, and only if, the reduction in transaction costs outweighs the costs of inefficient managerial behavior is governmental supply more efficient than private supply.[4] For the remainder of the paper, I shall assume that all bureaus satisfy this criterion.

THE DETERMINATION OF BUREAU OUTPUT

A legislative review committee determines each bureau's line of goods and services, the quantity of each good and service to be produced, and the bureau's budget allocation so as to maximize the net value of the bureau outputs based on the committee's marginal value function and the bureau's cost function. The marginal value function is in turn based on the committee's perception of voter demand for the output and the value placed on the output by the committee itself. In addition, the review committee periodically reviews the bureau's performance by evaluating its observable output and the productivity of its observable inputs. Finally, I assume that all bureau labor inputs are

---

[3] See Armen Alchian, "Private Property and the Relative Cost of Tenure," *The Public Stake in Union Power*, ed. Philip Bradley (Charlottesville: University of Virginia Press, 1958), pp. 350–371.

[4] Thus, any efficiency argument for governmental supply implies the presence of positive, unavoidable transaction costs for some privately determined allocations. It should be noted, however, that the converse is not true. The existence of private transaction costs does not imply that government production or distribution is economically desirable.

FIGURE 20.1

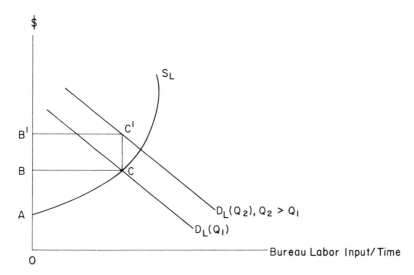

nonperfectly elastically supplied, noninferior, and are paid competitively determined salaries.[5] Thus, an increase in bureau output trans-
lates into an increase in factor demand, which results in higher wages
and higher economic rents for all inframarginal employees. In figure
20.1, for example, an increase in output demand from Q_1 to Q_2 shifts
factor demand to the right, increasing total inframarginal rents to current employees from ABC to AB^1C^1C.

Although at the formal level a bureau produces only those outputs
and quantities desired by its review committee, there is room in the
model for managerial discretion in determining actual output. First,
bureau performance in terms of output, especially quality, is difficult
to observe and measure. This is particularly true of outputs whose
benefits exist sometime into the future (dams) and those which have
poor market substitutes (social programs). Likewise, the productivity

---

[5] Gordon Tullock, *The Politics of Bureaucracy* (Washington, D.C.: Public Affairs
Press, 1965), argues that bureaucratic salaries depend on the number of subordinates
under each employee. Thus, if bureaucrats are noninferior factors of production, an expansion in output will increase *current* bureaucrats' salaries as (1) the total labor demand
is increased and (2) former subordinates become new managers. In a civil service context, this suggests that current GS-12's become GS-13's and likewise for other civil service ranks. Again, it follows that a bureaucrat's income will rise with bureau output.

of the bureau manager as both monitor and input decision-maker is often difficult to measure. For, unlike private firms whose outputs and production decisions are constantly being evaluated by stockholders and consumers, bureau output is evaluated only periodically by its review committee. This is not to say that the consumers of bureau output do not serve some sort of monitoring function, but the nature of the political process does tend to dilute the influence of unorganized or widely-dispersed consumers of governmental output relative to their influence in the private sector. Further, formal review is done either by disinterested bureaucrats with attenuated claims to the benefits produced by their investigative efforts or by legislators who have several interests to look after besides evaluating bureaucratic performance. The poor incentives to monitor bureau output, the difficulty in accurately measuring a bureau's performance, and the manager's attenuated profit incentives all imply that the bureau manager *can* produce an output that differs from the review committee's preferred output.

Given the structure of bureaucratic rewards and constraints, it seems likely that rational bureaucrats will seek to produce relatively large outputs in order to increase their factor rents. This is not to say that bureaus seek to maximize their budgets, a hypothesis that has come under strong attack.[6] Rather, I am assuming that bureaus seek to maximize their rents and that this implies an output and budget greater than those preferred by its review committee. One way a bureau can increase its output in the next budgetary period is to engage in current activities that shift out its review committee's perceived benefit function for the bureau's future output. Ryan Amacher, Robert Tollison, and Thomas Willett argue that a good deal of a bureau's expenditures is functionally equivalent to advertising (e.g., press releases, public demonstrations, and lobbying). Generally, these activities are not costless and require the expenditure of real resources out of a bureau's current budget.[7] But since actual output is not easily

[6] See Migué and Bélanger, "Toward a General Theory of Managerial Discretion"; Breton and Wintrobe, "The Equilibrium Size of a Budget-Maximizing Bureau"; and Thompson, "Review of Niskanen."

[7] Ryan Amacher, Robert Tollison, and Thomas Willett, "Risk Avoidance and Political Advertising: Neglected Issues in the Literature on Budget Size in a Democracy," in *The Economic Approach to Public Policy*, ed. Amacher, Tollison, and Willett (Ithaca: Cornell University Press, 1976), pp. 405–433.

observed, a bureau can divert some of its current budget resources to such demand-increasing activities and still meet its committee's current output requirement without violating its current budget allocation. That is, bureau managers can devote current bureau resources to securing larger future outputs that, in turn, increase their future factor rents.

CONFLICT AND COMPETITION AMONG BUREAUS

The review committee's budget recommendation depends on the bureau's cost function and the review committee's perceived benefit function, both of which depend on the outputs and budgets of all other bureaus and private sector output. Since the reward structure facing all bureaucrats is essentially the same, each bureau will seek to increase the demand for its output and consequently an increase in its budget allocation. As it is impossible for every bureau to increase its budget simultaneously for a given aggregate budget, there arises an interdependence of payoffs, and hence conflict, among bureaus. An increase in one bureau's output, either because of increased production or because of an expansion in its line of services, will generally have a negative effect on the rents accruing to other bureaus. Besides the obvious competition among those bureaus which produce close substitutes (for example, the various branches of the armed forces), all bureaus compete for the government's budget dollar. An increase in Bureau A's share of the aggregate government budget implies a reduction in Bureau B's budget share (and associated rents), *ceteris paribus.* For example, an increase in foreign policy spending will increase the State Department's budget at the expense of, say, domestic policy programs and the budget of HEW. Although in the private sector all industries do compete for the consumer's dollar, bureaucratic budget competition is more relevant to the individual behavior of bureaus, in that all bureaus deal with the same (small group of) buyers, the legislature. And it is the decisions of this set of buyers that determine the economic fortunes of all bureaus at a given level of government.

Note that competition also extends across levels of government. Ultimately, the source of all bureaucratic rents, at all levels of government, resides with the voter-consumer who demands government output. Suppose that one can disaggregate the demand for government output into demands for local, state, and federally produced output. If voter-consumers are indifferent to the level of government that actually produces the output they demand, then the individual bureaus at each of the various levels of government will compete for the voter-consumer's expenditure on government-produced output. For example, an increase in locally produced flood control services will, *ceteris paribus*, reduce the demand for similar services of the Corps of Engineers, a federal agency, and hence its factor rents. This will provide the Corps an incentive to prevent a loss of rents, for example, starting a campaign that questions the local agency's ability to cope with flood control. Multilevel competition can also create some interesting alliances. If a lower-level government can induce a higher-level government to assume part of the production (and financing) of services normally produced by the lower government's bureaus, a net gain accrues to the voters in the lower government, who receive a given output at a lower per capita cost because of the expanded tax base. The higher-level bureau also gains, because of the increased demand for its output. The losers in this case would be the lower-level bureaus (their rents fall). Current examples in the United States include education, environmental protection, natural resource management, and public welfare, each of which has become increasingly centralized.

To summarize, bureaus are viewed as individual production agents, "governmental" in nature, whose initial output levels are formally selected by their legislative review committees. Input levels and actual output levels are selected by the bureau manager, whose performance is costly to monitor and evaluate, thereby permitting the bureau manager the discretion to devote current resources to increasing the future demand for his bureau services and thus increasing his rents. As each bureau has an incentive to devote some resources to expanding its slice of the aggregate budget, every bureau must spend some resources simply to prevent a transfer of budget dollars from itself to other bureaus.[8] The remainder of this paper deals with some aspects and consequences of this competition.

---

[8] The interdependence of bureaucratic fortunes exists because of demand interdependence. It does not depend on whether the review committee or the bureau is a better bargainer with respect to determining the bureau's budget. In this regard we could, alternatively, adopt the model of William H. Niskanen, Jr., *Bureaucracy and Representative Government*, (Chicago: Aldine-Atherton, 1971), and "Bureaucrats and Politicians," *Journal of Law and Economics* 18 (December, 1975): 617–643, where bureaus act as interdependent, perfectly discriminating monopolists with respect to their review

Rents and Rights

Entry into the government production sector is not costless. Individual bureaus are "licensed" and "regulated" with respect to what and how much output they can produce. Before any rents can be captured, the *right* to produce given outputs in given quantities must be obtained from the legislature. A bureau cannot autonomously decide to produce an output not already allocated to it, or expand its output, without first obtaining what we will call a *production right* from the legislature. In addition, entry into the government labor force is also restricted and relatively free from competitive elements. Together, these institutional constraints imply the existence of significant rents in the government sector. So one would expect competition among existing bureaus for the production rights that generate these rents.

The right to produce does not mean that a bureau's rents are free from outside influence or protected from encroachment by other bureaus. As with any "property right," the right must be enforced to be meaningful. Each bureau's budget, output level, and rents depend on the outputs, budgets, and demand-increasing activities of all other bureaus. Consequently, each bureau generally must spend some resources just to maintain its current output level. The actual budget-maintenance costs of any given bureau depend on several factors—its political advertising technology, its control of specific resources, its influence in the legislature, and so forth. Amacher, Tollison, and Willett suggest that bureaus that produce insurance-type outputs (e.g., defense, environmental protection) have an advertising-cost advantage over other bureaus, given the presence of risk-averse legislators.[9] Also, if a bureau holds a specific technology not easily adopted by another agency (e.g., the operation of military hardware), then that bureau will face less competition for its production rights than a bureau with less specific technology. Finally, a bureau with influence over its

committees. One can also obtain interdependence by assuming that bureau managers and their review committees act as joint-profit-maximizing decision makers. In this case, the interdependence exists in legislator-bureau coalitions, which compete for shares of the government's general tax revenue. The entire budget process, including subcommittee review and congressional approval, could then be viewed as a single *n*-person, noncooperative game.

[9] Amacher, Tollison, and Willet, "Risk Avoidance."

review committee (e.g., a legislator whose district receives a large share of the bureau's output), and bureaus with a good "brand-name" will face lower rent-protection costs than other bureaus.[10]

Besides the expenditures to maintain *current* production rights, bureaus will also devote resources to obtaining *new*, previously undefined, or incompletely assigned, production rights. Meltsner has claimed that the assignment of production rights over new outputs is frequently made to the bureau with prior jurisdictional claim to the production right.[11] For example, it has been observed that bureaus spend part of their budget developing programs or projects that may possibly be implemented in the future. The bureau that can demonstrate it is able to deliver a new output *first*, rather than most *efficiently*, has a higher probability of being granted the rights to the production and thus the associated factor rents.[12] One consequence of this competition for new production rights is an expanding bureaucracy. The continuing incentive to create new production rights may provide a partial explanation for the observed growth of the government sector.

A bureau's demand-increasing activities, along with its efforts to establish future production rights, are examples of *rent-seeking*, defined as any expenditure of resources to acquire a transfer of wealth. In my model, bureaus devote real resources to gaining favorable treatment from their review committees in the form of increased budgets. This implies that bureaus also must engage in some "rent-avoidance"[13] activities, that is, devoting resources to protect rents from accruing to other rent-seeking bureaus. The consequences of these activities are analogous to the negative-sum aspect of intra-industry advertising on profits. That is, potential rents are dissipated by the resources expended in competing for them. Similarly, rent-seeking in the form of

---

[10] See Arnold Meltsner, *Policy Analysis in the Bureaucracy* (Berkeley: University of California Press, 1976).

[11] Ibid.

[12] Meltsner, writing for policy analysts, extols the tactic of having available programs ready for implementation if and when the demand for such programs becomes manifest (ibid.). See also Aaron Wildavsky, *The Politics of the Budgetary Process*, 2nd ed. (Boston: Little, Brown and Company, 1974), for a discussion of other budget-maintenance and budget-expansion strategies.

[13] Gordon Tullock, "Efficient Rent Seeking," chapter 6 in this volume.

trying to create a future production right often leads to resource usage with little or no net gain accruing to the final owner of the production right and the associated rents. Because of the differences in the rent-seeking abilities of different bureaus, however, one should not infer that no bureau realizes a net gain from rent seeking.[14]

The basis of these rent-seeking activities lies in the nature of the institutional setting underlying intrabureaucratic behavior. In the private sector, individual behavior is effectively constrained by a system of laws and property rights (a constitution). In the government sector, although there are also some constitutional constraints on a politician's or a bureaucrat's actions, the constraints do not appear to be as binding, particularly with respect to internal government behavior. Instead, one has a situation analogous to the distribution of property among competing nations, where what one nation "owns" is defined in terms of what it can defend. While these rent-protection expenditures, strictly speaking, constitute a deadweight loss and hence represent a non-optimality, this is unavoidable and of no policy significance within the current institutional setting, since rent protection is part of the cost of defining bureaucratic property rights.

Implications

An important implication of this rent-seeking hypothesis is that there are social costs of bureaucratic production beyond those identified in other models. Given the efficiency basis for government production outlined earlier, we must now add to the social costs of government production the social costs of bureaucratic rent seeking. It is no longer correct to measure efficiency in the government sector by comparing the savings in private transaction costs with the losses implied by attenuated profit claims of government production managers. Total so-

---

[14] It should also be pointed out that political advertising can have a positive social value as information to the potential customers of bureaucratic output. In the absence of rent seeking, the nonproprietorship of bureau managers implies that too little advertising will be supplied. Thus, the increased advertising due to the rent-seeking incentives may offset the former inefficiency to the extent that such advertising provides a positive benefit to the consumer-voter. This possibility, however, seems to be more relevant the less "public" the output, and less relevant where the consumer-voter does not have the option of buying the output (e.g., national defense).

cial losses also depend on the institutional environment under which the individual government decision maker is operating.

For this reason, it does not necessarily follow that making the bureaucracy more competitive by introducing several, smaller bureaus, each producing an identical line of services, will improve the economic efficiency of the government sector. On the one hand, increasing the number of producers of each output may well reduce the amount of rent seeking by any one bureau, as each bureau has a smaller expected gain at the expense of bureaus producing other products. But the introduction of several producers of each output creates greater substitutability between bureaus, increasing the return to political advertising with respect to a given output. Further, the introduction of several additional producers of each output will increase monitoring and evaluation costs for the various review committees, thereby increasing the ability of bureau managers to divert resources away from the production of authorized output and into demand-increasing activities. The net effect on aggregate bureaucratic rent-seeking cannot be predicted a priori. Further, one must take into account the increase in production costs caused by any forgone scale economies in production. Finally, proposals to replace the current legislative review process with a private market system, where bureaucratic production decisions are based on some sort of profit-maximizing criteria, violate the whole economic justification for bureaucratic production outlined earlier.

A major source of inefficiency, given the current institutional arrangement, lies in the way government production rights are assigned. The rent-seeking activities of individual bureaus can be viewed as internal attempts to determine the distribution of these rights, and because there is no exogenous government to allocate these rights, the rent-seeking costs may be unavoidable. In this case, if one accepts current institutions, policy recommendations should be addressed to finding ways of minimizing these costs for a given level of government output. Increased monitoring of bureau managers and improved measurement of bureaucratic output would, for example, reduce the resources available to managers for rent-seeking, and so reduce the amount of rent seeking in general.

Concluding Remarks

Any recommendation regarding the alteration of current bureaucratic institutions requires knowledge of how bureaus interact among themselves. Most previous analyses have looked only at the interaction between a bureau and the legislature, largely neglecting the issue of bureaucratic competition. This paper has attempted to address (1) the question of how bureaus compete and (2) the likely consequences of this competition. The main finding is that bureaus behave as a set of rational, rent-seeking individuals, trying to establish a prior claim to the factor rents associated with government production.

In closing, we note that our model has implications with respect to the so-called "unseen hand in government." It has been suggested that an "unseen hand" operates in government, generating an approximate optimal allocation of resources between the public and private sectors and *within* the public sector. [15] Despite the inefficiencies inherent in governmental organizations, it is argued, the presence of interpersonal bargaining induces individuals to weigh the benefits and costs of their actions, which results in approximately Pareto-optimal outcomes. Such an implication, however, requires that all property rights, governmental as well as private, be unambiguously defined. The absence of governmental property rights produces its own "unseen hand in government," which induces individuals to devote resources to establish these rights, resulting in a movement away from optimality. The actions of benign individuals may lead to nonbenign outcomes.

[15] See Ronald McKean, "The Unseen Hand in Government," *American Economic Review* 55 (June, 1965): 496–505.

21

Rent Seeking in Academia

by

H. GEOFFREY BRENNAN AND ROBERT D. TOLLISON

MANY academics are professionals in the business of analyzing the world around them but have rarely focused their analytical skills on the institutions they inhabit and manage.[1] This myopia may have a quite reasonable explanation. Perhaps universities are so odd or unpredictable as to be an uninteresting subject for analysis. We think not, however. Modern universities command a nontrivial amount of resources each year, and, moreover, represent a class of bureaucratic institutions to which the economist's expanding toolkit in the area of the economic approach to bureaucracy and other nonproprietary institutions can usefully be applied.[2] In this paper we hope to make a small contribution to this growing literature. Specifically, we will employ the rent-seeking model, as elaborated in this volume, to analyze the process of academic salary setting and the impact of certain policies (specifically, "sunshine" laws, which require faculty salaries to be published) on that process.

---

[1] There is a small body of literature that deals with the university as an institution. See, for example, Armen A. Alchian, "Private Property and the Relative Cost of Tenure," in *The Public Stake in Union Power*, ed. Phillip D. Bradley (Charlottesville: University of Virginia Press, 1958), pp. 350–371; James M. Buchanan and Nicos E. Devletoglou, *Academia in Anarchy: An Economic Diagnosis* (New York: Basic Books, 1970); and Richard B. McKenzie, "The Economic Basis of Departmental Discord in Academe," *Social Science Quarterly* 59 (March, 1979): 653–664. Moreover, this literature should be distinguished from that dealing with the so-called "economics of higher education," mainly devoted to rationalizing public subsidies to higher education.

[2] Much of this literature derives from William H. Niskanen, Jr., *Bureaucracy and Representative Government* (Chicago: Aldine-Atherton, 1971). For a pioneering study of economic behavior in a nonproprietary setting, see Armen A. Alchian and Reuben A. Kessel, "Competition, Monopoly, and the Pursuit of Money," in *Aspects of Labor Economics*, ed. H. Gregg Lewis *et al.*, (Princeton: Princeton University Press, 1962), pp. 157–175.

The paper proceeds as follows. In the first section we introduce and defend a basic assumption that substantial rents are earned by academics. The second section discusses the process of salary determination for academics. The third section presents a formal model of salary determination, based on the presumption that the department head is able to extract rents from faculty and reassign them in such a way as to maximize the academic value of the department. The fourth section considers the forms that rent seeking takes in the rent-extraction model. The fifth section examines the effects of salary publication on the rent-seeking process in academia. A final section offers some brief concluding remarks.

The Nature of Rents in Academia

In order to derive our model of academia, we must initially make certain descriptive judgments about the way universities operate. Our central observation is that the typical university or university department is characterized by substantial rents earned by inframarginal faculty members. More technically, there exists a significant range of salary structures consistent with retaining the same set of individuals as members of the department.[3]

We can, for example, associate three numbers with each faculty member, all expressed in dollars per year: (1) the member's actual salary, S; (2) the amount of money, M, below which the member would move to an alternative employment; and (3) the salary, C, that the member would obtain in his next best employment. We know that for each individual, $S \geq M$, since he would otherwise move to his alternative employment. We also assume that, in general, $C \geq M$, because there are positive costs of moving—both physical costs, such as housing transactions, and psychic costs, attributable to moving away from a preferred location.[4] Nothing can be said a priori about the relation of S and C. It is certainly consistent with locational equilibrium

---

[3] A salary structure is defined here as a vector of payments $(S_1, \ldots, S_n)$, where S_i is the salary accruing to individual i. In the analysis to follow, the discussion will be couched in terms of an academic department rather than the university as a whole, except where otherwise stated.

[4] It is, of course, conceivable that the individual would consider the stimulation of a new environment to be large enough to outweigh the costs of moving, but this seems

that $C > S$, and this condition may hold for every member of a department.

We should note here the relation between M and C. Presumably, the higher is C, other things equal, the higher is M. In fact, we can write: $C - M = K$, where K represents the cost of moving. If K is positive and constant over time (though not invariant between individuals), then an increase in C leads to a corresponding increase in M. We will have more to say about this relationship and its implications subsequently.

Of these four parameters, S, C, M, and K, the first is obviously directly observable—at least by the individual himself and the department head (it may not, of course, be known more widely in the department). The second is also observable in principle, though not necessarily directly. Its determination may require a competitive process among institutions for the individual's services. Since there are costs of recourse to the academic labor market for both buyers and sellers, a current value of C may not always be readily available. The parameters M and K, will generally be known, ex ante, only to the individual faculty member.

The difference between M and S is defined as the "rent" accruing to a given faculty member. The sum of such differences over all individuals in an academic department represents the total "rents" in the department. As in the standard geometry, we can depict these rents in a "supply-curve" type diagram. In order to do so, however, we first have to normalize for quality differentials among faculty, since some individuals embody more "academic quality" than others. There are a number of ways in which to do this, but we adopt the following procedure. We let C represent an index of the number of units of "academic quality," measured, for example, in terms of tens of thousands of dollars per year. Thus, if C, individual 1's market value, is \$26,000 per year, then C embodies 2.6 units of academic quality. On this basis we can convert individuals into labor units of more or less homogeneous quality, which can be added together to form a measure of the departmental labor stock, measured in standard units of "academic quality."

---

unlikely to be true generally. The fact that individuals usually move to positions carrying a higher salary provides indirect evidence of the validity of the assumption of positive moving costs.

This conversion procedure allows us to conceive of the ratio, S_i/C_i, for each individual i, as a measure of that individual's salary per academic quality unit embodied in him. Likewise, M_i/C_i is a measure of i's reservation price per academic quality unit, and $S_i - M_i/C_i$ is a measure of i's rents per academic quality unit. If we rank individuals according to their M_i/C_i measures, from lowest to highest, we can depict the departmental faculty salary structure in a diagram such as figure 21.1.

To understand the construction of figure 21.1, consider the case of the first faculty member. This member embodies OQ_1 units of academic input, as measured by the salary he would obtain if he moved to his next-best alternative. Per unit of academic input, his salary rate is S_1, and his total salary is the area, S_1Q_1. The lowest salary that he would accept without moving is M_1 per unit of academic input, or Q_1 in toto. The same interpretation holds for the other individual faculty members, from 1 to 10.

We should note that although we have normalized the differing academic capacities of the different faculty members by deflating the various salary measures by C_i, a certain amount of care should be used in interpreting the sum C_i (depicted by the area C_iQ_{10} in figure 21.1) as a measure of the total academic quality of the department. Nor should it be too readily assumed that the units of quality embodied in the various individuals are perfect substitutes for one another.[5] These matters need not concern us here, however. Our primary interest is in the existence of academic rents, depicted as the shaded area between S_i and M_i in figure 21.1. The total shaded area is the total rents that exist in the department, rents that arise from two distinct sources.

First, the university does not operate in an environment comparable with that of a competitive private firm. Universities receive much of their revenues through political processes, in which there can be no general expectation that a university's total output (and, a fortiori, the output of any department in a university) will be the output at which the demand for an additional unit will equal the cost of providing it. Indeed, there is no guarantee in this setting that at any

---

[5]See James M. Buchanan and Robert D. Tollison, "The Homogenization of Heterogeneous Inputs," *American Economic Review*, forthcoming, for a more detailed discussion of this and related points.

FIGURE 21.1

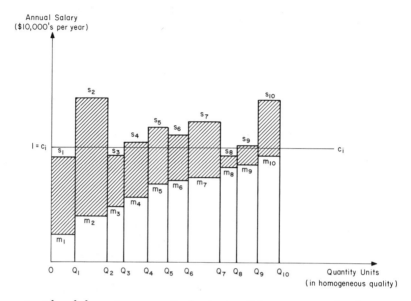

output level the price per unit of output will be constrained to lie at or
below any conventional definition of the "demand price." This absence of an outcome analogous to the equilibrium of a competitive
market reflects the institutional structure within which academic salaries are set and within which demands for the services of universities
are registered, rather than simply the difficulties of defining and measuring university output.[6] For this reason individuals within a university may *all* be paid more than is necessary to retain their services.
The wage for the most marginal faculty member (i.e., the one with the
lowest rents) may lie above the wage in his next-best employment,
without any marketlike pressures forthcoming to change the situation.
The way that we shall model the academic department in this setting
is to assume a "wages fund" model of the department.[7] The aggregate
salary budget is fixed and independent of academic quality in the department, at least over some significant range.

    This is not to say that universities are not competitive and that

---

[6] Although, to be sure, measurement and definition problems exist here and may
be exacerbated by the institutional arrangements.

[7] McKenzie, "Economic Basis of Departmental Discord," employs a similar
approach.

there is not an active market for the services of historians, economists, and other faculty. Yet this competition is not sufficient to dissipate the rents that arise in an academic setting, as it would be in a normal market context. Rents will persist in academia for the reasons we have stressed here. Universities are not run on the basis of the profit motive. Consumers of university output—students and the users of research output—do not pay directly for what they consume, and producers—teachers and researchers—are not paid directly for what they produce. A less productive institution or department may consistently have a larger budget than a more productive one, because allocations are not determined on market principles. Revolving majorities in the legislature, impinging on the fortunes of congressional or state electoral districts, may explain more of the fortunes of regional universities than of their academic accomplishments. Moreover, there is no presumption that, in our model, different demanders of faculty services will agree upon the "quality" of an individual scholar. For such reasons rents can persist in our theory, even though universities may be broadly conceived as competitive with one another.

There is a second and independent source of rents in the typical department, which is attributable to the costs of moving. Because individuals cannot move without cost to other employments, it is possible to pay an individual a lower salary than he could earn in a roughly comparable university (or other employment). For example, individuals 1 and 3, as depicted in figure 21.1, are both in this situation. These mobility costs will generally differ between individuals and will serve to generate differential "locational rents." Such rents can and typically will exist in perfectly competitive markets. In the academic setting, however, they seem likely to be larger than in most private settings. The academic market is widely dispersed geographically, and individuals will find it relatively easy to locate in their preferred environment. Any locational equilibrium will thus likely contain substantial elements of pure locational preference. Moreover, with the exception of universities in large metropolitan areas, it is difficult for an individual to move between academic institutions within the same location and even more difficult for most academics to find congenial and comparably paid employment outside universities. The decision of an academic to leave a particular institution therefore usually implies changing *location*, rather than moving to alternative employment in the same area. This is in sharp contrast to the situation with unskilled labor and many white-collar workers, for whom close substitutes for present occupations can usually be found without a significant change in location. In any case, even if locational rents in many other industries are no less substantial, in competitive markets there is no scope for those rents to be appropriated by someone else. In the nonmarket setting characteristic of academic institutions, however, these rents *can* be appropriated and reassigned.

Salary Determination in Academia

The distribution of rents, such as illustrated in figure 21.1, will be determined by those decision makers with the discretionary power to set salaries in the university, and various types of considerations will determine the amount of discretion they will have in this respect. For example, their discretionary power over salaries is increased by the fact that they have the power to adjust salaries on a yearly basis. In the absence of this annual redetermination, each faculty member would be paid that salary which he originally negotiated with the university. Since at the time of the original negotiation the individual would not actually reside in the area, locational rents would be restricted to ex ante local preferences, and total rents at any given academic location would tend to be minimal. Year-to-year adjustments in academic pay are thus an important source of the discretionary power of university officials over the distribution of faculty rents. The yearly increment to the aggregate salary budget, whether a real or a nominal increase, establishes the scope for adjustments in the salary structure, and thus for additional rent extraction and reassignment.

The power to determine salaries rests with the department head (or the dean, vice-president, or whatever), who will be constrained in a number of important ways in exercising this power. Since he has the power to distribute the rents, there is a sense in which the rents "belong" to him. He will not, however, have the power to appropriate rents directly as salary to himself, because he does not set his own salary. The department head will also be constrained in other ways. He can, for example, be deposed, if a sufficient number of department members are dissatisfied enough to seek his dismissal. He will, therefore, be anxious to maintain the good will of his department within broad limits. In addition, he may rationally seek to maximize the prestige of his department, because this in turn maximizes his own market value and his bargaining position in relation to his own salary. Or, finally, the decision maker may be constrained by internal "moral-ethical" rules, dictated by his conscience and general commitment to academic values.

In what follows, we will describe the implications of the existence of and competition for the rents that exist in an academic department, under the assumption that the department head attempts to maximize the academic worth of his department. In this setting we seek to derive some simple propositions about predicted outcomes.

Rents Versus Quality

If the department head is motivated to maximize the academic quality of his department, he will attempt to use the available rents to add additional members to the faculty or, perhaps more likely, to replace individual faculty members with others who embody higher quality.

Instead of a salary structure such as that depicted in figure 21.1, the department head would aim to achieve one in which each individual was paid virtually no more than his reservation price, M_i. In this case, the entire area, $(S_i - M_i)$ (shaded in figure 21.1), would be expended, hiring more academic quality at a price at or above C_i, and the salary structure would come to reflect that depicted in figure 21.2. Rents have been entirely obliterated, and the cost of the additional units of "academic quality," $Q_{13}Q_{10}$, is virtually equal to the original level of rents, $(S_i - M_i)$. No sycophantic rent-seeking will occur in this department, since there are *no* rents to be sought. There will, however, be a certain amount of potentially costly "rent protection," about which we will offer some comments in the next section.

For now, we want to focus on several aspects of the salary structure, as illustrated in figure 21.2. First, there is no reason to expect that individuals of identical academic quality will receive identical salaries. On the contrary, as simple inspection shows, the return per unit of academic quality will vary from M_1 to M_{13}. Thus, the arrangement that maximizes academic quality will not be congruent with popular equity norms: equal work will not yield equal pay. In fact, superior academics may well be paid less than inferior ones. On the other hand,

FIGURE 21.2

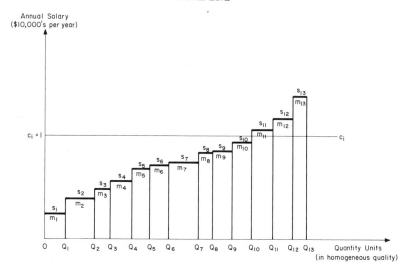

such a salary structure may not be as inequitable as it first appears. To the extent that locational rents are a nonpecuniary source of benefits accruing to the individual, the $S_i - M_i$ rule is closer to an equal-utility rule than the $S_i = S_j$ rule. After all, every individual is exactly indifferent between M_i and C_i, and the C_i's are the same for all individuals, normalized for quality differences.

The second noteworthy feature in this case is that the strategy at stake is a risky one for the department head. It requires him to predict the M_i for all individuals, and it is not usually observable. Further, the cost of providing an extra unit of academic quality via purchase from the market is much greater than the cost of retaining that unit from an individual whose locational rents are high. For example, to *retain* individual 1 as a member of the department costs M_1 per unit of academic quality, whereas to purchase an additional unit on the open market will cost C_i or more. For the academically motivated department head, therefore, a good rule of thumb is, generally, that it is cheaper to hang onto what you have than to buy replacements on the open market.[8] The cost in dollars of making a mistake in estimating M_1 is very much

---

[8] For much the same reason, it will be cheaper for a university to maintain quality in departments that are already strong than to attempt to build up departments that are presently weak.

larger than the costs of making a mistake in estimating M_{13}. One might therefore expect that individual 1—and other "high-rent" individuals—would be more likely to retain some of their rents than "low-rent" individuals, like individual 13. Notwithstanding this, however, a salary structure approaching that in figure 21.2 represents that for which the department head will aim. It represents the limiting case in which inframarginal faculty rents are used to maximize academic quality.

Rent Protection

Rent seeking, as normally defined, will not be absent from the academic world depicted by figure 21.2. Individuals will have an incentive to spend resources in seeking and protecting rents. Such expenditures will necessarily take the form of trying to make the decision maker's perception of the individual's M_i as large as possible. In this section, we wish to examine briefly some of the possible rent-seeking strategies in this regard.

Recall from above that $M_i = C_i - K_i$, where K_i is i's total moving costs, and C_i is i's best outside offer. Since K_i and C_i are not directly observable, the individual can increase the perceived value of M by increasing the perceived value of C and by reducing the perceived value of K. This can be accomplished in a variety of ways.

First, the individual academic should be continuously in the academic labor market, searching out offers and encouraging an active bidding process for his services. Such activity is not costless, either to the individual or to the schools that make offers and counteroffers to him. Moreover, the individual should advertise his offers as higher than they actually are. For example, he should emphasize the prestige of the alternative institution or the attractiveness of the alternative location when the bids are low, and the magnitude of the offer when the bids are high.

Second, he should attempt to indicate that his costs of moving are low. One way of doing this is to have a history of moving.[9] Another is to

---

[9] One testable hypothesis from this discussion is the prediction that academic mobility will be higher where the discretion of the department head, with respect to salary setting, is greater. On this basis we might predict that academic turnover is greater in U.S. institutions than in their U.K. counterparts—a prediction that seems to accord with casual observation.

spend a proportion of one's time "visiting" other institutions. Since there are advantages in terms of future rents obtained in any current decision to move, we would expect the extent of moving to be excessive, in the sense that individuals will move even when they would prefer the current location at the prevailing salary. Perpetual motion becomes a form of rent protection—rent seeking for the academic gypsy scholar.

Third, the individual should avoid those expenditures which tend to signal that he is locked into a particular location. He should consistently complain about his housing, the quality of the local schools, the lack of good restaurants, poor students, cultural deprivation, and the like, and he should avoid consumption expenditures of all types that are seen to make his present location more congenial. In this sense he will tend to underinvest in housing, garden improvement, sending his children to good schools, and so on.

These are only some of the ways that individuals may rent seek in a salary regime such as that depicted in figure 21.2. Of course, some of these effects may be irrelevant to the extent that individuals' demands for locational fixity, or goods that indicate locational fixity, are very inelastic. The individual who indulges such tastes must expect, however, to be exploited at the expense of those who do not.

Sunshine Laws and Rents

An interesting application of this analysis concerns the impact on the salary determination process of a requirement that faculty salaries be published. At one level it seems obvious that this requirement will inhibit rent seeking. The loss of the ability of the department head to negotiate salary levels and increments separately and privately means that conspicuous anomalies in salary levels between individuals of comparable academic quality are much more difficult to maintain. Salaries grossly out of line with commonly held notions of justice will cause dissension within the department and antagonism toward the department head. Scope for such discrimination is thus reduced in an open-pay regime.

This restriction on the discretionary power of the department head comes, however, at a price. It seems almost certain that common notions of salary justice will conflict with the "efficient" use of department resources, with "efficiency" defined in terms of achieving maximum academic output at minimal dollar cost. In this event it will no longer be as easy for the department head to discriminate among individuals on the basis of locational rents. Strong pressures to equalize the salaries of academic equals will result from salary publication. As a consequence, academic quality must decline in a university that is motivated to maximize academic quality via rent capture and reassignment.

A direct implication of this argument is that the measure of academic quality related to "market value," which we have used in our analysis, is, while economically justifiable, not the criterion that will be applied in an open-pay system. Judgments about academic value by appeal to external, nonmarket criteria are possible, and, indeed, probably predominate in academic institutions.[10] Consequently, the tendency for an academically mediocre law professor (or economist) to be paid more than an academically outstanding historian or English medievalist—with academic accomplishment measured by appeal to external criteria—is perfectly consistent with the market-oriented measure of academic quality that we have used. To the extent that publication of salaries makes it more difficult to sustain salary differences based solely on differential market value, higher-quality academics, in our market-value definition, will find their salaries squeezed, and the necessary overall outcome is for the quality of the institution to decline.

As another consequence of salary publication, it might equally be argued that the department head tends to be better informed about his department members' outside salary prospects than those members are about each others' prospects. The pressure established when salaries are published is for the measure of an individual's academic worth to approach the *median* of the measurements of his worth made by *all* members of the department.[11] To the extent that the department head is better informed about faculty members' market values, the postpublication measure of academic quality will be distorted, and there will probably be a trend toward narrowing the distribution of

[10]McKenzie, "Economic Basis of Departmental Discord," provides an interesting and entertaining version of the strategies that faculty members might employ in such a setting so as to influence the perceptions of their own and their colleagues' academic worth.

[11]We are indebted to our colleague, Roger Faith, for this point.

absolute salaries. Lower-quality academics will obtain a higher share of the aggregate salary budget, and higher-quality academics a lower share. Any such narrowing of the salary distribution will be inimical to retaining the higher-quality members and hence to the aggregate quality of the institution.

Salary publication therefore has certain predictable consequences in academia. It is also easy to see how such a pay system is related to rent seeking. Clearly, those members of the university who lie below the median level of locational rents have strong incentives to seek an open-pay system. This does not suggest that those seeking rents through salary publication will be a monolithic coalition (historians versus law professors). Rather, the salary publication coalition will be composed of an admixture of university members, who, for one reason or another, earn (but in our model do not receive) relatively large locational rents.

Concluding Remarks

We would like to stress that we have posited what must seem to many an unusual model of academia. Rent extraction and reassignment to maximize the "quality" of the university seems a far cry from the universities that we know. More to the point might be a model of departmental sycophancy, centered around the ability of the department head to redistribute rents arbitrarily ("rents up for grabs"). The rent-extraction model, however, provides an analytical definition of an "efficient" university, against which alternative models, such as more flagrant rent-seeking models, can be evaluated in terms of their implications for academic organization. In this sense our model constitutes a potentially useful vehicle for analyzing academic bureaucracy.

V.

Conclusion: The Rent-Seeking Society
in a Constitutional Perspective

22

Reform in the Rent-Seeking Society

by

JAMES M. BUCHANAN

RENT SEEKING involves social waste. Resources that could otherwise be devoted to value-producing activity are engaged in competitive effort that determines nothing other than the *distributive* results. Rent seeking, as such, is totally without allocative value, although, of course, the initial institutional creation of an opportunity for rent seeking ensures a net destruction of economic value. The distributive results are, nonetheless, important when we come to examine the political prospects for the institutional-legal changes that might be required to reduce the scope for rent seeking in modern society.

The community, the aggregate of persons in the defined political unit, loses value in two respects. First, there is the destruction of value when the initial decision is somehow made to create artificial scarcity and thereby to make possible rents over and above competitively determined rates of return to resource use. In the diagrams of basic price theory, this loss is measured by the familiar welfare triangles. Second, as the analyses contained in this volume have demonstrated, there is the loss reflected in the competitive struggles for the capture of the net rents made possible by the artificial scarcity. The appropriate measure for this second loss of value is less certain. Several contributors to this volume argue that this loss is measured approximately by the rents themselves, an argument based on the supposition that the rate of return on efforts to secure rents will itself be adjusted to rate of return elsewhere in the economy. As Tullock's paper on efficient rent seeking suggests, however, this equalization of rates of return between rent seeking and other economic investment does not necessarily emerge in some institutional settings.

In this concluding essay, my concern is not with the measure of the opportunity losses that the creation and the maintenance of rent-seeking institutions impose on the community. For my purposes, it is sufficient that these losses be acknowledged to exist and that they are or may be significant. My concern is with the prospect for community or collective action aimed at reforming the institutional structure so as to reduce or eliminate the opportunities for rent-seeking behavior. I shall demonstrate that the required shift from a set of inefficiency-generating to a set of efficiency-generating institutions may be particularly difficult to accomplish in a rent-seeking environment, relative to other settings that may generate comparable inefficiency.

Elementary Principles of Welfare Economics

It is helpful to commence with a brief review of some elementary principles of welfare economics. If an existing situation is shown to be "inefficient," by the standard meaning of this term, there must exist a means of moving from such a situation to one that is "efficient," with gains to at least one person in the community and without loss to anyone. To implement such a change, it may be necessary that the net gainers compensate the net losers, particularly if the potential losers must agree to any change before it is made effective. If we interpret the working of democratic process to require consensus on deliberately organized collective decisions involving major institutional change, the prospects for accomplishing efficiency-improving changes depend critically on the prospects for organizing the required compensations for the net losers.

If there are no net losers from a prospective change, if everyone is a net gainer, it seems evident that the prospects for collective agreement on a change aimed at eliminating an institutional barrier to efficiency should be relatively high. Even here, however, we should note that collective agreement may be required. Individuals acting independently cannot implement the changes needed, and, within unchanged institutional structures, rational individual behavior may continue to be that which generates overall results that may be judged to be inefficient.

One way of classifying or describing this setting of interaction is to say that the net gains and losses are symmetrical over the different persons or players.

The Classic Prisoners' Dilemma as a Fully Symmetric Payoff Structure

A familiar example is provided in the classic prisoners' dilemma, where the two persons involved are assumed to be identical in payoffs, whether these be positive or negative in the construction as presented. The structure of the game is such that both persons are led to behave in such a manner as to produce a "solution," where the payoffs to each person are lower than the payoff that could be secured from a joint and binding agreement to behave differently, hence to generate a different joint outcome. Figure 22.1 illustrates the familiar game here. Cell IV is, of course, the solution if the players are forced to play the game. Cell I is the efficient solution, on the assumption that A and B are the only members of the relevant community. Hence, a joint and binding agreement between A and B that involves each person in strategy (1) should be easy to secure.

A Prisoners' Dilemma with Nonsymmetrical Payoffs

Although less attention seems to have been devoted to it, most interactions that exhibit characteristics described by the prisoners' dilemma involve nonsymmetrical rather than symmetrical payoff structures. Players are not identical with respect to anticipated payoffs, whether these be negative or positive in absolute value. This absence of symmetry in payoffs is not relevant for my purposes here, except to the extent that it modifies the relative ranking of the individual payoffs in the differing cells of the matrix. In the illustration of figure 22.1, for example, both persons receive higher payoffs in cell I than in cell IV. So long as this relationship within individual orderings holds, there can exist some differentials between the absolute value of individual payoffs without modifying the structure.

Consider figure 22.2, however, where the asymmetry introduced violates this condition. Note that the payoff for A is now lower in cell I than in cell IV, the "solution," despite the fact that the combined

Figure 22.1

B

	(1)	**(2)**
	I	II
(1)	6, 6	1, 10
	III	IV
(2)	10, 1	4, 4

A

payoffs are higher in cell I than they are in cell IV. That is to say, cell I remains the "efficient" outcome in the standard sense. Note that row and column dominance still exists, ensuring that the solution under simple strategy is still cell IV.

When we examine the prospect for getting agreement on a proposed commitment to a behavioral change, a significant difference emerges between this game and that depicted in figure 22.1. Until and unless individual *B* makes a side payment or compensation to individual *A*, outside of and beyond the activity represented in the game itself, individual *A* will not agree to any change from the cell IV outcome, nor will he agree to modify the rules establishing the game. Gains-from-trade between the two players will continue to exist, but

FIGURE 22.2

B

	(1)	(2)
(1)	5, 7	−1, 8
(2)	8, −1	8, 0

A

the exploitation of these gains requires side payments. No such side payments are required in the game of figure 22.1; agreement can be limited to the parameters defined by the activities that take place within the game. Agreement clearly seems more readily attainable in a game like that shown in figure 22.1 than in that shown in figure 22.2.

Application to Rent Seeking

Rent-seeking "games" are of the nonsymmetrical, second type. There are "winners" as well as "losers," and the problem of getting consensus on institutional change to eliminate such games is relatively much greater than in other "games" that economists play at discussing. It is necessary, however, to distinguish carefully between symmetry and nonsymmetry in the ex ante and the ex post sense. Games that are symmetrical in the ex ante sense of expected payoffs may be nonsymmetrical in the ex post sense of realized payoffs. Consider the game depicted in figure 22.3; the payoffs in cell IV are (8, 0 or 0, 8) with the players having only a probabilistic expectation as to which one of these results will emerge. Note that, in this formulation, the game becomes symmetrical ex ante. Expected payoffs are identical as among the two players.

Suppose, however, that, once the initial round has been played, the payoff structure is fixed. Ex post, the structure is nonsymmetrical, and this structure is assumed to be anticipated for the continuing sequence of rounds subsequent to the initial one. The cell IV solution will continue to emerge; the relative "loser," B in the example if the payoff emerges as (8, 0), cannot do better by changing his behavior within the game itself. But, when consideration for a rules change occurs, when the prospect for eliminating the game arises, the game depicted becomes analogous in all respects to that depicted in figure 22.2. Gains-from-trade exist, but the exploitation of these will require side payments outside behavior in the game itself.

With rent seeking, however, it may be particularly difficult to get agreement on such side payments. Individual B, the "loser," may be extremely reluctant to acknowledge the "entitlement" that individual A seems to have secured in the nonsymmetrical game. The loser, B, may be able to observe that he has himself "invested" the same resources as A, the winner. The latter has merely been lucky in getting the relatively higher payoff, but does luck establish moral claim?

This reluctance on the part of losers in rent seeking to make the side payments or compensations that may be required becomes more intense if they think that the winners rigged the game from the outset, that is, if they think that the payoff structure was nonsymmetrical even in the ex ante sense.

Piecemeal versus Generalized Agreement

The simple exercises here serve to demonstrate a point that has long been familiar in the theory of economic policy. Attempts to eliminate efficiency-reducing institutional barriers to trade, which include all

FIGURE 22.3

B

	(1)	**(2)**
(1)	6, 6	-1, 8
(2)	8, -1	8, 0 or 0, 8

A

rent-seeking opportunities, are likely to founder if they are approached piecemeal, or one at a time. Those persons and groups who have established what they consider to be entitlements in the positive gains that have been artificially created will not agree to change, and those persons and groups who suffer losses will not willingly pay off what they consider to be immoral gainers. This moral barrier to agreement does not depend on the existence of positive transactions costs or on the relative disparity in the sizes of the members on the two sides of the potential transaction, an argument often adduced in this connection. Even if transactions costs are zero, the difficulty remains.

As more and more efficiency-reducing institutions come to be established, however, as more and more opportunities for rent-seeking behavior are opened up, resolution may become easier rather than harder. General agreement on major constitutional change may prove easier to attain than piecemeal agreement on changes made separately. Constitutional rather than legislative change may be possible. Whereas no single set of winners will acquiesce in relinquishing their own gains without full compensation, many groups may, simultaneously, agree to a generalized elimination of all rent-seeking opportunities, since, by so doing, each group gains more than it loses in net.

In order for such a "constitutional revolution" to become possible, however, it is necessary that the evolution of rent seeking take the form of different groups of winners in each new establishment of artificial scarcity. If the *same* group in the community become winners in each and every extension of rent seeking, losers may cease to play. They may reduce investment in rent seeking, but, at the same time, they may reject the increasingly disparate distributional outcomes. At some point, the search for agreement upon change will also cease, and prospects for "nonconstitutional revolution" emerge to replace those for its more orderly counterpart.

These points are familiar, but it may be useful to illustrate them geometrically, with a construction introduced by Robert Tollison.[1] Consider figure 22.4, where the wealth positions of two persons, A and B, are measured along the abcissa and ordinate respectively. P depicts the possibility frontier, and E is the fully efficient initial position. Assume that the introduction of what we may call symmetrical inefficiency pushes the position inward to any point within the shaded area. In such cases, as noted, agreement to return to E should be relatively easy to secure.

Suppose, however, that rent-seeking institutions emerge, and that the two-person group shifts to a position like that shown at E', on a new and lower frontier, P'. Note that, in this shift, individual A's position has been improved, but that of B has been damaged. Gains-from-trade exist at E', but to exploit these, B must first acknowledge A's net entitlement.

Suppose, now, that at a second stage in the evolution of rent seek-

---

[1] Robert D. Tollison, "The Prospect for Liberal Democracy: Comments," in *Fiscal Responsibility in Constitutional Democracy*, ed. James M. Buchanan and Richard E. Wagner (Boston: Martinus Nijhoff Social Science Division, 1978), pp. 177–180.

FIGURE 22.4

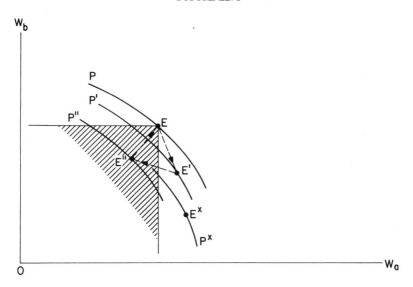

ing, individual *B* succeeds in winning a new and different game, shifting the frontier inward to *P″*, and to the position *E″*. Note that, at *E″*,
an agreement can be reached to shift back to *E*, with gains to both parties and *without* the necessity of side payments or compensations outside the activities that are depicted in the game itself. The "constitutional revolution" is depicted by the shift from *E″* back to *E*.

In a less hopeful scenario, however, suppose that the second stage
in the evolution of rent seeking shifts the group from *E′* to, say, *E**,
with individual *A* securing still further improvement in his own position at the expense of individual *B*. At *E**, exploitation of the gains-
from-trade required to shift back toward the frontier becomes more
rather than less difficult to implement than at *E′*. The distributional
disparities all but overwhelm the importance of the allocative gains.
The stage is thereby set for "nonconstitutional revolution."

Reform in the rent-seeking society depends critically on the history of its evolution, as well as upon the ability of political and intellectual leaders to think in terms of, and be persuasive about, general constitutional changes in the whole structure of social and economic
institutions. The classic American syndromes, incrementalism and
pragmatism, must be nonstarters in this search.